A LITERATE PASSION

Tuesday 3 P.m.

Had a frightful night. Went to bed exhausted about midnight intending to get up fresh at 8 = am. At one o'clock I woke up and lay in a half-dream state till 8 = am — then fell into a stupor until one to-day. Dreamed the most horrible dreams, among them that I saw my own grave with a tomb stone & a light shining on it. And a big dream about you — shattering. Feel completely wrecked. am trembling. Don't know what ails me. Tried phoning you just now but you were gone. wanted so much to see you. Feel terrible, terrible. Desperate. Disconsolate. am buying alarm clock to set my life in order. another night of this & I'd go completely mad. Jesus!! I'd give anything to see you now. I'm nuts. Harry.

A LITERATE PASSION

LETTERS OF

Anaïs Nin and Henry Miller

1932–1953

Edited and with an Introduction
by Gunther Stuhlmann

A Harvest Book
HARCOURT BRACE & COMPANY
San Diego   New York   London

For information about permission to reproduce selections from this book, write
to trade.permissions@hmhco.com or to Permissions, Houghton Mifflin Harcourt
Publishing Company, 3 Park Avenue, 19th Floor, New York, New York 10016.

www.hmhco.com

The editor would like to thank the Estate of Anaïs Nin for permission to
reprint excerpts from *Henry Miller: Letters to Anaïs Nin*, edited and
introduced by Gunther Stuhlmann, copyright © 1965 by Anaïs Nin.

Library of Congress Cataloging-in-Publication Data
Nin, Anaïs, 1903–1977.
A literate passion.
Includes index.
1. Nin, Anaïs, 1903–1977—Correspondence.
2. Miller, Henry, 1891–1980—Correspondence.
3. Authors, American—20th century—Correspondence.
I. Miller, Henry, 1891–1980. II. Stuhlmann, Gunther.
III. Title.
PS3527.I865Z49   1987   818'.5209   [B]   87-14950
ISBN 0-15-152729-6
ISBN 0-15-652791-X (Harvest pbk.)
ISBN 978-0-15-652791-0 (Harvest pbk.)
Designed by Judythe Sieck
First Harvest edition 1989
Printed in the United States
DOH 20 19 18 17 16   4500599229

INTRODUCTION

H E R E , published for the first time, is the private record of a passionate friendship and a literary romance which prevailed, against many odds, through the long course of two writers' lives. It began with a casual lunch on the periphery of Paris late in 1931, when Anaïs Nin, the twenty-eight-year-old wife of Hugh Parker Guiler, a young woman at that moment poised for intellectual and physical adventure, was introduced to Henry Miller, the "gangster author," as a friend had jokingly dubbed him, who would be forty years old the following December 26. They were, to all appearances, totally mismatched, but they had one thing in common: both were nascent writers and deeply enamored of the word. After a few months of heady intellectual exchanges—at Parisian café tables, at the Guiler home in Louveciennes, and in a flood of letters—the relationship burst into a tumultuous love affair.

For the next ten years the forever impecunious self-styled "Brooklyn boy" and the hypersensitive Spanish "child-woman" (as Edmund Wilson was to call her) tried to establish a life together. When these efforts failed, for reasons that become apparent in this correspondence, Henry Miller and Anaïs Nin, in the early 1940s, resumed their separate lives. But they remained tied to each other by a basic bond. Stripped of passing sentiment, of catering to each other's material and emotional needs, of a sense of adventurous comradeship in the breaking of social taboos, their relationship remained firmly founded on the shared need to create themselves through writing. As Henry Miller later wrote, it was the effort "to realize myself in words." For him, it was the obsessive, Proustian research into his past and the dubious role women had played in it. For Anaïs Nin, in a diary she had kept since childhood, it was the relentless pursuit of an ever elusive emotional present. "God, it is maddening to think that even one day must pass without writing,"

Miller wrote to Anaïs Nin in February 1932. "I shall never catch up. It is why, no doubt, I write with such vehemence, such distortion. It is despair." A few months later Anaïs Nin noted in her diary: "The same thing which makes Henry indestructible is what makes me indestructible: It is that at the *core* of us is a writer, not a human being."

Until the recent publication of *Henry and June,* a volume drawn from previously suppressed diary material, most of what we could glean of their relationship came from the edited pages of the published *Diary of Anaïs Nin,* the seven volumes spanning the years 1931 to 1974. Henry Miller, shortly before his death at eighty-nine, in 1980, had brought out some brief, revisionist reminiscences of Anaïs Nin in a collection portraying some of his female friends. But in his earlier published work, for all its seemingly self-revelatory frankness, there is little evidence of their long romance, their turbulent involvement, unless one tracks down emotions and incidents Miller has transposed into a different time and place: to the New York of the 1920s, into the saga of his "Rosy Crucifixion."

We have also had available to us, of course, the volume of Henry Miller's *Letters to Anaïs Nin* (New York: G. P. Putnam, 1965). At the time of its publication, he had finally won the battle against a Puritanical censorship which for almost thirty years had kept his most important books from being published in his own country. It was the start of a still rather reluctant rehabilitation of his image as a mere woman-degrading pornographer. The focus of the volume was on Miller's development as a serious writer. Anaïs Nin, then almost exclusively known for her "avant-garde" fiction, appeared only as the silent recipient of a torrent of letters, as the confidante with whom he seemed most comfortable. The intimate aspects of their relationship—as in the diary volumes published thereafter—had to be omitted.

Thus it is in the letters presented here, covering more than twenty years, that we have for the first time a two-voiced, kaleidoscopic record of two writers in love—in love with each other, for a time, but, above all, in love with writing.

For Anaïs Nin, since the age of eleven, writing had been the only way she knew of gathering in her emotionally splintered life following her father's desertion of the family. Possessed by a terrifying, self-observing consciousness, she felt separated from the "real" world and fragmented by unrealized potentialities. ("No wonder I am rarely natural in life. Natural to what, true to which condition of soul, to which layer? How can I be sincere if each moment I must choose between.

five or six souls?") The diary had been her refuge, her workshop, and the act of writing her only stabilizer. "The journal is a product of the disease, perhaps an accentuation and exaggeration of it. I speak of relief when I write—perhaps—but it is also an engraving of pain, a tattooing on myself, a prolongation of pain."

The diary long sufficed as her all-accepting friend, the comforting repository of her confidences. But by the time she had escaped from the courtships of her unimaginative Spanish-Cuban admirers into marriage to the "poetic" and handsome young Scotsman Hugh (Hugo) Guiler in 1923, she had also realized that to become a writer she had to emerge from the sheltering secrecy of her diary. In the early 1920s she worked on novels and stories, initially to be publicly recognized as an artist (like her beloved father) and later also to achieve a modicum of financial independence. From the start she had the steady support of her husband. She received encouragement from her brother Joaquin, and from her cousin Eduardo Sanchez (the first great infatuation of her girlish years), who eventually had come to live in Paris. But all her dogged attempts to succeed as a writer proved futile. In the diary her writing always flowed freely, unselfconsciously. When she tried to be "professional," when she faced an amorphous, uncaring world "out there," something, she felt, was missing. "I am terrified of my conscious work," she concluded in 1932, "because I do not think it has any value. Whatever I do without feeling has no value." What Anaïs Nin cherished most, in life and in art, it seems, was "feeling."

One might say, in fact, that the first two items she managed to get printed emerged from an overflow of her feeling. "The Mystic of Sex" (an essay on D. H. Lawrence published pseudonymously in *The Canadian Forum*, in October 1930), and its offspring, the "Unprofessional Study" of D. H. Lawrence, published in 1932, reflect her own urgent needs to express her sexuality, to reorder the framework of her marriage, as much, perhaps, as they were a passionate defense (the first by a woman) of a much maligned fellow artist. Indeed, one might regard them as the first successful attempts to transform details of her private agonies into "created" works that could be displayed publicly without the danger of causing hurt or injury to people she loved and respected.

"Have begun to open [the] diary and let it be read, to realize it's my major work, and seeking to solve the human problems of its publication," Anaïs Nin wrote to Miller in late 1953. We know that another dozen years went by before this enormous project—a constant theme throughout these letters—began to be realized. But even then, in 1966, Anaïs Nin had not found a solution to the "human problems." All she could do, at the risk of distortion and fragmentation, was to exclude from this lifelong record of her self-creation certain aspects that had been vital to her formation as a woman and as a writer: her marriage, her erotic adventures, and the depth of her involvement with Henry Miller. "To tell the truth," she had written, "would be death dealing."

At the heart of her concern, quite obviously, was the man she had married so enthusiastically, so idealistically in 1923, and to whom she remained linked until her death in January 1977. "My loyalty to Hugh is easily definable," she wrote in November 1932, at a time she already felt compelled to hide the handwritten volumes of the diary from her husband. "It consists in not doing him harm." It was a stance she would assume for the rest of her life. While she was able to slip with seeming ease across the conventional boundaries of her marriage, without any apparent sense of guilt ("There is no American virginal attitude toward sex in me"), a deeper loyalty, beyond mere self-preservation, prevented her from publicly exposing her husband—or anyone else—to her labyrinthian secrets. "He is among all of us the one who knows best how to love," she had written of Hugo, late in 1932, ". . . a vastly generous, warm man who has kept me from misery, suicide, and madness."

In her published fiction, which emerged not without difficulty from the emotional compression chamber of her diary, Anaïs Nin could disguise biographical facts, the truth told "as a fairy tale"—as she clued in readers of her first book of poetic prose, *The House of Incest*, in 1936. But when publication of the diary itself finally approached there was no way of transforming essential details into a "dream." They had to be omitted, suppressed.

Only the death of Hugh Guiler, on January 7, 1985, a few weeks before his eighty-seventh birthday, released Anaïs Nin's protective hand and finally resolved the "human problems." It also made possible the publication of these long withheld letters. Even Henry Miller, not exactly a paragon of discretion, never broke an honorable silence about the man who, directly or indirectly, had so decisively influenced his own life and work.

Though he had studied English literature—and Anaïs consistently appealed to the potential poet in him—Hugh Guiler, the Scotsman, had also obtained a degree in economics when he graduated from

Columbia University in 1920. Indeed, it was his long-time job with a bank, rather than poetry or literature, that provided the economic basis of their existence. It sustained Anaïs Nin's literary ambitions and allowed the "banker-poet" in later years to become "Ian Hugo," engraver and experimental filmmaker. It helped to support Anaïs Nin's family and funded her lifelong compulsive generosity, the unending need to give, of which Henry Miller was to become the foremost beneficiary.

When Anaïs and Hugh Guiler landed in France in 1925, even Hugh's modest salary, paid in U.S. currency, seemed impressive by local standards. It allowed them to live in the better parts of Paris, to employ a series of Spanish maids, to travel, to buy books and a radio, to maintain a car. When, after the Wall Street crash of 1929, they were forced to give up their fashionable apartment on Boulevard Suchet, they managed nevertheless, with Anaïs Nin's astounding capacity to conjure up illusions with limited means, to create another gracious home, at 2 bis Rue Montbisson, in Louveciennes, on the western outskirts of Paris, where they soon would encounter Henry Miller.

When the young Mrs. Guiler returned to the city where she had been born (on February 21, 1903), she had been appalled, at first, by the openly displayed eroticism, the wickedness of Paris: people kissing on the street, lovers silhouetted against hotel windows, whores freely patrolling certain neighborhoods. Her disdain and disgust, carried over perhaps from her strict Catholic upbringing, had even extended to some of France's amorous literature. But in 1928 she had inexplicably, confusingly fallen in love. The man who triggered this upheaval was John Erskine, best-selling American author of such books as *The Private Life of Helen of Troy* and a renowned pianist. Her husband's older friend and beloved former professor at Columbia, Erskine at first glance seemed to embody the two elements Anaïs Nin, in her fantasies, had always desired in a partner: a sexually strong man who was also imaginative and sensitive. ("There are two ways to reach me—by way of kisses, or by way of the imagination. But there is a hierarchy: kisses alone don't work.") Yet Erskine, already settled with a wife, two children, and a mistress of his own, seems to have proved deficient in both respects. The extended "affair," on the evidence of the diary, had remained mostly an affair of the mind. A reunion in New York between the Guilers and the Erskines sometime later dispelled the last vestiges of her infatuation.

But the experience had unleashed in Anaïs Nin, at the age of twenty-five, unsatisfied urges and latent needs which, when she at last confessed them to her husband, forever altered the basis of their marriage. She attempted to turn the experience into a publishable book. When she eventually abandoned the "John" novel, she noted in her diary: "Every word I wrote about Hugo [who appears as a character in the story] reveals his youthfulness and the religious aspect of my love for him. I write about him as one writes about God, with traditional faith. In dropping the constant effort of making my love for Hugo the most exalted of all, I also drop the last vestiges of my immaturity."

The discovery and admission of what she called her "mistress sensibilities," a devouring hunger for experience, obviously set up a conflict with her loyalty and love for her husband. It left her suicidal, "empty" and "dying." It was at this time of crisis that Henry Miller, broke and homeless, arrived at Louveciennes in search of the free lunch that his friend and benefactor, Richard Osborn, another budding writer, had promised him. "He set my feet in the right direction," as Miller wrote years later, when he dedicated his *The Wisdom of the Heart* to him.

Henry Miller's entry into the charmingly gracious world of the Guilers is enthusiastically reflected in the original pages of Anaïs Nin's diary. "I'm singing! I'm singing! And not secretly but aloud," she noted on December 1, 1931. "I've met Henry Miller. I saw a man I liked . . . a man who was likeable, not overbearing but strong, a human man who was sensitively aware of everything. He's a man whom life makes drunk. . . . He is like me."

In the first volume of her published *Diary*, which indeed opens at the time Miller arrived in her life, we get a detailed description of the man: "He was warm, joyous, relaxed, natural. He would have passed anonymously through a crowd. He was slender, lean, not tall. He looked like a Buddhist monk, a rosy-skinned monk, with his partly bald head aureoled by lively silver hair, his full sensuous mouth. His blue eyes are cool and observant, but his mouth is emotional and vulnerable. His laughter is contagious and his voice caressing and warm like a Negro voice." And she adds: "He was so different from his brutal, violent, vital writing, his caricatures, his Rabelaisian farces, his exaggerations."

Actually, when they met, both were writers of promise rather than of accomplishment. Though Miller had devoted himself seriously to writing since 1924, when he had married for the second time and quit his last and final paying job, as personnel manager of the Western Union Telegraph Company in New York, so far hardly anything of his had seen the light of print. ("Not because my work was larded with pornography," as he wrote in 1957, "but, as I am now convinced, because I had yet to discover my own identity.")

For a few years Miller and his second wife, June Edith Smith—the famous "Mara/Mona" of his subsequent obsessive literary re-creations—had led a precarious, hand-to-mouth existence in New York. While Miller tried to write, June—often mysteriously, and to his pain-ful vexation—provided their meager funds. A "windfall" from one of June's nebulous benefactors allowed the Millers to spend most of 1928 in Europe, traveling from London to Vienna, from Paris to Budapest (forever mythomaniacal, June claimed she had some gypsy blood). Back in New York, back in Brooklyn, in a grubby basement apartment now shared with June's female friend Jean Kronski, Miller sensed the trap closing around him once again ("In New York I have always felt lonely, the loneliness of the caged animal"). Even his writing seemed to offer no escape. With several unpublished manuscripts in his battered suit-case, he embarked for Europe again in 1930. June had provided the ticket, and the uncertain promise that she would forward some funds to the offices of the American Express Company. When no money arrived, Miller entered upon the most destitute, desperate period in his life, which also provided the impetus for his first published book.

Like other penniless expatriate "bohemians" who haunted the cafés and the dingy hotels of Montmartre and Montparnasse, Miller had managed (with the help, and sometimes under the name, of his Viennese pal, fellow refugee, and future roommate, Alfred Perlès) to publish a few short pieces in the Paris editions of the Chicago *Tribune* and the New York *Herald*. He had written about two of his favorite subjects: the circus and the six-day bicycle race. He had also placed an essay on Luis Buñuel and his first published story, "Mademoiselle Claude," in the unpaid-for pages of a "little" magazine, Samuel Put-nam's *The New Review*. But as Putnam recalled in his memoir, *Paris Was Our Mistress*, as a writer "Henry was more or less an unknown quantity."

But through his "wise and good-hearted friend" Richard Osborn, who worked with Hugh Guiler in the Paris offices of the First National Bank of New York, Miller had shown Anaïs Nin portions of the manu-script he was working on: the ribald, as yet untitled, celebration of his two miserable years in the City of Light, the hymn to his liberation from the dark shadows of his American past. "I don't care much whether it pleases or displeases," he had explained in a letter, "since (for the time being) it gives me some joy and satisfaction. But I have

trepidations. It is a crude thing. And I have not begun altering it yet."
He also passed on to her another unpublished manuscript, filled with
four-letter words and sexual descriptions, an obviously autobiographical
account of a young Brooklynite's "love" life with two older women: a
two-year romance with "Cora," and an unsatisfactory marriage to
"Blanche," who resembled the woman Miller himself had married at
twenty-six, his erstwhile piano teacher, with whom he had had a daughter in 1918.

At first glance there should have been little in these unfinished or
aborted manuscripts to appeal to Anaïs Nin's sensibilities. They bore
no resemblance to anything she had tried to accomplish in her own
unpublished writings. ("He does not write with love," she noted. "He
writes to caricature, to attack, to ridicule, to destroy, to rebel. He is
always against something.") Yet something in the raw realism of
Miller's efforts struck a cord. "Rub off the German realist and you get
a lusty imagist. At moments he can say softly the most delicate, or the
most profound things." Under the tough Brooklyn voice, challeng-
ing—like D. H. Lawrence, perhaps—the hushed taboos of a politely
repressed, gentrified literature, there was also the voice of a wounded
romantic rebelling against an essentially loveless, matter-of-fact world
of sex. "I share with Henry an anger not at the imperfection of women,
but at the foulness of living itself."

In turn, Henry Miller seems to have responded to her writing.
(For years thereafter he became a devoted editor and critic of her
work.) "Henry says I write like a man, with tremendous clearness and
conciseness. He was surprised by my book on Lawrence, although he
does not like Lawrence."

What occasioned Miller's surprise—and the disapproval of family
and friends when the book was published in February 1932—one
suspects, was the seeming disparity between the image Anaïs Nin
projected (or what people wanted to see in her) and the impassioned
voice here arguing, with Lawrence, against "a denial of the deeper
needs of our nature." Having been so perfect in her many roles—the
decorous, decorative wife of the rising young executive, the dutiful
daughter, the loving sister, the naïve Catholic girl striving for saintli-
ness, even the flirtatious socialite—Anaïs Nin had betrayed the tortured young woman of the secret diary to nobody except her husband.
But any perceptive reader would have noted the *cri du coeur* voiced as
a defense of Lawrence. To Henry Miller, what Anaïs Nin had to say
(here, slightly edited) might have sounded indeed like a defense of his
own work, which she later so vigorously championed:

If to some, his work is nothing but crude realism, to others who know poetry it is more than that: the prose is lyrical as well as sensual, the descriptions full of sensitiveness as well as crudeness, of beauty as well as obscenity. Why the crudeness and the obscenity of the language? First it was necessary to dethrone mentally directed love. He pleads for an instinctive beginning. He gives us an honest picture of all the aspects and moods of physical love. But he writes neither scientifically nor for the sake of pornography. Even when he is most naturalistic and apparently obscene, there is a reason for the obscene words. They are the very words by which he believed one could alone renew contact with the reality of sexual passion, which the cult of idealism has distorted for us. His war was against evasive, reticent language, which makes for evasive, reticent living and thinking.

Love has been travestied by the idealists. The words they used aroused lofty exaltations or timorous reactions in the head, which had no connection whatever with sensual love. He took the naked words and used them because they conveyed realities which we were to live out not merely in action but in thought. "I want men and women to be able to *think* sex, fully, completely, honestly and cleanly." Now this cannot be done if we are afraid of words.

We have no record, it seems, of Henry Miller's own immediate response to his introduction into the world of Anaïs Nin except for what has been filtered into or reflected in this voluminous correspondence. But a few years later, when with Anaïs Nin's support he was at work on *Tropic of Capricorn*, he wrote: "The woman you never hoped to meet now sits before you, and she talks and looks exactly like the person you dreamed about. But strangest of all is that you never realized before that you had dreamed about her." Ostensibly these lines recall a time when the first-person narrator invited "Mara/Mona," the taxi dancer he was courting in the New York of the 1920s, to share a booth with him in a cheap Chinese restaurant on Broadway. Yet these lines apply perhaps more accurately to the day in December 1931 when Miller first sat down at Anaïs Nin's luncheon table in Louveciennes.

In the unpublished pages of Anaïs Nin's diary there also is an entry, written on New Year's Day 1933, in Miller's handwriting, which directly evokes his own reactions to the new world he has entered:

Coming out to Louveciennes on the train the picture of the countryside so indelibly engraved in my mind—I know every foot of ground along the route and with each billboard, each sign, each crazy house or road or movie, even a chicken run, or a cemetery on a vacant lot, there is a welter of associations. And so when Anaïs remarks I have never made any notes, strangely, of my experience in Louveciennes, it is only, I think, because everything is still alive and meaningful, everything still so unconsciously exploited.

When I collect my notes for my first Paris book there is the tender sentimental regretful feeling of putting between covers what was once a rich throbbing life, and which literature will never reproduce, as indeed it should not. But as I was putting together these random notes what a joy when I found there were little souvenirs of Louveciennes which could be inserted into that chaotic mass of names, facts, events, incidents, phenomena—quiet strains of collective living, as it were—even a trifle like the handbill from the Louveciennes cinema, which will always remind me of my walks to the Village Tabac, or the Epicerie for a "good bottle of wine."

No, if I have not written about Louveciennes it is only because I am not writing history, I am making it. I am so aware of the fateful, destined character of this Louveciennes.

Here, in the big billiard room, where the rats once scurried, sit Anaïs and I—or I pace up and down, gesticulating, while I explain to her the bankruptcy of science, or the methanthropological crisis. Here at her desk, littered with shattering material for the future, I hammer out my impetuous thoughts and images. Here a thousand thoughts burst in my head over a simple utterance.

What I was thinking tonight is that Louveciennes becomes fixed historically in the biographical record of my life, for from Louveciennes dates the most important epoch of my life.

Inevitably, when Anaïs Nin took up Henry Miller's cause, when she—herself completely dependent on her husband's financial support—provided or organized, as best she could, some money for him, brought books, small gifts, food, a movie ticket, there were some among her family and friends who regarded him as an opportunistic sponger, a vagabond who had latched on to an impressionable, compulsive giver. They failed to see his charm, nor would they have appreciated the writings of this "cunt painter," as some of his more foul-mouthed café companions sometimes called him. Anaïs Nin's husband had gently warned her at times against her enthusiasms. ("Beware of being trapped in your own imaginings—you instill sparks in others, you charge them with your illusions, and when they burst forth into illuminations, you are taken in.") Even Richard Osborn, after engineering their first encounter, had wondered whether it really had been such a good idea to introduce Henry Miller to his boss's wife.

Anaïs Nin, so firmly convinced of the validity, the importance of Miller's talent, took in stride her own occasional doubts about his personality, his sincerity, his understanding. "When I first gave Henry and June a big sum of money," she wrote in her diary, late in November 1932, when the final act of Henry and June's disintegrating marriage was being played out, during June's ultimate sojourn in Paris, "and they spent it all in one night on drink, I was humanly hurt, but my understanding was disciplined. I gave because I wanted to—I gave them liberty at the same time. Otherwise I would not be giving, I would be taking." Looking back on her first year with Henry Miller, she added this: "Later I gave love. . . . Henry used my love well, beautifully—he erected books with it."

She knew then, and she continued to believe, that beyond the fallible sexual man there was the artist, involved—egotistically, to be sure—in an ongoing process of creation that was worthy of support, a process so familiar to her. ("Between Henry and me there is the diabolical compact of two writers who understand each other's human and literary life, and conflicts.") In a telling entry in her diary she pictured Henry, seated in a café, fully absorbed in his creation: "His eyes were blank and hard. He was the supreme egotist expanded, artist only, needing my inflation, my help—and how I understand him. There was no sentimentality. His work only, devouring all. His talk about June: she was completely discarded, rejected, because useless—as some day I will be too, when he has a new need." She did not exclude herself from this indictment: "I was doing the same thing on a minor scale . . . the pain I cause Hugo is tragic but inevitable to all living progression." For the sake of Miller's work she had been ready at times to give up her own, to postpone her own publications. When Jack Kahane, of the Obelisk Press, hesitated to bring out Miller's "Parisian notebook," she herself, with borrowed money, had underwritten the publication of *Tropic of Cancer*, which ultimately proved to be Miller's most important, most influential book.

Henry Miller, in turn, never flagged in his passionate advocacy of what he consistently regarded as her major work: the enormous diary.

In his impassioned letter to their common literary agent, William Bradley, in 1933, and in his first public mention of the early diary volumes, in T. S. Eliot's magazine, *The Criterion*, in 1937, he had predicted, correctly as it turned out, that if ever published, Anaïs Nin's diary would receive worldwide recognition. "It is a great pageant of the times," he had stated in his essay "Une Etre Etoilique," "patiently and humbly delineated by one who considers herself as nothing, by one who had almost completely effaced herself in the effort to arrive at a true understanding of life. It is in this sense again that the human document rivals the work of art, or in times such as ours, *replaces* the work of art." At the lowest ebb in their relationship, in the 1940s, when he had given up the always illusory hope that someday they would be joined together (Anaïs Nin, in October 1932, had already written in her diary: "Henry is thinking of our marriage, which I feel will never be. But he is the only man I would marry"), Miller had made the ultimate gesture. He had offered to share with her, to enable her to publish at least parts of the diary, the modest sum he had just received from an unnamed benefactor who had been moved by Miller's own desperate public plea for money. "I have always expected everything of the world, and have always been ready to give everything," as he wrote in *The Colossus of Maroussi*. "When I have been desperately in need, I have always found a friend."

In December 1931, a short time after Henry Miller had first met Anaïs and Hugh Guiler, his wife, June, suddenly arrived in Paris. It was only natural that he should introduce her to his new benefactors. On the last day of the year, Henry and June arrived at Louveciennes, and again something unforeseen happened. The woman who had just noted in her diary: "Henry interests me. But not physically," inexplicably became smitten by his wife, the "most beautiful woman" she had ever met. During the four short weeks of June's stay in Paris, the two women played out a strange and confusing courtship. Perhaps subconsciously imitating the Don Juanism of her father, Anaïs Nin—always regarded as the essence of delicate femininity—assumed the dominant role, while, at the same time, identifying with June's openly displayed sexuality, with the "femme fatale" who had so enchanted Henry Miller from the first and who had lain dormant for so long in Anaïs Nin's own convoluted soul. By emulating June, by becoming unashamedly "sexy," she could perhaps realize all the unexplored possibilities at the root of her restlessness. June, for Anaïs Nin as for Miller, had become a vital experience. She was, perhaps, the impetus that a few months later, in March 1932, prompted Anaïs Nin for the first time to climb the stairs to Henry Miller's room in a dingy hotel in Paris.

Looking back on her encounter with June, Anaïs Nin—a few weeks after her twenty-ninth birthday—drew up a summary of her sexual nature which reveals, perhaps, some of the dynamics of her interrelation with Miller also, as it is so vividly reflected in this correspondence.

Acting as a man (I have had masculine elements in me always) hurt me because I am extremely feminine. It would have been more feminine to be satisfied with the passion [of various suitors], to have let them love me—but I insisted on my own selection . . . which produced weaker men than I was. I suffered deeply from my progressive forwardness—as a woman. As a man I should be glad to have selected what I desired. That my first love was a homosexual, and Hugo partly maimed by moral fears, was my misfortune. Then I turned to the strong man, John, and he was unimaginative, unpoetical, and he did not understand me. I have discovered the joy of a masculine directing of my own life—as by my courting of June. But my body will die because I have a sensual body, a living body, and there is no life in the love between women.

Back from a short escape to a resort in Switzerland, overwhelmed by an almost daily avalanche of mail from Henry Miller the *artist*, Anaïs Nin was by now also prepared to embrace Henry Miller the sexual *man*.

Henry Miller, as we know, was an inveterate letter writer. He would rather write a letter, Anaïs Nin has suggested, than a novel, and some of his letters were indeed of novelistic proportions. One might even argue that much of Miller's published work—discursive, anecdotal, self-referential, self-relevatory and enlivened with some boyish bragging—resembled a gargantuan letter tossed at the world. Not unlike Nin's gigantic "letter" to a lost father, Miller's work remained open-ended, unfinished, to be continued. It could best be read in bits and pieces.

In the initial year of their acquaintance, as Miller wrote to his old friend Emil Schnellock (the recipient of another lifelong stream of correspondence), he had sent Anaïs Nin more than nine hundred pages, mostly typed—more than enough to make up a hefty book. Through the early years of their relationship, this astounding volume of mail hardly diminished. More astoundingly, it was produced in the midst of their hectic daily lives, filled with endless social events, travel, creative work and, last but not least, the long, if sometimes furtive, hours spent in each other's company.

The more than two-hundred-and-fifty letters presented here, spanning the two most important decades of their relationship, have been selected from this large body of correspondence, or, rather, from what has survived of it. It is a selection representative of the wide range of the originals and it has been limited only by the demands of available space. Through the spontaneous, uncensored words of both partners we can participate in the birth, the flowering and the inevitable maturing of a great, extremely literate passion. For all the hard-breathing steaminess of some of these letters, they remain anchored in the literary perceptions of two writers. Even "afterwards," as Anaïs Nin so delicately noted in her diary after a sexual encounter, "we talked about our craft."

The volume begins in Switzerland, in February 1932, when Anaïs Nin had escaped from the turmoil of her encounter with June. Henry Miller was in Dijon, at the Lycée Carnot (a dismal experience, so vividly recalled in the final section of *Tropic of Cancer*), trying to hold down the job as a *répétiteur* in English, which Hugh Guiler's intervention had secured for him, at the urgent pleading of his wife. It ends some twenty-one years later with what might be called Anaïs Nin's letter of "acceptance," a brief, conciliatory backward glance at their relationship. Providing new biographical insights, these letters lead us into the quiet days of Clichy, into the "black-lace laboratory" where two writers honed their craft, and made love. They give a sometimes farcical, sometimes moving account of the crisis of 1934–1935, when Anaïs Nin had left Paris to try her hand, in the shadow of Otto Rank, as a psychotherapist in New York, while Miller, in the wake of his first book publication, had stayed on, in his new home at 18 Villa Seurat, desperately missing her. They illuminate the background in the 1940s, of Miller's rediscovery of America, his "air-conditioned nightmare" trip, sponsored largely by Anaïs Nin, which spelled the end of his last hopes of a life together.

The letters have been chosen for their inherent interest and their relevance, and in an effort to provide a continuous narrative. They were deciphered and transcribed from copies of the handwritten or typed originals, or from carbons, some with marginal additions by one or the other writer. (The editor is grateful for the invaluable help of Barbara Ward in this long and painstaking process.) Space limitations, even after the initial often difficult selection, made it necessary to eliminate material peripheral to the personal story—lengthy discussions of Dostoevsky, Proust, Joyce, D. H. Lawrence; detailed critiques of one another's work-in-progress; ruminations on films, books, and so on, often encased in letters of twenty or more typed pages. Sometimes only portions of such letters are included, as indicated by editorial elisions. Some important letters, previously published in part or somewhat altered, have been restored to their complete original versions; some segments deleted from Miller's *Letters to Anaïs Nin* have been included here, along with a few letters essential to the overall narrative that also appeared in the earlier collection.

When Anaïs Nin, some years ago, entrusted the editor with a large box containing the raw materials for this volume (a box, incidentally, neatly decorated with copies of illustrations from her small volume *Solar Barque*), she also provided a rough breakdown into years of these mostly undated letters. But accurate dating often proved difficult, and some originals, unfortunately, defied all efforts of detection and could not be included here. Some letters bore dates supplied subsequently, apparently, but these dates did not always prove reliable when compared with available evidence. All dates given in square brackets are those of the editor. Anaïs Nin's original diaries for the 1930s provided invaluable clues, thanks to Rupert Pole, Trustee of the Anaïs Nin Trust. They often contained excerpts from, or references to, individual letters, but this evidence often appeared undated or in a retrospective context, which made accurate dating difficult. In fact, Anaïs Nin herself pointed out in her diary, in 1933: "If all my letters were put together they would reveal startling contradictions."

In the main, as any reader will soon discover, the narrative of these letters is self-contained, self-explanatory. Editorial footnotes and a biographical appendix have been supplied. Where necessary they provide relevant biographical or bibliographical information or fill apparent gaps in the chronology.

Occasionally, in this spontaneous dialogue, questions are asked and problems raised that receive no answer. They were quite obviously resolved in talk instead of letters. At moments of crisis, of mood swings, Henry Miller would be on his new bicycle on the way to Louveciennes.

And Anaïs Nin did spend a great deal of her time in Paris, especially after the demise of Louveciennes. These letters also rarely dwell on other relationships either writer may have had at the time, aside from the obvious one between Anaïs Nin and her husband. To unravel the labyrinthian complexities of Anaïs Nin's ties to her two psychoanalysts, Dr. Allendy and Dr. Rank, and to others, like Antonin Artaud and Gonzalo More, to name but two, or Henry Miller's quest for another June, another Anaïs, over the long years of their correspondence, is beyond the scope of this volume.

There are, inevitably, gaps in chronology. More than half of this volume is taken up with the letters of the early 1930s, the richest source of preserved material. Little or no correspondence seems to have survived from the later 1930s, and the flow itself, diminished by the writers' drawing apart, subsided to a trickle in the 1940s. But the essential, cyclical pattern of the relationship by then had already been established. In his book on Greece, written after war had forced him to return to America in 1940 (with a ticket provided by Anaïs Nin), Henry Miller dwells on what an Athenian soothsayer had pointed out to him: that his life had run in seven-year cycles. He had married for the first time in 1916. Seven years later he had discovered June. In 1931 he had met Anaïs Nin, and by 1938 the fires of desire apparently had been banked. "I had left Paris before the war," he recalled in *The Colossus of Maroussi*, a book devoid of women and filled with an elegiac sense of acceptance, "knowing that my life there had come to an end. In the last year or two in Paris I had been hinting to my friends that I would one day give up writing altogether, give it up voluntarily— at the moment when I would find myself in the possession of the greatest power and mastery."

Miller did not give up writing then, and during his American trip, from California, he tried once more—less urgently—to keep alive the flames of his involvement with Anaïs Nin. But the wild strength of his desire to write, to build a life with her was no longer there. "There is an estrangement, not on my part, but on hers," Miller wrote to his friend Wallace Fowlie in January 1944. "She has lost faith in me—and just at the moment (tho' she was unaware of it) when I was putting up the most heroic battle of my life, the moment when, had she been able to see through the airs, she would have been proud of me. She was to me, and still is, the greatest person I have known—one who can truly be called a 'devoted' soul. *I owe her everything.*"

In the last letter included here, Anaïs Nin writes: "I see you clear of distortions [now] and it makes me write you for the first time without the stiltedness due to hardening of the personal vision. Probably if I had then the sense of humor I have today and if you had then the qualities you have today, nothing would have broken."

The resolution of their estrangement brought forth, in the years to come, a reaffirmation of their friendship as writers and the continuation of the public silence about their romantic past. It validated, indeed, what Anaïs Nin had written in her secret diary so long ago, on July 23, 1932, on a rainy afternoon in the Tyrol, while her husband sat reading beside her:

> Henry is in my being for good even while I so wisely contemplate the end of our love. I still see the friendship lasting, the almost life-long tie. So it looks to me today—as if Henry is going to be part of my life for many years, even if he is my lover only for a few months.

GUNTHER STUHLMANN
Becket, Massachusetts
May 1987

A LITERATE
PASSION

Jan 4, 1935   1.

Henry, my love, my love, I don't know
if this letter will reach you, I don't
know where you are roaming. I've
lived dark days, feeling that you
were suffering and that nothing I
could write or cable would help
you. I said only I wish I were
here with you, I've been going through some
deep struggle on account of the
dusky heroine it reminded you of
other ghosts, and after resting in
my love peacefully, you have suddenly
been pushed into reality. I didn't
want to hurt you, yet because just
before I left I begged your for
activity I now have felt my love
you was becoming unreal... I wanted
to give birth to Henry Miller, and the hard
effort of that birth was to leave you

[Henry:]

Dostoevsky in Siberia! Henry in Dijon! From my fortress up in the place of frozen instincts (the Swiss), where I am not trying to find sanity but the power to conceal my madness, I sent you a telegram which will make you laugh, and 150 frs. The telegram is not unwise. Resign, Henry, that place is impossible for you. Hugh* is coming here Friday and when he reads your letter he will understand perfectly. Listen, old straw-Krans won't mind because he has other men for the job. You were sent down there under false pretenses, too. They had no right to say you would get 500 frs. and when you are there to say you will not get anything at all. I am sizzling with indignation as I write. I read your letter while I took a walk this morning. You *are* unduly sensitive too if you think your friends were relieved to have the problem of "you" settled, Henry. I think everybody honestly believed you were going to be given the one perfect chance to write, for a while, to digest the prodigious life you lead—or maybe, to make others digest it. I said: "Come home to Louveciennes," at least temporarily. I know it is no solution because it is another form of exile, and you are not free enough, and the house is too far from Paris. I say that because it means temporarily a place where you are sure to eat and sleep. Hugh will try and

*Hugh Parker Guiler (Hugo), A. N.'s husband, who with the help of Dr. Krans, of the Franco-American Exchange Program, had arranged for H. M.'s job as a répétiteur in English at the Lycée Carnot, in Dijon, an experience recalled in the final section of *Tropic of Cancer.* See Biographical Notes on Guiler.

find you another job. I said Wednesday because we will be home Wednesday, and also because I fancy you can't resign overnight. But if you want to run away from Siberia before, you can go straight to Louveciennes. Emilia [the maid] will be only too glad to take care of you. I'll write her a note today. Use our room. Perhaps Hugh has written you the same thing—I imagine not. Just as you know, when one is carried away the other must hold back, to create a balance, just as you hold back when June* is carried away. Dostoevsky got something out of Siberia, but from what you say, Dijon is not nearly as interesting. It is *mesquin*, meager, bloodless, small, petty. Don't stay there. Write me what you decide to do: Poste Restante, Glion sur Montreux, Suisse. Home Wednesday.

This letter must get to you immediately, so I keep all I wanted to write you about you, June, and other things. If you come back, will talk, if you don't come back I'll write you a lot. Don't worry about the criticisms you give me. I love them and I believe in them. You knew I cut out that chapter on whimsicality in the book on Lawrence?† You made me realize its foolishness. Also, you are right about the analytical part in the second book. You're helping me.

Anaïs

Lycée Carnot, Dijon
Thursday [February 4, 1932]

I don't know where to begin! My mind is flooded, saturated with material. *Alors*, I got your letter, the telegram. First of all, bravo! I am immensely elated by the interest you take—and that is quite enough to sustain me. It will not be necessary to return to Paris, or Louveciennes, tho' certainly I deeply appreciate your hospitality. Let us reserve the occasion—there may come a worse day. For the present I feel sufficiently fortified to stick it out. . . .

Perhaps I sounded like a crybaby. What a yawp I set up! Damn it, I wasn't supposed to fall into a bed of roses. So, if in the future I rave or rant, just set it down to literary ebullience. Everything has its compensations. . . . Now that I have cleared the deck with these

*H. M.'s wife. See Smith in Biographical Notes.
†A. N.'s first book, *D. H. Lawrence: An Unprofessional Study*, published in Paris by Edward W. Titus in 1932.

practical explanations (and hell how I detest them) let me make other apologies—and then to more interesting matters. First excuse the paper. I have good typewriter paper which I am holding in reserve, and if you do not mind the lack of formality why O.K. Maybe the random notes on the reverse side will titillate you. They are of no use to me any more. Secondly, excuse the absence of salutation. I haven't yet learned to call you by your first name, and Miss Nin sounds so stiff, like an invitation to tea. I should like to say simply Anaïs, but it takes time. (Osborn, for instance, is still Osborn.) How Germanic this is. . . .

Since I shall not be back to engage in long discussions (except perhaps during Easter, or will you be going away then?) why let's thrash things out by letter. The notes I sent you, after you read them, please hold them. As I said, so much was left out of the novel.* I want to return to it, supplement it by incorporating some of my material in the present book [*Tropic of Cancer*]. Naturally you have divined how precious this "Albertine" must be for me. Is not June very similar—perhaps much more complicated, orchestrated as it were? How many more enigmas are there for me to solve than was presented by Albertine? . . . God, it is maddening to think that even one day must pass without writing. I shall never, never catch up. It is why, no doubt, I write with such vehemence, such distortion. It is despair. . . .

Yes, I hope, Anaïs, that you will write. There is lots I have to say which does not fit into books. And I want to know what you think. I come back again to your book, to my first, vivid impressions. Certain passages are of an inestimable beauty. Above all a sureness, a grasp, a mature dexterity which I, alas, will never attain. The very composition of your blood, your inheritance, has without your knowing it perhaps saved you from problems and pains which most writers are obliged to suffer. You are essentially the artist, whether you choose a small or a big canvas. You have a power, through sheer feeling, that will captivate your readers. Only beware of your reason, your intelligence. Do not attempt to resolve. . . . *Don't preach.* No moral conclusions. There are none, anyway. Don't hesitate. Write! Keep on, even if you go from Switzerland to Timbuctoo, though why Louveciennes shouldn't suffice is an enigma to me. . . .

Sincerely,
Henry

---

*"Crazy Cock," a manuscript that remained unpublished.

[Henry:]

Last night I read your novel on life with Blanche.* There were some passages in it which were *éblouissants*—staggeringly beautiful. Particularly the description of a dream you had, the description of the jazzy night with Valeska, the whole of the last part when the life with Blanche comes to a climax. The last is *deep*, the feeling about illusion while Moloch watches Blanche's sobbing, the tragic desire for understanding in the center of the utmost emotional brutality—the tremendous struggle to *get deeper* into your own feelings. Other things are flat, lifeless, vulgarly realistic, photographic. Other things, the older mistress, Cora, even Naomi, are *pas dégrossis*—not *born* yet. There is a slapdash, careless rushing by. You have gone a long way from that. Your writing had to keep pace with your living—and because of your animal vitality, you lived too much. Now you feel the need of *appui* on what has been lived. You observe in Proust what it is to relive by retrospection and introspection. I say beware just a little of your hypersexuality! For you have that. You make me think of Casanova, except that in between the erotic, Casanova was boring, while you, in between eroticism and even because of it, you get profound. It astonishes me how delicately you can make *distinctions* between women. There was a marvellous paragraph on that. Among one hundred women you will distinguish five. It is more than Don Juan ever did. But I would say about fifty of these one hundred are the cause for that embryonic writing. However, that hypersexuality which Blanche used as an insult, I admire, because it is quite in proportion with the enormity of your mind, your outsized thoughts, your torrential style (oh, that magnificent part where you describe Moloch's sudden eloquence), the volcanic novels and the unanswerable letters!

I have a strange sureness that I know just what should be *left out*, exactly as you knew what should be left out of my book. I think the novel is worth weeding out. Would you let me? I'll give it a form, there is so much that is worth preserving and *publishing*. I'll chisel it out a

*An early, unpublished manuscript of a novel, originally titled "This Gentle World," written in the late 1920s, in which H. M., in the person of Dion Moloch, draws on experiences of his first marriage, to pianist Beatrice Sylvas Wickens (see Biographical Notes). Some of the characters sketched in this novel appear in his later fiction.

bit—you ought to be proud of it. I know how much you yourself would hate to do it, because it is dead for you. I know how much I have loathed working over the novel* you read because it is dead for me, how much we both love to work on living, palpitating stuff, at white heat only. But I believe it is only *after* the white heat that the story really *ripens*. The white heat re-creates the emotional experience, but *understanding* does not crystallize at white heat. For instance, it was only lately that I understand fully the experience I tried to describe in the book you read. I had forgotten to insert parts which were very important and very significant:

Why did I turn away from men who deeply loved me and love only Alan [John Erskine] for two years? Why did his mistress crumble after two years? Why did he love no one and was perpetually disappointed?

The woman [I] tells Duncan [Hugh]: I have sought a dominator.

Do I not dominate you? asks Duncan.

No, she answers, because you *love* me.

A man who dominates is a man who does not love. He has a tremendous animal vitality, a force, which conquers. He conquers, people are subjected by him, but he neither loves nor understands. He is just a force and he is filled with his own strength. If he loves at all, it is a force like his own, and so again he loves his own kind of strength, not the other, which is an infiltration. Watch the conqueror well, watch the man or woman who dominates another: he is not the one who loves. The one who loves is the one who is dominated. You love me, and so you cannot dominate me, and I being a woman sought domination. But it is all over now. I see it as an impersonal force, an animal force, which no longer has power over me. I even hate it now. I hate its lack of subtlety!

And then sometimes, you know, that power one is born with is not in accord with one's desires, it is outside of one's self. I have sometimes suspected Alan of being annoyed at the effect of his force. It flatters his vanity to be loved, yes, but in reality he does not want to be loved because if you are loved you must love in return and that he cannot do. Women make the mistake of loving him because they are dominated by him. He prefers, deep down in himself, to be *resisted*,

---

*An unpublished novel dealing with A. N.'s relationship with the writer John Erskine, a friend and former professor of her husband's. See Biographical Notes and *The Early Diary of Anaïs Nin*, 1923–1927 and 1927–1931. The manuscript subsequently underwent numerous revisions but was eventually abandoned.

on his own grounds, with almost an indifference to love as you and I understand it, with a certain toughness. He hates the way women crumble before him, he hates it. I have seen him hate Mary too, because she too has crumbled.

I don't know what you'll make of this, because such "dryness" is so far removed from your own character. Though I think you can destroy a woman, too, but for other reasons.

Anaïs

Can you work on my portable! Will it solve your problem for a while? Do you know anybody I could sent the prospectus of my book on Lawrence to? It will be out in two weeks.

Lycée Carnot, Dijon
Friday [February 12, 1932]

Anaïs:

At midnight last night my table was so littered with notes that, unable to digest it all and frame a coherent letter, I gave up in despair and went to bed. The room has become infinitely more habitable since (after two weeks) I discovered that the light could be manipulated. I must tell you that the big coal box in my room is an object which I look at with a deal of affection. It is the best object in the room. . . .

One of my notes says: "Correct Anaïs' English." Do you want me to do that, or would Hugo consider that I am encroaching on his private domain? Furthermore, and this is more important, would it "cramp your style" if I were to do so? I think it fairly important to apprise you of your errors, since you are making English your language. Nothing is more embarrassing at times, and more provocative of ridicule, than these queer twists which betray one's ignorance of the language. I suspect you want to come as near perfection as possible in this matter; and you know I'm no stickler for grammar, syntax, commas etc. No, it is only when the meaning is distorted or the beauty marred that I would hazard a friendly counsel. . . .

I sent a second letter to Switzerland, same address, did you get it? And did I enclose the book list I had promised? Don't be terrified by the avalanche of mail. It is a bad habit of mine, and as I can do no work with the pen it is just a way of letting off steam; Hugo, I hope, is not annoyed. Please have him say so. He must not. In any case, I am not dropping them on his desk. They arrive at Louveciennes, when commences a new life. But, I know how it can be sometimes. I should hate to have him saying to himself—"More mail from that guy? What's the meaning of all this? I hope to Christ he croaks."

And having written this I immediately perceive that it sounds a little like having a bad conscience, which I haven't at all, my conscience being practically defunct. No, I want Hugo to like me, to trust me always, to believe in me. It's a little harder to get at him, and then it was not he who put the first foot forward. That always makes things awkward. But damn all that, Anaïs, but it is all for Hugo too, absolutely. And if I can write freely—without fear of planting worms in the fruit, why fine. Hugo will either like me tremendously after a time, or detest me. I think he will like me. And, if I may sound just another note before finishing with this subject—you see I am extremely touchy, because I myself was so often placed in Hugo's role; the scars never seem to heal. But between you there is understanding. That is the big victory. I am where Proust was, only with more complications, more facts, more mysteries, more terrors, more of everything, except genius. You almost make me weep with your flattering words. No, I am far from being the artist you imagine. Maybe there are in me possibilities—they have not yet come to fruition. But your friendship, your wonderful sympathy is everything. . . .

> *Sincerely,*
> *Henry*

[Dijon]
Saturday [February 13, 1932]

Anaïs:

Just received your two letters and realize that you did get the second letter sent to Switzerland. . . . If the typewriter has a standard American keyboard I certainly will be able to use it. . . . That you found the old novel good in parts and that you think it could be doctored and made publishable is well. Sure I would be delighted if you would go over it and prune it. Even if only a hundred pages remain and they are good, why O.K. Perhaps I could reciprocate sometime by doing the same for you. . . .

You . . . make me laugh talking about Casanova. You don't know yet what men are like, pardon. I am fairly normal. It is true I swim in a perpetual sea of sex but the actual excursions are fairly limited. I think it's more like this—that I'm always ready to love, always hungry to love. I'm talking about love, not just sex. And I don't mind at all saturating my work with it—*sex* I mean—because I'm not afraid of it and I almost want to stand up and preach about it, like that nut in [Robinson Jeffers's] *The Women at Point Sur.* He was cracked and people forgive that, but I am quite sane, too sane almost, madly sane. No, I'll stop explaining myself. I'll let you explain me to myself—that sounds intelligent and fantastic. Don't worry about offending me—that's quite impossible. . . .

Henry

P.S. I must seem pretty nonchalant in the way I pass over your gifts and aid. . . . It hurts me to know that you are pinching and scraping to aid me. I think sometimes I am nothing but a big bum. Damn it, if I could find a way to earn a living I'd sell myself for the remainder of my life. That's honest!

[Louveciennes]
Feb. 13, 1932

Please understand, Henry, that I am in full rebellion against my own mind, that when I *live*, I live by impulse, by emotion, by white heat—June understood that.* My mind didn't *exist* when we walked insanely through Paris, oblivious to people, to time, to place, to others. It didn't exist when I first read Dostoevsky in my hotel room, and laughed and cried together, and couldn't sleep, and didn't know where I was . . . *but afterwards*, understand me, when all basis, all awareness, all control has been knocked out of my being, *afterwards* I make the tremendous effort to *rise* again, not to wallow anymore, not to go on just suffering or burning, and I grasp all things, June and Dostoevsky, and *think*. You got the thinking. Why should I make such an effort? Because I have a *fear* of being like June *exactly*—I have a feeling against complete chaos. I want to be able to live with June in utter madness,

*June Miller had returned to New York, after a visit to Paris of less than four weeks, in late January 1932.

but I also want to be able to understand afterwards, to grasp what I have lived through.

I may be wrong. You see I can give you a proof that the *living madness* is more precious to me than my thoughts: however much I think of you I couldn't *give* you what *feelings* I've lived through with June. I could give you explanations, general talk, etc., but not the *feelings* themselves. I can also give you the only criticism I could make of Dostoevsky, and there are in my journal four pages of my incoherent feelings about the reading of *The Possessed*. Can you understand that? Only thought comes to the surface, though very often, when your letter moves me, as I told you the very first time, I am almost ready to give everything, just as that day when I was so upset and beside myself—the first day you came—I was about to read you everything I had written in my journal—because your own despair aroused my confidence in you. Forgive me. Do you remember what was the first thing we did? We went out—I raved about the "healing" quality of the place. It was laughable. We weren't seeking to be healed, but I sought my mind again. I knew you were suffering torture—I evaded plunging, because it meant plunging into my own torture, too. I say again, I may be wrong. Yes, I am wrong. Today I exploded into fearful rebellion against analysis. Even if the second movement in all my sonatas is extricating myself from chaos, even if I have much of Gide in me, and that I may someday, like Lawrence, turn around and write my own explanations of my books (because other people's explanation of what is conceived in white heat by the artist sickens me), even if I do that, understand me, what comes first is the artist, the sensing through emotion, that *envahissement* by sensations which I feel and which breaks me to pieces.

You ask contradictory and impossible things. You want to know what dreams, what impulses, what desires June has? You'll never know it, not from *her*. No, she couldn't tell you. But do you realize what joy June took in my telling her what our feelings were—in that special language. How could I do that? Because, because I am not *sunk* all the time, I am not always just living, just following all my fantasies. Because I come up for air, for understanding. I dazzled June because when we sat down together the wonder of the moment didn't just make me drunk—I lived it with the consciousness of the poet, mind you, not the consciousness the dead-formula-making psychoanalysts would like to put their clinical fingers on—oh, not that, no, a consciousness of acute *senses* (more acute than the drugged ones). We went to the edge, with our two imaginations. We died together. But—June continues to live and die—and I—(oh, god, I hate my own work, I'd much rather just live)—I sit down and try *to tell you*—to tell you that I'd much rather go on living ecstatically and unknowing to you—to all—and you beat your head against the wall of our world, yes, and it is I because of my demoniac creative power of realization and coordinating mystery—I who will tear veils. But not yet. I don't want to. I love my mystery, I love the abstract, *fuyant* world I live in as long as I don't begin my *work,* the forcing out of delicate, profound, vague, obscure, voluptuously wordless sensations into something you can seize on—perhaps never. Perhaps I'll renounce my mind, my works, my effort, and merely live, suffer, wallow, elude your knowledge, your *seizure* of either June or me. Why do *you* want more clarity, more knowledge—you do not ask it of Dostoevsky—you thank god for the living chaos. Why then do you want to know more about June? Because you too are a writer, and mysteries inspire you but they must be dominated, conquered.

A little irony. It was you the writer who gave June the words with which she praised & described me. It was something about "her figure bore a faint resemblance to the beautiful Byzantine moths in silk and fur. . . ." I found it in the first novel. For the painters I had always been "a Byzantine." I was amazed at June's uncanny description of the "splendor of subtle oriental sophistication" etc.

She had promised to write me a great deal. She has not written. Has she written you, and do you have an address you can give me? Yes I want to write her.

Don't worry about the effects of your correcting my English. Nothing could make me *conscious*—but you will not be *rewarded* because on days like today I would write you any way at all—and I don't really care, as long as you understand. I don't care about beautiful or perfect English. If it comes out perfect or beautiful—very well—and I'm willing to work, but you know, I don't *care enough* about just that—I'm so full, so excited, so feverish—language will always drag and lag behind. I don't even read over my letters to you. Your poor sensitive English ears! The kindness in your help, I realize that.

Please buy extra coal and wood.

I'll answer the rest of your letter tomorrow.

Anaïs

[Dijon]
Sunday [February 21, 1932]

[Anaïs:]

Encore une et c'est fini, la grande correspondance.

I'm quitting—happy as a convict getting his release.

I received a telegram and letter from my friend Fred [Perlès]*
saying that the editor offered me a permanent job on the *Tribune* as
assistant finance editor.† Salary to start 1,200 frs. [about $ 45.00] a
month (*pas beaucoup!*) but a chance for an increase soon. The hours
are 8:30 P.M. to 1:00 A.M. (my hours) and the work easy.

What could I do but accept? It means a sort of independence,
Paris, and *life.* I will be able to write as the day is mine. And I get a
day off a week. . . . My address temporarily will be c/o *Chicago Tribune,*
5 Rue Lamartine, Paris. Excuse haste—mailing this in a hurry.

Henry

[Louveciennes]
Feb. 22, 1932

[Henry:]

When you said about Dostoevsky: "It is a pity that we shall never
have the opportunity again to read or see a man placed at the very core
of mystery and by his flashes not merely illuminating things for us, but
showing us the depths, the immensity of the darkness . . ." I thought
how much this meant to me, and that it was what I really felt about
D. H. Lawrence, and that it was the darkness which attracted me
. . . don't you think it *is* so about Lawrence? And another reason why
I could not live with Dostoevsky alone, and had to find something else,
is that in Lawrence the "darkness" was mostly sexual—and there is not
quite enough sexuality in Dostoevsky. Implied, yes, suggested, shown
by passions, proved by death—*mais la sexualité presque toujours dans
l'ombre,* whereas it is that which Lawrence tried to bring out of the
darkness. And you too—I love that about your work as much as I love
life itself. I use the word "sexual" in the sense which includes love—
that is why when I talked about Casanova I didn't mean to compare

*See Biographical Notes.
†Actually, the job involved mostly proofreading.

at all his sexuality and your frank sensualism or sensual love. You had a right to say that if I could find a resemblance I didn't know men. The resemblance only occurred to me numerically speaking!

And then you say: "Gide has mind, Dostoevsky has the other thing, and it is what Dostoevsky has that really matters." For you and for me, the highest moment, the keenest joy is not when our minds dominate but when we *lose* our mind—and you and I both lose it in the same way, by love.

We have lost our minds—to June. Both you and I would follow her into death . . . at moments. She has destroyed reality. She has destroyed conscience. (You say you haven't any—I say I haven't any, but it is not so true about us as it is about June. Example: Why are you always so thoughtful of Hugh, so considerate?) June is not bothered by truth. She *invents* her life as she goes along—she sees no difference between fiction and reality. How we love that in her—she takes the imagination seriously. At moments you want to follow June into death, but at others you react violently with a vigorous assertion of your own magnificent livingness. Unknowingly, you have been pushing me into the darkness. I didn't need much pushing. One little word from you against mind . . . Do you understand? My being is breaking up, crumbling. I thought my reason for being was mind. I thought it too easy (at least for me) to be exalted, to live on the edge of death as June does, to give until death . . . the hardest thing is to stop suddenly, to stop because someone appeals piteously to your reason as to one's greatest gift. I wanted, when someone turned pleadingly to me, to *understand*, lucidly. *Pouvoir, au milieu de la folie, redevenir humaine et pitoyable.* But every day I have less power to do so.

He who has the courage to hurt . . . for great reasons . . . he alone does good. That is June. Someday I may share June's madness entirely, entirely. Question my mind before it is gone!

I'm raving—you won't mind. I sometimes have the feeling you go through the same *tiraillements*.

I was trying to answer your warm, gorgeous letter.

Goethe—it's amusing how we agree about Goethe. The man who sought out serenity and sanity. I hardly know him, and I hate him.

But I also hate Nietzsche. I wish you would tell me something that would make me understand him. I began with *Zarathustra*—fatuous language, and the world full of "tougher and merrier" men! Alan [John Erskine] was a superman who wrote letters like this: "Mary has found a good outfit of servants and so the household is running smoothly. We will move uptown in October. I showed your letters to Mary and she thought they were charming, and *so* foreign. You must write me often and tell me how you are etc." (I'm sorry, I shouldn't tell you this except that you told me about Bertha [Schrank]'s* letters!)

Apropos of "gifts"—*une fois pour toute,* please pass them over nonchalantly—don't even say thanks—will you? Or I shall have to balance our accounts and show you what I *owe* you. I don't want any accounts.

Do you know, I wish you were called *"Heinrich"* (I saw the notes on your ancestors). German has a flavor for me such as French has for you. And what about Russian? I'm learning Russian. Yet my friend Natasha [Troubetskoia]† swears that Dostoevsky was a great liar and you could hardly find a Nastasia, an "idiot," or a Stavrogin in Russia. It's the *somberness* she denies. She is highly temperamental, cruel, perverse, tyrannical, fantastic, but not somber. Her lover is a "tough and merry" superman. She is trying to take away from me my image of Russia, as I try to dissolve your image of France.

Tell me something. You have a feeling for the macabre—your imagination is attracted by certain grim images. *Did* you tell Bertha that living with June was like carrying a corpse about? Do you really mind June's neuroses, and illness, or are you merely cursing at what enslaves you?

I wanted you to get this letter when you were about to begin the calculations. It might help—or again, it might not!

Did you observe the difference between the *colors* June and I love? She loves violet, which is the symbol of death. I love warm tones, blood tones, red, which is life. What do you expect me to *give* June?

Anaïs

---

*The wife of Joseph Schrank, an American playwright living in Paris, a woman to whom H. M. was attracted.
†See Biographical Notes.

Henry:

Perhaps you didn't realize it, but for the first time today you shook and startled me out of a dream. All your notes, your stories of June never hurt me. Nothing hurt me until you touched on the source of my terror: June and influences on June. What is June? *Is* there a June? When you talked about hating "Broadway," and that when you first met June she was just about to go Broadway—that without you she would have; when I realized that you met her and gave her most of what made her dazzle me, your influence—the terror I have when I remember her talk and sense through it how much loaded she is with the riches of others, all the others who love her beauty. Even "Count Bruga" was Jean's creation.* When we were together June said: "You will *invent* what we will do together." I was ready to give her everything I have ever invented and created, from my house, my costumes, my jewelry to my writing—my imaginings, my life. I would have worked for her alone.

The words she used were yours, the fantasie belonged to Nastasia.

Understand me. I worship her. I accept everything she is, but she must *be*. I only revolt if there is no June (as I wrote the first night I met her). Don't tell me that there is no June except the physical June, don't tell me, because you must know: you have lived with her.

I never feared until today what our two minds would discover together. But what a poison you distilled—perhaps the very poison which is in you. Is that your terror too—do you feel haunted and yet deluded, as by a creation of your own brain? Is it a fear of an illusion you fight with crude words. Tell me she is not just a beautiful *image*. Sometimes when we talk I feel that we are trying to grasp her *reality*. She is unreal even to us—even to you who have possessed her, and to me whom she has kissed.

I didn't know why I couldn't write her. Now I know: I doubt what I mean to her except when she is *here*, by my side. I haven't written because I sensed Jean in the background—June showing Jean my letter—a *different* June, another June, not *mine*. And I want to let her move on, as you move on, I don't want to hold her. Pride perhaps.

*A puppet made by June's friend, Jean Kronski, which she carried with her on her visit to Paris, when A. N. first met her.

These days I live only either in ecstasy or in maddening pain. Tonight after our talk, it was pain.

Anaïs

[Louveciennes]
[February 26, 1932]

[Henry:]

This will be a test of the efficacy of writing you care of the *Tribune*. Unfortunately we won't be able to meet on Sunday. There is an internal revolution at home. My mother won't live any longer in the house of a person capable of writing such a "dirty" book as my study of Lawrence. She is in terror of my influence on Joaquin.*

This may all seem laughable, almost naif to you. It is almost incredible. There will not be peace until the third "divorce" is settled (first from Father, secondly from my older brother because he showed interest in his father, then from me). Sunday we have to help them look for a home.

Call me up as soon as you find time to come, or we can meet in Paris and have a talk. Next week almost every afternoon I'm posing for a Russian painter in Montparnasse.

If this gets to you I'll mail you [Rainer Maria Rilke's] *The Notebooks of M. L. Brigge* and I'll finish answering your last letter.

A.

[Louveciennes]
[March 1, 1932]

[Henry:]

I never wrote you a small enough letter to send you this—something to amuse you, like the nails!

I can't see you Thursday because it is a holiday but Hugh wants you to come Sunday evening for supper—and I can be at the [Café] Rotonde Friday about 4:30. I forgot to tell you yesterday that Hugh does not read all the letters I get. Don't tear anything up: it creates blanks, silences—like the dashes of [Paul] Valéry.

Can you read this ink, made of distilled Andalusian blood?

---

*A. N.'s younger brother. See Nin-Culmell in Biographical Notes.

Did the chameleon change color again yesterday in the Rotonde?

What a contrast between our lives. Last night your notes overwhelmed me. So much stuff to be assimilated and transformed and brooded on—and you want peace so that your imagination may penetrate all that heavy material, and I am running away from peace and have begun to live like you and June. And both kinds of lives lead to the same madness.

Anaïs

Look at my coat of arms and the symbols on it.

[Louveciennes]
[March 2, 1932]

[Henry:]

The woman will sit eternally in the tall black armchair. I will be the one woman you will never have . . . excessive living weighs down the imagination: we will not live, we will only write and talk to swell the sails.

[Anaïs]

Chez les Vikings, Taverne Scandinave
29 et 31, rue Vavin, Paris VI
[March 4, 1932]

Anaïs:

Three minutes after you have gone. No, I can't restrain it. I tell you what you already know—I love you. It is this I destroyed over and over again. At Dijon I wrote you long, passionate letters—if you had remained in Switzerland I would have sent them—but how could I send them to Louveciennes?

Anaïs, I can't say much now—I am in a fever. I could scarcely talk to you because I was continually on the point of getting up and throwing my arms around you. I was in hopes you wouldn't have to go home for dinner—that we might go somewhere to dine and dance. You dance—I have dreamed of that over and over—I dancing with you, or you alone dancing with head thrown back and eyes half shut. You must dance for me that way. That is your Spanish self—the distilled Andalusian blood.

I am sitting in your place now and I have raised your glass to my lips. But I am tongue-tied. What you read to me is swimming over me. Your language is still more overwhelming than mine. I am a child compared to you, because when the womb in you speaks it enfolds everything—it is the darkness I adore. You were wrong to think that I appreciated the literary value alone. That was my hypocrisy talking. I have not dared until now to say what I think. But I am plunging—you have opened the void for me—there is no holding back.

Without you realizing it, I have been living with you constantly. But I have been afraid to admit it—I thought it would terrify you. Today I had planned to bring you to my room and show you the water colors. But it seemed so sordid, leading you to my miserable hotel. No, I can't do that. You will lead me somewhere—to your shack, as you call it. Lead me there so that I may put my arms around you.

And I lie, Anaïs, when I tell you that I do not want to worship you. Did you expect me to tell you these things? When I saw [Marcel Pagnol's film] *Marius,* I was dreaming of you—you are like that boat going out to sea, and your sails are full spread, and the sunlight is playing all over you. And like Marius, I have joined the boat at the eleventh hour—I have jumped out the back window and raced to the wharf.

Still, I don't know how much I dare write you in spite of your permission. I have a feeling that I may be committing sacrilege, but then that can't be. My instincts must be right. Nevertheless, I await hungrily some word from you. Yes, you have told me, over and over again, in a hundred different ways, but I am slow, Anaïs, slow perhaps because it is such delicious torture. It is like waiting to see you rise from your throne.

And about Hugo—Anaïs, I can't think of Hugo. It is impossible to think of him and of you. Please don't lie to yourself now. Not before me!

I may call you tomorrow and let you know that this is waiting for you. I would call you immediately, only that Hugo will be there.

There is a telephone at my hotel, but I don't know the number, and I am afraid it is not listed in the book. At any rate, if you should succeed in calling, the number of my room is 40.

Then I won't see you Sunday. That is hard, too. But it is better—you are right.

Henry

[Hotel Central, 1 bis Rue du Maine, Paris 14]
Sunday, 1:30 A.M. [March 6, 1932]

Anaïs:

The most gruelling pace tonight. Have just been to the Trois
Portes for a couple of beers. Trembling as I swallow them, from the
pace at which I worked. Absolutely dizzy with figures . . . dizzy, dizzy,
I tell you. And the strange thing is I don't mind it. I got keyed up. But
all the while I'm working I've got to tear myself out of a coma. You
called me just after I had started and luckily I was switched to a private
room. But I couldn't think about the figures afterwards. I had blind
spots. I called you this evening, not about the telegram but to tell you
I had sent the letter, and as you will know when you get this, I sent
it from the Viking immediately after you left. And today, bundled up
in a bathrobe, an overcoat, a muffler and hat, I sat down and wrote ten
pages more for the book [*Tropic of Cancer*]. The woman I described
leaning out of the window—I wanted to say that she was Spanish. I
am filled with Spain. You don't know how often I encounter the word
"Madrid" or "Barcelona"—even here at the office. When I come to
dollars against the pound, the lire, etc. I come to Madrid and then I
halt. I go dead. But it isn't just here, it's everywhere. I go to the
Rotonde bar and there are Spaniards shouting and arguing. Spain
again. Anaïs. I go to the bar for a drink and the messenger who delivers
me the Havas [news agency] reports mentions a girl he wants to introduce to me—he is a pimp on the side. She comes from Seville. I was
in the Café l'Avenue the other night and there was a pregnant woman
sitting beside me. She opened her coat to show me her stomach—
eight months under way. Some dirty Spaniard, she said, deserted her,
and there she was high and dry, would I give her a hundred *sous* so
that she could eat. I won't have time to say everything. I'm a little
crazy from the excitement of the day. I talked to your maid over the
telephone and she didn't understand me very well, so I said, *"Vous
êtes espagnole, n'est-ce pas?"* Alors, je suis M. Miller. Bon! Crazy,
crazy. [. . .]

Anaïs, you've started the sap flowing. I am not responsible for
what I say or do any more. Listen, you will get the letter and you may
be disappointed. It is such a small part of what I had to say to you, and
I haven't still the courage that I should have. Why, damn it, why? You
have given me permission. But do you expect all that I am going to say?
You read me your notes—yes, yes, there is a difference between what
I write and what I say, what I do. Let us say, there has been.

Anaïs, I am being constantly interrupted. I will try to continue at home. They are curious here that I should be writing so often. They think I am a glutton for punishment. They ask me why don't I go home. Anaïs, I could stay here all night writing you. I see you before me constantly, with your head down and your long lashes lying on your cheeks. And I feel very humble. I don't know why you should single me out—it puzzles me. But I don't want to examine too closely. You have fired me and now I can never again be what I was before, just your friend. Was I ever just that? It seems to me that from the very first, when you opened the door and held out your hand, smiling, I was taken in, I was yours. June felt it too. She said immediately that you were in love with me, or else I with you. But I didn't know myself that it was love. I spoke about you glowingly, without reserve. And then June met you and she fell in love with you, and I was a little unhappy, not because of June, but because of you. And when I came and wept in your house, when I walked through the woods with you, underneath all my sorrow and despair was a deep desire to put my arms around you, to have you love me. But almost your first words froze me. You said *"we* miss her." There was a moment of horror—you know all that, I don't have to explain. But I did not turn away from you. For the first time in my life I was listening to someone say these things without hating that someone. I could have forgiven you anything . . . I can still.

Back in the room and still feverish. Have looked everywhere for the letter. I can't write you yet. I hear the dynamos going outside the window. And there is a strange phenomenon outside—a building glowing like hot metal and beyond it a house pure white, milky, the rest floating in charcoal. I look around my room to see what I can offer you; I see only my silly water colors and notes—notes everywhere, and on the backs your name—show this to Anaïs, ask Anaïs, see Anaïs. . . .

I have been to bed and can't sleep. Up again, shivering, with a desire to write you. It is dawn and everything is bluish. In front of me are some excerpts from Thomas Hardy. They are almost the last I have been guarding, and now here, what do I see—"He returned to the room and sat as watchers sit on Old-Midsummer Eves, expecting the phantom of the Beloved." I will bring the notes with me. They are for you. And you, will you make me a copy of those lines you read from your journal? They were magnificent—and I think it is their magnificence that inhibits me more than anything. How, after listening to them, can I ever write you anything adequate?

Fragments race through my mind—I can't think anything through. Your saying once that the Spanish woman liked her man to come to her with the smell of wine on his lips . . . Saying that you wanted to know a "rake," to understand what such a creature was like . . . Description of yourself walking through Paris and the tips of your breasts taut and tingling. Feeling, as I read your book, that for the first time I was going to know what are a woman's sensations in love . . . Asking myself over and over, does she look at men always with those steady eyes? . . . And then, invitation to walk through the country—to walk, not through the country, but to some obscure inn, to waylay you with wine, smell out your Arab blood. Your blood—I want a smear of it to put under the microscope. Once you came within a foot of me, face to face, the back of a chair between us—how did I ever restrain myself? And there were other times I felt only your mind, and your mind is slippery, it gets between my thoughts and I have to squirt sand or the wheels will slip. . . . Fear that you are coming close to me as you would to some monster, that you are studying me—heretofore *I* have always done the studying. [. . .]

Henry

[Louveciennes]
[March 9, 1932]

[Henry:]

I did not mean to burn you yesterday—I was lying as in a dream— and so dissolved I could not hear you rising—I clung to a prolongation of that moment. When I think of it now I feel a kind of pain to have burned you—say that you forgive me—it was unconscious.

I can't write to you, Henry, though I was awake last night telling you—all night—of that man I discovered yesterday . . . the man I sensed with my feelings the first moment—all the mountains of words, writings, quotations have sundered—I only know now the splendor, the blinding splendor of your room—and that unreal moment—how can a moment be at once so unreal and so warm—so warm.

There is so much you want to know. I remember your phrase: "Only whores appreciate me." I wanted to say: you can only have blood-consciousness with whores, there is too much mind between us, too much literature, too much illusion—but then you denied there had been only mind. . . .

My face makes you think that all my expectations go up, up . . . but you know now that it is not only my mind which is aware of you.

Aware of you, chaotically. I love this strange, treacherous softness of you which always turns to hatred. How did I single you out? I *saw* you with that intense selective way—I saw a mouth that was at once intelligent, animal, and soft . . . strange mixture—a human man, sensitively aware of everything—I love awareness—a man, I told you, whom life made drunk. Your laughter was not a laughter which could hurt, it was mellow and rich. I felt warm, dizzy, and I sang within myself. You always said the truest and deepest things—slowly—and you have a way of saying, like a southerner—hem, hem—trailingly, while off on your own introspective journey—which touched me.

Just before that I had sought, as I told you, suicide. But I waited to meet you, as if that would solve something—and it did. When I saw you I thought, here is a man I could love. And I was no longer afraid of feelings. I couldn't go through with the suicide (idea of killing off romanticism), something held me back. I can only move wholly.

I don't know if it was love—there was a long moment of interruption—the love for June. Henry—the love for June is still there. I couldn't bear seeing her [photograph] yesterday. She possesses us both—everything else is only a temporary victory.

I thought I was in love with your mind and genius (I read you what I thought of your mind and writing)—chaos only with June. I felt your mind watching me. I didn't want love because it is chaos, and it makes the mind vacillate like wind-blown lanterns. I wanted to be very strong before you, to be *against* you—you love so to be against things. I love to be *for* things. You make caricatures. It takes great hate to make caricatures. I elect, I love—the welling of love stifles me at night—as in that dream which you struggled to make *real* yesterday—to nail down, yes, with your engulfing kiss.

When you will feel me veiled, holding back, Henry, it is June. What power you had that first day, tearing from me pages from my journal about her. You do not know to what extent I guard myself, and my feelings. It is strange how you get truth from me.

Henry, I too want to sit and write you a long time, as if it represented a closeness to you. I didn't tell you the joy I felt at your return from Dijon, what a joy, acute, I feel when you act spontaneously as I do. And what a joy again when, in the center of the madness, you say unexpectedly something very deep, the sudden illuminations of living, the lantern never quite blown out—I love that too. Dark living and that awareness—I appreciate that—don't you understand—like an intensification of all pleasures. I love the creator in you, too—who enriches and expands living in ways nobody else understands. I love the sincere and the insincere (I was delighted when you wrote me once and in the middle of the letter became aware it would make a preface!).

On se penetre non par les sensations mais par la pensée, I wonder.

I won't be at Natasha's place tomorrow—write me—or call me at home in the evening just to tell me what you want to say or do. I'll just say "yes" or "no" if anyone is around. I'm afraid I can't see you tomorrow, Wednesday, and yet I have so much to tell you about that portion of your book—the last—which is *extraordinary.*

A.

[Hotel Central, Paris]
1.30 A.M. [March 10, 1932]

Anaïs:

I was stunned when I got your note this morning. Nothing I can ever say will match these words. To you the victory—you have silenced me—I mean so far as expressing these things in writing goes. You don't know how I marvel at your ability to absorb quickly and then turn about, rain down the spears, nail it, penetrate it, envelop it with your intellect. The experience dumbed me. I felt a singular exaltation, a surge of vitality, then of lassitude, of blankness, of wonder, of incredulity . . . everything, everything. Coming home I kept remarking about the Spring wind—everything had grown soft and balmy, the air licked my face, I couldn't gulp down enough of it. And until I got your note I was in a panic . . . I was afraid you would disavow everything. But as I read—I read very slowly because each word was a revelation to me—I thought back to your smiling face, to your sort of innocent gaiety, something I had always sought for in you but never quite realized. There were times you began this way—at Louveciennes—and then the mind crashed through and I would see the grave, round eyes and the set purse of your lips, which used almost to frighten me, or, at any rate, always intimidated me.

You make me tremendously happy to hold me undivided—to let me be the artist, as it were, and yet not forgo the man, the animal, the hungry, insatiable lover. No woman has ever granted me all the privileges I need—and you, why you sing out so blithely, so boldly, with a laugh even—yes, you invite me to go ahead, be myself, venture anything. I adore you for that. That is where you are truly regal, a woman extraordinary. What a woman you are! I laugh to myself now when I think of you. I have no fear of your femaleness. And that you burned—I want that—I would not have it otherwise. You see, in spite of all my intimations, I was not quite prepared for the tempest you invoked. That moment in the room when, standing and swaying, you clung to me with your very womb, it seemed, that blinded me. And then do you know what happened later—you will forgive me, I hope—the blood on your face kept reminding me of the garden scene in [Luis Buñuel's film] *L'Age d'Or* and I was growing frantic and hysterical. Then I remember vividly your dress, the color and the texture of it, the voluptuous airy spaciousness of it—precisely what I would have begged you to wear had I been able to anticipate the moment. I was aware, too, of all that you hint at but tremendously relieved that you treated these things (I am about to say brazenly)—but no, it was nonchalantly.

And today, in the most precious good health, I had very languorous, pleasurable sensations of aches in my arms—from holding you so tightly. It dawned on me very very slowly. I wish I could retain it.

Anaïs, I am sending you this note to the other address.* In my crude way I have a certain feeling of delicacy which prevents me from sending such things to Louveciennes. You will understand, I hope. I am enclosing more of Fred's manuscript, and some more of mine, too. Note how you were anticipating what I wrote today—I refer to your words about "caricature . . . hate etc." I will call around noon tomorrow, and if I don't succeed in getting you I *may* phone you again in the evening. I am timid about that sort of thing, or is it false delicacy? I don't know. When I phone I shall be able to say if it is possible to meet tomorrow—you see I am not yet straightened out with the police about my working card—the red tape is endless.

Henry

[Paris]
Friday [March 11, 1932]

[Anaïs:]

Before starting—just begged ten minutes for this note—terribly, terribly alive, pained, and feeling absolutely that I need you. Allowed the silence deliberately, feeling a great need to withdraw into myself, to write, and a thousand things intervening.

Switch to another machine, frightful; the French machine::: god

*Apparently, Natasha Troubetskoia's studio.

damn, and me drunk with desire to write you. listen; I'll call you in the morning: tonight I'll write or bust: But I must see you. I see you bright and wonderful and at the same time I have been writing to June and all torn apart but you will understand: you must understand. I'll go down in the break and put in a call. Anaïs, stand by me. Don't let the silences worry you: you are all around me like a bright flame. nothing but semi-colons can't find periods or apostrophes. No carbon of this either: fine: drunk::: drunk with life::: Anaïs by Christ: if you knew what I am feeling now.

This one was [written] on arriving [at the office]. Now 3:20 A.M. in Fred's room—all the zest gone & destroyed by figures. Fred is in bed with Gaby of *chambre 48*. She's laid out like a corpse. I feel sorry for her. Tell her to sleep.

Have just read Fred's pages on me—they are good—I think you will say so too. (You know I would like all his mss. back—they are for me, and he would be hurt if I didn't keep them.) Wanted to telephone you tonight but when I was free to go out it was a little after ten and I was afraid you would be in bed. It seemed strange not to see any mail from you, not to hear your voice. Now Saturday and Sunday will have to pass without sign of you. All day yesterday I spent dealing with the police and the real estate company. Nothing is certain yet about my working card. Today I stubbornly refused to let anything interfere with writing. I thought I could carry on after work but no, I was quite exhausted.

I don't like writing you scratchy notes like this—I want space and time for you—but now it is Paris and everything is squeezed up like an *accordéon*. One must elbow even for time.

Anaïs, drinking the wine diluted now—it is near the end. Overpowered again. This table is so rich—everything imaginable on it—typewriter, food, water colors. Gaby's belt and sweater. Fred's mss., flatiron, Rona's medallion, alcohol lamp, Goethe, dossiers, pocketbook, pipes, etc. etc. Inards. I have a sandwich in my hand. Gaby is dead to the world. I'm sitting on her fur coat—Fred says it's alright.

I want to get more familiar with you. I love you—I loved you when you came and sat on the bed—all that second afternoon was like warm mist—and I hear again the way you say my name—with that queer accent of yours.

You arouse in me such a mixture of feelings. I don't know how to approach you. Only come to me—get closer and closer to me. It will be beautiful, I promise you. I like so much your frankness—a humility almost. I could never hurt that.

I had a thought tonight that it was to a woman like you I should have been married. Or, is it that love, in the beginning, always inspires such thoughts? I don't have a fear that you will want to hurt me. I see that you have a strength, too—of a different order, more elusive. No, you won't break. I talked a lot of nonsense—about your frailty. I have been a little embarrassed always. But less so the last time. It will all disappear. You have such a delicious sense of humor—I adore that in you. I want always to see you laughing. It belongs to you. I have been thinking of places we ought to go together—little, obscure places, here and there in Paris. Just to say—here I went with Anaïs—here we ate, or danced, or got drunk together. Ah, to see you really drunk sometime—that would be a treat! I am almost afraid to suggest it—but, Anaïs, when I think of how you press against me, how eagerly you open your legs and how wet you are, God, it drives me mad to think what you would be like when everything falls away. Yesterday, going to the police, waiting in line here and there, I thought of you, of your pressing your legs against me standing up, of the room tottering, of falling on you in darkness and knowing nothing. And I shivered and groaned with delight. I wanted to run and telephone you—and then it was my turn to march to the window.

I am thinking that if the weekend must pass without seeing you it will be unbearable. If this letter reaches you on Saturday—if I get up in time—or can phone you—tell me whether we can meet, and if needs be I can come to Louveciennes Sunday—anything, but I must see you, be near you. *But act,* Anaïs—don't be afraid to treat me coolly. It will be enough to stand near you, to look at you admiringly. Don't venture too much. Just let me be there—if possible, arrange so that we can all go into Paris together. Oh, I don't care, don't arrange anything. Don't do anything that will hurt you, compromise you. I love you, that's all.

Henry

[Paris]
Sunday, 9.30 P.M. [March 13, 1932]

Anaïs:

The gate was locked and I had to turn away from Louveciennes. Foolishly I thought you would be waiting for me! In the afternoon I tried calling you but was told the phone was disconnected Sundays. At six I gathered up my copy and rushed away—caught the train without.

a ticket. Figured it all out, what I was going to say to Hugh—I was going to sweep him off his feet and carry you both back to Paris. The last thing in the world I expected was a dark house. I couldn't believe it. How different it all seemed then when I paced the station platform—I remembered distinctly each time I had waited for the train—your gestures, your words. And now I saw only the stars. My night off! Christ, I couldn't believe that I would not see you. I called my hotel to see if there was any message. *Rien!*

Now I am at [Café] Monsieur Paul's. This is the place—and I find in the writing tablet a photo, which will show you Mme. Paul's honest face. What am I going to do tonight? This will be a restless night. I don't care what happens. I am cruelly disappointed.

[Henry]

[Paris]
Thursday, 1:00 A.M. [March 17, 1932]

[Anaïs:]

Have had about six hours' sleep in the last two days. As you will see from the *pneumatique* I am installed temporarily at the [Hotel] Cronstadt, just across the street from the office. The Cronstadt looks like what a French hotel should look like. But let me go back a pace. I begin somewhere either yesterday or day before, sitting in the anteroom of a physician's office at eight o'clock in the morning. Expect a long examination—for my working card—but instead am asked to take off my shirt and be vaccinated; thirty francs, and *voilà*, I'm *en règle*. At ten o'clock M. [James] King is waiting with his Ford downstairs at the Hotel Central. We are going to Suresnes for some beds, etc. It's a wonderful day, and though the house is locked at Suresnes, we are not deterred. First, M. King drives me up to a villa that he was to own, on the street called Rue de l'Hippodrome, I believe. The villa is called "Villa Henry," and *à côté* is one called "Villa Andrée." We start for Marly le Roi, where there is a cabin in the woods with two divans. In order to take a short cut M. King drives through the woods itself, on the soft greensward. The car bucks like a bronco and we shout and sing as we knock down the underbrush. Then we come to a gate at the edge of the woods; the gate is locked, but M. King, who can accomplish everything, has a big key for the gate. There stands the little shack—no windows, but the roof is tar-papered. We pile the beds and mattresses and a folding table and three chairs on the automobile and start back. On the way we stop off at the gas company and the Lumière Nord and we register and pay deposits. We visit the bank so as to put in enough money to cover the check we are going to give the Société du Champ de Mars. We visit every conceivable sort of company which caters to *locataires*. M. King is only loaning us the divans. He prizes the mattresses even more, though they have big holes in them, because of sentimental reasons. The wool was sheared from sheep who grazed on the plains of Armenia, where M. King comes from. M. King is a pseudonym. He is "Peter Pickem" in the *Chicago Tribune*. He picks the winners at Auteuil and other places.

I forgot—on the way to Marly he told us a story. It was a story about a *plongeur* who was poor and illiterate. He was in love with an Armenian girl who worked as a *bonne*. One day they decided to get married, and it was then that M. King's mother insisted on the girl and boy having some property of their own. So, with the ten thousand francs which the groom had accumulated *plonging* they bought a little house and a tract of land. The point in this story is that today the ground is worth over a hundred thousand francs! These are the sorts of stories M. King specializes in. But wait. M. King can do everything. He ties sailor's knots, cooks good meals, makes reeds for musical instruments, and installs electric fixtures where needed.

We arrive at the apartment [4 Rue Anatole France, Clichy] in the late afternoon, after paying all and sundry, and find that the bathtub is not connected. The place has not been cleaned. A few doors need to be settled on their hinges. The chandeliers are not there. O.K. With M. King's car we go back to the Rue du Faubourg St. Honoré and search his possessions for electric wiring equipment, tools, plates, glasses, etc. Fine. We haven't stopped off anywhere yet for a drink. While M. King mounts the stepladder and tries out the connections, Fred and I fall asleep—sound asleep. It is dark now. When I hold the candle to Fred's face to shake him I see something crawling over his face. I wake him up and he complains of being bitten, shows me the welts on his arm and cheek. We call M. King. This is important. Examine the mattresses and divans—a few live ones crawling sluggishly over the things. Then we get busy and inspect. Hold the candle to the walls. Marvellous! The walls are alive! Big ones, egg-layers, nests, nits, cocoons, spider webs, dead ones, comatose ones, active ones . . . We take matches and burn them alive. But it is hard work—they are coming too fast. M. King pulls me away—"You've killed enough for one afternoon," he says. We go down in the cellar and turn on the water. Tell the concierge, who is a new concierge and like a child. She says it's terrible. We agree. Then we move all our luggage into one room and flee. M. King is worried about his Armenian wool mattresses. They were in the family a long time—the sheep used to graze right near his home, at the foot of Ararat.

It is too late to call the Société du Champ de Mars. We decide to write them a nice letter. At Levallois-Perret we stop off for a *casse-croûte*. Here is where [Blaise Cendrars' character] Moravagine went after he had explored the mouth of the Orinoco, or was it before? I have always wanted to look upon the men of Levallois-Perret. Fine. We order cold pork and plenty of potato salad. We eat it, and wash it down with the rarest of *vin blanc ordinaire* I have ever tasted. M. King knows about wines, too. He confirms my judgment. We order Camembert and Gorgonzola and a little Brie for Fred. Fred is upset about the bedbugs. He remembers them from the Rue Mazarine. But the wine. We consume several bottles, and then we order coffee and Cointreau. It's just a little snack before going to work. A *casse-croûte*. Upstairs there is a hotel and the female lodgers are permitted to come downstairs, back of the dining room, and do their laundering and ironing. That's how it is at Levallois-Perret. And if you ride in a car along the Seine, which the *bateaux mouches* miss on their quotidian journey to and fro. You see wonderful things in M. King's car, especially when the windows are cleaned.

After work I walk home with Joe.* He is going to put me up for the night. We get to the Oasis and we have another little snack, a *plat du jour* with a glass of beer. I am very tired and aching to lie down. But while we are eating—we are just through, really—a young woman comes in and greets me. I recognize her. "Oh, my dear sir, you are so kind, it must be Heaven that has sent you to me. May I sit down? May I order something hot?" I give Joe a big horse wink (here is a column, Joe!) and order an *épaule de veau avec pommes nouvelles* for the girl. This is something hot—for four francs! Yes, she has the same story to tell me. She cannot go back to her room until she pays a little money down. Just a few francs, say twenty or thirty. She says she is Irish—Nell

---

*Wambly Bald, the young Chicagoan who wrote a weekly column for the Paris edition of the Chicago *Tribune*, apparently called everybody "Joe." Miller jokingly picked up the habit and called Bald and Alfred Perlès "Joe," and Perlès also referred to Miller as "Joe." See Biographical Notes for Bald.

O'Connor, but she was born in Latvia and talks like a Greek. If you question her closely (which I have done several times) you discover that she is nearly Irish. Anyway, Joe is listening with a big smile. He has never heard her line before. And while she eats she whispers in my ear. I tell her no. So she orders some cake and a cup of tea. When I go to pay I haven't enough money. Joe pays. Then we stand on the corner outside the Rotonde and try to shake her off. She's begging Joe for twenty francs. She has never sold herself, you understand. She knows now that I can't give her anything so she concentrates on Joe. But Joe says he's married. Then he asks her if a hundred francs would be enough. "But, my dear sir," she says, "why do you ask me that? I only want twenty or thirty francs." Joe says, "But if I had a hundred francs I would like to give it to you. But I haven't." And then suddenly a man without a coat or hat comes up, his lips all slavered. He says he has had fever for five days. He shakes my hand warmly. "You're a gentleman!" It is the waiter from the Bar Dominique—he remembers me because I am always so polite to him. He is very sensitive tonight. So he insists on going to the Dôme Bar and buying me something. I don't want to go but I want to get rid of the girl. So we go—but first I tell him only on condition that it is one drink, no more. At the bar he won't let me order coffee—I must have something good. We order and then he begins telling Joe what a fine guy I am—that I'm better than any woman, etc. The girl talks Russian to him. It seems to be near five o'clock—they're closing up soon. Just then a burly fellow with a brief-case puts his head in between me and the girl, who is chewing my ear off about her hotel bill. He looks at me strangely, then at the girl. He insults her. He says she has been talking to niggers. I smile a little, but he stands there and grows more insulting. My blood is growing cold. I wonder how long it's going to last. Suddenly he moves off, and then suddenly he turns again, near the door and hurls a few more words in her direction. This gets me. I go up and give him a terrific shove, smashing him against the door. I know my face is white, my lips are twitching. I yell at him. I tell him to shut up. And the funny thing is he shuts up. He opens his mouth but he can't get a word out. He is dumbfounded, and I even more than he. I get so wrought up because he refuses to come to blows that I run out of the place. I don't know where to hide my rage. And as I turn the corner the Russian is after me. And behind him is the garçon demanding his money. The Russian turns on him savagely and tells him he'll be back in five minutes. The garçon is going to call the gendarmes. I don't know what to say. I grab the Russian by the arm and lift his head up. "What's the matter, are you ill?" "No," he said, and apologizes piteously. "I haven't enough money. Lend me fifteen francs and call for me at the bar tomorrow." Joe pays again, but I get the thanks. I have the warm heart. That licks Joe completely. "Damn these Russians," he says, "they're yellow dogs." This gentleman stuff! *D'accord!*

So we're too excited to go to bed. We walk around for a half hour and dawn comes up. Then we go to Joe's room and while I snore he sits up and reads. And during the night I accidentally twine my legs around his, thinking it's a woman. That makes Joe nervous.

Only a few hours' sleep and Fred is knocking at the door. Time to go to the Ministère de Travail. Bang, like a cold douche, up and out. On the line at Rue Vaugirard, listening to the interpreter talk to the applicants. Talks Russian, Czech, Hungarian, Arabic, German, French, Spanish, English. "I don't know whether the application will be favorable or *dis*favorable, but go please now to buy an envelope and stamp. Next time, you bring certificate of domicile, passeport and five photographies without hats." *Je suis presque en règle maintenant.* O.K. Subway to Rome, Société du Champ de Mars. What about the disinfectors? Haven't started yet. But they telephoned. Only the second case on record. O.K. Back to Clichy and remove some of our belongings. A few semiconscious ones lying around here and there. Flick 'em off nonchalantly. Look for a hotel. Then I step into a booth and telephone Louveciennes. But you are not there. Around nine o'clock every time the phone rings I think it may be you. Hot wire from the Associated Press: "Margery Latimer on a honeymoon with Jean Toomer—to favor miscegenation." Nobody here seems to know who Margery Latimer is. Steel goes up a few points. The pivotals are soft today, and the volatiles firm up after yesterday's slump. Abitibi is in shape again.

So I'm at the Cronstadt and you have the telephone number. I will be here at the office in the afternoon. If you don't find me at the hotel try this joint—editorial room. I want you to see the Cronstadt. Probably won't get back to Clichy until the end of the week. I don't think my vaccination took. My arm has not swelled up. All I have is a little fever, but that may be from the excitement. In the morning I will take a bath and disinfect myself. I'm dog tired. We locked the gate at Marly all right. Tonight M. King was wearing a tuxedo. Did you know that today was St. Patrick's day? *Erin Go Bragh!*

Henry

[Louveciennes]
[March 20, 1932]

[Henry:]

Je pense à toi tous le temps.

Persecutions have begun. My friends—a Spanish painter, a guitarist, the tenor who has been staying with Joaquin, a poet, a homosexual, a Roumanian painter, an American composer, etc. etc.—they are all pained, injured, that I should defend Lawrence. *Una mujer tan ideal, que lastima!* which means "For such an ideal woman, what a pity." They look sadly at me. A little like Fred's eyes, swimming in illusions. You see, I had been carved in copper and set with jewels for a legend of Pushkin. For the guitarist I was as tender as his instrument. For the composer I was Mélisande, who sings about the world: *Je ne suis pas heureuse ici.*

And do you know what I think? I am filled with *your* livingness, and I expect with impatience the day when I can defend your writing! It gives me exultation to think of your writing and of how I'm going to defend it, as you defended Buñuel.

I am glad I didn't blush before Fred. That day was a high peak of my love, Henry. I wanted to shout: today I love Henry! Perhaps you wish I had *acted* well, pretended casualness. I don't know. Write to me. I need your letters, as human assertions of reality. When I come home at night to a peace-wrapped house, to dream, to the demonstrations of joy from the dogs, I am sure I am living in a dream. No, I feel your livingness in my body, I still hear your words. I want to hear them again. I too want time with you.

One man I know wants to frighten me. When I talk about you he says: "He cannot appreciate you." He is wrong. Only one detail—a small, small one. About costume. You have got the sense of it. What is costume? Not what Fred said—but a manifestation of art, of imagination, another aspect of creation, that's all. What is a house? The same. Manifestations of one's ideas, feelings, nostalgias, evocation of countries, atmospheres, etc. Expression. Something that has a *meaning.* Now you see it is all *more* than clothes, more than a house. Besides, however moth-like or elusive, I don't feel that I slip between your fingers—do you? I need your letters. Yet I can't write you as much as before, for lack of time!

We are not going away.

Someone said something I liked about my book. It shows that a woman is not really a *critic* but a penetrator. She does not judge, she understands.

Interruption. Visit from Walter Pach, translator of Elie Faure.* Serene, austere, civilized conversation about art. He reads [E. E.] Cummings only, among the moderns. Remembers meeting you in N.Y. He has a light touch, sense of humor too. Peddled the *History of Art* for *7 years* before it was accepted.

Tomorrow I'll write you about the manifesto.

Anaïs

Keep Tuesday afternoon free.

[Clichy]
[March 21, 1932]

Anaïs—

All I can say is that I am mad about you. I tried to write a letter and couldn't. I am writing you constantly—in my head and the days pass and I wonder what you will think. I am waiting impatiently to see you. Tuesday is so far off. And not just Tuesday—I am wondering when you will come to stay overnight—when I can have you for a long spell—it torments me to see you for just a few hours and then surrender you. When I see you all that I wanted to say vanishes—the time is so precious and words are extraneous. But you make me so happy— because I *can* talk to you. I love your brightness, your preparations for flight, your legs like a vise, the warmth between your legs. Yes, Anaïs, I want to demask you. I am too gallant with you. I want to look at you long and ardently, pick up your dress, fondle you, examine you. Do you know I have scarcely looked at you? There is still too much sacredness clinging to you.

Your letter—ah, these flies! You make me smile. And you make me adore you too. It's true, I don't appreciate you enough. It's true. But I never said that you don't appreciate me. I think there must be a mistake in your English. That would be too egotistical for me to say.

Anaïs, I don't know how to tell you what I feel. I live in a perpetual expectancy. You come and the time slips away in a dream. It is only

*See Biographical Notes.

when you go that I realize completely your presence. And then it is too late. You numb me.

I try to picture your life at Louveciennes but I can't. Walter Pach? A drunken dream—and besides, I dislike him, why, I can't say. Your book? That too seems unreal. Only when you come and I look at you does the picture become clearer. But you go away so quickly—I don't know what to think. Yes, I see the Poushkine legend clearly. I see you in my mind as sitting on that throne, jewels around your neck, sandals, big rings, painted fingernails, strange Spanish voice, living some kind of a lie which is not a lie exactly, but a fairy tale.

I put on my corduroy trousers tonight and I saw they were stained. But I can't for the life of me associate the stain with this princess in Louveciennes who holds court with guitarists and poets and tenors and critics. I didn't try very hard to get the stain off. I saw you coming to the washroom and laying your head on my shoulder. I can't see you writing "An Unprofessional Study."

This is a little drunken, Anaïs. I am saying to myself "here is the first woman with whom I can be absolutely sincere." I remember your saying—"you could fool me. I wouldn't know it." When I walk along the boulevards and think of that. I can't fool you—and yet I would like to. I mean that I can never be absolutely loyal—it's not in me. I love women, or life, too much—which it is, I don't know. But laugh, Anaïs, I love to hear you laugh. You are the only woman who has had a sense of gaiety, a wise tolerance—no more, you seem to urge me to betray you. I love you for that. And what makes you do that—love? Oh, it is beautiful to love and be free at the same time.

I don't know what I expect of you, but it is something in the way of a miracle. I am going to demand everything of you—even the impossible, because you encourage it. You are really strong. I like even your deceit, your treachery. It seems aristocratic to me. (Does "aristocratic" sound wrong in my mouth?)

Yes, Anaïs, I was thinking how I could betray you, but I can't. I want you. I want to undress you, vulgarize you a bit—ah, I don't know what I am saying. I am a little drunk because you are not here. I would like to clap my hands and, voilà—Anaïs! I want to own you, use you. I want to fuck you, I want to teach you things. No, I don't appreciate you—God forbid! Perhaps I even want to humiliate you a little—why, why? Why don't I get down on my knees and just worship you? I can't. I love you laughingly.

Do you like that?

And, dear Anaïs, I am so many things. You see only the good things now—or at least you lead me to believe so. I want you for a whole day at least. I want to go places with you—possess you. You don't know how insatiable I am. Or how dastardly. And how selfish!

I have been on my good behavior with you. But I warn you I am no angel. I think principally that I am a little drunk. I love you. I go to bed now—it is too painful to stay awake. I love you. I am insatiable. I will ask you to do the impossible. What it is I don't know. You will tell me probably. You are faster than I am. I love your cunt, Anaïs—it drives me crazy. And the way you say my name! God, it's unreal. Listen, I am very drunk. I am hurt to be here alone. I need you. Can I say anything to you? I can, can't I?

Come quickly then and screw me. Shoot with me. Wrap your legs around me. Warm me.

[Henry]

[Louveciennes]
[March 21, 1932]

[Henry:]

The manifesto* is magnificent—outrageously ironic sometimes, startling of course, comical, inconsequential, and effective, stimulating. One is half tempted to subscribe to it, to work on it, because of it. It is specially effective when you and Fred are *for* things, in your two contrasting ways of approaching them. [. . .]

What a powerful duet! What a mixture of significant irrelevancies, illuminating incongruities! [. . .]

The beginning, "a proclamation of rebellion against the puerilities in the arts and literature etc.," arouses my enthusiasm. I take this seriously: "They were afraid to recover, to tamper with, to approach the steel tabernacle containing the sacred, explosive essence of destruc-

---

*"The New Instinctivism (A Duet in Creative Violence, 1930)" had been composed by H. M. and Alfred Perlès in response to the many manifestoes issued by various literary groupings (Dada, Surrealism, et al.). Originally intended for the summer 1931 issue of *The New Review*, while it was under the supervision of Peter Neagoe, it was killed in the galley stage when the editor, Samuel Putnam, returned. Advertised again in *The Booster* of October 1937, to be "published shortly" as a "Booster Broadside," it apparently did not get printed because H. M. and his friends lost control of this short-lived venture. See Biographical Notes for Neagoe.

tion." It is one of those phrases one would live and die for. I want to wave it like a banner. It is one of the prefaces to your work, Henry. *J'en suis ébloui.* "Because it failed to liberate the element of violence in man without which he ceases to be creative," another pregnant phrase. I believe in it, I believe in you. I believed in it before you worded it, *instinctively.* I urged you on—you remember? I'm an instinctivist, even if it is too late, and today you are something else, even if today you laugh at yesterday. There is something all through the manifesto which is permanent, indelible. I subscribe to its indelible truths! You must please do the same, especially when you write: "We are against all obscenity which has not for its ultimate goal some high purpose, some reason of state, some religious significance." [. . .]

The quotation on "The sway of alcohol . . ." I took that seriously. I was trying to say something like that to you one day, only it was not so clear: there are two worlds, two states of being—alcoholic or nonalcoholic, and without alcohol, you seemed to have taken me into the second, which I love: the Yes-function. "It brings its rotary from the chill periphery of things to the radiant core." To you the triumph of having done that to me without alcohol. But you will see me drunk, too. "The drunken consciousness is one bit of the mystical consciousness." I know that now. It is *your* revelation. It is your effect on me. And June's effect. (Because, as I wrote in my book on Lawrence, "alcohol alone does not release the blood consciousness—passionate feelings accomplish the same thing.")

Remind me to tell you something about the "puerilities" of certain violent attacks of yours! Occasionally, oh, rarely, I find that I prefer them to the puerilities of tasteless things, of hypocrisies, of mincing femininities, but I ask you, half-jokingly, why, after you glorify Mlle. Claude's naturalness, why do you [inveigh against] her rinsing of the bidet? But that's logic. I am against logic! Besides, I think I understand. Certain gestures (I felt that in the Rue Blondel*) destroy the magic. But you are against magic too!

Anaïs

---

*A. N. and her husband had visited a bordello at 32 Rue Blondel on H. M.'s recommendation. See *The Diary of Anaïs Nin,* 1931–1934, pp. 59–60, where H. M. has been substituted for Hugh Guiler.

[Louveciennes]
Saturday morning [March 26, 1932]

This is strange, Henry. Before, as soon as I came home from all kinds of places I would sit down and write in my journal. Now I want to write *you*, talk with you. Our "engagements" are so unnatural—the spaces in between, the set hours, when I have, like tonight, a desperate need of seeing you. I hinted to Hugh we might go out with you tomorrow night but he wouldn't hear of it.

We have just seen the *Beggars' Opera*,* in German, at the Ursulines. Have you seen it? It is wonderful in spots, some fantastic settings, the skeletons of sailing ships, little sinister streets, gigantic barrels of beer, cellars like bandit caves, the macabre faces of the beggars. The sound of German arouses a curious nostalgia. I loved the wedding scene with the stolen trappings, the chair with the bullet hole, and the woman singing a Russian song. In between, when it was slow, realistic, literal, I thought of other things—of Fred's portrait of you. Tell him again how much I like it. I thought that your enthusiasm and mine resemble each other. I love when you say: all that happens *is good*, it is *good.* I say all that happens is *wonderful.* For me it is all symphonic, and I am so aroused by living—god, Henry, in you alone I have found the same swelling of enthusiasm, the same quick rising of the blood, the fullness, the fullness . . .

Before, I almost used to think there was something wrong. Everybody else seemed to have the *brakes on.* A scene in a movie, a voice, a phrase was not for them volcanic. I never feel the brakes. I overflow. And when I feel your excitement about life flaring, next to mine, then it makes me dizzy. What will we do, Henry, the night Hugh goes to Lyon? Today I would have liked to have been sewing curtains in your place while you talk to me. I have the *European Caravan* † for you. You may have found [Alain Fournier's] *Le Grand Meaulnes* a little pale perhaps. (I spell "god" with a small "g" because I do not believe in him, but I love to swear by him, which shows what a Christian fear of sacrilege I have.)

Note: "Correct Anaïs' English." I *feel* it so very quaky tonight. But I have no time to read it over!

*G. W. Pabst's film *Die Dreigroschenoper.*
†An anthology edited by Samuel Putnam.

Do you think we are happy together because we feel we are "getting somewhere," whereas you had the feeling that with June you were being led into more and more obscurity, mystery, entanglements? And suppose the "getting somewhere feeling" meant simply reaching a clarity, a knowledge, the very opposite of Dostoevsky—and that the clarity I have I may throw away, discard, repudiate entirely. . . . You see, I often return to this conflict—the passion for truth, and also the passion for darkness.

[Anais]

[Clichy]
Monday [March 28, 1932]

Dear Anaïs:

I've been in a state of morbidity the last few days. I wanted to write but there was cleaning to do, or else we had to sit in the kitchen and twiddle our thumbs while the men papered the walls. Now everything is in order—my windows are clean and I look out on that delightful little *cité* with the low houses and feel the surge again.

There is a danger, if one doesn't write habitually, that one will lose the habit. I am always in fear of that. And when you are thinking constantly, writing in your head, writing while you undress, wash your teeth, scrub the dishes, etc. you get roiled and everything turns to mud.

When I saw your letters coming I got panicky. How would I ever answer them? The night you left me in the Hotel Cronstadt I was in a fever. I made so many notes, and I was going afterwards to the office to write . . . but I didn't. I think I saw *L'Amoureuse Aventure,* and though it was insignificant it was full of meaning for me. Sometime you will see it and tell me what you felt. There is no use now, going into it.

I have a large envelope before me on which are the notes I scribbled after you left. I want to give you an idea. . . . "Ask some rector for a copy of the *Apocrypha*" . . . "Read Rabelais in old French." "Reread Cervantes" . . . "Write Joe's column in the morning." "Include dream of Aunt Annie—see the dream book." "Make the Last Book the first of a series—a life job, like Proust's." "Anaïs must see *A Nous la Liberté.*" . . . "Read the *Golden Ass* of Apuleius and *Les Diaboliques* in French." . . . "Go to Russian Church on Rue Crimée for the music." . . . "Get back the first volume of *Albertine* and make annotations . . . write copiously, there is time for everything" . . . "Read Jacques Maritain." . . . "Tell Anaïs how I stumbled into Anatole coming out of the Gare St. Lazare that afternoon . . . Anatole is a beautiful character." "Begin the book with paean to Buñuel." "Go with Anaïs to the Franco-Czech restaurant on the Rue St. Anne."

I was glad you liked the Thomas Hardy excerpts, and now I think of it, I want to make a copy again for myself. Remind me to show you something on "Decadence" from Havelock Ellis' Introduction to [J. K. Huysmans'] *Against the Grain.* You will like it.

After you left the other day I had an experience. As I was finishing work my friend Ned Calmer, of the *Herald* (the fellow I mentioned regarding the book review), came to the office expressly to look me up. He had a fellow with him who was in love with Bertha and this chap wanted to talk to someone who knew her. He was lovesick. Well, we began in the Chope Cadet—Calmer and I alone, at first. A rush of talk—commencing with *Sorgen und Sorgen*—that singer in *L'Opéra de Quat'sous.* * And ever since, I have been mumbling phrases from that thing—saying half quixotically, half ruefully, to myself: "They who walk in the light do not see those in the shadow." That was quite beautiful, if you remember (sticky, though), when toward the end the light closed down gradually on the retreating figures. I too have lots to say about the picture. What gripped me when I saw it (I went alone) was the melancholy, that pervasive, insidious German despair which the French know nothing about. I want to flee from it, naturally, but it is part of me, and it always chokes me. And when you wrote once "I would like to call you Heinrich," I appreciated it. I am more *Heinrich* than Henry. I was always "little Henry," *der kleine.* I was impish, and I was very good but I brought sorrow. And oh, someday, what a treat you will have when you read Thiess . . . Frank Thiess. I want you to read his two books, and in the order I suggest. The title of the first escapes me; it is sensational, a sort of recrudescence of Dumas (which [Samuel] Putnam talks of in connection with a branch of French modernists).† The second, *Interlude,* will make you weep. And this I

---

*The French version of G. W. Pabst's film based on the Bertold Brecht / Kurt Weill musical play *Die Dreigroschenoper* featured a cast different from the German and English versions. Albert Prejean played Mack the Knife; Margo Lion, Jenny (created by Lotte Lenya); and Antonin Artaud, Peacham.

†H. M. apparently refers to a novel by the German writer Frank Thiess (born 1890),

applaud and admire in the German spirit. Not Goethe or Schiller, not the great Germans. But this other is like their music, the music of Schubert perhaps, or even Schumann. Fred is singing something of Schubert's always—a very beautiful thing—and when Fred is singing it, it is at once comical and pathetic—it makes you weep as clowns make you weep. You blush before your tenderness. But I remember this song from Vienna. That walk one evening before the Graben, before the Hotel Muller, with June, debating whether I would go back next day and look up the hotel register to see if she had slept there in the same room with a certain individual. That whole Vienna episode was a nightmare to me—I gave a little of it in the novel, I think—the part about the Ferris Wheel, the Jew who talked about God continually, the woman in the café playing the zither with long nails, the whores under the gas lamps, creating for me that imaginary scene which I inserted in the novel. Vienna! The name is magic to me (no, I don't destroy magic!) and I wanted to be so happy there with June, with Vienna, with her women, her lovely boulevards, her desuetude, her softness. But everything turned out differently, as everything always does. I lived cooped up in a ghetto, in a vile little flat with bedbugs and everyone was dying of poverty, of misery, around us. And all the while there was that infernal hotel register and I didn't have the courage to find out— the truth was too much for me.

And night before last, when Fred came home, we talked till six in the morning about June, and about you. You see, Fred likes you tremendously. He thinks you are quite wonderful—the first woman whom he could admire—for me! And then he goes on to talk of June—*she is evil,* he says. She is bad for you. But you are blind . . . you want to be tortured. And yet you are intelligent, too. You see things. Yes, I know all her good points, but they don't interest me. I see her bad points. She's a fake. And then he gets conscience-stricken. He thinks he is hurting me. But I urge him to go on. (I might learn something!) But no, I learn nothing. We agree, at the end, that we are both right. Only, afterwards, there are seeds which germinate, poison- ous little seeds. I see all right—only too clearly. I see everything. I know

---

which achieved notoriety for its theme: incest between brother and sister of an aristo- cratic family (*Die Verdammten,* 1922). H. T. Lowe-Porter translated the book as *Devil's Shadow* (New York: Knopf, 1928). *Interlude (Frauenraub)* was translated by Caroline Frederick (New York: Knopf, 1929), and was part of a series of novels written between 1924 and 1931, published under the overall title: *Jugend (Youth).*

more than anybody will know about her. But I am two beings. With my seeing eye I rend her—I could stab her over and over . . . one death would not be good enough . . . I would resurrect her in order to kill her again and again. There is no limit to my fury. And then there is the other me, maybe it's little Henry again, I don't know, but it is a me that is absolutely trusting, *naïf*, child-like, and that me accepts all the stories, all the lies, all the treachery. When she says "I love you," everything else vanishes—in that moment I live eternities. With that June I want to live. (But of course that June is seldom.) And then there is a June who sees all my facets—who sees me as a first-rate clown, as a liar, as a hero, as a god, as a son-of-a-bitch, as this and that. Is it her intelligence that is lacking? Why doesn't she adhere to that vision? Why does she get angry and hurt and jealous and spiteful and malign and cruel? That, I can't understand.

And so, when I read Proust (I am about finished now) I begin to perceive things, things I already knew, things I refused to bring to the surface. Like him, I could cry out in anguish because my instincts are so sure. But like him, the mind deflects me. I can make the most extravagant allowances. I have a dubiety that is incredible. For example—apropos of June—Fred mentions a letter from Roland which he discovered in a book I loaned him. He read the letter—it was irresistible. "Well, you read the letter, too," he says. "What did you make of it?" Make of it? I look at him blankly. I never made anything of Roland's letters. We used to read them together and laugh uproariously. The more passionate he became the funnier it seemed. (His letter, I must add, ended with "kisses.") Well, the idea of June kissing Roland seemed preposterous to me always. She had no difficulty in convincing me of that. But I get to thinking about Roland. How June said one night, in a rage, "I ought to go back to America and fuck Roland—he's the one I ought to give my love to . . . he deserves it." "To fuck Roland"—you can't imagine how coarse, how vile, how brutal that sounded to my ears. She could envisage the idea, then fucking someone like that—even if only in revenge? Let me think about Roland. Was he so terrible to look upon? No. Was he a fool? Yes. But a poetic fool. One could be so terribly sorry for Roland that one might surrender to him as one throws a bone to a dog.

Again . . . does a man who is represented always and only as a blind worshipper . . . does such a man throw kisses to a woman in his letters? She says he wouldn't dare to talk that way to her (but there are things she forgets about these conversations). No, there is no solution to this problem, no solution to any of them. I ask her once, when everything is soft and melting, when she is absolutely one with me, I ask her—"about Pop now, was all that true you told me?" She nods her head. "Come now . . . maybe once or twice?" "Ah no, Val, it was more than that . . . too many times for me to remember . . . all Summer, or all Winter, I forget which it was. Night after night." This, mind you, she says slowly, reflectively, as something to be regretted but not gainsaid. But I won't believe this. Why won't I? Is anything too preposterous to believe? Of June I should believe anything because she is capable of anything. But I see myself departing from America. A few days before I sail, a discussion by the window—a cold February day, dreary Brooklyn, dirty snow in the streets, the floor unwashed, pins in her skirt, and in the lavatory expensive bottles of this and that. "You are unhappy here," she says. "Why don't you go to Europe? I will follow you soon." And then she unrolls the scheme. Pop is just a tool. . . . She handles the subject with the most amazing callousness . . . with an indifferent cruelty toward Pop. But I refuse to go at first. And yet, just that word "Europe" made something rise in me, tempted me severely. We came back to the subject later. It boiled down to a choice between her and Europe. She threw herself away. Magnanimously. (All this came back to me in seeing *Marius*—the final scene by the window when the girl talks to the father.) Well, I went. And that morning, as I rush downstairs for a taxi, a man is standing in the hallway, talking to the landlord. He is asking about a Mr. Miller—just as I pass by them. And ordinarily, the landlord would have stopped me—why this is Mr. Miller—but I forestalled that. I sensed something wrong and rushed into the street. So this then was Pop—and what an odious creature! And Pop was jealous. Was that it, or was Pop simply making sure that I was going? And whom did Pop think I was? (He too was torn with lies—he had been told she was my wife, but I can see now that he didn't believe that either.) And while the trunk was tied to the taxi—it took an interminable time—Pop stood across the street on a corner and watched. He even sent a man over to read the address on the trunk. Oh yes, I caught it all. And it was agonizing. June upstairs hanging out the window for a last glimpse of me. And there I sat in the taxi, not daring to look up—I the husband not daring—can you picture that? And Pop saw June and June saw Pop, and what exchange went on between them I can't possibly imagine. On the boat I pace the deck feverishly before she starts. I am half minded to go back. Strongly minded to. The moment she starts I am convinced I should have returned, but it is too late. Always too late. In the stateroom I toss around on the bunk. Misery, anguish. How will I ever pass the ten days at sea? And then London? What am I going to do in London? And not enough money in my pocket to get to France. I must wait in London, stall, kill time, fake it again, until June wires me money. And meanwhile Pop. What happened that night after I left? What explanations? And perhaps that night—that very night—she bought the champagne which Pop always kept on ice for her in order to drown her sorrow, in order to give herself to Pop. Don't you see what torture that is? And no matter what she says, not even if she swears by her mother's sacred blood, can I be sure of her. And this is one little incident. Well, I am not crazy. I am living, eh? Yes, I am living, but all that is boiling, stewing inside me. I shall never be able to sneer hard enough, and if I hurt anyone it will not be her. When I see women with lying eyes I adore them. What right has a woman to look at you with truthful eyes? Woman brings pain. Woman is evil. There are no exceptions. I tell you, even the angels are liars. What does Proust say? "We lie all our lives, and more especially, only perhaps, to those whom we love." Open your Proust. I have underlined it for you. What is not underlined is worthless. I see all the rubbish that annoyed you. It annoys me too. Fuck the Princesse de Parma and the Duke de Guermantes and Mme. Villeparisis. And Monsieur Norpois. Sorgen, Sorgen . . . Somebody is sitting on a wall all the time, like Humpty Dumpty, and below there is an organ grinder. When the music plays it is like someone is turning a coat inside out and you see that the lining is stained with perspiration, the lice drop out, there are buttons missing, the sleeves have shrunk.

But I am happy, Anaïs. I am happy about you, for you, with you. I want no more of this dark, groaning, wailing love. Fred brought your picture home last night. He stole it from the office after Waverley Root had written the review of your book [on D. H. Lawrence]. I am going to present you with the original text—a little souvenir of my days on the *Tribune*—because they are short—I have been given notice already. But there is your photo. I hung it on the wall immediately. I went up to it and kissed it on the mouth. It is just the right height. And the eyes are grave and downward looking. Yes, it is you, and I am in love with you and I am going to be frank with you, brutally frank, because when you have an equal you can afford to be frank. And now you are like sunshine that bathes me, like a song. (Oh yes . . . very important!) How was it that when I stood by the window, listening to June, I said suddenly, "No, I don't want to go to Paris; I want to go to Spain!" And June insisted on Paris (because I think she felt that I always hated it—I used to say so then). But I was thinking of Spain because I had had enough of Nordic climes, of dreary faces, of cold streets, of studio debauches, of odious tippling. I wanted the sunshine, the oranges, the fragrance of the earth, and then the bleak, stark hills, the scabrous rocks, the severity and violence of Spain. I wanted to hear women with musical voices, women soft and undulating, women all women, slaves maybe, dupes too, but what matter . . . *women*. Did she sense that? I said nothing about it, I know. But she sent me to the French women because she was sure they were unattractive. When someone loves you do they send you away? "Yes, Val, more than I can remember . . . all that Summer, or Winter, every night, night after night." Christ, not for this could she have sent me away? Or is she an angel who made this sacrifice in order to have me as she wanted me, as her lover, as some flower removed from an unhealthy soil? That is where Rilke comes in . . . his angels. But Rilke is crazy. He has invented these angels. They are his angels, not of this world. They are German angels, with romantic wings and they float over the world in love until the wings are melted by the sun.

So I can look at you now every day. Anaïs Nin, an unprofessional study. O.K. But the first paragraph of Root's makes me jump. "She must have something of the man in her to . . ." No, don't say that. This is untrue. This is shoddy thinking, journalism, quick escapes. No, Anaïs is all woman and she has no wings, thank God. But there is a devil inside me. I know one Anaïs. Let June come. Then what? Prepare yourself—ah yes, I keep saying that all the time. Prepare yourself. And yet, this time it wouldn't hurt so much. This time I would accept it as Fate. That is how life is, then. *C'est la vie.* So that's it. . . . I nod my head ruefully, I gather up the pieces, I weave another poem. I cut off my head and walk the streets regarding the head with my navel. This is my head now and it no longer belongs to my body. I will see with my navel. I will see perhaps like a horse sees—instead of jalousies accordions flung open, instead of hats sceptres. Is that June coming down the street? No, it is a bottle of absinthe. Is this Anaïs? No, it is a hydrangea. What do I see beneath their dresses—a dream of Aunt Annie—wooden flowers in a glass of water, flowers that open only in H_2O. I open the dictionary and being a horse with only a navel it appears that certain words are missing. It is a dictionary for horses. There are no such terms in the dictionary as "truth," "loyalty," "justice." Love? You buy it in paper packages from the Japanese, you drop it into a glass of water. Love is something that goes on only in H_2O. This means that libraries have to be destroyed. This means that when a woman slips between your legs it is only for the sake of slipping a snake into your entrails. When she sings with joy the organ grinder is standing outside behind the wall. *Sorgen. Sorgen.* She will do anything for you but cut off your head.

How will we spend the night when Hugh goes away? That I was thinking about too. I will be working most likely, but you could meet me when I'm through—between 12.30 and 1.00. You wait for me in the Chope Cadet or any place you like, and we will go to Montmartre and sit down somewhere for a drink. And then we will come back here and we will eat. And we will drink again and talk. And the rooster will be crowing. He is crowing now. He crows all the time. And now my room looks beautifully austere. Only there is the smell of dust in it. I don't know how to get rid of that. Maybe you clean the room again. But it looks clean. My blanket, you see, is a horse blanket—it has a peculiar odor—an ineradicable one. And this divan does not resemble a divan, but a cot in a hospital. Yes, I have a feeling that I am living in an asylum of some sort, where they allow you liberties, special privileges. You clean your own room, of course. But you are free to do as you please—you can write, or paint, or sing in your room. In the next room lives a nut who is writing about dogs. He must write about dogs because Marcienne loves dogs and he has promised Marcienne that he will write a chapter for her—on dogs. Someday Marcienne is going to come with the baby. I propose to him that he take Marcienne in, with the baby. It would be wonderful to have a baby in the house—then the floor would have to be clean because babies pick things up from the floor and swallow them. But we don't need a *femme de ménage* just yet. When I leave the *Tribune* I can devote myself assiduously to the cleaning. Fred will go to work and pay the rent and buy the food and hand me cigarettes. He will keep me like a mistress. I will make a good mistress, because I am not jealous or exacting. And I will have time then to get the dusty smell out of the rooms, do the laundry, run errands, cash the bottles, perhaps time too for a little *raccommodage.* It is bad to put on holey socks—it gets your feet dirty.

I forgot what I started to say earlier, about meeting Ned Calmer. It seems that he himself writes the book reviews occasionally, and when I suggested that he write up yours he assented willingly. So, if you want it, send him a copy of the book: Edgar Calmer, *N.Y. Herald,* 21 Rue de Berri. Add a little note saying that I suggested that you send him it and that you would appreciate his doing it, etc.

When Calmer left that night I sat up talking until seven, I think it was, with two newspapermen. I was obliged to read aloud the last chapter of a novel which one of them had written. It was not very good, but he assured me it was masterly, that his book would create a sensation, and showed me a letter from Simon & Schuster urging him to get finished with it as they were waiting for it eagerly. And Calmer too has a publisher for his first novel, the John Day Company.* There must be a publisher for everybody apparently. One has to take up the scent, like a dog. When I get the dust out of my nose perhaps I will pick up the scent. Anyway, I have a good table to write on and a tin trunk to file away my papers. When Summer comes I will throw the horse blanket away. Until tomorrow, Anaïs.

[Henry]

[Clichy]
[April 3, 1932]

Anaïs—have just left the cinema and am waiting for it to stop raining so that I can run home & write about *Kriss.* I am afraid to say a word about it for fear of breaking the spell. I think I will do something *magnificent* on it. And if I fail, I will go again and again to see it, because it is extraordinary.

You recommended it so casually—how was that? Was it just another fine picture for you?

However—I'll try to spill it on the machine.

You know why I am sending this? I want some help—forgive me—after all that rot I wrote in the letter.

Absolutely broke and will be until Friday. Could you send me a little tomorrow—to the office so that I would find it when I arrive? Anything will do—there isn't a bit of food left.

I sent you a tremendous batch of mail earlier this evening—it should last you several days.

I think if I were to make a trip around the world armed with a

---

Beyond the Street, Edgar Calmer's first novel, was published in New York by Harcourt, Brace and Co. in 1934.

portable machine I would produce something stupefying. I know now I'm truly possessed—*fou.* Good Christ, how everything is boiling in me. Words aren't enuf. I want to bite into things, with my teeth. *Foutou!*

I adore you. You make me believe that everything is possible.

Yes, let's drink to the full. I have great need of you. June will come and June will open her eyes—very, very wide. I'm not going to let her go, but I'm not going to let you go either. I don't care what sort of situation develops—only you must not betray me. I love June and I love you. There you are. I can't add a word beyond that.

Only this—that you are giving me something rare. I don't dare speak about it because then it would be dimmed.

Anaïs—just stick to me, defend me—even with June. Be a woman with June—don't trust her too implicitly. This is wisdom I'm giving you—not fear or cowardice.

I look for something big to result.

And Tuesday prepare to be raped. Wear that beautiful dress you had on when you first came to Clichy. I want to see the white of your flesh against it. I want to commit excesses. Passionately yours,

Henry

P.S. We'll go to see *Kriss* again—together. Take me to everything that's splendid. Spoil me. I'm sick of this white poverty, the vulgarity of my daily life.

[Louveciennes]
[April 3, 1932]

[Henry:]

The "frescoes" must absolutely be finished by Wednesday and so I must pose all day Monday & Tuesday, & perhaps Wednesday. Perhaps it is good, as I have the tragic sense of life these days . . . if I can I'll write you what I have been feeling. Reading *Albertine Disparue* because you asked me to. I had wanted to preserve as long as possible the exultation you gave me, and now I descend again into infernal regions. I had a dream about the lepers, mixed up with the idiotic priest's words: "His novels, instead of raising the soul of the reader, drive it down by the brutality of character and description." *Au contraire, au contraire!* I understand your wanting the lepers to invade the world. One's soul is not "raised" by detachment from life, which is like leprosy—embrace them, embrace them . . . and then see that you will only have lived if you die first.

I love you.

Anaïs

Write me at Natasha's.

[Louveciennes]
Saturday [April 9, 1932]

Henry, I don't want to say much on the Montparnasse article until I see the end of it and the *whole*—but I can say that it is too good! Never mind about [Wambly] Bald's "smartness": you give a few elliptical, ironic, and over-intelligent phrases there which I am sure the readers of *Vanity Fair* (not being sure of their meaning) will accept as pure glossy flippancy. Everybody will be satisfied. (I refer to all you write about Cocteau, [Eugene] Jolas & Goethe—with the changefulness of tone, the mockery of the "pomp" in the next paragraph.) Very fine the way you do not overemphasize anything, so nothing seems too serious—very good, the changefulness and transitions in tone—banter, digs ([Edward] Titus' bookshop), descriptions (mention of photographer for background is masterly). Just right to give that kaleidoscopic aspect. Perhaps I feel the need for a word more about Cocteau. You drop him a little too abruptly. I found only one thing which has been said perhaps too often. It's just at the beginning, from "The most sophisticated New Yorker" to the end of that paragraph. Think it over. It seems to me you found your *own* tone from the next paragraph on.

I'm returning the MS. though I would like to have it back if you don't need it. If I had my typewriter today I would write you a book. The Lawrence book excited *me* too.* Mark it as you wish—I also found similarities and dissimilarities. I admire her extremely for one thing: the complete frankness—a really courageous frankness. I want to tell you where I read you into it—or contrasts with you. I thought at the time that a document about you, June, me, or [Michael] Fraenkel† or Fred or Jean [Kronski] would never be as *petty.* Isn't that true?

*Mabel Dodge Luhan, *Lorenzo in Taos.* New York: ALfred A. Knopf, 1932.
†See Biographical Notes.

Listen, I have found my "happiness" again. The awareness of the danger which threatened it (which came fully with the reading of Proust and after a talk with Fred) at first tortured me. I am just as aware today, but I have more courage, or rather I don't care about tomorrow, or any future, only about *today*, and enjoying acutely what we have *today*, Henry. Henry, we are going to taste *all* we can give each other before June comes, quickly, deeply—we are going to lie together as often as possible. It is all fragile, but for every day of it I am thankful, thankful! I don't know why I am thinking much of Tuesday. Perhaps it is wrong that I should be so oyster-like and so obstinately clinging to my shells—and Natasha's studio is like one of my shells. Yet I love to go to Clichy, and I love sitting in the kitchen with you and Fred, and all the books on the table. If you ask me I'll come Tuesday to Clichy!

Did Fred tell you about our talk?

Tonight I'm going to call you up to know if you have received the *European Caravan.* Monday I have to pose all day. Bring the Lawrence book Tuesday. Ask Fred if he would be interested in a book on Goethe by Calvin Thomas. And in a study of Colette by Jean Larnac. I have something interesting for you, "The Language of Night," by Jolas—a booklet.

Anaïs

[Clichy]
Saturday Night [April 9, 1932]

[Anaïs:]

I'm slow-witted, Fred is right. I meant to ask you to call me back after midnight so that I could talk to you again and without restraint. Now you're gone and there is no way to get you back, and I'm quite desolate . . . quite. [. . .]

But I'll tell you what—if I write these two articles on Montparnasse and on Lawrence I'll send them out. I'll ask Grace Flandrau,* perhaps, to intercede for me with Horace Liveright, her literary broker. Why not? Perhaps I could earn a hundred dollars. Who knows? I may not be altogether foolish or hopeless.

You will see the remainder of the Montparnasse story herewith.

*See Biographical Notes.

It gets duller, heavier perhaps, but I lost interest when Bald felled me with his cruel remarks. I began to write as though I was myself writing. And so now, after I see what is left of my work (I can't infringe on his copy, naturally) I will try to do it over in more devastating style. As for the Lawrence thing, I am almost afraid to embark on it. I want to say so much that I am afraid it will be too long to fit any magazine or newspaper. Maybe you will teach me a little restraint. How would you like to collaborate with me? I'm collaborating with you already. Tonight I bought *à crédit* two tickets for the Sweepstakes in June. Better, one ticket and a half. With the whole ticket I go splits with you. Maybe we will pick a winner. That would clear up a lot of difficulties. You see, I'm good to you! (How I would love to hand you a cool 50,000 dollars.)

Excuse me, this sounds a little indelicate. Only I'm a little elated tonight. I would like to call Louveciennes and say: "Come to Paris immediately and let's go places." Yes, I've got lots of places in my head where I'd like to spend time with you. I always imagine I could have a wonderful time with you, if you didn't have to think about catching the 6 o'clock train. What I envisage, for instance, is a long, lingering meal *(soit à Clichy, soit à Paris)* and you just beginning to bubble over, and maybe Fred looking on with that foolish, anthropoid grin of his, now hurt, now flaming, now tender as a dove. And we could go absolutely Surrealistic, plumb to the bottom all those burning questions we now skim over or postpone for a better day. We could even write a few pages in your journal for you and draw diagrams or anamyths or psychographs. We could go Mantic and do a Thomas Aquinas—anything you will.

Yes, I think too much about going with you, drumming it into you, laughing with you, listening to you. And at the same time I have a strong urge to protect you. For instance, that rendezvous with Root. You mustn't keep it. It's a mistake and you'll rue it if you go. Why? [. . .] Root, cocksure, greasy, self-sufficient, figures that his review [of *D. H. Lawrence: An Unprofessional Study*] must have flattered Miss Nin's vanity. Powerful man, Mr. Root. And Miss Nin is Spanish . . . exotic therefore.

But Miss Nin, let me tell you, is a little idiot to write letters to Mr. Root. Miss Nin is not equipped to combat the [. . .] Roots of this world. No matter. Miss Nin must reconcile herself to playing another role. Once Mr. Root has laid his greasy eye on you, it is all up. Your reputation will be ruined. Seriously, you have no idea of the depths to which conversation hereabouts [at the office] descends. You may think you know something about the masculine mind, but I can tell you you don't. You would squirm if you could listen in for one night. [. . .]

I'm not going into this further. Just trust me. You have everything to lose by risking a meeting with Root. Keep away from Montparnasse and newspaper men. Remain enigmatic. Let the professors visit with you, and the Walter Pachs, but don't soil your skirts by sitting with this other crowd. I know what I'm talking about.

Maybe it sounds funny to you, my talking this way. But I can't let you be pawed and fingered by these slimy devils. And that's what it'll amount to. Similarly, it would be all right to meet Fraenkel—excellent in fact . . . you would probably appreciate him. But it would be disastrous to meet Walter Lowenfels,* who is writing the longest poem in the English language. It's all right to know Fred—it's a duty in fact—but to meet Wambly Bald would be fatal. And so it goes.

It is this that infuriates me about June—her going out to meet all sorts and rhapsodizing about the wrong ones. If you knew Bob McAlmon, for example, how would you feel, I wonder, if you heard June talk about him? It would make you retch. Why she even handed me a couple of his stories to read, thinking no doubt that I would find some good in them. Bob McAlmon is one of the vilest creatures alive. And then there is [Maxwell] Bodenheim—you should see how he greets June! Well, if I saw you making such errors I would lose faith in you. [. . .]

To change the subject. I was immensely pleased that you dallied with Fred that afternoon and forgot about the curtains. Fred came home radiant. For a space I was almost jealous. Christ, he must love you to go on about you the way he does. What did *she* say, I wanted to know. But Fred, in his imbecilic, his best imbecilic manner, couldn't remember what you said. Apparently you said next to nothing. *"I talked!"* he said. He was proud of it. [. . .]

Do you know, I don't do very much for you. I have been thinking a lot about it recently. It seems to me I must cut a very selfish, egotistical figure. And what galls me is that you are still deprived of your machine. Drat it all—withhold some of your gifts and rent another machine, a decent one, until this matter is cleared up. I'll tell you where to go and it can be arranged simply and for next to nothing. It's all rot, your writing in pen and ink, or not at all, just because your machine

*See Biographical Notes.

is lost or stolen. And this posing [for the painter Natasha Troubetskoia] . . . why? I want to know. It's on my account, I suspect, and nothing else but. Well, it's too much. Christ, you aren't figuring in things at all. You're just making a slave of yourself. Why, your book is practically finished. And here weeks are rolling by and it lies on your desk untouched. Damn it, I thought when I would lose the job [as proofreader] that I would be able to help you with it. Now they tell me that I am to remain up here until the 24th, and on the 1st of May I can go downstairs. I think they'd really like to keep me. That's how things go with me. But, whether I get a vacation or not, I want to see you get that book out. I can help you a great deal, I believe. And your work won't be hard. Heavens, with your facility to write I think you could turn out a book every six months. As for me, I never get them out. You're wasting time trying to help me. Someday I may muddle through, but it doesn't seem as if money or kindness or sympathy or understanding help any. I'm just slow, or feeble-minded. So please go back to your quiet ways and work for yourself. Just to know that you are interested in what I do is enough. The curtains and the linoleum and all that stuff will come along in due time, by act of Providence. After all, I have a table and a typewriter. What more does a writer want? I'm just pampering myself, or letting you pamper me, I don't know which. And I adore you for wanting to do so, don't misunderstand that. In fact. I'm weak that way. Nothing is more to my taste than having people do things for me—particularly those I love. I don't think I ever gave much, except love—and Fred is even suspicious about that. He says I don't know the meaning of love—that all I really experience is gusts of passion or sentimentality. (But I don't always agree with Fred—in this certainly not.)

Once I tried explaining myself on this score to June. There are times, you know, when she accuses me of being the most selfish person on this green earth. These accusations never center around money, to be sure. It's when I want my blooming way all the time that she balks. Well, it's true. I want my way. I don't give a damn about the other person's way. I say, let our ways coincide—that's the best we can hope for. Trying to give in, to compromise, to go fifty fifty and all that bunk strikes me as idiotic, as inefficacious in the long run. June, of course, is more subtle about having her way. She makes it appear that it is you who want it, not her. That's the old way of women, and as a man I rather detest that. When I try to protect my ego it seems crude to her, and no doubt it is, but what do you expect, that I should turn soft and feminine? No, I want the utmost that anyone can offer me, and in return I will give the utmost—if I happen to be in that kind of mood that day.

Mostly you've seen me quite complacent and yielding. It's because there hasn't been anything to fight over. What you say goes pretty well with me . . . we're treading the same path. But, if I have to balk, then, good God, I'm afraid you'll see something of that odious behavior mentioned in the Lawrence book. I can become very nasty, very petty, very vicious when I'm rubbed the wrong way. And I can take it out on perfect strangers. Well, I'm beginning to talk like Mabel Dodge Luhan [in *Lorenzo in Taos*] herself!

I am enclosing herein also some more pages of Fred's manuscript, and I beg you to return them to me when you're through. It is this I really started writing about, when I began this letter. How his language affected me. You know, he makes me hunger for a sort of beauty that is absolutely out of my reach. He said to me the other night: "If you really knew what love was—it is the only thing you lack—you would be a genius, another Goethe perhaps." Well, standing by the window and reading his manuscript today (your pneumatique arrived in the very midst of it) I felt that I knew what Fred meant. I don't believe that he ever loved Marcienne—or anybody for that matter (it is *he* who is incapable of love), but I believe that he loved what Marcienne did for him, how she made him expand, warm to the world, etc. [. . .] Why, I would like Marcienne to come here immediately and live with us, live with Fred, of course, I would almost like to teach him how to love her, to put their two hands together, and make Fred, who is so childishly selfish and withdrawn, sacrifice his whole life for Marcienne and that kid. [. . .] There is room in me for all the Marciennes in the world and all their brats, particularly if their brats are bastards. I love little bastards. I would like to create a whole litter of bastards and be able to roam the world saying hello everywhere to my sons and daughters.

[. . .] I hand you these pages with the most delicate, chaste, reverent feelings. I think them exquisitely beautiful, matchless in their way, and I want to say that whatever it is I lack Fred has shown it to me here. My eyes melt and I know that there is a beauty in the world which is utterly out of my reach and I bow down before it. It is a world on which I have slammed the door and I will never try to open that door, but I must confess that in the night I go back now and again and I stand wistfully before it and I know I left something precious there.

I halt here only because it is 2 A.M. & Fred is waiting for me to walk home with him. Now Montmartre—other thoughts. Jesus, it's wrong to stop. That's where I'm weak. I always believe I can summon it when I want.

[Henry]

[Clichy]
Sunday afternoon [April 10, 1932]

[Anaïs:]

Too beautiful a day to remain indoors. In the most wonderful spirits but unable to decide what to write about—the book, Lawrence, continue this letter, more on Montparnasse, a letter to Grace Flandrau or what. Haunted by time again. This is my day off—I need this day off. But there's nothing I can do unless I buttonhole the Russian waiter. He has been putting me off on that eleven francs debt for weeks. [. . .]

Do you think *we* could do anything with this Montparnasse stuff? Would you like to rewrite it with me? If you think your name would put it over better, and if you wouldn't be ashamed of signing it, why that would suit me swell. Same with the Lawrence thing. All I care about is the money. When I finish the book I think I will make it "Anonymous." I think probably it's more fun. [. . .]

[Fred] is getting ready now to write some more about Goethe, to slam hell out of me. I think he will do an excellent job. It doesn't matter whether one is for or against—the writing it is all that counts. And with your permission, I think I will lift the last page of my letter to you (on Fred's manuscript) and insert it in my book, with more to follow. You will notice I have scrupulously kept you out of my book, though it is hard. One of the first things I have to take up with June when she returns is the question of freedom, the privilege to put down my thoughts somewhere and not permit anyone to pry into them. This occurred to me in reading about Lawrence. The situation with Frieda was perfectly analogous to June and myself—when Lawrence tried to collaborate with Mabel [Dodge Luhan] and Frieda squelched it. Lots of things about Frieda, about her behavior, reminded me of June. I believe Frieda was good for Lawrence, but I see too how she hampered him—perhaps that too was good. I can see him dancing around her furiously, whaling her now and then, cursing her, and then getting on his knees to her. Yes, that's us! Only I never struck June—do you think I should? [. . .]

At five-thirty [Fred] was sitting on the edge of my bed and we were planning to take a trip to Rouen or Provins on his day off—the week between April 24th and 30th. Stay overnight there—a holiday. We want you to come along with us. Yes, we saw ourselves walking through some strange town with you in the middle—no thought of trains, of dinners etc. How would you like that? Could you do such a thing? I'm seeing you Tuesday at 2 o'clock at the studio. I wish it were today.

Henry

[Louveciennes]
[April 28, 1932]
[Henry:]

[. . .] Yesterday you said there were flaws in my goodness. Won't you tell me what they are so that I may accentuate them? In that knowledge lies my salvation. Save me from goodness, Henry.

When I come next week and you read my journal you are going to be happy. I said to a Frenchman the other day: "I love genius." He answered: "A woman gives genius to the man she loves."

I didn't tell you that after reading *The Well of Loneliness* I combed my hair back and put on a tailored suit. And immediately someone who bores me happened to come and cut into my day and intrude on my work and I had the courage to pack him back to Paris—pitilessly, as I have rarely done, and perhaps it would be good if I could keep such a spirit up (I can while I wear the costume).

Have you given my wine-colored handkerchief to one of the whores who says you have a good heart? (You have.)

Someday I will tell you something I found out about how a whore practices faithfulness, and how I profited from the knowledge. I cannot believe that Fred wrote that letter I saw yesterday. Sometimes, however, I have the feeling that I myself will write something so truthful about the feelings of a woman that you will not believe I wrote it. You tempt me. With you I never feel truthful enough. I have an implacable desire for truth. But at the moment of writing I get exalted and I rush for the beauty, and the *rest* is dispersed. Out of the journal, and out of my body. Washed. Washed. But I would like to come back like a miry detective and collect what has fallen off.

Anaïs

Café de la Régence
161–163 Rue Saint-Honoré
Friday [May 13, 1932]

Dear Anaïs.

I don't know how to express my feelings on reading your Journal. I have not finished it yet. I put it aside because I want to be able to read more and more. It touches me deeply. I think it is one of the most beautiful things I have ever read, and if I were you I would never leave it out of my hands—not even for such as Fred and myself to read. I had no idea, when I begged for it, how precious it was.

Tonight I came here hoping you would remember last Friday night and perhaps manage to get here somehow. I sat a number of hours correcting my manuscript. I reread the letter I wrote you in French and then rushed home to write you some more. But it is so quiet here that the noise of the machine seems too much. And besides, I have too much to say to you—I would be writing all night.

But this I want to say—that you are becoming more and more divine. You *have* become all those things you wished to be, when you wrote your secret thoughts in your little *cahier*. Anaïs, it makes me weep, your Journal. It makes me love you beyond words. I am trying to make notes of all the beautiful utterances I find in it, but there are too many—I want every line of it, every *"bon soir,"* every *"me voici à nouveau"* etc.

Why, from the very outset you showed your genius. It amazes me. Or rather, nothing about you amazes me any longer. If they said to me tomorrow, "Did you hear that Anaïs Nin et Culmell just performed a miracle" I would not look astonished. I expect miracles from you!

Alors, je tombe de sommeil. Je sais bien que vous me pardonnerez—n'est-ce pas?

Heinrich

P.S. *Mon rêve? Aller à l'Espagne, à Barcelona, avec Anaïs, aller aux Brussels aussi, pour voir les bonnes soeurs qui ont soigné la petite Anaïs. Encore un rêve—voir le petit coeur d'Anaïs, goûter les larmes au dedans, les larmes de son triste enfance. Anaïs, Anaïs, je t'aime. Je t'aime à onze ans, je t'aime à vingt-neuf ans. Je t'aimerais à cent ans. J'aime le Dieu que tu as aimé si pieusement. Je comprends maintenant pourquoi tu dis toujours—j'aime, j'aime. Tu aimes parce que tu es bon. Aucun mal en votre petit coeur. Rien que la bonheur, la tendresse pour le monde. Oui, je comprends. Tu peux me faire comprendre tout. Tu me fais voir comment arrive-t'il un miracle. Toi, toi même est le miracle!*

Am holding all MSS. because I expect to see you surely Monday or Tuesday.

au Sans-Souci, Comptoir-Glacier
65, rue Pigalle
Sunday [May 15, 1932]

Anaïs!

Just finished the Journal. Please bring volume II. *Je ne demande le Dieu rien plus!* I must go back & back away some more on the pages. *Quel travail!* Came out to rest my eyes, but alas your script is blinding.

I enclose some notes I made while reading the Journal. They may not convey much to you now—later, when you return them, and I have a chance to expand, you may find them more interesting. But just now I thought it might please you to see what attracted my attention.

(Have I permission to refer to your Journal? I never stopped to consider that! If not, I will give my remarks to you—not to any book. I promise!)

Certain lines seem prophetic. Some things already fulfilled. Remarkable, all this! I have a feeling of its tremendous importance later—when you are known and have your readers, as you will!

The pages in French which accompany this will indicate how strongly the very first pages of the Journal affected me. (I can give you the original copy—I only keep the original because everything hurts my eyes.)

I am missing you tremendously. And your silence! That hurts. Are you terribly occupied? I suppose so. *Certes,* I am looking forward to next week with impatience. You've added a bit to your stature meantime.

Saturday night I went with [Walter] Freeman (after discussing [Richard] Osborn's* plight) to see *C'est le Printemps.* † I am much impressed. It is very German—and that perhaps left you indifferent. *Les Boches!* How do you happen to like me, *Heinrich? Un mystère!*

*See Biographical Notes.
†A 1929 film based on Frank Wedekind's *Fruehling's Erwachen,* directed by Richard Oswald.

Yes, I will tell you what I thought of the film, or write you about it, later. With the pen I move haltingly.

(Note: Miss *Bring!* The name of my protagonist in the novel. A *rare* name in America. It is one of June's family names!)

In the movies *(Actualités),* * I saw Mona Paiva herself! She danced in a lion's den, clad in a tiger skin. Very supple. *Pas mal.* Rather intriguing—from a distance. You are going to help me frame a letter to Candide & Gringoise for information about the *real* Mona Paiva.

Hectic this. I'm rather jumpy. I wish I were finished looking at my MSS. *C'est embêtant!*

Anaïs, believe me, I love you dearly—more, much more, than ever. You left something with me. Our place seems empty. Did my "curiosity" hurt you—afterwards. I hope not. I regret all that very much. I am going to impose silence on myself.

Heinrich

P.S. Mailed you a letter to Natasha's Saturday night. Do you like this stationery? *Voyez—Lacaze, propriétaire.* †

[Clichy]
Sunday [May 22, 1932]

Anaïs, Anaïs—

I am dazzled by your beauty! You looked at me so strangely, I thought, as if I did not appreciate thoroly the marvel you had wrought. Oh, but I did! I lost my head. I felt wretched. "I have been blind, blind," I said to myself. You stood there like a Princesse. *You* were the *Infanta!*

You looked thoroly disappointed in me. What was the matter? Did I look stupid? I probably was. I wanted to get down on my knees and kiss the hem of your dress. So many Anaïses you have shown me—and now this one—as if to prove your protean versatility.

Do you know what Fraenkel said to me? "I never expected to see a woman as beautiful as that. How can a woman of such femininity, such beauty, write a book like that?" Oh, that pleased me no end!

*The weekly newsreel which preceded the feature film.
†Under the name of the establishment, the stationery shows a line drawing of M. Lacaze, smiling, with hat and bow tie, a black cane tipped upward under his right arm, wearing an overcoat with a handkerchief pocket.

The little tuft of hair coming up over the crown, the lustrous eyes, the gorgeous shoulder line—and those sleeves I adore, regal, Florentine, diabolistic! I saw nothing below the bosom. I was too excited to stand off and survey you. How much I wanted to whisk you away—away forever. Eloping with the Infanta—ye gods!

So that was a rug, or a tapestry? A magic rug. Did the Infanta go home and sit on her throne afterwards? I hope you didn't go back in a Chevrolet. (Do you know what I was thinking of all the time? That no accident should befall you. I was worried about you going home in a car.)

Feverishly I sought out the father. I think I spotted him. His hair was the clue. Strange hair, strange face. Strange family. Presentiment of genius. Ah, yes, Anaïs. I am taking everything quietly—because you belong in another world. I see nothing in myself to recommend your interest. Your *love?* That seems fantastic to me now. It is some divine prank, some cruel jest you are playing on me.

What a mood you were in the night you came to Clichy. Why, you swept in like a Philipornan woman. You are the most surprising of creatures. Chameleon-like. And do you know what I liked? Your asking in the taxi "Are you rich, Henry?"

Yes, Anaïs, I am rich! The richest man in the world. I am rich for knowing Anaïs Nin et Culmell. Ask Fraenkel if it isn't so.

Maybe this will reach you while Fraenkel is there. Ask him about the conversation we had after the concert—in the lobby of Freeman's hotel.

Items: Spengler, Money, Hermaphroditism, Catharsis, Psychoanalysis, Death, the Black Plague.

Fantastic night! I must rehearse it for you. Fraenkel astounded me. There is a *mind.* I hope you form a favorable opinion of him. Last night made me more than ever certain that he is an exceptional person. He will be good for you—you will know what it *really* means to think when you grapple with him.

Incidentally, he does not like the new revision of the book. He almost crushed me by his criticism. Said I had castrated it—made it a *literary* thing—destroyed the flow—etc. etc. until I almost wept.

Ah, Miss Nin, the critic, where are you? Are we both blind now? I was afraid of that. Afraid that your love would kill your critical faculties. Nevertheless, I am not altogether convinced. If what he says is true, then I have very bad artistic instincts. Then, indeed, I am nothing but a poor Dutchman, a pedant, an artisan, a plodder . . . *a failure,* in the last analysis. And yet, I think my instincts were correct when it concerned your writing. Am I all at sea when it concerns myself? That would be quite terrible.

I want to add that I did not say enough about the red journal. That it didn't matter to me at all about the diminution of language. The ideas were rich. The bravery of it again! You make me wince sometimes. I think you are capable always, when you choose, of exerting greater strength, greater cruelty. I think I am always closer to literature than you.

Anaïs, I adore you. It is just possible that I may take it into my head to come out there tomorrow. I ought not, of course, but I may.

Henry

P.S. I have a vague feeling that you are going to talk business with Fraenkel. Don't, for God's sake, add to your burdens. Everything can wait. I am great or bad whether I am in print or not.*

I would be a thousand times more pleased if Fraenkel published something of yours first. After all, where are you coming in? You are making a martyr of yourself—and for whom?

P.P.S. I'm going to print—anyhow. See Neagoe's letter.† I don't want to go to print. *I want you!*

Dis Bon Jour à Papa! Oui, je n'aime que toi, cher Caron. Te quiedo. Te amo. (Teach me more!)

[Louveciennes]
Saturday [May 28, 1932]

Heinrich,

did you know that Lawrence wrote some verses he called "Nettles," which certainly did prick me disagreeably one day and I wrote some "Counter Nettles" which ran like this:

---

*Apparently A. N. wanted to explore the possibility of privately printing H. M.'s work, as Fraenkel and his friend Walter Lowenfels had done with their own work under the imprint Carrefour.

†Peter Neagoe was co-editor, with Samuel Putnam, of *The New Review*, where two short pieces by Miller had appeared ("Buñuel or Thus Cometh to an End Everywhere the Golden Age," Vol. 2, May–July 1931; "Mademoiselle Claude," Vol. 3, August–October 1931) which represented his first acceptances by a literary magazine in Paris. The magazine ceased publication in April 1932, before anything else by Miller could be printed.

You did say with touching frankness
That a mood or a poem
Is only true for a moment.
When a woman happens
To come for a moment
She's only a nuisance
For a moment
Why did you then
Eternalize the nuisance aspect
Through many moods and many poems?
Was it so often true
That it must remain
Always in the files
As a final truth?

And another:

The women who talked to you
About their feelings
Did you really mind them
Or did you put all the feelings
Into a book?
How often did you endure
A boring hour
And then come home
To write a poem?
What annoyed you
Was your impatience
To get home
And write that poem.

And so on, and so on.

I am enclosing a story partly in imitation of American stories. This is just to fatten up the letter. Read it only after four glasses of beer. I should be working on my novel but what I really want to do is to write you such a love letter that you will require a safety vault in the style of the man-sized one we saw in the movies yesterday. But I have only six minutes before Hugh comes home, and though I often write in my journal sitting a yard away from him, on the floor, almost at his feet, typewriting is different, more noticeable. Ah, listen, Henry, I sound so very nonsensical today, and I am, because I have promised myself not to think, not to become lucid. I have a terror now of the lucid moments. Last night, when I said to you: "I will see you a moment Monday," you don't know what flashed thru my mind: "Perhaps between tonight and Monday June will arrive. Tonight may be our last night."* Do not believe the red journal. You don't know yet when and how I fell in love with you. That's in the purple journal. Listen: on the seventh of June we are going to have a Spanish night. We are going together to see L'Argentina dance, and then we'll have supper in a Spanish restaurant, and you'll read the purple journal. Letters. I owe you many, but I cannot write letters. I have forgotten how to write, forgotten pain, learning and thought. The only books I am interested in are the ones you have marked. There must be a *you* in them.

Anaïs

The last part of your book is immensely satisfying, gripping. Everything you write about June is *foudroyant*. I am making notes. The coordination seems to me absolutely inspired. I feel you are doing it with the same instinct which made you write the book itself. Go on, go on, Heinrich. And listen, if a security in my love can serve as an *aliment*—then be secure. *En ce moment tu remplis tellement mon être il n'y pas de place pour personne d'autre.*

I am holding back notes on your book because of that idea I have that one should not discuss a work in progress. Perhaps you want to—I don't know. Isn't it enough for you to know that I am petrified with admiration, that the pages on Matisse kept me awake last night. Besides, Henry, my notes are no good to you. Something has happened to me. I cannot be objective enough. I begin to *think* about the book, deliberately, detachedly.

Sending you notes on [Dr. René] Allendy† so that you can show them to Fraenkel.

"Je viens à Clichy à 5 heures."

The bell rings.

Christ! says Henry.

---

*June had cabled from New York to H. M.: "Miss you—must join you soon."
†In April 1932, A. N. had begun analysis with Allendy. To pay for her sessions she eventually arranged to do research for him and work part-time at his office. See Biographical Notes.

[Clichy]
Tuesday Night [June 7, 1932]

Dear Anaïs—

I love you madly, madly. I ran into Hugo during the intermission (I saw you come in, you know) and when Hugo spoke to me so gently, so kindly, and so innocently, I felt wretched. I hate this lying and deception when a person is so fair, so generous as he appears to be. I hated myself violently. I was sorry I went. I wanted to run away. And so, during the second intermission, I just couldn't pull myself together. Moreover I felt that he would be a little ashamed to introduce me to these society people. I felt that he was embarrassed meeting me there— that he knew everything.

As you went out for the second intermission I saw you look up—and you did it so well, such an actress you are!—that I don't know what came over me. I adored you. You were so soft, so diabolically angelic looking.

Anaïs, I'm crazy tonight. I rushed away from the theatre because for once I couldn't act. I don't know what I would have done had I met you in the lobby.

I looked at you from up there as if I had loaned my wife out to play a part. And all thru Ruth Draper's performance I kept thinking of your words—"No, it's not so good!" What was that to signify? I looked at the woman in amazement. I saw a rather dried-up New England type, with a voice I distinctly disliked. Her arms and chest I disliked. I disliked the whole program, tho' I admit she did splendidly at times. But a talent wasted on that trash—that I couldn't appreciate. And you said she was beautiful, in an American way. I was trying so hard to see what you saw, but I couldn't. I was jealous of her. How could she attract you? And then I saw those sweet, innocent-looking punks you were sitting with. No, I want to take you out of all this—let's get down to real things. I felt tonight that I was committing a sin. A man who has been as hungry as I have has no right to idle time away in those places.

And the old fool next to me kept saying—"It's genius! Have you ever seen anything like her?" I merely grunted. When you saw me talking to him it was only because he said—"I came to Paris in 1891"— which was the year I was born. There were 25 francs to the pound then and a leg of chicken cost only one franc ten. Now it costs ten francs.

I liked the way she did that three-act impersonation—the secretary, the wife, the other woman—especially *the other woman*. And the way her voice changed, and her posture, when she did the beggar woman—that was quite unexpected. But of what use all this? Drivel, isn't it? Doesn't she know that the world is cracking?

Anaïs, you have become so vital a part of me that I'm completely upside down, if this means anything. I don't know what I write—only that I love you, that I must have you exclusively, fiercely, possessively. I don't know what I want. I've got too much, I guess. You've overwhelmed me and you've spoiled me. I keep asking harder and harder things of you. I expect you to accomplish miracles. You don't know how I miss those nights we spent together—how much they meant to me. Other times you are just a phantom, a wraith. You come and you make me sick with desire, with a desire to possess you, to have you around me always, talking to me naturally, moving about as if you were a part of me.

[Henry]

[Louveciennes]
[June 8, 1932]

Heinrich, *amor mio,* I was in an infernally black mood last night. To see you up there and not to be able to talk with you (1st entr'acte the lady wouldn't go out—the second I was going to find an excuse to go alone upstairs but then Hugh knew you were there and would have guessed . . .) that added to my despair. And you? Last night at the cabaret the gaiety and the music only made me feel worse. Today I'm too tired to work for Allendy. I'm going home to sleep a little. If for any reason you are not in the mood to write this afternoon come to Louveciennes. Otherwise meet me Friday night at Gare St. Lazare at 8:30.

Ruth Draper—what a disappointment! An actress yes, but what flimsy material—insipid and when you know her personally an ordinary American woman—*tirage en gros.* Yet she was beautiful as the mistress and as the Italian girl. Did you notice the *"te amo, te adoro"?*

Heinrich, Heinrich—*Toutes les tristesses du Journal* are nothing compared to a day like today.

A.

[Louveciennes]
[June 11, 1932]

[Henry:]

Things I forgot to tell you: The *quena* is an instrument like a flute used by the South American Indians. It is made of human bones. It owes its origin to the worship of an Indian for his mistress. When she died he made a flute of one of her bones. It has a more penetrating, more haunting sound than the ordinary flute.

That I love you, and that when I awake in the morning I use my intelligence to discover more ways of appreciating you.

That when June comes back she will love you more because I have loved you. There are new leaves on the tip and climax of your already overrich head.

That I love you.

That I love you.

That I love you.

I have become an idiot like Gertrude Stein. That's what love does to intelligent women. They cannot write letters anymore.

Anaïs

[Clichy]
[June 14, 1932]

Anaïs!

The letter will follow! Came home, stripped down, and scrubbed and polished everything in sight. Wonderful form of indoor exercise. I'm going out tomorrow and buy myself everything I need. And I'm going to see Osborn. And I think it is wonderful that Jeanne turned out to be a *femme du trottoir*. They make marvellous wives. Was Hugo sore? Did you put over the deal? Everything was marvellous, the woods, the warm beer, Amelia,* the mosquitos, your blue-green oriental dress, your little purse—and that very wicked thing you did under Hugo's chin!

I'm crazy about you! Every time I see you I discover new marvels, new hip lines, new *ceintures,* new smiles, new dimples, new wickednesses. The last bothers me frightfully. You are becoming a Medici.

*The Guilers' Spanish maid, Emilia. H. M. persisted in calling her "Amelia."

But your writing desks intrigues me most of all. Ask me to write about it someday. The geography of it!

If you were poor, do you know what I would do? I'd work for a living—become a barber or a taxi-driver—or a *femme de ménage*. I'd be wife, husband, poet etc.—all at once. Because I love you madly, madly.

Heinrich

[Clichy]
Friday [June 17, 1932]

Anaïs—

When I got home last night I found a woman there—a Mlle. Paulette, *dix-neuf ans, une amie de Fred*. No more housecleaning for us. Paulette will do everything. You ought to have seen her dry the salad in a towel—marvellous! She's going to economize for us. Had a dispute with her father and so she won't go home any more. She's quite adorable. Fred's already worried that he won't write any more. She can do anything. *Dix-neuf ans!* Maybe we'll have dinner together Monday. Paulette must change her hours—she's used to getting up at 7:30 A.M. She makes me very happy to watch her—just like a child. *Alors, lundi chez Fraenkel. Tout va bien?*

Henry

[Clichy]
Monday [July 18, 1932]

Anaïs:

Fraenkel is lying on the bed, his trunk packed, waiting for a cable with money from America in order to go to America. I have arrived at the last ten pages of the book and halt there, hoping to make a whirlwind finish—lay down for three hours yesterday thinking it all out, and if what I wrote when I lay there could be put on paper I guess it would be another book. It was a mad conversation, mostly a monologue between June and myself, a complete trajectory of our life together packed into a last chapter and me surrendering to all the dark invisible gods; you can have her, I am a saint, a Christ as far as Coney Island. Your telegram arrives and upsets me, that is exhilarates me, drives me crazy, opens another bottle of wine and the dark gods and the rim of pallor all going to waste and I don't care about punctuation or spelling except that Fraenkel tarry just long enough to take with him a copy of my book and show it to all the fucking goddamned sons of bitches who would do me dirt and not recognize me. Yes, I'm going completely nuts these days, not knowing whether I have failed again or not, but feeling as I wrote certain passages that they were fine, splendid, the best I ever wrote, only nobody will take the pains to read them. And so there we are, or here I am in Clichy and you're some thousand miles away in the Tyrol with healthy peasants and mountain air, and a husband who adores you and stays by your side and doesn't let you write even a *pneumatique.* I longed and longed all this week for a letter, a cable, a telegram, anything that would tell me where and how you were and did you miss me, and when the telegram arrived I went wild and I am still wild and I don't know what I am saying because Fraenkel is lying on the bed reading stock reports and about men who have had their Adam's apple slashed by third-degree methods and I have just rehearsed for him the whole story of *L'Age d'Or* and he says it's all very intelligible and what lies at the basis of it is just "fuck, fuck, fuck . . ." and I think that's about right, only this time I believe you won't call me a Casanova. I hope not. Imagine, he, Fraenkel, was on his way to the lawyer's to hand over all his property and possessions to his wife. He had sneaked out of the house like a convict and missed the lawyer, and then on the Avenue de l'Opéra he ran into a woman with hair down to her buttocks, long, golden blond hair and she smiled at him. They went to a hotel which cost fifty francs for the room and he opened his heart and his wallet at the same time and he said there is the story of my life, my wife, my children, I'm going to America and that's what's in my wallet, take what you want. And she took only fifty francs and then he waited around outside the hotel to see where she would go and she didn't appear again and he is in love with her—madly, madly, would take her to America, but she wouldn't hear of it, etc. etc. And in that condition he comes to me and lies on my bed and I write letters and stuff Mss. in fancy envelopes to be delivered by hand when he reaches New York.

I can't send the letter until your letter arrives as I don't know whether this is the Poste Restante address or not. But in the meantime I have read your book on Lawrence and I marked it up and I went nutty over it and asked myself what was wrong that I hadn't understood all this the first time I read it. I have the book open right before me and every page is marked . . . but especially I remember the rim of pallor, the monks walking in the garden, twilight in Italy, the most gorgeous page of prose that a man ever wrote and I think of you saying to Caresse Crosby* that this is better and bigger than Lawrence and I think it is all crap because no man could be better than those marvellous pages, except Anaïs Nin in her diary when she was sixteen years of age and nobody loved her.

It is the desire of the human male to build a world! *Soit.* Who said that? Anaïs Nin? Not merely useful, something wonderful. Also, Anaïs Nin. O.K. Everything Anaïs Nin says is swell, wonderful, and the world is wonderful and I am wonderful and America is wonderful.

Big break here during which I bought oodles of paper and carbon and strong envelopes, etc. Had my hair completely shaved off and look like a convict. Why? Feeling of humility, abasement, wanting to slink through the world even more inconspicuously. Long intermission during which Fraenkel traversed all the discoveries of psychoanalysis, for Fred and myself on the terrace of a café. All the insanities, the neuroses and the psychoneuroses . . . the burning of the ship "Youth," why the Nordic races discovered the machine, the philosophy of work, Lutheranism, etc. In the *Actualités* there was a man beating a drum with a mechanical drumstick—he turned something like a pencil sharpener and there was a fine and continuous two-four-flam. Fraenkel is going to take a copy of the novel to New York with him and see three publishers for me. The other copy I will send to Putnam as soon as I hear from him. So, perhaps you will have to wait and see the original when you get back. Anyway, you must be wearing your eyes out with all the books you took along. Fred is reading *Les Chants de Maldoror* and finding it swell—full of violence. I have just finished the book on China (which was interesting indeed) and then read [Claude] Farrèrre's *La Bataille*, about which I would like to say a great deal, though it is a cheap and poorly written book. But the woman, the Japanese Marquise, Mitsouko, and the old Chinese philosopher, appealed to me. Interesting thing was that he makes the rich American woman, who is a stunner, a Lesbian. That is, she has a lover in the great French painter, but he is jealous always of her women friends. It is all trash, what he writes about the Americans. But when it comes to the Chinaman it is very good.

*See Biographical Notes.

And then we had a strange session—Fraenkel and I—with King, the race-track man. King undertook to read two pages of the "Weather" article* (which I am sending you), after rewriting it again for Fraenkel; King grasped it amazingly well, better than I did on a first reading, though I doubt that he gets the overtones. At any rate, I have come to the conclusion that the use and knowledge of words acts sometimes as a stumbling block rather than a clarifier. All those things which King saw through at first glance are like thick forests for me. You will see from the last page or so how important the article is to the writer, the artist. (And, apropos of dreams, Fraenkel gave us a perfectly marvellous account of the psychology of dreams, and of *artificial* dreams, which is even more important than real dreams. And of *lies.*) At any rate, Fraenkel would very much like to have you show his article to Hugo without explaining a thing, and see what his reaction to it is. And I too would very much like to hear about that. (Incidentally, he got your letter, but there was a page missing, he said. It is not vitally important, but if you should run across it, why send it to me and I will forward it to him.) He goes back to New York practically penniless, with all his possessions signed over to his wife, and no idea of what he will do when he lands there. But when [someone like Fraenkel] says he is penniless it must always be taken with a grain of salt.

But I am going to write you about the *Unprofessional Study.* I may not finish it in this letter, but I will begin. [. . .] [Here follow several pages of detailed comments.]

Your letter arrived just a little while ago and I was elated—but now I am depressed, horribly depressed—not because of anything you wrote, but because of a disagreeable scene here with Fred, which is too petty to write about, but which gets under my skin just the same and exasperates me. Yes, I succeeded in finishing the book—just yesterday. There were interruptions. I rewrote Fraenkel's article and will send you a copy in a few days. I want to be sure of your address. That's why I didn't answer immediately when I got the telegram. You say "Achenseehof, Tyrol." Is "Achenseehof" the name of the town? Fred either doesn't know or won't know. To get information from him is like getting water out of a rock.

The Weather Paper, as Fraenkel recalled in 1946, "was an attempt, in stenographic form, to bring up to date the spiritual and psychic climate of our time." (Cited in *Death: A Literary Quarterly,* edited by Harry Herschkovitz, Vol. 1, No. 1, Summer 1946.)

And so, please excuse me from writing more today. I'm glad you enjoyed the trip—you gave me quite a thrill reading about your philologist. It's good that there are some romantic people left in the world.*

I'll go on writing you about your book shortly. Not the way I started. That's picayune, when I look back on it. No, I liked the book immensely. I got much more out of it than I did on the first reading. I tell you, I'm absolutely disgusted today, sick of humanity.

Notice the letters enclosed from [Jacques] Calmy† and [Paul] Morand.‡ I saw Calmy yesterday. He says if he had money he would undertake to publish it himself, because he believes there is money to be made on it. He admits that it would be very difficult to translate into French. But he added that in France there would be at least ten thousand readers for such a book. Well, I am trying to catch Fraenkel today before he sails for America and hand him the copy of the book in order to show it to my pseudo-rich friend George Buzby,§ who, if he had a little common sense and an iota of guts, would bring it out himself.

And now I'm going to rewrite that Buñuel article, to put as a foreword to the book. I'll make it even more savage, the way I feel at this moment.

No, June isn't back, nor do I want to see her back.

All this is spread over about four days and in four days—you know my tempo—there have been many ups and downs. I feel apologetic for introducing this black mood. Perhaps by tonight I'll have swerved round, and will write you again.

Henry

[Hotel Achenseehof
Tyrol, Austria]
Friday A.M. [July 22, 1932]

[Henry:]

Today I was really anxious when the man at the desk said: no mail. I wonder if you received my telegram Monday. And then I wrote you

---

*According to her diary, A. N. had met an Austrian professor of philology on the train from Munich. Her first letter from Achensee has, apparently, been lost.
†An acquaintance of H. M. who worked for a French publisher.
‡For Morand, see Biographical Notes.
§Editor of a small magazine, *USA*.

a note the same evening. Mail is extremely slow to come here. What I write you one evening doesn't catch the train to Paris until the next night. But I should have news of you by now. Perhaps you are working with Fraenkel. I came away with such a deep feeling of his importance. I would love it if as soon as you are finished with the article you would send me your copy so that I might read it here deliberately.

Have been reading Spengler *exultantly*. I never expected to experience such a sense of wonder, of vastness and richness. I wish we could talk about it. I am going to read nothing else. I want to absorb it deeply—even what I do not altogether understand seems beautiful and arouses the imagination. I'm so thoroughly awake again, sizzling and fermenting. I wrote you such a mad letter after the note—did you mind it?

Just before I left I received this announcement of something written by Lowenfels on Lawrence [*Elegy for D. H. Lawrence*]. Is it worth getting? Shall I get it for you, or will you be given a copy? Let me know. I am not writing except in the journal. I am stuck with the novel, but it is a good healthy stop; it is the minute when I choose forever one kind of writing from another. It's a desperate moment, but beyond the temporary paralysis, I feel already the joy of a good bold cutting out of the mediocre. And the novel? It seems a long time to wait to read it, but I prefer to be patient and read it all at once.

I wish you would get that lamp from [Lawrence] Drake. It will be better for your eyes.

Anaïs

P.S. I got a letter from Rebecca West and we will meet in Paris when I return. No news of Caresse Crosby but as soon as I return I will hunt her down with "social" instruments. And Paul Morand?

[Achensee]
[July 23, 1932]

[Henry:]

Dabors, when I did call you a Casanova you made the mistake of thinking perhaps I didn't like Casanova, though I admit it was a hasty and superficial comparison. And if it looked like a criticism that was only because I thought at the time you were not giving enough time to writing. But now I am completely satisfied, and you will not be angry if I tell you I thought of you again while reading *The Brothers Karama-zov* (The Sensualists). Everything I read now has a different meaning, a terrible meaning; the way I read Dostoevsky anyway is not reading, it is actual passionate experience, as when I read you. *Je suis boulever-sée*, as after an earthquake. I remembered your saying to Fraenkel: "No, I do not think of people in terms of ideas; I think in terms of a leg, a mouth."

What you write me now about the last pages of the novel makes me want to see them. I must see those last pages. Couldn't you mail me those from your own copy registered and I will mail them right back? I wish you could tell me too what Fraenkel told you about dreams, the *artificial dreams,* and of *lies.* I have been obsessed with those two things for two days. You have noticed from the [*Unprofes-sional*] *Study* that I am predisposed to Fraenkelism, that I am if anything a Fraenkelist already. I am touched that you should be reading my book so carefully. But please spare me a discussion of it. I don't know why I dislike this so. I have written a thing in white heat, with terrific intensity, in a state of visionariness. . . . I cannot retrace my steps, I cannot expand on what I have said, nor say it in another way. It is a cold thing to me now. I cannot explain why I can't do it. It isn't lack of enthusiasm, it is perhaps a change in me, I'm rushing on. I'm taking Lawrence along, not all of him, a sifted Lawrence, a great part of which I have outgrown. Or perhaps, Henry, I hate to think. Perhaps, as you say, I am not a thinker. I've written in ecstasy and in enthusiasm, a bit like a medium, if you wish, a bit in a trance. I feel that if I sit down now I will do some bad thinking about Lawrence. Remember Gide on Dostoevsky—"When he began to explain himself he showed himself a bad thinker." Don't ask me to explain myself. That is the way I feel. That is why I feel that Fraenkel overestimates my book. It is done in a dream. I am not lucidly responsible for it. Do you mind this? I must warm up to something that is somehow finished for me. Today I am set off by Spengler. And yet there are some things you said I must answer, and which I like to answer. You say that the blood-conscious-ness of Lawrence seems very different to you from the last knowledge of Dostoevsky's heroes who have "conscious depths—the nightmare of the intellect." I say it is exactly the same, only differently worded. The liberation of the instincts, of the inchoate etc. (except that with Law-rence it is restricted to the sexual problem and Dostoevsky was larger). By the word "transcendental" I mean: beyond the obvious, the deepest significance, transcending in the sense of the almost visionary acuity.

It is a word I *love* and which is the best I ever got from Emerson. It means so much to me that I can hardly give a definition of it.

Whenever you wish I had expanded, I agree with you. This is not a book, and I have the same trouble as Fraenkel; it is a form of shorthand. I also agree with the *merde* if it is applied to puritanical hearts. Page 13. I seem to be warming up, growing more amenable, though I am skipping the real issues. Ok about the hundred years.

Maybe I wanted to frighten the slow ones. When I use this for Fraenkel it is Latin exaggeration, though I must explain to you that Fraenkel is harder for me to understand than anybody because as he writes "essence" the way I do, when I read him I in turn apply my extraction habit to what I am reading, adding complications to his, and in the end becoming entangled as no one else might. It was a revelation to me what you said about King, and "I have come to the conclusion that the use and knowledge of words acts sometimes as a stumbling block rather than a clarifier." From now on I am going to read Fraenkel more simply, with an effort at diluting rather than intensifying what he says, which is already intense enough. I would love to see your markings in my book, yes. Most of the time you praise what I write thinking it is Lawrence's, which flatters me. The truth is Lawrence was a very confused and contradictory thinker, and you can't question him step by step as you are doing; you can only extract a general meaning, as I have done, dropping the rest. If you take him too seriously or too logically he is impossible.

Don't keep your bad moods from me. I am writing you now out of a lead tomb. It's the rain, which disgusts my tropical and cat-like nature. And Hugh's talk about our finances, which make him contemplate the idea of going to a wild place in Brazil to try his fortune in the precious woods business owned by a friend of ours. Your letters would take a month to get to me!

No, I don't believe in deep grooves of living, and you don't either. You may admire it, but you know you could not fit yourself into one. You have broken down all formal order, grooves, more than anyone I know outside of Dostoevsky's books. You should know what a fluid, mobile system offers by comparison.

(à suivre)

Thousands of mountains, heavy clouds, mists, rain, mountainous Austrian quilts, blankets, then me. Asleep. I am still asleep, though I would love to write you a letter. I am still dreaming that Joaquin was playing not on a piano but on the lake, and the symphonies fall down in white torrents, and there are notes of a blue you have never seen in any woman's eyes. Women fail even to have eyes the color of an ordinary mountain lake. Now, said the professor of philology, I will tell you about the "Uhland Ballads,"* *"Des Sängers Fluch."* The exact meaning of your name in Greek is "ascension," élan, going up—*"Ana"* means rising, to rise, *"is"* is up high. I am still asleep, Heinrich, I was very tired. So much *Sturm und Drang.* I would like to know why June took drugs. I know why I would. Awareness, too much awareness. The day I left you at Gare St. Lazare I could have said to the taxi driver: Drive me right into the Seine, because I am leaving Henry, and I *know* I am leaving Henry. The next best thing was to sleep.

I hide my journal in the ash receiver of the Austrian stove. But yesterday when I returned from a walk I found that the maid had obeyed Hugh's order and changed our things to a better room. How to explain in German that I had to be allowed in the first for a moment? A comic moment. Another comic moment before the framed pictures of the people who have been killed by stones falling from the mountains on the road. Photographs with the story underneath. Besides all the Christs and Virgins. No humor. Ungainly looking people, but lovable. All smiles.

You are like a bear, Heinrich, softness wrapped in roughness, that delicious rough suavity which melts me. I am sorry you did not read on in the journal, there were many soft things written about you. I still do not understand very well what stopped you.

Last night I wondered how I could show you . . . show you . . . by what costs me most to do . . . that I love you . . . and I could only think of sending you money to spend on a woman. . . . I thought of the negress, I like her, because at least I can feel my own softness melting into her. . . . Please don't go to too cheap, too ordinary a woman. And then don't tell me about it, since I am sure you have already done it. Let me believe I have given it to you.

Anaïs

*The German poet Ludwig Uhland (1787–1862), whose late-Romantic texts were often absorbed into folk songs.

[Anaïs:]

Continuing—it is too late to type. And then I can say some things better when the pen moves noiselessly over the paper. I miss you terribly. I don't seem to know how to kill the time until you return. I couldn't think of your going to Brazil. That's impossible! Will you be coming back ahead of Hugo—will you be able to spend a few days with me—alone? I dream so often (daydreams) of those last hours in Louveciennes. I don't know of any more golden hours than those. Your saying "cripes" was so funny—and the way you wake up—just like you go to sleep—peacefully, with sleepy wonder in your eyes—but so quiet, peaceful, gentle. Even the way you get in and out of your clothes. Noiselessly, like a cat. And what fun that was dancing in the hallway— with nobody in the house. I could spend such precious hours with you. You would never bore me and I—would I you?

I was so thankful that you showed me those photographs. I wish I had one. I can close my eyes and see you perfectly. Only now I can never close my eyes and visualize you as separate from that lovely garden—always I see you before the mirror, in that golden ambiance— the peculiar diffracted light falling on the lawn, the sombre trees, the silence and the fragrance wrapping you about. As you said on Christmas day in your diary, "I would sacrifice all etc.," so I feel about you. I would sacrifice everything to keep you where you belong, in that beautiful frame which fits you so perfectly. With you, Anaïs, I could not be selfish. I want you always to be happy, to be secure, protected. I have never before loved a woman with this unselfishness.

I am not doing much. I am restless. I am lost without you—that's true. I know it's only for a short time, but I can't adjust myself to it. I was greatly moved by the letter you wrote, enclosing the "suggestion." You do the most surprising things. I have been wondering how I could go to the Tyrol, near you, even if I didn't see you—or yes, maybe see you while you were out walking—from behind a rock or a tree. But think as I may, all that is out of the question.

Anaïs, it only required that you go away to make me realize the full measure of my love for you. I have been withholding much in my letters for fear of "accidents." But now I can't hold back any longer. I just trust that you will have enough discretion not to put this under your pillow. I would write you every day, but that I know would look bad. I've come to such a state of passion that anything I might write now would burn up the paper. I keep constantly reviewing in my mind all the episodes beginning with the [Café] Viking and ending with the lawn-mower. I wonder do you still talk in your sleep? I wonder what you think of when you are going through the act now.

Write me about all that—frankly—if you can, and tell me do I dare to do likewise.

I can't write more because my head is all jammed with it. I just see you in my arms, writhing, and feel myself deep in you and staying there forever. I'm hot as hell now—you're no longer the Anaïs I wrote to from Dijon. You're not Anaïs of the diary, either. You know which Anaïs I mean. I'm all yours.

Henry

[Achensee]
July 28, 1932

[Henry:]

We have a funny way of anticipating each other's thoughts. Today I got your letter in which Lawrence is beginning to irritate you. Just then you must have received mine in which I say: "I'm taking Lawrence along, not all of him, a sifted Lawrence, a great part of which I have outgrown." *Alors tout va bien.* It isn't Lawrence we are going to quarrel about. But then what? About "this tenderness it is, as well as the rejection of his tenderness, which makes him violent," you say you are tender without being violent. I would like to remind you, however, that you reject your tenderness and *write* violently, which is the same thing!

I am absolutely certain the Buñuel article is not sick. I wish I were there to prove it to you. To prove my sincerity I will agree with you that the first hundred pages of the first novel do not indicate what you were going to write later except by their fullness!

I have also outgrown the idea of perpetual solitariness. I laughed about that in my novel, don't you remember? You noticed that Spengler spoke of this feeling as characteristic of the Faustian soul. The illusion of solitariness is necessary to the artist; it is the space he creates by which he obtains perspective, individual realization etc. It seems quite obvious that they make no effort to seek the opposite. Lawrence and Waldo Frank knew each other and never became intimate, though they were obviously meant to understand each other. Each one was taking care of his solitariness.

Yes, there was a time when we had absolute love, that is before consciousness. We *believed* it was *absolute* love. Those eternal, inseparable famous lovers of history *(sic)*. Sometimes I believe it was Dostoevsky who discovered the relativity of it! Again in the *Brothers Karamazov* this astounded me. Mitya is visited by Katya. He has just been telling his brother how much he loves Grushenka. And now Katya says: "You love another woman and I love another man, and yet I shall love you for ever, and you will love me." And he answers: "All my life! So it will be, so it will always be. . . ."

In answer to a "fine old phrase" I used (an answer which will do for all the rest of the writing I do): I never weigh a phrase against another, nor think about it, nor am conscious that there is a better one. When I stop to do so it is only when Hugh or you make me aware of the imperfections.

You say: "I can't conceive of one arriving at a feeling for homosexual relationships through his thinking things through." On the contrary. It is by thinking about taboos that we have become aware of their foolishness. When we began to do some healthy thinking about morality, we discovered it was ordained by fashions, no higher dictate than that, and when we began to think about "abnormal" acts, we realized we could not say they were against "nature" because nature gave us a million examples of worse abnormalities than we ever invented for ourselves. It is *thinking* which shows us that the *feelings* we have against certain acts have been acquired (like the puritanical feelings inculcated in the old Anglo-Saxon generation). What I mean in my book is that I see nothing to be said against homosexuality, but I point out that Lawrence, to satisfy his idealism, evolved a complicated law that there should not be a sexual connection, and launched himself into explanations about the mystical. . . . Altogether a noble form of self-deception, since the ultimate truth is that if a man is sensual, he will carry sensuality into his friendships too, into everything, including his enjoyment of music and painting etc. Lawrence, who was in reality not at all sensual, experienced a condition of exaltation in the presence of men, and so was able to conceive of an exalted-mystical enjoyment of them. If, occasionally, he submitted to a physical urge, it bothered his idealistic conscience. That is the way it looks to me. On cynical days I envisage the "exaltation" as an idealistic sublimation possible only to those who know sexual restraint, but a humanly shattering and futile condition. I cannot add any more because it will bring me to a discussion of an analogous subject which you and I have discussed to tatters: lesbianism.

Don't be against Lawrence, not only because of all I wrote *for* him, but simply because he was not a writer who wrote for the sake of covering paper, but because he was miserable, and tormented, and he had a lot to say.

About the "Religious Man" chapter I will only say this: I was explaining and stating simply Lawrence's attitude. I wash my hands of it. For religion I myself have nothing but bitterness in me, even hatred. Fury if you will. So nothing that you say can annoy me. It is one of the things I detest [John Middleton] Murry for: he is still discussing Christ.

Erskine's erudite contribution to your talk is every day less probable. Our correspondence, though weighty, actually *steams* with discord.

About Spengler: I stutter when I mention him. I have only one more chapter to read [of *The Decline of the West*]. I want more. Where is volume two? How glad, how glad I am you made me read him! I am so overwhelmed, impressed and stimulated that I cannot make any comments. Here is the transcendentalism, profundity! The deepest realization, the widest perspective. How I bow to the visionary who fires the imagination. I have never known a book like this, Henry. Let me assimilate it. I want to talk it over . . . I am going to read it twice.

Your pages on my journal move me . . . to see you bending over it so tenderly, taking so much time to understand me, writing such beautiful things about it. It makes me wish I had had a much more tragic childhood. . . . It is so terribly sweet now to be given what you give me in exchange for the calendars and handkerchiefs. Think of it, Henry, now you understand my exclamation in the last journal: "Henry has given me all the world, *toute la terre!*" I alienated myself from it, at the first taste of pain, and then you came and tore the veils down. Do you remember in the Viking your saying: "Yesterday you were so *human*, so warm. Today there is a veil around you." The day before, only with my journal, I was able to break through and say to you: here is the *human* me. The next day there were veils again, but you broke through them. And then the kiss, and then . . . and then. If I had known then in 1914 how you would give me the world, the street, laughter, the dawn, rare books, talk, fat radium letters, your life, wine, *nuits blanches* dipped in Anjou, understanding, new words, new worlds. Never like this, you asked the night of the Quatz Art Ball, and I said: "Never like this."

Anaïs

P.S. Spengler's definition of becoming *is* better than Heraklitos', whose version I used in my book.

P.P.S. Henry, I'm working a little, but I don't know whether what I am doing is good or bad.
     The journal is suffering from an ash-suffocation.
     This is my 5th letter. Are you getting them all?

[Clichy]
[July 28, 1932]

[Anaïs:]

     That was the longest letter you ever got, eh?* I love you—and that's only warming up. I love you—and I want you back here. Woman. I may come and drag you back by the hair. This is the shortest letter I ever wrote. I love you! I'm going to bed and dream about you. You give me prickly heat. I'm all wrought up since you went away. I ain't good for nothing.

Henry

[Clichy]
Friday [July 29, 1932]

[Anaïs:]

     I thought maybe there'd be a telegram saying "Come to the Tyrol." I got that way from sitting beside a mirror and watching people

---

*In a letter of more than thirty typed pages, written over several days, H. M. had commented at length on D. H. Lawrence, James Joyce, Eric Portman's film *Stuerme der Leidenschaft* (*Tumultes* in French, starring Charles Boyer), Fritz Lang's film *Metropolis* (starring Brigitte Helm), and on sundry friends and acquaintances. He had also included letters from Richard Osborn, as well as copies of letters to Peter Neagoe (criticizing his book of stories, *Storm*) and others. A. N.'s responses are scattered through a number of her letters.

pass; there are no climaxes in life like in mirrors. People fall in and out of the picture and you don't have to touch them. I was awake nearly all night sleeping in Fraenkel's ten-franc hotel room, packed his grips, and saw him off at the St. Lazare this morning. On the way he lost his hat and we had to stop off and buy another one. The biggest problem he had was where to put his toothbrush. Before leaving he explained to me quite thoroughly what a "bond" was, and I decided in my own mind that government bonds are worthless—especially German government bonds. And just as I write this there is a telegram from him, dated Cherbourg, asking me to make sure that Mrs. Fraenkel has received the package he left at the door last night. A package containing bonds, notes, bills, receipts, leases, and money. I had to help him decide whether to leave twenty dollars or 350 francs for the boy's operation.

And so now you are alone for a few days, something tells me, and I am wondering if you will have time to write a big letter, also if you are getting mine because I still don't puzzle out the address—Achensee or Achenseehof or Jembach or Zillertal. I guess Achenseehof. I found your letter under the door when I got home and I think it was marvellous of you to suggest what you did, but I have no intention of acting on the suggestion. Instead I shall have a little surprise for you on your return, and if you study your German faithfully it will be all the more pleasant a surprise for you. I feel clean and bright and washed out, and I hope I shall have some clean, bright, washed out pages to show you (something new) when you return. I do hope I can send you at least a copy of a few pages from the novel before you return. I hit a streak toward the end that I think is me at my best. And I am sure that if I could write an entire book with nothing but pages like that I would be all that you expect me to be.

Do you remember the lawn-mower and how wonderful it sounded? I passed a hotel named after my favorite wine [Anjou] the other night; the electric sign threw a strange red glow over the windows, and when I looked up I saw a woman parting the curtains. I imagined her to have a strange foreign name. I'm getting delicate, you see.

I don't know any more than you why I stopped reading at a certain point. You may be sure I regret it. I can only say that it was an impersonal sadness, things turning out badly not because of evil or maliciousness but through a sort of inherent fatality. Making even the most cherishable and sacred things seem so illusory, unstable, transitory. If you substituted X for the character it would be just the same.

As a matter of fact, perhaps I was substituting myself. How are your characters coming along—are they developing in the dark room? And what sort of bath do you give them? Does philology spoil the plate? You see, I'm still delicate. I'm so delicate now that I'm almost fragile.

Do you want me to go on writing you about the Lawrence book? And do you want Symbolism or Euclidian proofs? I'm referring to the first line on page 2. It is very difficult for me to answer except that you were mistaken about me. I believe until I get hit on the head. Don't hit me on the head. I am crazy about you.

[Henry]

Don't forget to put "Clichy (Seine)" on envelope. Letter was delayed.

[Clichy]
Saturday [July 30, 1932]

[Anaïs:]

[. . .] I think I have discovered a title for the book. How do you like either of these—"Tropic of Cancer" or "I Sing the Equator." (2nd volume would be "Tropic of Capricorn." The last book ought to be just "God.")

This evening at sunset I lay on my couch and watched the clouds sailing by my window. You can see nothing but the clouds when you lie there and clouds are wonderful when they are punctured by cerulean blue. (Time and Space—what these things are beginning to mean to me. I'm just waking up!) There was one blue hole about eight light-years away into which a sparrow dove. I was intoxicated by it. Why is it that distance in itself is so enchanting? [. . .]

Sunday morning and no letter from Anaïs. Desperate. Is it possible you didn't receive the big letters I mailed? One of them was sealed, the other was about of equal size—I think I have sent you about three thick ones, this will make the fourth. My eye, if all that stuff is lost or strayed it will be a pity. [. . .]

A letter this morning from William Aspenwall Bradley,* the literary agent, asking me to come and see him. Dr. Krans had told him about my book. I will show him the novel. I just wrote a three-page letter to Krans which will amuse you highly when I show it to you. I

*See Biographical Notes.

am not going to enclose any more copies of letters—it's too damn egotistical. You must be laughing at me. Nevertheless, I am writing nothing but letters, and typing out excerpts. I must be a nut. But the letters are a link between me and the world. I can make people read letters. Etc.

This [*European*] *Caravan* is proving a veritable treasure to me. Now, not only the introduction, but the contents interest me. I don't know how much you read of it, but there is a lot I am going to talk to you about when you get back. For one thing, I think you are going to revise your opinion about the sterility of French letters. [. . .] Contrasted with England and America the French appear much more favorable. I think what you needed (pardon the air of superiority!) was a key to this writing. You saw things in Lawrence—because you had a preference for the Anglo-Saxon? But there were bigger, better things being said here all along and much before Lawrence. I tell you, I don't wonder that the French are sore or envious over the success of Lawrence. It really wasn't deserved! I don't care if they only wrote a page—if that page gave us something it was sufficient. Anyway, what I see in the French writers is a superior attitude. Lawrence is so childish in many ways. I mean that all his fanaticism, his preaching, etc., is infantile. You and Fraenkel have succeeded in giving me a complex about Lawrence. Nothing, for instance, annoys me more than when Fraenkel says: "When you write like that you're as good as Lawrence"—sometimes he says "or better." Shit, I don't want to be compared to Lawrence. I don't say "better" or "worse"; just different, totally different. And if I am to be measured, then pick a better yardstick, that's what I say. (You see what an egotist I can be!) [. . .]

Now—listen to me! I discovered another good guy in the *Caravan* last night—José Ortega y Gasset, professor of metaphysics at the University of Madrid, a man who says that he believes "that Spain's normal state is a permanent decadence." This man has written the very finest thing on Proust which I have yet read. If you ask me what I consider good criticism, what I call thinking, then I refer you to this brief essay which once appeared in the *Nouvelle Revue Française*, and which is called "Time, Distance and Form in Proust." If you ever write another critical work, let this be your model! The subtitle reads "Merely a Contribution to Proustian Studies." Oh how I wish for a brain like that! [. . .]

Gone mad with a desire to hear from people, to read things, to communicate. Feel as though I were marooned here. Fred is no use to me anymore. His ideas are stale. I need someone to exchange thoughts with. Someone of equal stature. When you return I am going to give you one literary fuck fest—that means fucking and talking and talking and fucking—and a bottle of Anjou in between—or a Vermouth Cassis. Anaïs, I am going to open your very groins. God forgive me if this letter is ever opened by mistake. I can't help it. I want you. I love you. You're food and drink to me—the whole bloody machinery, as it were. Lying on top of you is one thing, but getting close to you is another. I feel close to you, one with you, you're mine whether it is acknowledged or not. Every day I wait now is torture. I am counting them slowly, painfully. I don't know when you return—the 7th or the 15th? But make it as soon as you can. Be unselfish—yes, I am asking you to. Make a sacrifice. I need you. This long Sunday—*how will I ever get through it?* [Marginal note: "(1:00 A.M. Got thru by reading Unamuno.)"] It is just killing time. Tomorrow there may be a letter. Everything hangs on tomorrow. God, I want to see you in Louveciennes, see you in that golden light of the window, in your Nile-green dress and your face pale, as frozen pallor as of the night of the concert. Let the hair wave—expose it to the sun—let the color return. I love you as you are. I love your loins, the golden pallor, the slope of your buttocks, the warmth inside you, the juices of you. Anaïs, I love you so much, so much! I am getting tongue-tied. I am even crazy enough to believe that you might walk in on me unexpectedly. I am sitting here writing you with a tremendous erection. I feel your soft mouth closing over me, your leg clutching me tight, see you again in the kitchen here lifting your dress and sitting on top of me and the chair riding around over the kitchen floor, going thump, thump.

Henry

P.S. The excerpts will follow in the next mail. Just read Unamuno! My Unamuno! Where is that *tragic sense of life?* I want it. I may write on Gide's Dostoevsky tomorrow. Everything is stirring in me—Fraenkel, Proust, Unamuno, Osborn, Lawrence——

[Achensee]
Sunday [July 31, 1932]

If Morand does not need you just now perhaps you would like to go away, Heinrich? Are you tired? Are you in the mood for Spain?

Please write me immediately if that is what you want to do. By return mail I will arrange things. I am writing to [Edward] Titus to see if I can get any money from him. *Tell me the truth.*

I am sorry about Calmy's letter, but here is one from Caresse Crosby which sounds very friendly. I even wonder if you could not go with this letter and introduce yourself to her, and take your manuscript to her so that she may read it and answer me when I return. She is bound to like you immensely, and if I know women well, she would rather be given a chance to judge for herself than be told by another woman. . . . What do you think?

You sent me a small note in praise of your last book, but who wrote it? It is good.

You did not mind all I wrote yesterday? Today in reading over your letter I notice that you liked something I wrote to which I attach great importance. Page 20. It is symbolical of the creative . . . etc. This pleased me acutely. Tell me why you wrote *no comment* on: "It is inequality of sexual power which causes disintegration in sexual relationships." Is it something well known, obvious? I often wonder how I ever wrote anything at all on Lawrence when you consider that most of what I said on sexual matters was guess work. I am checking up now!

I was going to write a whole lot more yesterday on the "groove" idea, but the letter had to be mailed before eight. I may add to this one if Hugh goes fishing this afternoon.

You begin so quietly. You feel the weight of the pack. Peace. Then you pick on a word, a word which you repeat each time your foot stamps the earth. In Paris, on the asphalt, I have often walked saying: wild, wild, wild. Crescendo. You just say it, and walk, walk, walk. It makes everything rise, swell, burst. Here I say: strength, strength, strength. Then I am so happy I cannot bear it any more and I begin to sing. You sing because you lose your identity. It is a cause for bliss. You have become mountain, torrent, and valley. You can get drunk on walking.

When you come back and read the longest and most extraordinary letter, you think: "Well, I have got terribly behind in the pursuit of madness." But that is what Henry wanted: that I should get behind in my writing. . . . That way I live more *for* you, I can give more time, more adoration to the man who is helping the world to crack, or who has already split it open!

Poor Bertha! What are you going to do about it? If you ever find a solution for the "anguish" let me know. I need one. We both use our own life and friends, and lovers too, undisguisedly. I don't mind that it should bring about tragedy, but *gossip*, oh, that I mind, that is unbearable, that every fool or idiot in Montparnasse should be given the chance to discuss either you or Bertha, or any of us, . . . Gossip, that is ignominious, intolerable. I always hated that. To avoid it (Richmond Hill gossip, Cuban gossip, society gossip, painters and models gossip) I chose solitude. Do you feel that? It arouses a fierce pride in me, an enormous contempt. It is terrible if your book can give Mr. Calmy such a pleasure, and Mrs. Calmy, and others. . . . I know *you* so well, Henry, that I know this was not in your mind. But that is what has happened, and it is hateful. Tragedy is O.K. but not *talk*. Tragedy is healthy and interesting, but talk is petty and humiliating. It is like women's fights.

Your speech to the Hungarian is fine, but naïve. How do you know but what his sweetheart or sister might not thoroughly enjoy what you describe as a vengeance?

I am a little jealous that Fraenkel got you interested in Jung and Freud. . . . Perhaps what I said about all this was not vehement enough. I've read them both *completely*. I wanted you to be interested, but I sometimes thought you were jeering. Don't go to the Library for the books. I have most of them, or Eduardo* has all I do not have.

Tea, which means beer on the terrace, and watching the curious types who come from Munich. Beethoven heads. Perhaps Spengler himself. (They tell me he lives in Munich.) Why not? Half of these rotund men in short Tyrolian pants, monstrously ugly but determined looking, are either Professors or Doctors. They come here for the day with their families. They are all infantilely enthusiastic over nature. They pick the little mountain flowers. They take photographs of the group and it is a wonder to me how they can all fit into one snapshot. Henry, if you would only be a little patient and wait two or three months. I would come back obese. I loved the *short* letter, but I cannot answer it. *Tu comprends?* Hugh is changing his clothes. We walked out for a while after tea and were caught in a hailstorm. His shadow sometimes covers the letter I am writing. *Si tu savais* . . . Our plans are indefinite. We may return next Monday. Hugh may stay a day in Paris and then go to Vienna etc. Or he may begin his business trip from here. You will get a telegram Monday. Perhaps Monday night I will be in Clichy.

I did not find as many defects in *Metropolis*, but that was over

*Eduardo Sanchez, A. N.'s cousin. See Biographical Notes.

a year ago, and I was very young then. I did feel that the story theme was very thrashy, but I liked the background, the atmosphere, and the emotion of terror aroused by the implacable machinery. And of course, Brigitte Helm . . . That pose in the dancing which you noticed is not only African, but Oriental. When I studied Hindu dancing I realized it was the basic difference, and the animality of it startles one at the moment of doing it. European women hold their legs like Gothic spires in ballet dancing etc. The Spanish gypsies alone took over that particular gesture.

Wonderful, the Gorgulov trial. Dostoevsky would have put it into a book. Here is where the French mind *fails.* Gide will understand. "Take my life but save my idea!" And "This man has understood my soul—now I can die." I was thinking of Natasha's vehement dislike of Dostoevsky because "he was a morbid man and there were no Russians like those he wrote about!" Gorgulov should not die. I'm keeping the clippings for you. I wish we could have gone to the trial. I know someone who could have made it possible. It was so strange to read his fantastic remarks just after finishing Mitya's trial in *The Brothers Karamazov.* "Everybody here is glad that I killed my Father. Everybody wants to kill his Father." You remember?

Osborn's letter did not sound so very mad to me. If you see him ask him to give you back my *Salavin.* If he is still in Paris when I return I would like to see him just to thank him, *tu sais pourquoi.*

I wasn't laughing at you. Your "fragile" letter was amusing. It may have been unconscious humor.

And now I get one of my letters back—the very one I wrote you the day Hugh was in Paris. You are not such a good detective after all, not to have missed it.

Tumultes and June I keep for the day I see you. I have a lot to say about it.

Your letter to Neagoe is not due to any *tumulte,* but to your everlasting mania for hanging yourself. Yes, you love to hang yourself. It was a useless letter. Criticism is good when you apply it to someone who carries a *seed* of talent. Applied to Neagoe it only means the loss of a man who wished you good. When you say you believe in his next book you know you don't mean it. *Storm* cannot lead to anything else that you would prize reading. Oh, Henry, I would like to be there when you rush like that into pure self-destruction. But it is such a strong impulse that I still marvel, when you write me about our "golden hours," how it is you haven't done anything yet to destroy them! You will. *Tu te défends d'être heureux.* It is because of that there will always be *tumulte* and June, *always, always, always.* June knew that when she chose her eternal husband!

I don't know if you are really in trouble or entertaining Emil!* In case I am not back Monday, I am enclosing a check, and dating it Friday instead of Monday. But oh, Henry, I do *hate* that you should *feed Paulette!* Instead of yourself! I can't help myself. Before I came away I gave my best hat and black dress and shoes to a woman who needed them, but I *could not have given them to Paulette. I think you understand.* Fred must understand it is too ridiculous.

Anaïs

P.S. Do you know what touched me? It was Rebecca West, who asked if she could meet me—not I who asked her.

[Clichy]
Monday [August 1, 1932]

[Anaïs:]

Up at 8 o'clock, ahead of the mail. Yes, the letter came. I don't think it's the fifth—I seem to miss one in which you asked why I didn't write—I would have remembered that one. And in one letter you put a postscript about Rebecca West which I didn't understand. Anyhow, I'm all enthusiasm—today I will surely start a new book. You will see.

Sorry I am still writing about Lawrence—had I known how you feel I would have dropped the matter. You are a few letters behind. By this time you must know that I have gone into other things. Where are we in this correspondence? Better tell me when to stop, as soon I figure you'll be leaving there.

One item—of jealousy: "though our correspondence is still weighty" (meaning the Erskine–Nin et Culmell correspondence). How does one write long letters to a lost love?

You speak of a "time before consciousness." Can't imagine such a time? About *when* was it? B.C. or A.D.? Or is it prehistoric time. Unamuno says: "The prehistoric is unconsciousness; it is the void." (This of course is literature, but it sounds convincing.) Nobody knows anything about the prehistoric!

You misunderstood me about "thinking things through" in con-

*Emil Schnellock, a long-time friend. See Biographical Notes.

nection with homosexuality. It was thinking *versus* feeling I was talking of.

No, I won't be against Lawrence any more—more especially because "he was miserable, and tormented, and had a lot to say." Not because of all you wrote *for* him! That wouldn't deter me one bit. (That to you, Miss Nin.)

Give me a little of that steaming discord of the Erskine correspondence. I would like to see how he *steams*.

How I laughed going down the street for the croissants this morning—thinking of you saying that you were going to read Spengler *twice*. Read him six, seven, eight times. He'll stand the test. But I am delighted you found it so good. Volume 2 can surely be had. Volume 2 deals with gold, etc. Double-entry bookkeeping. (One of the great discoveries of all time!)

The journal—well, if you didn't have a too tragic childhood, you at least had something infinitely better—the tragic sense of life! I hope to write an imaginary preface to your diary some day this week.

Whenever you ask me "do I remember," remember that I remember everything. I am a sponge.

Funny that we both mentioned "calendars and handkerchiefs" at the same time. Mention the lawn-mower next time—or the dirty wine bottle.

Do you really mean that I gave you all those things you mention? I must be an interesting guy. I must be rich! Are you rich today, Henry? Sure I am. I'm the richest guy in the world. Sprinkle a little *eau de javel* on me. I'm going to write today. I wish I were leaning over your shoulder reading those fat letters I sent you. I hate to stop, but I must go out and perform an important financial operation. Ortega y Gasset will follow. And Unamuno. And Dostoevsky. And the preface. Let me know the date line. Everything is on the stones, as they say. I'm still crazier about you.

Henry

[Achensee]
Aug. 2, 1932

[Henry:]

The last pages of the novel [*Tropic of Cancer*] are magnificent. There could be no better end. Not reality, not suicide, not Tony killing either one of the women, or himself, but the man swept down by a "lucid madness" in which all the feelings and acts of the book swirl in fevered antediluvian symbols. Also, no climax, no pause, and no conclusion, just the simoom wind and all things withering. Spengler says that what we attach words to, we in a sense conquer, and in this, since the words are not attached to anything, since it is simple delirium, it tells what you want to tell, defeat. Certainly if the world is cracking (which I do not believe) you are the master destroyer. These pages prove it. Everything you write proves it. It is Spengler's prophecies you are materializing, with each novel.

You knew this. You said: "If I always wrote as I did in these pages I would be all that you expect me to be." Have I understood?

I have just this minute come back from a three days' hike to the German frontier. We went there walking with packs on our backs. I liked the idea of standing for a few hours on German soil—only because it is yours. When I read the longest letter I have ever received, and also the most extraordinary, I wanted to answer immediately, but it will take me days! Hugh says: "What are you doing?" I answer: "I have an idea for my book." He says: "The hike was a good thing then. But you won't be long? It is time to go down for tea." And tomorrow we are off again, to climb mountains! Listen, I wear pyjamas and a gypsy handkerchief, and I look like a pirate. What I enjoy is the rhythm. It begins with regularity, harmony, and it ends in ecstasy. You walk until you walk *over* the world.

Afternoon.

I am still laughing over your "delicate" letter! I love it. How did you ever guess that I was alone for a whole day and two nights. Something told you I would be alone for a few days indeed! Did you see Hugh in Paris Friday? He was suddenly called by telephone to attend a lunch for a big client, rushed away Thursday night and was back Saturday morning. Friday I wrote you the short letter in which I mentioned being anxious because I had no news of you. I didn't mention Hugh's absence because I thought you would immediately imagine . . . a philological entanglement. As a matter of fact the two Austrians who wished to console me were finally discouraged by our dialogue . . . or the briefness of it, with only shaking of the head on my side. As I was not sure what they were asking me (one of them offering his arm and pointing to the boats on the lake), I said *"Nein."* The only word I got out of their conversation was *gemütlich* which means charm, to which I also said *"Nein."* All these *neins* mainly because their heads were shaved, and this is a warning to you! The impossibility of conversing would not have hampered me in Spain for instance. I did imagine wild things like asking you to come over in an aeroplane. Two hours. But I can't get over your *expecting* a telegram: Come to the Tyrol. Tell me *really* how this happened. It amuses me so much I can't go back and finish the other letter. And oh, Henry, don't mention surprises to me. I am like a child. It keeps me awake at night with excitement! If I study my German faithfully . . . Impossible to know what "page 2" you are referring to. Please expand. Symbolism or Euclidian proofs? "It is very difficult for me to answer except that you were mistaken about me. I believe until I get hit on the head. Don't hit me on the head." If by any chance you happen to know what you mean by all this, I would love to be told. You don't know how I love this loose mad kind of letter writing which I believe I owe you originally. It is full of surprises, no tapestry weaving, no arduous mountain climbing, just diving. You don't absolutely have to be fragile. I am always dressed first and it is I who go down for the mail. I read it coming up the three flights of stairs. The Austrian No. 2 is always there with green Mephistophelean eyes to *read the barometer* for me, slowly, portentously. That is another reason I say *"Nein"* to him, and *"Verboten,"* and all the other porcupinish adjectives I know.

Anaïs

Hugh said just now we might not return until Tuesday. Will try to send you this letter by air so you won't be so many days without news.

[Achensee]
Aug. 3, 1932*

[Henry:]

I like your letter to Buñuel. It is direct and definite, and effective. What you tell him struck me even more deeply now that I have read Spengler. If each civilization produced one particular form of art, it does seem as if the movies were the only logical expression of the last. But Henry, I do not believe everything Spengler says. I don't like his cursory treatment of psychology, objecting to the fact that in talking about the soul no other language but the physicist's has been found and

*Dated subsequently, apparently, in A. N.'s handwriting.

that shows psychology has achieved nothing. (Incidentally, the only thing that is very wrong with psychoanalysis is the jargon, the visibility and obviousness of the terminology. If an artist ever *absorbed* the significance, made the filing invisible and undetectable, as Dostoevsky does, it would be wonderful and fertile. Psychology has not been absorbed and transformed yet. Who will do it?)

And then the end of one civilization *is* the beginning of another; they dovetail each other, just like the falling of withered flowers produces the seeds for the Spring. Why does Spengler stop at the indication of a decay which it is impossible to feel as a finality. All finality is defective. To persist in a theme without swerving is defective. It is perhaps good to emphasize the decay so that we may become more conscious of our *beginning*. Are you aware of a beginning? While Spengler chants pessimistic requiems I hear the vigorous birth-throbs of Picasso, psychoanalysis, the new mystical sciences, the Negro soul pouring into America's steel magnitude, Fraenkel's resurrection of death, the *fecundity of disintegration,* and I don't understand why we should stop painting, building houses, writing. Henry Miller, the master destroyer will write scenarios. [. . .]

[Spengler] is profound and at his best when he writes about music and painting. I have so much to ask you about certain things he says.

Henry, there are only a few rare moments when I am proud of myself: when I realize that I figured out Lawrence *all alone,* without help, talk or nourishment, background, or the smallest connection with the outer world and ideas, and I find that a few things in the book connect themselves automatically, mysteriously, with a great whole.

[Anaïs]

[Achensee]
Wednesday [August 3, 1932]

[Henry:]

Did you mind what I wrote you yesterday? So much literature, so many ideas, which cover up without replacing the human moments when we sit in a café, without talking, and I lean my head on your shoulder and say: I don't want to go home now, Henry. It isn't Hugh's physical presence which prevents me from leaning my head on your shoulder instead of telling you about Neagoe; it is just his closeness, the closeness which grows up again between us when he wins me back with his faith and fervor. I can say to you now what you wrote me once: I am all torn apart, but stand by me. And also when I am away it is the doubts which come to the foreground, and what preys on me is what you told me one night about Bertha, and what I prophesied. Will you believe it, I have promised to stay in Paris a few days and then go to San Rafael in Segovia to spend the rest of the summer. And then everything will be "ideas" again, and what do you think of French literature, etc.

Anaïs

I'm coming back Tuesday alone. We'll have a week together. *Peut-être tu me feras oubliée tout ceci. Je suis malheureuse.* Write me by air-mail in a post office—there's a special box.

[Achensee]
Thursday [August 4, 1932]

I have not been able to answer your letters the way I wanted to, Henry, and they move me and interest me and excite me so much—you cannot ever imagine how much. It discourages me to see how much I want to respond to, dwell on, and how pressed I am for time. We are never in the room, even when it rains, and that is every day; we are out walking, or rowing, walking, walking. I managed to read Spengler at night after dinner. I have not worked at all, neither for Allendy, nor on the book, only ten pages in the journal. About the old love and the weighty letters, that was exaggeration.

Observe the indecision. I rarely change my mind about a phrase. [A. N. had x-ed out the preceding paragraph.] I wanted to tease you, but I love you so much I can't, Henry. I tried twice, you see. *N'en parlons plus.* I can't think of anything but of Louveciennes, and of your ringing the bell at eight—not at nine. The plan is this: when I arrive in Paris I have to take a taxi with my trunk and valises and go straight to Louveciennes and get my cousins to move out first, in the same taxi. This will be done about seven. And then you must eat dinner before you come because there won't be any food in the house. Emilia only arrives the next morning for breakfast. I can't go to Clichy because I will be all dusty from the trip, and because of the baggage.

It didn't seem at all egotistical of you to show me the letters you write. On the contrary, I liked your wanting me to see them. I'm interested, terribly so, in every word you put down, and I enjoyed your letter to Emil. I have the same feeling when I read a book you have marked. (*Cahiers de Brigge* [Rilke's *The Notebooks of Malte Laurids Brigge*].) I love the sharing. I feel with extraordinary vividness your presence, as if you were reading with me. I actually experience again the sensation of my leaning over your shoulder and kissing your hair and neck while you are reading or writing.

I must get down to literature. How I laugh when you take sly digs at "Miss Nin." When you write this name I feel as if you were mentioning *another person.* It is like Joaquin writing to me in old pompous Spanish: *Mi distinguida autora y hermanita.* He admired Ortega y Gasset. I have read a book of his, beautiful, limpid style and thought, and very modern.

Brigge reminded me of Fred's writing. Very much so. Did this resemblance strike you at all? At its best it is poetic and sensitive, sometimes profound. But as a whole it is puerile, a little like a woman's writing. The total impression was feeble.

It saddened me when you wished to exchange ideas with someone of your own stature. It reminded me of all that I have sworn to myself about your life: I want to work my head off to make it marvellous—I want to get you outside of all mediocrity. Clichy, flatness, drabness, everything which doesn't aliment you, which isn't good enough for you. You will see what a winter we will have, and how much dynamite there will be in *Tropic of Capricorn.* The passage about the clouds—is that the beginning?

I see you are getting serious about Lawrence. I never compared your writing to his, as Fraenkel does. No. But I don't like your comparing him with *any* Frenchman on the basis of "superior attitudes." I don't like superior attitudes based on well-poised intellect. I hate well-poised intellects. Lawrence may have been childish etc. etc., but like Dostoevsky he at least went to the *bottom* of feelings, what no Frenchman will disturb himself to do. Everybody who keeps cool is superior. But who likes the man who keeps cool? Not I. If you go on like this I *will* fight! Dostoevsky also gets childish when in the *Brothers* five people get hysterical fits, two epilepsy, and two others brain fever within a month . . . but you can forgive exultation a great deal, and I can't forgive the *lack* of it. If this is not enough I will say more! So fanaticism, preaching, petulance, nerves, exaggerations, irrationality, etc. are all to be forgiven because of the *intensity.* It is after all only the intensity of feeling which makes *Lady Chatterley* superior to any French book on the same subject (even *Lucienne* by Jules Romain) and to this statement I will stick until I die. It is the same intensity which makes me love Spain and a few Anglo-Saxons with all the strength of my blood and flesh, while for France I feel a mental admiration which only stirs the tip of my hair, like a message through a telegraph [wire].

Only it is better for you to cherish the French, yes, because you are rich enough in exultation, and the cooling process only brings out of you deeper, wiser, new and wonderful things. I can see that—I've been noticing that. I remember your great admiration for French Olympian detachment. I understand it. But I have had enough of it! It is new to you and stale to me. I never told you about a famous French writer I knew—that was long ago, I had almost forgotten—five years ago. He was like Anatole France. When I see you, remind me to tell you all about him.

What I meant by "the time before consciousness" was really the time before introspection. Spengler tells how the Greeks never knew introspection [. . .]. He designates this as a Faustian malady. He is too fond of the Faustian soul, Spengler, did you notice? But how magnificently he writes about de Vinci, the painter I love best.

Unamuno wrote a book of sly, paradoxical, tart comments on *Don Quixote* which you would love. Grim Spanish humor. You know he reads English, is widely read in *Anglo-Saxon* (Another!) literature, a specialist on English poetry . . . so you can write to him. When he was exiled from Spain for political vehemence, he used to sit at the Rotonde. You were in America then. Let's go and see him in Spain. Let's go and hear Ortega y Gasset lecture in Madrid.

I believe you have improved the Buñuel article *immensely.* Yes, it is hard straight thinking, but not *cold writing.* It is far more effective because it is better *aimed* than the first. The first draft now has a random air . . . it does not go off as well. A few small portions of the first draft, I was sorry to see, were completely omitted from the last. That is the only thing which bothers me. We'll talk it over when I come. It's a powerful and great piece of writing, Henry. A worthy ushering in of your book. You are quite right about Buñuel, I feel, altogether, as well as in what you write about the film [*L'Age d'Or*] and about him personally. (Yes, I knew about the word "fuck" used as a swear word. When I first heard and read of it in *Lady Chatterley* I told Hugh I *loved* the word. Hugh made a grimace, and told me how it was used in general. *Bon.*) I find, too, that you have brought out more interesting emphasis—on the destructive, negative etc. That was very important.

How impatient I am to hear about Bradley, Crosby, etc. I'm afraid of Bradley. Krans wishes you success. I wish you had sent me your letter to him. We'll see Buñuel so that we can present *your* film when it is ready. In the train I'll have time to underline what I want to talk over with you in *L'Age d'Or.*

Henry, there are moments when I am almost frightened at the way you have *invaded* me. Don't talk about *others,* for instance; it is all external—contrast, not penetration. I cannot understand yet how I gave you my journal to read, which *no one* has read all through. Each secret I have kept, you have slowly unravelled. Sometimes I feel strangely *exposed* before you. Sometimes I seem to stand aside and marvel at your way of touching me now here, now there. Things you say and write almost hurt me. I always carry, with a curious sense of independence and pride, a hidden side. There is always a hidden side . . . are you going to go on? The last arrow was your mention of the *tragic sense of life.* You have heard me laugh. You said first of all that *laughter belonged* to me. Then why do you connect now Unamuno and the tragic sense of life and me. That was a feeling which Joaquin and I preserved. He has it too. And the same shell of outward gaiety, too. That is why we don't even talk to each other: *we know.* Once we gave a big party at which a trio of his was played, and after it I was going to dance Spanish dances. I had heard the trio often and knew it well. It was a more vehement, more spontaneous thing than he writes now. [After it was] played, I couldn't dance. Impossible. I was in a terrible mood. Joaquin came up to me and said: "I'm glad you can't dance. Dancing doesn't suit you." He was always against it. Hated it. *"Ce n'est pas serieux."*

Anaïs

[Achensee]
[August 5, 1932]

Henry, my love, tear up the letter I sent you today. Between two of Hugh's caresses I want you desperately. I want your strength and your softness, your hands, all of you; you don't know the things I remember and crave. But it drives me wild to imagine, to feel, or to word all this with Hugh's face thrust constantly between me and the paper—"Pussywillow, what are you writing? What are you thinking?" He has a trick of asking me every hour or so: do you love me? All this torments me and paralyzes me. Tonight I dreamed my return—perhaps you would like to come to Louveciennes. We will be all alone in the house. Henry, Henry, I remember everything—the day in the woods, and the nights in Clichy, and the lawn-mower. (It doesn't matter what you said that night. I want *you* from *me* to have the experience of being loved.)

[Anaïs]

[Achensee]
[August 6, 1932]

Oh, Henry, I was so upset by your letter this morning. When it was given to me all the artificially pent-up feelings overwhelmed me. The very touch of the letter was as if you had taken me all into your arms. You know now what I felt when I read it. You said everything that would touch and win me and I was *moist,* and so impatient that I am doing *everything* to gain a day. This note I'm enclosing, which I wrote you last night two hours after mailing my letter, will help you to understand what is happening. Anyway you must have received the telegram almost at the same time. I belong to you! We're going to have a week such as we never dreamt yet. "The thermometer will burst." I want to feel again the violent thumping inside of me, the rushing, burning blood, the slow, caressing rhythm and the sudden violent pushing, the frenzy of pauses when I hear the raindrop sounds . . . how it leaps in my mouth, Henry. Oh, Henry, I can't bear to be writing you—I want you desperately, I want to open my legs so wide, I'm melting and palpitating. I want to do things so wild with you that I don't know how to say them.

Hugo is calling. I'll answer the rest of the letter tonight.

Anaïs

[Clichy]
[August 14, 1932]

[Anaïs:]

Don't expect me to be sane any more. Don't let's be sensible. It was a marriage at Louveciennes—you can't dispute it. I came away with pieces of you sticking to me; I am walking about, swimming, in an ocean of blood, your Andalusian blood, distilled and poisonous. Everything I do and say and think relates back to the marriage. I saw you as the mistress of your home, a Moor with heavy face, a negress with a white body, eyes all over your skin, woman, woman, woman. I can't see how I can go on living away from you—these intermissions are death. How did it seem to you when Hugo came back? Was I still there? I can't picture you moving about with him as you did with me. Legs closed. Frailty. Sweet, treacherous acquiescence. Bird docility. You became a woman with me. I was almost terrified by it. You are not just thirty years old—you are a thousand years old.

Here I am back and still smouldering with passion, like wine smoking. Not a passion any longer for flesh, but a complete hunger for you, a devouring hunger. I read the paper about suicides and murders and I understand it all thoroughly. I feel murderous, suicidal. I feel somehow that it is a disgrace to do nothing, to just bide one's time, to take it philosophically, to be sensible. Where has gone the time when men fought, killed, died for a glove, a glance, etc? (A victrola is playing that terrible aria from *Madama Butterfly*—"Some day he'll come!")

I still hear you singing in the kitchen—a light, niggerish quality to your voice, a sort of inharmonic, monotonous Cuban wail. I know you're happy in the kitchen and the meal you're cooking is the best meal we ever ate together. I know you would scald yourself and not complain. I feel the greatest peace and joy sitting in the dining room listening to you rustling about, your dress like the goddess Indra studded with a thousand eyes.

Anaïs, I only thought I loved you before; it was nothing like this certainty that's in me now. Was all this so wonderful only because it was brief and stolen? Were we acting for each other, to each other? Was I less I, or more I, and you less or more you? Is it madness to believe that this could go on? When and where would the drab moments begin? I study you so much to discover the possible flaws, the weak points, the danger zones. I don't find them—not any. That means I am in love, blind, blind. To be blind forever! (Now they're singing "Heaven and Ocean" from *La Gioconda*.)

I picture you playing the records over and over—Hugo's records. *"Parlez moi d'amour."* The double life, double taste, double joy and misery. How you must be furrowed and ploughed by it. I know all that, but I can't do anything to prevent it. I wish indeed it were me who had to endure it. I know now your eyes are wide open. Certain things you will never believe any more, certain gestures you will never repeat, certain sorrows, misgivings, you will never again experience. A kind of white, criminal fervor in your tenderness and cruelty. Neither remorse nor vengeance; neither sorrow nor guilt. A living it out, with nothing to save you from the abyss but a high hope, a faith, a joy that you tasted, that you can repeat when you will.

All morning I was at my notes, ferreting through my life records, wondering where to begin, how to make the start, seeing not just another book before me but a life of books. But I don't begin. The walls are completely bare—I had taken everything down before going to meet you. It is as though I had made ready to leave for good. The spots on the walls stand out—where our heads rested. While it thunders and lightnings I lie on the bed and go through wild dreams. We're in Seville and then in Fez and then in Capri and then in Havana. We're journeying constantly, but there is always a machine and books, and your body is always close to me and the look in your eyes never changes. People are saying we will be miserable, we will regret, but we are happy, we are laughing always, we are singing. We are talking Spanish and French and Arabic and Turkish. We are admitted everywhere and they strew our path with flowers.

I say this is a wild dream—but it is this dream I want to realize. Life and literature combined, love the dynamo, you with your chameleon's soul giving me a thousand loves, being anchored always in no matter what storm, home wherever we are. In the mornings continuing where we left off; resurrection after resurrection. You asserting yourself, getting the rich, varied life you desire; and the more you assert yourself the more you want me, need me. Your voice getting hoarser, deeper, your eyes blacker, your blood thicker, your body fuller. A voluptuous servility and a tyrannical necessity. More cruel now than before— consciously, willfully cruel. The insatiable delight of experience.

HVM

Café Terminus, Gare St. Lazare
Tuesday night [August 16, 1932]

[Anaïs:]

I hope you won't chew me to bits when you read the enclosed. You wanted it.

Came home to find two guests for dinner—M. King & Wambly

Bald, and they persisted in hanging around, and besides it's so terrifyingly hot this evening. I don't think you can picture it quite—out there in the country.

One of the printers at the *Tribune* has a beautiful, almost new wheel, which was especially made for him, and worth 800 frs., that he is willing to let go for 250 frs. I am going to look at it Saturday. I think Providence is still looking after me.

I hope the Fraenkel letter doesn't disturb you. I'm nervous about it. Maybe I said too much—all that about the house—I had no right perhaps to talk that way, and yet I felt somehow that you yourself would have said just that.

Anyway, I very seriously mean that what I would like *is to invite him to our home*—do you understand? Sometimes I have the audacity, or unreality, to think of Louveciennes as *our* home.

Tho' I didn't write a line yet I thought of so many things going home. I know now how and why everything fits. Again everything becomes grist for me. I will send you the first few pages [of *Tropic of Capricorn*] immediately they are written. I am almost as feverish as you about it. I think it's marvellous of you to throw yourself into my work as you do. You'll be in it too—watch and see. You make me completely happy. You are inexhaustible. The diary must go on. It seems to me it's getting richer, thicker. Don't worry about Allendy's interest in it. And don't type it out yourself. I'm thinking that when we see Bradley and the wine flows I'll be making a grand speech and Bradley will want that diary so badly. Don't do anything but write in it. Some of the things you say are sublime and monstrous at once. No woman has ever before said such things. Believe that!

Henry

P.S. Erskine with his grand *Helen of Troy*—fiddlesticks! This is a Helen who will launch a thousand ships! Nobody has ever told us how and what women think. It is a revelation.

[Louveciennes]
[August 18, 1932]

My Love—

Today I'm collecting my wits! I'm going straight to the film store and will have the snapshots for you tomorrow night. I'm free tomorrow night. Where do you want me to meet you?

Allendy's wife made a desperate move and he was whisked away to Brittany for a while. We had a beautiful scene which I will tell you about—profoundly interesting—right here in Louveciennes, an hour ago. So I'm going to work on other things. *Your* book swells up inside of me like my very *own*—more joyously even than my own, for *your* book is for me a fecundation, while mine is an act of narcissism. I say let a woman write books but let her above everything else remain *fecundable* by other books! Do you understand me? I'm *glorying* in your immense plans, in your ideas—those talks of ours, Henry, how they *rebound*, they are so firm—Henry there will never be drabness because in both of us there is always *movement*, renewal, surprises. I have never known stagnation. Not even introspection has been a *still* experience. . . . Even into *nothing* I read marvels, and in the mere act of burrowing earth, not gold mines, I can generate enthusiasm. Enthusiasm, change, expansion are encrusted on me like the glowworm's sulphurous tail. And how it glows in the *night life!* Then think, if this is so, what I find in *you* who are a gold mine! Henry, I love you with a *realization*, a *knowledge* of you which takes you *all in* as you were never taken in, with all the strength of my mind and imagination besides that of my body. I love you in such a way that June can return, our love can be destroyed, and yet nothing can sever the fusion that has been—no June, no space, no thousand miles, no hatred even— something has been started like a *mouvement perpetuel.* Don't think when I read you riotous pages of my journal that I am unaware of the depths—yesterday the *transition*, the completion of the circle seemed in itself beautiful to me, fuller than anything I have ever imagined. A kind of double climax always. Do you understand me?

Anaïs

Just got your letter to Fraenkel. I *like* it. I like its *assertiveness*, possessiveness—it's *you* too. I like the feeling for Fraenkel that it shows—Louveciennes, as a symbol of much else, belongs to the one who takes it, penetrates it, understands it. I love that idea of the house open and sheltering Fraenkel—your prodigality satisfies me, answers my own feelings.

Have you written about the *flies* yet?! I have *seen your* diabolical face these days in Louveciennes—yes. And I think today of what you said: I will help you. I want to make the *feminine scar.* Helen of Troy was, after all, unfecundable. She was one of the rigid ones, like [Virginia] Woolf and [Rebecca] West.

[Clichy]
Sunday [August 21, 1932]

Anaïs—The enclosed [cable from June] was lying on the kitchen table this morning. I haven't answered it because I don't know what to say. Should I just ignore it? Or what? I'm stumped. You have to help me decide—it concerns us both now. Notice that there is a slip for the payment of a return answer. If you want me to cable enclose the telegram with the slip in your letter. Naturally, she won't come the end of October—this is just a preliminary barrage, as usual.

Fred says she probably did it to impress the guy she was with—and I think that's almost right. It certainly wasn't anguish that prompted it.

I have rewritten all the pages I took out for revision. Made a fine mélange of Salavin and Buñuel, which I think you will approve. Wrote Bradley that I would see him Tuesday noon.

Also received two good letters from my friend Emil Schnellock, saying that he met Fraenkel & was much impressed. He said some fine things about the MSS.

Emil says one funny thing—"When Shakespeare painted a horse it was a horse for all time."

And he asked especially to say to you that he *needs* that Lawrence book. Evidently he saw the copy which Fraenkel was to give Buzby. He wants to know more about you—I guess Fraenkel gave him an earful. He says that Fraenkel is incapable of writing me because he is only thinking of things *immediate & material.* Poor Fraenkel!

And only now it just occurs to me that perhaps the reason for June's cable is that she met Fraenkel. I didn't give him her address nor did I tell him to see her, but he is frequently in the Village where no doubt she is living and I wouldn't be surprised if they met. And the rest is jealousy, no doubt. And if that's the case, god damn her soul. I'm disgusted. So don't let the cable excite you. I'm almost sure now that this is the explanation.

Do you expect to be coming to Paris in the next day or two? Could I meet you somewhere, or would you have time to come to Clichy? Remember that I see Bradley Tuesday noon unless he rules otherwise. I'm all cured of my ills. I'm working well again and taking lots of exercise. And I love you more than ever.

Henry

P.S. I can't see the typewriter people Monday as I promised because I haven't paid my bill for this month yet and I don't want to just yet. Could you telephone them? I'm sorry!

P.P.S. I'm sending you herewith one of the pages from Emil's letter. He inked out the lines himself.

[Louveciennes]
[August 28, 1932]

Henry,

I am coming out in the open. I want to explain to you, if I can, the reason why I did not have much voice or much naturalness over the phone today. You telephoned in the middle of a crisis. To understand it, try and remember some of the questions you put to me about June, the comparisons you made. One night you said: "*You* would not do that to me." Always comparing June's way of loving you with my way of loving you, and wondering if and how much June loved you. Very much the same thing happens to me with Allendy. He forces me almost to believe that if I compare his way and yours, you do not love me at all. This is not nonsense, Henry. Allendy could not stay away a week even, whereas you could play with the idea of our living together a month in Spain and relinquish it immediately, which is what I realized afterwards. To live together for a month! But that was not what was in your mind the other day either: it was just to save yourself, or that I should save you from June. Don't you see what an admission you are making? The one I would never make. I have been wilfully blind. I wouldn't have anybody open my eyes to the fact I know now, that you love me as a consolation, as a way of enduring life between June's absences, for the happiness I can give you. More than to love, you have let yourself *be* loved. Very often I have had the feeling of your seeking June in me, a reflection, a possible resemblance. Until now I didn't care whether yours was a half love, or whatever it was. I could live. Now I have the same temptation that I was to you: someone who loves me wholly and can give me a *human life*. Until now I have demanded nothing. You happened to dwell on this once when you read my journal: if Anaïs has any defect it is to be too easily satisfied. That was possible when I was not a human being, just the ghost of a writer living in fantasy alone. See, I am still a little inhuman: look what I have written during those very days when I was most humanly tormented by your return to June. Look at the way I can surpass the petty human being! But Henry, that trifle, that mere trip to Spain so easily relinquished, what a way to open my eyes! That, and my knowledge that with Bertha you could easily go to Russia, risk losing June, everything, and *also while* you were in the middle of a book! And now, such wisdom, such thinking, such hesitations—from cool men, yes, that is the way it comes, but not from men like you. Henry, I want you to admit today that this is all true. I want you to give me up, to let me go, just to admit all this and *free* me. I have often doubted you—it is you who have made me doubt. Don't play a comedy with me, Henry, because the quietest people like me are those who do the most unexpected and violent things. *I prefer the truth*. Unwittingly you are acting towards me now exactly as June acts towards you. When you are here, as when she is next to you, no doubts are possible. You never *demanded* anything from June—that is not my way either. But in sheer self-protection I asked Allendy today what you asked me to do for you (save me from June). I asked him to save me from you. And this is my first effort. I don't want to go on living in this nightmare. Take the talks we have, and the books and the writing we incite each other to do—all this can be kept, but be honest with me. Don't just do what June does: send the cable now, and then just to keep the thread from breaking— that's all. *I love you too much*, Henry, and that is something to be feared, you know. *I have come too close to you.* You may say I am fighting a destiny, something which cannot be fought like this. But I want to try. Say that you do not love me, that you love the closeness and the intimacy and the understanding between us, and the bouts. I am fighting a mystery, Henry. You have never done that, you have let yourself be swallowed by your great slavery to June, until it became unbearable, until you exhausted the pain. Well, I have done that, only I have done it within a few days. I have lived through a century in a few days. You cannot ever imagine it all—with Allendy coming at the end, looking on just as other people looked on at you and June, knowing all the while, *from the very beginning,* that you did not love me! That *those four days are not a necessity to you.* The terrible part of all this is that I come to it too quickly . . . terrible because it shortens all the joys! At least you had years of blindness!

I am leaving for Segovia to get back my sense of humor, which I have lost. I am not *asking* for anything from you, only to stop asking of me my *whole* love, to stop me from being wrapped up in you too much. That's all.

[Anaïs]

[Louveciennes]
[August 30, 1932]

Henry,

I am again coming out in the open. I do not want to see you for a few days. You have asked things of me which are *humanly* unbearable. You have asked me to thrive on a half love, and also to give you my understanding of June so that you could add this to yours and write your book out of both. I have wanted to give you the impossible, the gigantic, the inhuman. I thought I could stand the arrival of all these pages in which you do every day more justice to her wonder. You are testing my courage to the full, like a torturer. How to extricate myself from this nightmare? I have only one source of strength (*humanly,* I have no strength), I have only writing, and it is this which I am doing now with a desperation you can never conceive of—I am writing *against* myself, *against* what you call my imperfections, *against* the woman, *against* my humaneness, *against* the continents which are giving way. Two things may happen: in a few days I may be dauntless again, and you can go on with your interesting and monstrous experiments; or I may send you a postcard from Stamboul. Don't come and show me the immediacy of your *humaneness*—behind your humaneness there is always a great evaluator.

I may not send you this letter. I still have the instinct that the most important thing is your book, and that I must not disturb your work on that. The rest is just human life.

[Anaïs]

[Louveciennes]
Sept. 6, 1932

Henry,

you have just left. I told Hugh I had something to add to my work. I had to come upstairs [to] my room again, and be alone. I was so filled with you I was afraid to show my face. Henry, no departure of yours has ever left me so shattered. I don't know what it was tonight, which drew me to you, which made me frantic to stay close to you, to *sleep* with you, to hold you . . . a mad and terrific tenderness . . . a desire to care for you. . . . It was a great pain to me that you should be leaving. When you talk the way you talked about *Mädchen* [*in Uniform*], when you are thoughtful and moving, I lose my mind. To stay with you for one night I would throw away my whole life, sacrifice a hundred persons, I would burn Louveciennes, be capable of *anything*. This is not to worry you, Henry, it is just that I can't keep from saying it, that I am overflowing, desperately in love with you as I never was with anyone. Even if you had left tomorrow morning the idea that you were sleeping in the same house would have been a very sweet relief from the torment I endure tonight, the torment of being cut in two pieces when you closed the gate behind you. Henry, Henry, Henry, I love you, love you, love you. I was jealous of [Jean] Renaud* who has you all these days, who sleeps in Clichy. Tonight everything hurts, not only the separation, but this terrible hunger of body and mind for you which every day you are increasing, stirring more and more. I don't know what I am writing. Feel me holding you as I have never held you before, more deeply, more sadly, more desperately, more passionately. I kneel before you, I give you myself and it is not enough, not enough. I adore you. Your body, your face, your voice, your human self, oh Henry, I can't go now and sleep in Hugh's arms—I can't. I want to run away just to be alone with my feelings for you.

[Anaïs]

[Clichy]
Wednesday [September 7, 1932]

[Anaïs:]

I'm enclosing the copy only of the first five pages which I have just attempted to rewrite for you—I'm not so pleased with the results of my efforts. I'm afraid I have frequently so distorted your original thought as to make it unrecognizable.† But this will only show you, prove to you, how difficult you made your language, and how much *work* it requires sometimes, to say what one has to say, after one had

*A student at the Lycée Carnot who became a friend of H. M.
†A. N.'s manuscript of "Alraune," which eventually became *House of Incest.*

said it. I don't know what you'll think of this draft. You may see some improvement in the language, or the way of expressing yourself, but with a corresponding diminution of force. Because I can't penetrate your thought deeply enough, and so appropriate it and refashion it. Yet, with this in your hand, and the only copy to compare, you may write it once again and restore the lost vigor, the tattered thoughts, etc. That's my only hope. I'm somewhat disappointed in myself—that I could not do better. Nevertheless, I will continue with the remaining pages—and I beg you to send to me, as the work progresses, all the pages you write, and allow me to revise them. What I have done has been done in a few hours. I would go on only Wambly Bald is coming for advice and I want to duck him. Renaud is seeing one of his friends today and I am free—free to rest up—to think in English for a change.

Your wonderful letter arrived when I was out. The three of us [including Fred] had been to Versailles on bicycle and came home exhausted from the hills. But it was a glorious trip through the forest— the best bicycle trip I have made around Paris. I fell on the couch and slept like a log until almost midnight. I went to the Dôme with Renaud and tried to write you, but I couldn't.

What you wrote me is so beautiful that it hurts and I can't answer it yet. I will only tell you that just as you were filled with me so I was with you, that the moment the gate closed behind us we began talking about you and it continued in to Paris and all through the night as we sat quietly conversing on a *terrasse*. I was touched by Renaud's quick and deep appreciation of you—he said marvellous things about you, all the things you would like to have said about you. And when he read Fred's pages, on Anaïs, he was disappointed. They were not good enough. He wants to write about you himself. He adores you. All that made me feel wonderful. You know, I didn't want to go that night, but I felt that Hugo was not too pleased with the idea and I didn't want to hurt him. I know just how you must feel about Renaud's sharing things with me—and yet what he is sharing with me is something in which you would probably not participate. I assure you it is nothing. But when I proposed Spain that time it was with just that feeling—of wanting to share something with you exclusively—no interruptions, no dread of telephone, no quick return to other roles.

He will be leaving Saturday morning and I will be relieved after all, because though I have enjoyed the vacation, it is a little too protracted. It has been almost like work.

Will you be free any time before Saturday? We have only one big date ahead of us, and that is Thursday night, to spend with Fred and Paulette, at the Bal Nègre. Afterwards to go to Les Halles.

I am running now to get away before Wambly Bald arrives. If you have a free night let me know; we can make any arrangements you like.

What did Renaud observe that was interesting? Costume, gesture, voice—plus the most natural charm, the most exquisite intelligence, a deep generosity, a hospitality unknown to Frenchman, etc. etc. Oh, you will be greedy to hear it all. I am congratulating myself over and over. No, don't you kneel to me—it is you who are great, and I am just a sort of reflection, a light you had kindled.

Henry

[Louveciennes]
Thursday Evening [September 8, 1932]

Oh, Henry, I don't know what is the matter with me. I am so *exulted.* I am almost mad, working, loving you, writing, and thinking of you, playing your records, dancing in the room when my eyes are tired. You have given me such joys that it does not matter what happens now—I am ready to die—and ready to love you all my life!

How are you? I have been anxious about your cold. Hugh is leaving Sunday night for London for two nights. I'll write you again about it. I would love it if you would put your typewriter in a taxi and ride over—or if you are tired after Renaud's visit just come for a rest. I will need one too. Write to your Mother *today* asking for exact date and *hour* of your birth. *Je t'aime.*

Anaïs

One evening I must give to Allendy & the journal business—that's O.K. *n'est ça pas?*

Friday A.M.
Just got your letter. Not free any evening. Hugh leaving Monday night. Call me up Monday to make plans. I'm sending you 100 frs. tomorrow.

[Louveciennes]
Saturday, Sept. 24 [1932]

[Henry:]

Astrology certainly went to my head Thursday—I realized afterwards I had let Fred pay for the dinner and felt so badly about it. Then yesterday I could not get away to send you anything. This morning Hugh is home but Emilia is going to send two hundred francs by telegraph from Louveciennes.

Am very happy about the last pages. Felt that you wrote *beautifully* about the stars and planets. Wonderful passage. Eduardo [Sanchez] saw it and admired it. You made wonderful use of the spider idea, and how well you linked that idea with the description of the place you lived in. That was artistry!

Please send me the others. I expect you Tuesday as early as you can come, for lunch unless you tell me otherwise. We must make the most of October and November, since the planets are going to separate us in December! Eduardo is fiendishly exulting over the future catastrophe. But Allendy told me something remarkable the other day: one person or one will cannot fight the predestinations, but *two* wills can do it. Two persons against a planet's influence can alter its course. Allendy meant that an analyst and I, for instance, could defeat all malefic forces, but I thought to myself: Henry and I can too, Henry and I and Libra.

Anaïs

[Clichy]
Sunday [September 25, 1932]

[Anaïs:]

A lot of things have happened, or it seems that way. I've been wanting to write you a long letter and have been putting it off in order to go on with other things—the pages will testify. I don't imagine you will find the *first chapter of our book* very hot—on Nudism—but it's a start. I could improve it a lot if I wished to. At any rate, I want you to take the idea seriously (of the book); I have already broached it to Bradley in my letter to him. You will want to write about your own films most likely—that is, your choice will be different than mine frequently. Why don't you start off with *Lumière*

108

Bleue, * since you got a kick out of it the first time? And besides, I can see you writing a good introduction to the book—in your best abstract vein, with all the dire implications of your recent philosophizing and astrologizing. And some things we will write jointly, no? It is time we wrote a book together—it must be sooner or later.

Last night I went to a very wretched theatre on the Rue D'Avron—most interesting morbid neighborhood, most interesting morbid theatre (The Family Cinema)—and I got a great kick out of it. I should almost like to write about the theatre itself, the audience, the posters on the wall, the asbestos curtain with its advertisements, the song that came over the loudspeaker, that wonderful song which the prostitute sang standing by the window in *L'Opéra de Quat' sous*—do you recall it? Imagine, I thoroughly enjoyed the first film—*Coeurs Farouches*—a Wild West thriller. I would write about it if only you weren't sitting there laughing at me—I know it must sound ridiculous. The second film was [Jean Renoir's] *La Chienne* and this you must go to see by all means—it is a story of La Fouchardière's and well played, particularly the role of Michel Simon's. The story too has qualities and overtones which will delight you, recall all sort of things, and lead to inevitable comparisons. (For instance, that in an Emil Jannings' theme the French handle it even better, much better!) But don't go to the Family Cinema—I'm afraid they would lynch you. (Yes, I'm going to write about that theatre!)

I spent a whole day making notes for the book, collecting my papers and my wits, and everywhere I saw notes for you—buy Anaïs the "Fire Bird," ask her to hear *"Molchi, grueszt Molchi"* at Poisson d'Or, make her read *Magic Mountain* and *Gay Neck,* read *The Inferno* of Strindberg, borrow or steal for her Hamsun's *Wanderers* and *Mysteries,* buy Stokowski's "Love Song" for the piano. And Fletcher's *Gauguin,* and van Gogh's *Letters,* and the first volume of Elie Faure in French. Etc., Etc.

Les Frontières Humaines [by Ribemont-Dessaigne] came and I looked at the jacket and I do not read it. It looks too good. I am saving it for a rainy day, a day of despair, when one wants to eat his fellow man. I love the looks of it. I believe in it before reading a page. And I want to thank you for your thoughtfulness and beg you never to write me again a letter like the last, saying that you apologize for not paying the meal. Do you want to rob us of our last pleasure? I wish I could starve for a week, like Gandhi, so that I might get you at least a few

*French version of the Leni Riefenstahl/Bela Balazs film *Das Blaue Licht.*

of the things I keep promising you all the time. The radio makes me laugh. Maybe it's wonderful. Maybe. But I see New York written all over it. Ennui. Futility. Dreary nights. Sad jokes. Creamy voices. Crooning melodies. I have to laugh. Anaïs sitting by the radio—impossible! Is this then the end of the long circuit? Or maybe you don't sit by the radio—maybe you lie in bed and turn out the lights and listen to those creamy yellow voices?

Domino was rotten. I can't get over it. You must explain it to me.

Paulette has gone for good—it's all over. Yesterday her mother came, with an official of some sort, and Paulette, too. They took her few belongings and warned Fred not to try to get in touch with her. She was only fifteen. The man said that Fred was not a malefactor—he could see that at once. Paulette said: "He was very good to me." And the mother was quite beautiful, tastefully dressed, quiet, reserved, *genteel*. She could never have been a whore, or even a dancer. She was a lady. I think Fred is lucky. And I feel good, too, that we are not living in a stable any more. I have cooked some good meals since she left—she had us on short rations, you know. It would be O.K. now if you wanted to come here a few days when Hugo goes away. (I asked for an envelope just now & the waiter brings me a "rum"—do they sound anything alike to your ears—even in French?)

I'll call you up tomorrow morning about Bradley. Did you mean for me to bring him out Tuesday for lunch—or did you want me to come in advance and have him follow later by himself? I wrote him that it would be Tuesday or Wednesday. I said I'd phone him Monday after talking with you. I praised you pretty highly—as a writer—mentioned the diary and the unfinished novel. My thought was that perhaps he could place the complete diary. It might go fine in instalments. I also said you were the one who would back my book, if it were necessary, but I told him that that was confidential. He seemed to think it a pretty simple matter to publish and distribute one's own book—said many French writers did it. I told him I wanted to see [Jack] Kahane* before coming to any agreement with him. I have a feeling I won't like him & that nothing will come of it there. I'm not going to let the book go for a song—and I'm not going to let Kahane get the idea that he's doing me a favor by publishing it. I expect to treat him rough.

About the stars—you know, I think Eduardo and Allendy are a little foolish. I am not taking this stuff seriously—as prognostication! I think that with some knowledge of one's character (plus a lot of other

*English publisher in Paris. See Biographical Notes.

data: heredity, race, environment, experience etc. etc.) one can trace a tentative chart for oneself. I am not a believer in magic or witchcraft—never will be. And Eduardo, sitting back and gloating over his astrolabe, awakens a sort of pity in me. So far as my path crosses his, if he is relying on his soundings, he's making a grave mistake. And Allendy talking about a "combination" to defeat destiny—that too sounds highly ridiculous to me. I refuse to become involved in such claptrap. Sure, everything depends on you and me—it's what we deeply want that will determine things. I am opposed, very strongly, to sitting back and waiting for a December to roll around. We make the Decembers ourselves. October may be our December—or December may never roll around. That's how I look at the stars! That's where I shake hands with Jesus Christ—"the kingdom of heaven is within you!" Absolutely. Not only the kingdom of heaven, but the whole cosmogony, and God and the angels. I want to get all the data I can get on the stars, and on psychology, and on history and philosophy. But I'm not going to let it rule me. That's why I keep telling you that when June comes I'll face the issue soundly, with a clear head, and a strong will. In fact, my will is unimportant now. I am a different being than I was a year ago. She'll feel it. I won't tolerate any drama, nor any compromise. I'm going to keep on being myself now that I've found myself. Is it clear?

Henry

P.S. There is a *documentaire* on "India" (I forget the exact title). You must watch for it. It is very rare. I have also listed a few of the films we might write about. Are you going ahead with your book? Don't let it grow cold.

[Louveciennes]
Sept. 29, 1932*

[Henry:]

I want to *damn* you and to love you at the same time for what you have written me about psychoanalysis. You have said *exactly* what I wanted to say, and have been struggling to formulate for the last two weeks. It's wonderful, how you put it!

---

*Dated subsequently, apparently, in A. N.'s handwriting.

Do you remember the time I told you I was in great revolt against Allendy and analysis? He had made me reach just such a point where by great efforts of logic on his part he had *solved* my chaos, established a pattern, etc. I was furious to think I could be made to fit within one of those "few fundamental patterns." I felt exactly as you described: "Life's problems were too limited, that it was a pity, that the function of the artist was to increase these problems, to cause upheavals in the brain, to make people wild and free so that there would be *more* drama to their lives."

For me it was a question of upsetting Allendy's pattern. I set out to do this with the most *ingenious* lies, the most *elaborate piece of acting* I have ever done in my life (someday I will give you the details), I used all my talent for analysis and logic, which *he* admitted I had to a great degree, my own ease at giving explanations, etc. As I hinted to you, I did not hesitate to play with his own personal feelings, *every bit of power* I had, *I used,* to create a drama, to elude his theory, to complicate and throw veils, I lied and lied more carefully, more calculatingly than June, with all the strength of my mind. I wish I could tell you how and why. I tried to when I asked you: "Wouldn't you find an interest in whatever happened to me, an *objective* interest, which would be stronger than your jealousy?" Anyway, I did it all without endangering our love. It was a battle of wits in which I have taken the utmost delight. And do you know what? Allendy has beaten me, Allendy has known the truth, he has analyzed it *all* right, has detected the lies, has sailed (I won't say blithely) through all the tortuousnesses, and finally proved today again the truth of those damned "few fundamental patterns" which explain the behavior of all human beings. I tell you this: I would never let June go to him, for June would simply cease to exist, since June is all ramifications of neuroses. It would be a crime to *explain her away.* Oh, God, today I pray [to] you on my knees for Dostoevsky's obscurity, blindness, the most sacred and precious of all things. And tomorrow I go to Allendy and we start another drama, or I start another drama, by a lie or a phrase, a drama of another kind, the *struggle to explain,* which is in itself deeply dramatic too (are not our *talks* about June sometimes *as dramatic as the event* we are discussing?) and I find that I do not know what to believe, that I have not decided yet whether analysis simplifies and undramatizes our existence, or whether it is the most subtle, the most insidious, the most magnificent way of making dramas more terrible, more maddening. I don't know whether I was more alive the night on board ship when I was planning to jump overboard, or the nights I spent with you, or the hours with June, or when I walk out of Allendy's booklined cave with a word-born drama inside of me of which I will only know the outcome next Thursday at four thirty when Allendy wishes me to know it! I tell you I don't know. All I know is that drama is by no means dead in the so-called laboratory, that it depends on where your sense of voluptuousness is centered, and that for Allendy to discover, to interfere, to guide, to talk, to insinuate, to hint, to explain, to penetrate, is as passionate a game as it has been for you to live with June. And then when you see the analyst *alive,* and himself caught in the currents, hurt, deluded, strong, weak, etc., then you are ready to believe that there is drama everywhere if you are of a dramatic caliber, in alchemy as well as in drunkenness, in the moments when we *understand* life as well as in the moments of orgasm, in the moment when you and I sit down to write as well as when we are reeling with fever. Perhaps because I am an artist I act as every other artist will act, I make use of another new instrument to create *more and more complications.* In other words, psychoanalysis, when grasped by the artist, becomes another device by which to create chaos. The primal formula was to tangle up a bunch of people, place them in difficulties, and then the novel was begun. But if every day we become aware of greater and deeper tangles, greater and deeper and more diabolical difficulties, why I can only see the birth of greater and deeper books, that's all. [. . .]

Don't forget how you yourself are seeing every day more aspects of your June story, every day a new face, a new detail which assumes importance. Think for a moment how one of the first novelists would have told this story (I can't think who myself) and why it is we cannot read these books any longer. I am so tired I can't give you an example. My great battle is over. I have just come home. I find on the mantelpiece a gift, a marvellous gift from the simple pattern maker: "A writer could completely baffle a psychologist." A writer and a woman, a woman with imagination, too, and a psychologist half blinded. Oh yea?

Friday. Was so disappointed when Hugo telephoned I couldn't go out tonight because he wasn't feeling well! Have so much to tell you about your work, your letter to me, Emerson, Puritanism etc. Was secretly hoping you'd come today—suppose you are working. Saturday 8:30 [Gare] St. Lazare Café. There were no qualifying clauses in my *pneumatique!*

Anaïs

[Clichy]
Thursday [September 29, 1932]

[Anaïs:]

Only got your *pneumatique* just now, this afternoon, after I had telephoned you to say that Bradley could not come Friday, he is ill, but that I would come and fetch your machine—the typewriter people convinced me that was the best thing to do—you can have it back next day. But now that I see your *pneumatique* I don't know what to do. I will call you in the morning and what you propose is fine, that's the thing to do. I am writing with a rubber finger on my hand. Anyway I'm a little drunk. I had to go out and drink a little because I was going nutty writing this stuff. You can't imagine what a turmoil is in my head, how much I want to say, and how little is coming out. My head is bursting. I have to calm down or I will go mad. I tried to telephone you to tell you about the machine, but what I really wanted to say was that I had reached a high point and that I couldn't stand the rarefied atmosphere. Everything you said—and more—I was going to write you myself and I desisted for the same reason—only I had no qualifying clauses like you. I mean what I mean. So here are the pages of today, and no dream, because I couldn't remember it, though I know I dreamed violently. Also want to urge you to bring the first volume of your diary in English.* It is my intention to type these volumes for you, up to the point where you decide not to show me it. It is important for you—you will never get two better typists than Fred and me. We are devoted to your diary and we will guard all your secrets, particularly those you don't reveal. No vain curiosity inspires us, just a desire to aid you. So don't fail to give me the first volume in English. Further—all that I am sending you today seems to me important—to show Allendy. This is how artists make literature of their woes, their reveries, their dreams. I have unravelled a lot more about the dream, and about the book, than I am revealing. I am simply curious to know how much Allendy will reveal. Is he equipped with better vision than me, that's the question. There is more coming about this little incident at the café. So much happened to me internally at that moment. It seems almost fateful. Every day I grow more and more egocentric. Is that weakness? Am I going mad? Do you like these last pages? All this is dreadfully important. Yes, do come tomorrow evening for dinner. Come and stay. Wash the dishes. Watch the dawn come up. Never

---

*Until July 1920, A. N. had written her diary in French.

go back. I don't care whether Hugo sees this or not. I don't care what happens. I love you and that's what I wanted to say over the phone. That's what I wanted to write. Everything you say is so true and I felt it even more than you. But without the qualifying clauses. You are still a hypocrite . . . a weeny, weeny one, but a hypocrite. I love you. Let Hugo read it. Let things go to smash. I love you. I'll call you tomorrow morning.

Henry

[Louveciennes]
Thursday, Oct. 6 [1932]

How you fired me the other day, Henry. As soon as Mother and Joaquin were gone* I began to work. Did nothing good, but it is a beginning. Have done a great deal of copying. Found I had already copied out that first volume of the English journal. Will let you have it, and am now doing the second volume. Struck always by the same deficiency: wisdom and seriousness and understanding in relation to books, studies, contemplation etc. but great inadequacy before real life, naïveté and a deep inequality in the *age* of my mind and the age of my experience. Too bad—if I had known you then you would have made the experience catch up with the mind's maturity. *I wish I had known you always.* How much I owe you, Henry. Let us try and stay wise. The other night, after you left, I was completely unnerved. When Hugh turned on the music I began to weep. What I want to remember is that I can make you much happier and give you much more and enrich you in every way far more deeply by staying *here* and giving you nothing to worry about except your work. As to analysis, here is what I find in Allendy's book which is entirely applicable to your future facing of the problem June represents. I may have felt that analysis would simply help you. Was not conscious of my reasons for wanting you to have that experience. Listen to all this: *"Le névrosé a tendance à répéter indéfiniment un comportment vicieux, anormal, à susciter indéfiniment des situations critiques analogues dont il est chaque fois victime. . . . J'ai indiqué comment d'éclairer à la lumière de*

---

*A. N.'s mother and her brother Joaquin had moved to an apartment in Paris, since they no longer wanted to share the house in Louveciennes.

l'analyze le mécanisme intérieur de la destinée. Une telle répétition comporte d'ailleurs une finalité; c'est une obstination à revenir sur l'obstacle dans le but de le dominer à la fin, mais c'est dans le cas du névrosé, une obstination vaine comme serait celle de l'acrobate paralyzé s'évertuant indéfiniment à tenter un exercise devenue impossible pour lui: l'instinct à de ces constances inexorables. Or la cure psychoanalytique a pour but de rééduquer le névrosé suffisament pour l'emmener à dominer une fois et sur un point la situation critique."

This corresponds in a sense to your wanting to face the problem with June and wanting to dominate it once and for all. Now the question is: For a human being who wants to dominate life and not be devoured such help might be precious. For beings like Eduardo and Hugh, for example, it is absolutely unnecessary that they should suffer, be homosexuals or otherwise paralyzed. But for *you and me* it seems to be that the problems are entirely different (because we are writers and make art out of our struggle). It is true that I create over and over again the same difficulties for myself in order to struggle over and over again to master them; it is true that you have put yourself in critical, harrowing situations [with] women over and over again, and have not won. But I may say (and you can see I am talking very objectively *as a woman* because if you were to free yourself of June's power I would of course be in ecstasy) that the struggle against your own inclinations (self destructive or others) is the very stuff we live on and work with. (This links up with [Ludwig] Lewisohn's art as catharsis, confession etc.) Ours is no paralysis at all, because our neuroses created your novel and my journal. However, here Allendy would answer: to continually struggle against the *same problem* and to continually fail to dominate it brings a feeling of frustration and a kind of paralysis. What is necessary to life, to livingness, is to move on, in other words to move from one kind of problem to another. Jung has mentioned this. The neurotic is obsessed with *one* kind of problem. He cannot move on. Certainly there must be a great exultation to move on, not towards a stupid happiness (don't worry, that will never come to *us*) but towards *other* difficulties. The effect would be somewhat like that of travelling, of encountering new experiences, of expanding, whereas in the long run the effect of the persistent obsession with the old problem might be one of defeat, discouragement (not to speak of suicide etc.). I would say that you (as you have said yourself) sucked the very best out of your last critical situation. You lived out your old problem with Woman on the greatest and most magnificent scale imaginable and it may be time to move on, not to avoid, absence of drama, etc., but to the grappling with other kinds of dramas.

It seems to me for example that if John [Erskine] had not spent forty years of his life struggling against Puritanism, he would have passed on to richer struggles. That if I had not spent most of my life fighting with a single problem, I might have been enjoying others, as I am now. To move on *is* living. To be caught in a round cage, in a wheel, in that "inexorable constancy of the instincts," in the likeness, resemblance of our crises, does seem like death. Fraenkel, you can now see, is also dancing on a red spoked wheel. I did the same in my journal. You did it with June.

But what is wonderful about you is that you seem to be arriving at all of this alone, without anybody's help. What you said the other day about the futility of running away was very profound; and very courageous. Listen, Henry, I believe you *should talk with Jung*. I don't care if I ruin myself [so that you can] do it. Whether it changes nothing in your life, it will have importance. You will know what you are about. I beg you to go to Zurich. I will get you everything you need. You will be able to continue with your book because you will be talking about it, and will have much time on your hands. I think you are ripe for all this, this illumination of one's destiny with intelligence, with the deepest, obscurest, most intuitive intelligence.

Anaïs

Sometimes I have this desperate attitude towards analysis. Let Allendy give me *all* the wisdom and courage he can. It will only be more stuff to give away, to sacrifice at the next crisis—more to give to whoever I want to offer my happiness and life to—whoever I may want to die for. Is this clear?

4 h. Gare de Louveciennes—on the way to tea at the Ritz with Eduardo, his sister Ana Maria, [and] Marqués de Aviles y de Casa Real, Señor Alonso Patino. While I dance I will be thinking of Clichy and the lustiest passages of your books and of my passion for you.

Can't write you about Lewisohn's quotations because Joaquin took [the book] away by mistake with other papers in my desk drawer. Will see you Saturday.

[Clichy]
[October 13, 1932]

[Anaïs:]

It was presumptuous of me to want to alter your language.* If it is not English sometimes, it is a language nevertheless and the farther one goes along with it the more vital and necessary it seems. It is a violation of language that corresponds with the violation of thought and feeling. It could not have been written in an English which every capable writer can employ. It required your own intimate imprint, and in the measure that one understands and appreciates you, one understands and appreciates the strange language you have used. Above all it is the language of modernity, the language of nerves, repressions, larval thoughts, unconscious processes, images not entirely divorced from their dream content; it is the language of the neurotic, the perverted, "marbled and veined with verdigris" as [Théophile] Gautier put it in referring to the style of decadence. It has all the elements of consumption in it which Chopin introduced into his music; it is diseased as are the finest passages of Huysmans, it is a concentrated poison which only those may quaff who have been inoculated through too much living. There are lines in it which are immortal—not lines only, but whole passages. There are passages which seem to defy all explanation, which hover on the borders of hallucination, madness, utter chaos. There are some which are so cruel and revolting that they seem inhuman—they are not thoughts or feelings any longer, but the raw essence of pain and malice. The whole thing is like a bloody emission, the orgasm of a monster, cluttered with snakes and jewels and bile and arsenic.

When I try to think to whom it is you are indebted for this style I am frustrated—I do not recall anyone to whom you bear the slightest resemblance. You remind me only of yourself, of the later books of your diary in which you reveal your development.

Mighty dissonances, in the superhuman effort to dissolve the plexus of the medium. You have worked with an almost satanic glee, with a corrosive force, you have broken down the veils of flesh and all the cushions that protect the nerves—you have played on the raw

---

*In an early draft of what eventually became *House of Incest* A. N.'s "Mona" pages represented her reaction to June and underwent numerous rewrites before the book was published in 1936. H. M., at various times, worked on the manuscript.

nerves, the very tenderest filaments of our sense organs. The effect is delirium, ecstasy which becomes unsupportable.

What lies behind the confused welter of images, the ideas pyramided one on top of the other to infinity? A woman stripped of all femininity, a woman with the raw, devastating power of her sex, a woman tearing from her symbols all the human masks which have made men behold in the monster the dangerous and unfathomable allure of his counterpart. Back of the glazed and shimmering lesbianism stands the spectre of undivided sex, the original complete entity which has no need for the male to reproduce its kind, back of all the legends of friendship and love between man and man, woman and woman, or man and woman, lies this hideous narcissistic image of the single, all-sufficient self, the primitive generative force which fecundates itself, which in its irrepressible ebullience threw off a planetary system that forms the whole corpus of mythological worship and love. "In the beginning was the word and the word became flesh." It is as though you were repeating this story of creation. The duality which you divine is the despair, the bankruptcy of logic and philosophy; it is the illusion which holds the human planetary system together. It is the great lie of creation that lends the piercing note of sorrow to all the great works of art. The lie which you expose sounds the death of art; it is fatal to trespass beyond a certain point. Since you are a woman and since art is masculine, you as an artist rid yourself of the riddle by explaining it. In this inhuman struggle which your language reveals, you are crucifying the world. This is not language, this is the world being turned inside out, not mathematically in super-dimensional planes, not artistically in violaceous daring, but biologically, atomically, so that not even the creator can any more recognize his world.

The investigation that will follow the launching of your words will never end. Every line is pregnant with meaning and however much the meaning is ransacked, the riddle will remain because only you can explain it, and this riddle is your last triumph—you will never reveal it. "I wait for a light as sulphurous as before the burial of Pompeii." That means for death, for the final catastrophe in which everything will be buried, because in the dissolution of death a flame is born whose secret is imparted only to those who are then and forever escaping the mould. The secret is incommunicable; it is that last knowledge to which we are driven by our most vital forces, the mystery which makes death not only supportable but desired. Etc. etc.

[Henry]

[Louveciennes]
[October 16, 1932]

[Henry:]

The reason why I stopped writing on "Mona" is because I went mad, in Fraenkel's sense. I went insane *with pain,* and then you came along (the day you came to say how much you loved me) and restored me to sanity! And since then I have been too happy, and happiness is bad for one. That is why this book must progress slowly. It is a book composed solely of mad moments.

Yesterday morning I half woke up and kissed Hugh ardently telling him I loved him because I thought it was *you.* He has been very happy ever since. He will tell Allendy about it.

Your writing on my writing is extraordinary. We won't write a book on movies, but maybe a book of dreams, or a book of writing on each other's writings, bouts, questions and answers. Better than Valéry's banquets. It will be a banquet of two persons "surcharged with life, saturated with sex." I retained these two phrases of yours the other night. I am cajoling Hugh to travel. I need liberty, oh, so much liberty. What is so strange is that together and alone we are so human, so softly warmly human (those hours in the kitchen), and in our writing turbulent, turgid, spectral, febrile, monstrous; drenched in homoerotic carnalities. My enameled style and your muscular one, wrestling, drawing sparks from one another.

Have finished Lewisohn.* Did not like the confused and briefer passages. He never comes up to his three full-length portraits again. Too much material. Too hasty. Great book.

Rushing this so that Emilia can telegraph you money. There must be real food at our banquet. Next time you will tear my dress at the top.

[Anaïs]

Clichy
Friday [October 21, 1932]

Anaïs—this is my very first opportunity since June has arrived. She is now on her way to meet you. I can image that you had a splendid talk last night—June seemed to be very happy, very contented. I hear

Expression in America (New York: Harper, 1932).

rumblings of change of mind about my book, and wonder whether you were really convinced by June or whether you capitulated for political reasons. In any case, it's all right. I want you to get the whole picture, for your sake as well as mine. June has said some profound, most profound things in the great welter of talk which has rolled over me like a steam roller these last few days. Our sessions have lasted until six in the morning—that's why I fell asleep, drugged and exhausted last night. There is a radical improvement in her physically and nervously. I think even the talk will abate as she gets over the idea of combatting me. We had some illuminating discussion on this subject only last night. And I think I can go on with the book, even in her presence, with perhaps some fantastic and even more sagacious or penetrating sidelights thrown on the whole work. You will see. At any rate, thanks to you I am not being crushed this time; the difference is so marked, now that we are living under a sheltered roof and can act like human beings. Had we to live outdoors again, from café to café, I would have been cracked, no doubt of it. June immediately wanted to "do things"—practical things (which sound rather impractical to me), but I am discouraging her for the time being, urging her to just take it easy, and I hope you won't think this selfish of me. I understand how much more difficult it must be for you now, but please realize that I, or we, are content with anything. June is deeply appreciative (and I suspect she would still be if she knew the whole truth). Don't lose faith in me, I beg you. I love you more than ever—truly, truly. I hate to put in writing what I wish to tell you about the first two nights with June, but when I see you and tell you you will realize the absolute sincerity of my words. At the same time, oddly, I am not quarreling with June. It is as though I had more patience, more understanding and sympathy than ever before. All this may mean a protraction beyond what I originally anticipated, but I think it for the best. I can't be mean or spiteful, or anything, but just what I am. June, it seems to me, is making heroic efforts to be what I should like her to be—and I can't help but to be touched by that. There is, too, a sort of tacit realization that another scene, such as last Christmas, would completely destroy us. Not a word about love has been mentioned, no cross-examinations, no prying curiosity—we're just taking each other for what we are as well as we can. For June's own sake I am very glad. She needed this sort of equilibrium, this new confidence in herself. Instead of criticizing her I am praising her when possible, and it affects her admirably.

As to a way out! The other night, in referring to the book which

Bradley has, I mentioned that there was a possibility of it being printed privately, through you, and June immediately grasped for that in preference to the other. Said that she would like to go back to America with a number of copies and dispose of them for me—which it is quite possible she could do.

Of course, Anaïs, I don't know at all how you feel now about June, whether that first exultation is there and deepened or the reverse. I'll only say to you that you are free to do with her as you will—that's my gift to you, my love for you. I find it impossible to be jealous. I know that better than ever now. When I see June returning and smiling radiantly, and I hear little fragments of your words with her, I feel beautiful about it—and Hugo's attitude makes me sick and only more conscious of how wrong, how absurd, how futile it is. I am hurt that he should have treated you as he did—not because it may affect me adversely, believe me, but that it is so humiliating for you, so small, so lacking in human sympathy. But I too was that sort of man once, and I should forgive, only now it seems incredible that I ever was that. (At least, I had more grounds for my behavior—all that June tells you to the contrary notwithstanding.) June is perhaps not lying to you—nor I either; you are seeing, or going to see, how far apart two human beings can be even though they live together and love one another. I am listening to June attentively and seriously, when she speaks of the book and my lack of insight. Sometimes she is right, but often too she is wrong; I do know things that she doesn't know herself, about herself. And if I do not defend myself too strongly it is not because I am overwhelmed by her but that I want to spare her future pain. I can afford to be wrong, because I am more right—that's all.

I think it is quite possible for you to say to June that you want to make a rendezvous with me, at Louveciennes, and that ought to disarm her even more. I am not appearing too anxious to see you, because I am acting. But I have missed you greatly, and I have been thinking of you at moments when, God help me, no sane, normal man ought to. You can't imagine how terrible it was to get your letter, with all that it breathed, at that moment when it was impossible for me to do anything. And I had to destroy the letter, having merely been able to rush through it, which saddened me much. I suggest that you write me through Fred, either here or at the office, and allow a sufficient interval of time for me to respond because he cannot always hand it to me at once. If the letters come here I will probably get them first; don't put your address on the back (because June knows you haven't much in common with Fred) and address them on the typewriter. If you write to the *Tribune* (5 Rue Lamartine) they will be delivered to me next afternoon, you understand.

And please, dear, dear Anaïs, don't say cruel things to me as you did over the telephone—that "you are happy for me." What does that mean? I am not happy, nor am I greatly unhappy; I have a sad, wistful feeling which I can't quite explain. I want you. If you desert me now I am lost. You *must believe in me,* no matter how difficult it may seem sometimes. You ask about going to England. Anaïs, what shall I say? What would I like? To go there with you—to be with you always. I am telling you this now when June has come to me in her very best guise, when there should be more hope than ever, if I wanted hope. But like you with Hugo, I see it all coming too late. I have passed on. And now no doubt I must live some sad, beautiful lie with her for a while, and it causes me anguish, and that pains me terribly. And perhaps too you will be seeing more in June than ever, which would be right, and you may hate me or despise me, but what can I do? Take June for what she is—she may mean a great deal to you—but don't let it come between us. What you two have to give each other is none of my affair. I love you, just remember that. And please don't punish me by avoiding me. Why not occasionally come to Clichy? Do you think you can act it out here, or is it likely to prove too great a strain? Only do what you think best, what it is humanly possible for you to do. And tell me if you think I am asking too much of you?

I understand you are to meet again tomorrow night, but there is no mention of me. I feel badly. Not to deprive you of anything, but that I must be excluded. Please don't make of me another Hugo.

Henry

P.S. I stole the Elie Faure book *for you.* It is grand. It will make you delirious.

The diaries I am holding—the big one is in Fred's room and you are to ask him for it. I didn't want it to be here in my room because I don't remember what I wrote in the review of it. And I stopped working on your little diary, only because you insisted. But please let me have the other—I want to do them all for you. I want to do everything for you.

[Louveciennes]
[October 25, 1932]

You don't know the wild things I wrote the first day June was here, Henry. What I imagined I could *give* you—that I would make superhuman efforts to give you a more selfless June and to give June her Dostoevsky—you. And I was between you and June like between two torturers. When I told June I loved you I felt I made you my greatest gift—I knew it would augment June's love! I was giving you to each other by *revealing* you to each other. And so yesterday I was again so dazed that things didn't turn out as I expected. It was so good that we laughed together, Henry. Anything that exists between June and me only brings out in relief my deep deep love of you. It is as if I were experiencing the very greatest test of my love for you—the greatest *test* of all life. And I find that I can be drunk, drugged, ensorcelled, everything that could make me lose myself, but that there is always always always *Henry* . . . that what I would fling away for you is every day more tremendous, yet I would fling it away for an hour like yesterday's. I need to see you again. I won't hurt you anymore with mention of others. You don't need to be jealous. I belong to you, Henry.

Anaïs

Can't you telephone me Friday morning before I leave . . . perhaps come Friday afternoon—I didn't know until June came *how much* I loved you!

I cannot write you as much or as freely as before—you understand why.

Your last pages are strange. There are some phrases which are terrible for June to see. Don't *show* them to her. The quotations are extraordinary and how they apply to you, describe you.

Have read a fecund book—*Gide* by Ramon Fernandez. Have marked it for you. Will bring it Thursday. It raises a big question about your work. Observe marks and what I wrote on last page. We must talk it over. It seems as if in the last book you were doing a Gideian multilateral trick—novelist, dramatist, critic, writer and analyst all in *one*—revealing all.

Fernandez says Gide failed because he sacrificed the art of the novel to his criticism, *and* because he lacked *passion*. Now as you are surcharged with passion it seems to me you can keep your book *moving dramatically, alive,* while yet being *critical* within the book and revealing the work in the novelist's head. To me a *unique* combination. Is that clear?

[Louveciennes]
Oct. 30, 1932

Henry,

I am excited and upset by Elie Faure. I see so many vital truths, superb proclamations, prophesies, revelations, that I do not know where to begin. I believe deeply in most of what you have underlined. I have been running toward all this, these days, by contrast with the life I am leading, by reaction against the wisdom which engulfs me and I must fight off, for the sake of life and of drama, and of passion. You represent all that Faure attributes to the great artist; it is to describe you that these lines were written. Some of those words are your own words, and that is why they inflamed you, and they inflame me. I see more clearly than ever the reason and richness of the wars you carry on, I see why I have given myself to your leadership. "About the passionate and dangerous play of a great soul, or a great intelligence, or a great will, men form a circle . . . becoming confusedly intoxicated by the illusions. . . ." All this is an explanation of yourself as the mould-breaker, as the revolutionist, the man you describe and assert in the first pages of *Tropic of Cancer.* I would use some of those lines to defend your book. [. . .]

Your Hundred Years' war with June—"this war succeeding to the most splendid outburst of lyrical power . . . seemed to dry up the source for ever." No. In order that the "flame should be reborn from the warlike effort . . . it was necessary that ruined France should seek in Italy gold and bread." And I gave you gold and bread, and you resuscitated, until the next upheaval. And upheavals won't come from me. We need each other to nourish each other (in the vastest sense of the word). What June called your "dead period" was your reconstruction through thought and work—in between the bloodshed. The fruitful period following the war. The period of the lyrical outburst. And perhaps when you have exhausted all wars, you shall begin one against me, and I against you, the most terrible of all, against our own selves then, to make drama out of our last stronghold of our ecstasy and romance. Notice this: "War is always just for him who conquers." It was necessary to conquer. "The important thing is to set the passion free. The drama is everything, the cause of the drama nothing."

This summer, after your great drama, "for the first time you fixed upon your own interior life with poignant attention." I tell you this man Faure has written your novel into History. He is the man who will recognize it. "The hero is the artist."

Anaïs

More coming!

[Louveciennes]
[November 8, 1933]

[Henry:]

I have so much to tell you. I can see now that you are a thinker who deviates too easily; when you are not *distrait* by anything, you reach everything in one bound. You think well with me because of my attentiveness, because I do not interfere but follow you. I give you that thread of cohesion by which you will achieve continuity.

Your work. In the second book [*Tropic of Capricorn*] you will probably end by telling the truth about June, that is, about your *creation* of June, the crumbling of the creation, the appearance of the real June, the conflict, the most tragic moment of all life, when a circle is completed and we are thrust into a new one, without a rest in between, the dovetailing of your books, the excrescence of books and stories, the swift and monstrous course of the writer who discards what no longer serves his work. I see the road indefinitely. I hear repercussions on the moon. Listen. Your first book plays the demoniac role of the artist who brings experience and pain, war . . . it is against all wisdom achieved without struggle . . . and then I see the line mounting, and your touching both the bottom and the top of the world, and abstract wisdom will be made ridiculous, and what will survive is only the great force which has destroyed the world so that only strong men could survive, or resuscitate. . . . I mean that you will plunge men and women into danger and darkness, as if to say, *only* those who have *burned through life* (as you have done) have the right to look down into the lower steps of the spiral. There is a spiral, in you, and in your books. Rich, richer than any writer or man yet known to me. You only need to do enough thinking to know where you are going, that is all. The rest is movement, movement, which is your sundering of crystallized moulds.

Reflecting on your "brochure" or book. Please stop quoting so fully. It appears clearly even here, and more so in your books, that you are *revealing the writer in the process of writing.* That seems to me intensely interesting. But do not reveal the exact source of the alchemy of opinion by over-quotation. That is German. (The passion for footnotes.) Either restate the thing in your own terms, or quote in some condensed form, like the key phrase: "inability to make it move" (Joyce) etc. Be a little more shrewd—or a little more assimilative. I mean, do not drag in the criticisms of others so obviously, even to contradict, or eschew them. Speak for yourself, always. It is *lack of confidence. You* can say things as well as Dostoevsky, Elie Faure or anybody you quote. Dare *to speak for yourself.* Let the other people lie in your blood, but faceless, nameless, diluted, masticated by you, reproduced etc. You listen to too many voices. Listen only to yourself. The best parts are yours, not your putting forward of other men.

Also, *I entreat you:* do not show your work in progress to any *outsider.* I mean Bradley or Kahane, or anyone who is not working *with* you, following your thought, entering into it. It is confusing. These men are not your co-workers or even friends. These men are outsiders. Keep to yourself. You need a deep cohesion, a strong forward continuity. Admit no opinions until you are *through.*

[Anaïs]

[Louveciennes]
[November 26, 1933]

[Henry:]

Was thinking last night apropos of "Mlle. Claude" and Germaine that it was a pity that women could not enjoy gigolos in the same way as men enjoy a whore. It is a fact that they don't; that the only women who make use of them are women who can't get anything else. Man needs reality, and woman illusion. Man needs illusion, too, but the woman who gives him illusion also gives him less reality—in proportion. Why did the ancient whores of Greece and Babylon and India study also the art of speaking, of culture, of *artifice* (see *Kamasutra*)?

Please lend me (mail them to me) your green carbon copy of my "Mona" pages. And what about this calling June "Alraune"? Would it be cheap? June, Louise [de Vilmorin],* and I should be Alraune, number one, two, three. Yes? Is the legend too current, too banal (I wish I had never seen that movie†), too cliché? Please tell me. It is new to me, and so I can't tell.

The three Alraunes. The men who loved them were guilty of zoolatry!

Listen, I believe the disturbances last week of self-consciousness etc. which were so unlike your lusty, healthy self were due to too sudden and intensive an introspective life. Don't work so hard; go out. *Spend this money on anything you want to do, see, on anybody.* All I care about is *you, your* joy, *your* ecstasies, *your* work. You are over-sensitive about June knocking on the door, over-sensitive about pleasing me etc. (I was so completely satisfied as long as you did whatever you *wanted* to do! Willing to talk a week or a year.) Maybe by now you are singing and attacking analysis as a revenge. *Tant mieux.* Telephone me if you want me to go to the movies with you. To hell with consciousness. I leave home at five now. Jung speaks of tender minds and tough minds. *Soyonne* tough. I love you more than ever. I feel guilty. You gave me reality and I gave you introspection. But we have to keep ourselves balanced *against* each other—that balance is what we found that summer week here.

Write down what you said about Dick's eyes, it was good.‡

Funny this: you are always *ahead* of your writing. My writing is ahead of me.

If you call me up we can meet and go to the Printemps [department store], where they have thick woolly rugs that will delight you. Cheap. From French Algeria.

[Anaïs]

---

*See Biographical Notes.
†A German film, based on Hans Heinz Ewers's novel *Alraune*, starring Brigitte Helm. "Alraune" became A. N.'s pseudonym for June, and she adopted the French title of the film, *La Mandragore*, for her own pseudonym, "Mandra." Both were used in various attempts to "fictionalize" the diary for possible publication, and "Alraune" became the working title for the *House of Incest* manuscript.
‡A friend of June, with whom she stayed at times while in Paris. H. M., it seems, had described him as having "the eyes of a waif."

[Anaïs:]

Continuing the little note—I don't remember saying a thing about Dick's eyes, not a thing! You ask me a big question about the whores of Babylon, Greece and India. Maybe Putnam has answered this in his brochure called *The Psychopathology of Prostitution,* mentioned in one of his footnotes. You know he translated an immense work, called *The History of Prostitution.* Should I inquire? I remember distinctly what [Pierre] Louÿs said in *Aphrodite.* There is more to your question than you imagine, I believe. Just as, in referring to the *Querelles des Femmes,* which Putnam mentioned *(Hundred Years' War)* I had an inkling of something far deeper and more complicated that was felt then than latterly, in the 19th century with Shaw, Ibsen, and Strindberg. Don't ask me these questions too lightly please!

You see, I realize now, just now, on my way home, the progress we made "Intellectually." If our heads have been a little tired and dizzy, remember that we have taken for food some of the knottiest problems possible. I feel that there are certain subjects we have come to grips with in masterful fashion, and it was tremendously important for both of us. Such as Time and Space, Psychology, Form in language, the problem of Destiny—more, more, I can't recall them all. (Allendy's book [*Le Problème de la Destinée*] is terribly disappointing; I am dropping it—he contributes absolutely nothing to the problem—it's just a rehash of other men's ideas, a smug, easy solution. You've got to show me something immensely better to make me respect him now.)

When I think of what you have done for me (*not* introspection, as you say!), but through your resisting your too facile syntheses, your feminine mind, as it were, causing me to really *think,* think almost everything over again—but with new vision, with a wisdom that I owe to you (even tho in a letter to Emil I attribute it to Fraenkel)—I say, when I think of this, I realize the value of what you represent. Part of a lingering oversensitiveness in me is a fear that, in showing you the tough work to be done I may paralyse your easy stride, that enthusiasm with which you rush into things, and despite an insufficient knowledge, nevertheless accomplish miracles. We spoke of this one night on our way home. It seems I must do the heavy sledding—that's what my mind is built for. Don't be discouraged by my tenacity, my desire to exhaust things. (It wasn't Jung, for example, who coined "tough" and "tender" mindedness—it was William James—doubtless he got it from Aristotle.) And as for "Alraune," again—why don't you look up the legend in a reference book? Then you would probably discover things—astounding things. [John Cowper] Powys wrote a book called *Mandrake and Mandragora*. It is one of the great myths; I think the plant is native to Greece. That big Funk & Wagnalls dictionary had a huge portion on it if I remember rightly. Anyway, it's in grappling with things at the source that you can tell best whether a thing is worth continuing with or not. Any mystery, like that, in tracking it down I always discovered amazing detours, sometimes a field of reading that would occupy me for months, and when finished, would piece out a missing link in the chain of things. In other words, everything is worth investigating, wasting time over, if it interests you. There is always a deep, unconcealed reason why it interests you. (Psychology again—rats!)

Yes, I'm singing about the coming attack. I am working up steam. My antagonism increases. But don't let that interfere with your work. Be a healer. Healing precedes psychology. I'm dropping with fatigue. Tomorrow I'll wake up a new man.

Henry

[Clichy]
Dec. 18, 1932

Anaïs—

The trip is off.* Came home and found June sitting here, eating what was left. She knew I was going away. The bags were packed and folders on the table indicated England. Fred was in his room and probably admitted it. He left almost as soon as I arrived. I hardly know how to tell you what happened then—after a bitter, nauseating conversation of several hours—but I emptied my wallet. She said she would never bother me again—that that would see her through until she left. Whether this is true I don't know. In any case, I will not run away.

*To avoid further quarrels with his wife, A. N. and Alfred Perlès arranged for H. M. to go to London over the Christmas holidays. When this attempt was foiled, he stayed for a short time at Louveciennes and eventually made a second attempt to get to England. June left Paris, apparently, during the final week of December, and H. M. did not see her again for more than a dozen years. They obtained a Mexican divorce late in 1934.

I will face anything that's coming to me—and there may be worse to face. But this thing is clear—no more help from you until she goes. I feel humiliated, deeply ashamed. The gesture was thru you and you got no credit for it. Instead you were covered with mud. It was agony, what I endured, and why I stood it I don't know unless it is that I have feelings of guilt I don't wish to recognize. But I am sick of trying to analyse things. There is the rotten fact—I gave it to her and you're horribly disappointed in me. Don't think that I handed it over lightly. It was a last resort. I know what it cost you to write out that check. If I said nothing to June it was because she is beyond reason. She has become a mad woman. The vilest threats and recriminations—so disgusting that I listened fascinatedly—awed by it.

I gave in only because of fear that she would try to punish you. She is capable now of anything. That is why it is better I remain and bear the brunt of it. If I go away she is crazy enough to do anything— she might see Hugo and tell him everything. I was in a quandary—a great quandary. When I handed her the money I broke down (thinking of my betrayal of you) but fortunately she callously interpreted it as a sign of weakness, that I had been robbed of a pleasure, or some such thing. I tell you, I stood for terrific insults. I could have killed her—and I know she felt likewise. So now it appears to her probably that I was "tricked"—that's her favorite word—and she is probably rejoicing over her cleverness.

Probably this all sounds hectic. It was serious—and I did what I thought best. I purposely made it appear that I was doing a heroic thing, and looking cheap about it at the same time. She thinks I'm some worm now. But that doesn't matter. Two things I recognize— that her pain must be terrific to come here and to put on these scenes, and secondly that you can't hate or fight when you understand what's at the bottom of such behavior. Watching her I saw myself when I was being tortured, and God knows I would never want any one to go thru that if I could prevent it. I think she's getting a joy out of harassing me and since she isn't big enough or brave enough to take her medicine why should I try to defend myself.

But, Anaïs, I feel dreadful about you. All your good acts seem to go for naught—and June reaps the benefit. Bear with it. Consider all I might have done had I been free and independent. If you feel sorry for me that I have been cheated, don't. Anyone who does things with his eyes open isn't cheated. I've had my trip to London—I don't feel badly in the least about that. It's only you I'm thinking of. *You* were tricked—and she had to sue me to trick you. That's why I broke down and wept.

Don't bolster me up any more. I've got to act out this gesture. I really must pay for what I did—and I intend to. You know I won't die. And let me keep you out of this. She would like to drag you in but I won't let her. I told her I was doing the utmost I could and no matter what she threatened I could do no more. I think she realized it. At the end she wanted to return half of it but I refused. Why? Perhaps I should have salvaged something—but I just couldn't. If it were in my power to aid by depriving myself I would. She doesn't believe that at all. She thought I was sneaking away in order to avoid helping her. But I want her to know that I can't and won't do anything more than is possible for me—and my only possibility is to go without.

She said that with a little more money she might have had enough to return—as tho' we might at least have done that for her. I said that didn't concern you at all. She thought you ought to be glad to do it to get rid of her etc.

Anaïs, I can't go into it all. It was horrible. I hope you'll forgive me for using your money this way and believe me when I say that I want to pay the penalty, that I must or else feel still more humiliated.

And now I am angry. I want to stay and see it out to the bitter end. I've done what I thought was kind and just. If that doesn't appeal then I'll use harsher methods. If I were to go away she'd make it miserable for you. And there's no need to suffer that. I can face the music. And please don't think as she does, that it's love of suffering (masochism) that prompts this attitude. I'm sick of suffering. I'm disgusted. Write me please immediately & don't worry about me. I love you and that's all that matters.

Henry

[Clichy]
Sunday [January 1, 1933]

Anaïs:

I'm writing you from 4 Ave. Anatole France, to my great surprise and your own no doubt. I never got to London at all. Was held up by the immigration authorities at Newhaven, the English side, subjected to a gruelling cross-examination as a suspect, locked up overnight and sent back the next morning. It's a long story and I want the pleasure of recounting it in detail to you. [. . .]*

I arrived last night, quite exhausted. Wanted to call you up immediately but was afraid I might get Hugo on the phone again. At any rate I will call you up in the morning, probably before you get my letter.

Fred has told me about the mysterious phone call you received. I hope you're not too worried. I feel good to be back in Clichy, good to be sitting at the typewriter again. My only thought now is to stay here in peace and work. I feel as though I had been through an ordeal. The thought of packing my bags again makes me sick. I don't fear anything from June any more; she can do her damnedest now—I'm ready for her. The very worst she could do would be to get in touch with Hugo, but I think that is remote and even if she did, probably little would come of it. If she reports me to the police for non-support I can answer that charge too. And if she wants the divorce I'm going to let her get it. I'm not going to talk to her any more. I'm not interested in anything she has to say. I think I've been a damned fool, taking all her nonsense. [. . .]

Henry

[Louveciennes]
[January 16, 1933]

[Henry:]

Answer to the riddle: Hugh is hostile or anxious because he is not *sure* of me—so he is suspicious of my writing. He would destroy this *joy* whose source he suspects. As you would destroy June's joys because you suspected their origin. You and I, though no less jealous, are more *sure* of each other—more aware of our possession of each other. Being sure, we can afford to be very generous, very tolerant, very lenient! We are sure of the *core*. When one fights, one fights one's fears, and one attacks windmills, as you attacked June's apparently harmless stories; as Hugh suspects my writing, my stories. *Voilà?* Is that too pat, my

---

*H. M., again with A. N.'s aid, had made a second attempt to leave Paris while June was still there. He later dramatized the experience in the story "Via Dieppe-Newhaven," first included in *Max and the White Phagocytes* (Paris: The Obelisk Press, 1938) and subsequently in *The Cosmological Eye* (Norfolk, CT: New Directions, 1939).

profound Heinrich-Otto-Oswald-Beethoven-mask? Too pat, too gullible, too facile from the Marquise de Pomponette?

[Anaïs]

[Paris]
[January 17, 1933]

[Henry:]

Rushing this off to you from Paris because I'm starting today on a Herculean job for Allendy—hours of work—am settled in top floor studio with kilos of notes to be expanded for his book—working with Mrs. A. I need the money so I couldn't refuse but this means that I won't be able to see you all week—terrible—going out every evening for Hugh, including Saturday night. I assure [you] this time I am not being yielding but simply forced. Please write me how you are doing. We'll make up for this next week. I think Hugh is going to Brussels for two days. Will have interesting things to report—met a crazy Marquise who takes drugs, a lesbian countess who wants to adopt me (this at Louise's). *Je pense à toi.* I'm not even home in the mornings. Don't worry about the faithlessness of women—you've got a *Spanish wife* now—*famous* for their faithfulness! (See Encyclopedias, histories, guide books.)

Will send you a check tomorrow.

A.

[Clichy]
Tuesday [January 24, 1933]

Anaïs:

I am only finishing my revisions tonight, though I have been working steadily on it since I saw you. I could stick on it forever, it seems—an endless task, cutting, adding, transposing, etc. Disgusted with looking at it. But now that I am almost through, and much more pleased with it than when I left you, I have a desire to write [Dr. Otto] Rank* a letter, which will explain a lot of things he will want to know. A good letter, which will expose some of the problems in my mind.

*See Biographical Notes.

Putting away the 1932 correspondence, labelled "Anaïs," I am amazed at the mass of it. What will 1933 bring? Yesterday I bought you *A Rebours* and afterwards I had a great attack of conscience. What have I ever bought you? Why, when I got that check from my friend, [Dr. Emil] Conason,* didn't I cash it and get you something? I am always thinking of myself. I am, as June said, probably the most selfish person in the world. I am amazed at my own selfishness. When I bought the book I felt like a worm. So little. I could have bought up the book store and handed it to you, and it would be nothing. I miss you a great deal. If you come for dinner Thursday and it looks dull here we will go out—go out and dance, or anything you want. I miss you terribly. I think sometimes that I must live a great part of my life in a trance, or in some sort of anesthetic state. The moment I leave Louveciennes I am in another world.

[Henry]

[Clichy]
Monday [February 20, 1933]

[Anaïs:]

Here's wishing you all sorts of "macrocosmic" happiness upon your arrival at the climacteria [A. N.'s thirtieth birthday]. Fred & I are getting you *Ulysses* together—he *insists*. Saw Kahane today for a few minutes only. He is still enthusiastic and is going ahead with the printing of *T[ropic] of C[ancer]* in short order—getting it out as a private edition at first. And about the brochure—I'll tell you later—the fat's still in the fire.†

And now (from *L'Art et la Folie*): "*Chez les paranoïaques (orgueilleux, méfiants et persécutés) la poésie devient un moyen de protester contre leur sort, mais ils lui préfèrent habituellement la prose.*"

Going strong!
Love

Henry

*See Biographical Notes.
†Jack Kahane, of the Obelisk Press, had suggested that H. M. write a short book—the "brochure"—about D. H. Lawrence, which could precede publication of *Tropic of Cancer* and establish Miller as a "serious" writer before his novel appeared.

[Clichy]
Friday, March 3, 1933*

[Anaïs:]

Just received a letter from Rank saying that he had really been ill all this while and asking me if I still care to make an appointment. Damned glad now I didn't write. You have good hunches.

Spring is in the air—radios going full blast. Why go to Tahiti or Bali? Only sad, defeated people do that.

Am eager about next week. You'll let me hear *instanter,* won't you?

Henry

P.S. Looking at that nail-polish stain on kitchen floor—was eating alone, meditatively, this evening. That meant, according to Freudian wisdom, that I wanted a break between you & June—is that it? And if it hadn't meant that, it would have meant something else, eh?

P.S. What tickles me is that I wake up from a sound slumber writing the lines for the Brochure. *Economy. Pleasure-pain* bunkum.

[Louveciennes]
Friday [March 3, 1933]

[Henry:]

Enclosing roughly written, careless notes on your work, done in the train. 2 months ago. When I have time will make a better job. This to amuse you.

I'm in the grips of my favorite, unique, particular illness—a little ironic trick played on me by life, that I, so alive, breezy, active, undaunted by bigger obstacles should be paralyzed by neuralgia because Eduardo opened the window of the car last night. But I'm glad because it gives me time to read your pages carefully, to finish Nietzsche.

[Marie] Bonaparte last night [at a lecture given at the Sorbonne] was psychoanalysis at its worst, barren, precise, arid, clinical. Created a revolt in me. Point was that Poe's mother died of consumption when he was 3. He sought the *image* of her in several other women, including

*Dated in A. N.'s handwriting.

the consumption, the lingering death etc. The dying women haunt his work, dominate it (perhaps as *cruel* women have haunted and dominated you). Dying women arrested the living flow of his sensuality. His sensuality became necrophilic. *Et puis après?*

Tell me this, however: What were your mother's *dominant* traits. As far as I can see, criticalness, sharpness, hardness, tyranny?

Anyway, it's *all* necrophilic—Mme. Bonaparte too—I agree with you—more and more. Wherein I don't agree is that the study of necrophilia, for people like you and me, is a great incentive to become more and more Dionysian. I'm absolutely brimming with effervescence even though I can't move an inch!

Seems to me you have *escaped* the fatality of repetition in your destiny by escaping *cruelty* in women. As I escaped mine by finding you, in place of my former penchant for dead or half-dead men!

Did I leave my face powder & engagement book *chez toi?*

Will manage to see you Monday somehow or other.

[Anaïs]

[Louveciennes]
March 8, 1933

Henry—

Was sad yesterday not to be able to stay with you and enjoy our day, Rank, your pages *à fond.* But tomorrow I am coming for the evening. Please get Fred out of the way. Or telephone me if you can meet me elsewhere for the evening. I am inordinately proud of your over-generous letter.* Inordinately proud of you. Inordinately happy. Enclosing more pages on Louise. Why I objected a little yesterday to your saying the astrologer was so surrounded by people—because I feel always that you over-estimate his life and his power in comparison with yours. Because I felt that you aggrandize the lives and doings of others and minimize your own. But perhaps Rank is right and humility is an

---

*In a long letter, dated March 7, 1933, H. M. reported on his first, and only, interview with Dr. Otto Rank. "What I needed was the high challenge, the acid test, and I got it. And where Rank stands after thirty years of struggle, diligence, research, exploration, etc. there I stood, equally firm, firmer I'm telling you, despite all the temperamental diffidences and all the questions and obscurities and contradictions in my soul." See *Letters to Anaïs Nin,* pp. 80–86 (New York: G. P. Putnam's, 1965).

atonement for your great inner pride and knowingness about your self!

I found my powder, notebook etc. behind the seat in the car. Enclosing *prix réduits* for a Spanish piece. Don't know anything about it except that Martines Sierra is one of the Shakespeares of Spain, which means nothing to me, but may interest you as a curiosity. Who was telling me about the museum made of things of no value and of no interest whatever to anybody? It takes genius to fill it! I feel that way about banks, bankers, stocks, bonds, gold. . . . This is a strange moment for the artists, when they feel their strength and the power of their possessions, the enduring quality of them.

Anaïs

A year ago today . . .

[Louveciennes]
[March 9, 1933]

[Henry:]

You did me so much good today. I felt so close to your *joyousness*—it is that I feel in you which is in me, a joyous tragic sense of life, a love of catastrophes even; it is the darkness and weight of Hugh which it costs me to live with, the eternal darkness, the heaviness, the heaviness. I have been so burdened, have fought so hard to liberate him of fear. Tonight he is happy. He says: "Let the worst come now, we are philosophers." I said to myself: "We are artists," thinking of you and of how you turned and blunted the edge of our talk at that mere word "Worry," which does not exist in our vocabulary. "In this book does not speak a tremendous hope?" Agreed. But a tremendous ecstasy, a joy. That is what I meant by saying you and I could handle necrophilism without fear of contagion!

Another thing makes me happy. That you are looming so tall as a thinker that I have to strain to follow you. In fact, I am falling behind, which you desired on one of your Germanic-masculine days. And I am delighted, delighted as a woman. I feel my neck getting strained, from watching the immense, immense curves you are taking in space. And I am hypnotized!

Great idea on the arrangement of my work. It will make a difference to me to disentangle certain passages, bring certain phrases in relief, help me to find my own bearings. The literalness is not to be attributed to the high and noble reasons I gave you (all that stuff on Rimbaud, metaphysical-artistic imperatives), just sheer laziness, between you and me. I'm going to work like hell.

Tomorrow lunch with the Poe worshipper. A tea meeting with Comtesse de Vogüe and Edmond Jaloux. Dinner *chez des banquiers.* Saturday night meeting [Antonin] Artaud. *Everywhere* I miss *you.*

Anaïs

There *is* money in the bank—you can cash this any time!

[Louveciennes]
March 11, 1933

[Henry:]

Comtesse de Vogüe. Nellie. Like Brigitte Helm and Clara Bow. White satin armchairs and divans. Butlers. *Très frileuse.* Fire in the room in the Spring. The magazine is to appear April 20. Her venture with Edmond Jaloux. She herself will translate a chapter from my book. Lost her taste in life and blindly expects me to give it back to her. We talk as people do in books. Strange, brittle, arrowed. Tall, tall windows covered with lace. Pillows under our feet. And life tasteless. And so eager, so eager that I should accomplish a miracle. People always expect miracles.

In the evening we are taken to see *Rain.* I discover Joan Crawford. I think you told me you loved her. So do I. Her face haunts me. The dream-like exaggeration of features, the big mouth, the mouth. The story is ridiculous. The French are jeering. Absolutely jeering and there is almost a scene. The Americans are weeping. Joan Crawford as slut and as angel . . . magnificent. We all step out nonchalantly, with refined indifference, sit in the Colisée, lorgnetting everybody, but I am simmering.

We are saved from disaster by the Cuban poet. I do not have to write the Poe book, because it is not for literature, it is for politics. So I very politically and tactfully evade the nauseating job. Prefer any job to that. But the politics-minded poet saves us from ruin, anyway. He is very fond of us. Knew me as a child etc. In return we have to help him put across a magazine which is no good. And we have to praise poetry which is no good. Pfew!

This afternoon Eduardo, Gustavo [Duran] and Hugh, and then Artaud, and I always thinking of you, like a plant stretching out always in an unexpected direction, its head stuck out through the neighbor's fence, and all the sticks in the world cannot make it turn its face where it should.

[Anaïs]

Wrote you a note the evening you left which I could not mail until this morning.

Henry, I'm afraid of the adulation I'm getting. Be *severe* with me. Don't let me get spoiled. I knew I should live alone as I did before. It is good for one.

[Clichy]
Wednesday [March 22, 1933]

Anaïs:

In spite of my desire to hold back these copies until they were more rounded out I send them—because you may be wondering what has happened to me. Today I have cracked. A most awful headache from lying awake all night thinking. I am running out on the work for a spell. Don't understand it, as it is not lack of desire or ideas—rather a superfluity; I guess I am disturbed only because so little strains through the meshes and I am thinking in such violent floods. The few pages on Lawrence represent only the commencement of a big inundation, for which I have all the notes carefully made—big clarifications. I got terribly excited about *Extase* * and wrote the pages on it all in one breath, much more to follow. In fact, I was hipped by the idea of starting yet another book and was racked by the thought of being divided between so many books. There's the conflict. There is no patience in me. Just a raging tempest all the time. The Lowenfels eulogy I did out of a stricken conscience because I had promised to write him something—is it rather too thick? (It hurts sometimes to let out such steam on someone else—wait till I unloose my dogs on your preface!)

I got out a library card yesterday for a year, at 150 frs. I would have had to pay the 150 for six months (they [would be] keeping 50 as a deposit—this other way there is no deposit required). The red envelopes were from Lowenfels—I'll get you some.

*Gustav Machaty's film, starring Hedy Lamarr, who appeared nude in a ten-minute sequence.

I telephoned at noon today but couldn't understand Amelia. You're not giving me the silence, are you? No imaginary ills or grudges? I thought everything was *swell* when I left. How come the sadness? Sadness. Hateful word. Yank it out. I assure you it was never finer—*it*—the world, life, work, love, you, everything. I still have a rotten headache and if I can write this you must realize that there are no phantasms of June, the German, or such nonsense in back of my head. The Proust in me would like to *know* a little more, but the volcano smothers the Proust perpetually. I'm afraid I'll never get to know German and hence June and a lot of other things—incest, trauma, etc.

Incidentally, thinking out the scheme of my film book—have a glorious idea for the section devoted to stars. Purpose is to reveal their appeal, their inner symbolism for the public, in terms of this death nonsense. Can you see what I would do to Greta Garbo from the standpoint of corpse anatomy—corpse buggerers—sadistic jakes who rip with the corn-cob, etc. etc.? Can you see me handling John Barrymore, or any of the great screen lovers (Valentino, for example), as the Don Juans of the Unconscious Psychology? Jung furnishes me with marvellous ammunition for this theme—the tragedy of Don Juanism. (It has almost the importance of the "Hamlet" theme.) And then there is the "omophagic" aspect of stardom. Eating the holy wafer in the dark halls, the catacombs of Christian robotism. The machine men going for their Holy Communion, their joints stiff, their tongues hanging out with thirst. "This is my body broken for thee—eat ye all of it." *And drink!* I could make a marvellous maggot feast of it. . . . But listen, I must finish Lawrence, Joyce & Proust. It's driving me nuts. I feel like a slacker. I'll spit them out alive, if necessary. I'm screwed up to a frenzy. *Vino, vino* . . . I wish I had the taste for it. *Vino* isn't strong enough. It's blood I want.

Henry

Jesus, say something—I feel you are secretly angry about something.

P.S. And I had to write a ten-page criticism of Osborn's junk.* I think he'll stay *quiet* now!

---

*Since the beginning of the year, Richard Osborn had sent H. M. numerous manuscripts of his own writings, including material on his relationship with "Janine," the girl he had wanted to marry and who turned out to be, according to H. M., a prostitute.

[Anaïs:]

Still plowing along, as you see. Am I getting anywhere, saying anything? What a struggle! I seem always to arrive at the edge of something and then fall off. Only approaching the "Fantasia," notes piled up, the desk cluttered. I seem to be moving through a sewer. I'm worn out with it, but principally because I'm not sure if I am ramming things home, or if I am just repeating myself, or if I am not saying anything at all. I don't quite know where I'm at, except that I am full up and the end nowhere. I'm in a morass. I'm dead tired. These ten or eleven pages seem to have used me up more than any ten pages I remember. The bastard is driving me nuts. I'm beginning to doubt seriously whether he was worth all this.

So much for my agonies. Other things don't exist just now. I got your letter this evening and I think you asked me some things but I am too tired to remember. I never want to try and be a thinker again. I'm *not* a thinker. I'd really like to read what somebody else wrote about Lawrence, and, by God, hereafter I will.

I'm remembering that you're free Friday. Maybe I'll call you up some morning before then. If not, you tell me when and where. Steer me along. Nourish me. My blood's running out. Every time I think now of your book, of how you wrote your Lawrence in three weeks I take my hat off to you. You're a wizard. You ought to write my books. How can anybody do anything in three weeks? To do that one must be a god. God took a week to create the world. I take my hat off to him too. It's stupendous. Unbelievable. Let it stay that way. Hurriedly,

Henry

Jesus, don't think this is cold. I'm just simply functioning as mind. The whole thing is going to collapse soon—the mind, I mean.

[Louveciennes]
[March 29, 1933]

[Henry:]

I wish I could see you. It is so easy for the *other* to see clearly into the "morass," to prove to you that you are not only getting somewhere but to *high, high spots*. Cannot go into details. I'm writing this surreptitiously between two translations for Allendy. Will have much to tell you on Friday. Am *pleased, enormously pleased,* I tell you. You don't know what you are writing. You're like a painter who has gone blind to his work. Go out. Get on your bicycle. You need movement, rest. Have much to tell you that is good about *your* pages, more so after reading Hale,* who is fine. I can see why you were excited about Goethe. Hale and me. I writing on Lawrence in three weeks. But don't you see it is done by a process of elimination, of clarifying, of sifting, of cutting a narrow path into a mountain. You take so much bigger an armful. Too big sometimes. But in the end, what you give, how much you give! I go along like a horse with ear-holders. I give you a carved apple to eat. A neat apple. No Spengler. You have tackled a herculean task. And then you are astonished to be perspiring.

Too much mind, though, Henry! I do not like Goethe's *complete* transference into ideas. I do not like his second metamorphosis. That is not for you. You must, like me, turn it *on* and *off.* Let us go to Spain. Perhaps next week Hugh may go to the Riviera and you may come here. It is celestial, in the garden, as it was last summer. You need a *human* life . . . in between.

Friday. Come as early as you can. I'll expect you.

A.

[Clichy]
Monday [April 10, 1933]

[Anaïs:]

Been cleaning up odd jobs all night. And so I came upon "Alraune" again—original version. Numbered the pages, as well as these last pages of yours—curse you!

Anyway—"Alraune" is something to still marvel over. When you come again, and every time you come, until you get blue in the face, I'm going to trot it out and we're going to work over it—slowly, patiently, lovingly, scathingly. This is your great work—86 pages or so, but of such intensity that they are worth several hundred. As I read it over—parts of it only—I felt sure it could be brought to some state of near perfection. And that it must be done. It must not die, in the way

---

*William Harlan Hale, *Challenge to Defeat: Modern Man in Goethe's World and Spengler's Century* (New York: Harcourt, Brace and Co., 1932).

things do, through oversight, laziness, neglect. A lot of the neglect is my fault. I haven't been back of you arduously enough. And now I am going to show you that I am in earnest.

I propose going over it together, a page at a time maybe, in order to teach you what you have to learn. With just a little more mastery you would make of "Alraune" one of those rare, unique works, such as are attributed to Rimbaud, and to the author of *Six Immoral Tales*, whom very justly you admired so. Because you have a lot in common with him. (Can't remember his name.) (I sent you something from Pound on him recently.) It is difficult writing—this which you have in common with him. It is either flawless, or else it is gibberish. I mean there are no intermediate degrees. A rocket, a shooting star—or else cinders. Do you get me? Now *La Forgue* (that's his name),* tho' only 20-odd years and a sick, poverty-stricken bastard, had the genius required. You have the genius too, but you have no language in which to express it. And that can be tragic, if it is not overcome. There is no question of *pedantry* involved herein. You must firmly, decisively, once and for all, acknowledge that to yourself. You need to take *language lessons* from me, regularly and obediently, until I pronounce you cured. Otherwise—well otherwise you will make no progress whatever. You will simply turn out marvellous abortions.

I'm talking to you like a Dutch uncle because I know and I fully value your genius.

But here is the crux of the matter: art is not the translation or the representation or the expression of some hidden thing. It is *a thing* in itself—pure, absolute, without reference. In whatever medium you choose to employ, the *mastery* of the medium constitutes the art. There are no rules, no guideposts. But one can detect bad art from good art—or better, one can detect *art*. Now then, language, the *English* language, is your medium. If you do not handle it—I won't say "properly" (because school-children are supposed to be able to do that)—but "masterfully," i.e. *as artist always*, you can not produce a work of art. You might as well expect of Brancusi that he give us his masterpieces in fried bread crumbs or apple sauce. Can't be done. The choice he makes—of wood, or steel, or marble—together with the instinctive knowledge of how to manipulate each material, is what produces said

---

*Jules Laforgue (1860–1887), who, like Rimbaud and Lautréamont, was influenced by Baudelaire, wrote several volumes of poetry and the collection of prose pieces *Moralités légendaires*.

Brancusi's works of art. *Soit?* If he said, "Well, first let me do it any old way, in bird seed or pigeon shit, because I'm not in a mood to make a marble egg today," you know he would not make a marble egg. He has sometime to tackle the egg. So with you! I am going to make you tackle "Alraune" here in my presence, as though it were a golden cockerel and you were creating it—the first golden cockerel ever created.

If you look at language *merely* as craft you are committing *lèse-majesté* towards your own sacred tools. You've got to have the proper respect—you've got to feel awed in its presence (see, I say "awed," not "sacred").

I suppose you will be a little peeved at all this and accuse me of doing just what you requested me not to do. I have not forgotten. I read the last installment with considerable pleasure—some delicious things about myself—I'll show you where. No, I don't wish to ride you. I'm not thinking of these particular pages. I'm thinking of you in general, as a writer, and what I can do to save you, that is, to aid you. I ought (so I feel, anyway) to correct every letter you send me, correct every statement you utter. Not tyrannize over you, as your father might, for sheer love of power or whatever it be, but for the sole purpose of keeping ever uppermost in your mind the one thing you must conquer—your defect. There is no petulance in my voice, as I state these things. I understand fully how it came about. But you don't need my understanding. You need help, encouragement. You need constant goading.

I tell you, this all started with "Alraune." It's so damned wonderful, and it's so damned aborted yet. I don't want you to drop what you're doing. I want you to go on, because you're doing it well. One word of caution—*don't cut to the bone!* You can let loose once in a while, you know. You are almost too conscientious in your new resolution. I liked the way in which you inserted some of the original text of "Alraune"—that bit beginning: "At night she sank into the dream." (Page 32, my pagination.)

You have been doing a hell of a lot of work, I see that now. Working like a nigger. Fine. I know you can work. But I want you to sweat still more. To give birth to stars and gems. You can do it.

Anyway, when you come, we'll get "Alraune" out and dust it off. Don't write silly letters to Eduardo. You don't need to cultivate your "imaginings." You need to manicure your tools. You should be asking me all sorts of questions—as I told you, *technical questions.* No matter how silly it may seem to you. Don't hesitate to betray your ignorance. It's no crime.

I hope you're not sore. I want to do things for you. Love,

Henry

[Clichy]
Thursday [April 13, 1933]

Anaïs:

Fred has finished [typing] the Diary—do you want to meet me somewhere in town and get it? He says it is the worst of the lot—sometimes unintelligible, and that you will have to read it carefully for corrections. He means also that it is the most sugary—a bit nauseating. I haven't had a chance to glance over it, but tell you this so as to be on your guard.

Am going to the library to renew my Proust books; I won't get the [Thomas] Mann book for you just yet as I imagine you are going to be very busy for the next week or so. If I can dig up any more on "Alraune" I will.

What you said about Narcissism-June-yourself-Alraune the other night was excellent. If you do attempt a preface (I see in my letter that I suggested the book ought to be "explained") don't forget this theme. The preface should be stunning, and if written in an unscientific language, interesting to everyone. If I raved about that letter of criticism it is only because I realized once more, and more completely than ever, how much your little book contains. It is loaded with dynamite. You'll see—the books written around it will be huge! You've given the bare bones—the quintessence.

The dream—rather fantastic, eh? What a Spain!

Henry

[Louveciennes]
[April 15, 1933]

[Henry:]

Fred is *all wet* about the journal, which shows he bears me a grudge for some reason or other. It is the one you read from MS. and from which you culled many phrases, the visit to the woman writer who was so kind, the reading of Turgenev at 14, comments on love, *"un de ces jours je devrais dire: mon journal, je suis arrivée au fond,"* passage on the petals, *"suis-je comme tout le monde, voilà la question."*

In fact *most* of what you commented on and sent me to the Tyrol. What I regret is that this is not the one Bradley saw—it is better than No. 2.

Now I know Fred hates me, but that is good!

But I felt *bitter* tonight that Bradley should love the journal while Kahane delays your book—it is you the *force* that is feared. But I tell you this, Henry, not another book of mine comes out before yours does! You and your work mean more to me than my life. I want the world to know *you*, the value of *you*. I swear it will. Today I loved the selflessness with which you enjoyed my successes. You are great, great, great, Henry. I will never tire of saying it. My journal has become the journal of *you*. It's full of you—brimming full.

> *Anaïs*

I'm coming to Clichy Monday if that suits you, with an idea for [Rudolf] Bachman's* plight. Tell him to get his valise ready to come to Louveciennes for a holiday and we'll find a way out. Not to be afraid.

> [Clichy]
> April 20, 1933†

[Anaïs:]

I've taken a tremendous liberty. I hope you won't be angry. Here are a few pages, the opening, which was so difficult and still baffles me. I tried to rewrite it, but I feel I have worked some kind of sacrilege on you. You must try to understand. On re-reading your pages last night I had a feeling of despair. It is not what you wanted to say. It is off-key. Or so it seems to me. Perhaps my version is still more off-key. Perhaps I make it difficult, with these improvisations, for you ever to find the right key. And yet, annoyed that you had somehow failed to convey *all* that you wished, I felt it my duty to see if I could convey it. I don't think I have succeeded, but I offer you these pages as a witness to the difficulties you must still encounter.

*See Biographical Notes.
†Dated in A. N.'s handwriting.

And then I want to add—maybe I'm wrong to criticize your work. I begin to doubt my own ability, or my own vision. Certainly I found it an awful struggle to rewrite these few pages. Why? Is it that I don't clearly understand what you are trying to say? Do you understand yourself? You are attempting to express such inexpressible things.

I elaborate, as you notice. That is the only way out of these *water-tight* abstractions of yours that I can find. Break through them, divest them of their mystery, and allow the core to flow.

I am terribly disappointed not to be able to come tomorrow. I had hoped to thrash this all out with you in great detail. It's hard for me to state the subtleties which make your writing so enigmatic. One thing I know—it will pay to rewrite this damned thing fifty times if necessary—just to find out what you wanted to say. And to learn, at the same time, how to say it. I feel it all very keenly because I want you to be neither humble nor enraged, but to look at it coldly and critically with your eyes unscaled.

Oddly enough I have come to a strange conclusion about your writing—I have given a great deal of thought to it in the interim since I left you. I think that, instead of being so Pisces as you imagine, that you are, on the contrary, quite bound up, knitted, restricted. Now and then you break it and you rush on with convincing power and eloquence. But it is as if you first had to break diamonds inside you, powder them to dust, and then liquefy them—a terrific piece of alchemy. I think again that one of the reasons you have lodged so firmly in the diary is because of a fear to test your tangible self with the world; surely, if what you had written were offered to the world you would have already altered your style. You have gotten ingrown, more and more protected, more and more sensitive—and that produces poisons and gems, the clotted, spangled phantasmagoria of neurosis. I want to be harsh now—in order to liberate you. I don't want to ever see you write another Alraune 1, 2, 3. It's as revelatory and symptomatic as my *Tropic of Cancer*. These things are bridges to something.

But it must be a firm bridge. Otherwise there's no crossing. I'll call you tomorrow—I hope you get this beforehand.

I'll also make arrangements for Bachman to meet me in Paris before coming to the house, as I don't want him to be seen returning. I don't think I shall be able to see Kahane before next week. It won't matter too much. Had a card from Bradley saying what a great find you were—he considers the diary remarkable etc.

I hope this doesn't make you feel bad. It doesn't militate against my praise the other day—all that is just and not too extravagant. Now I am seizing on the weakness, that is all. I am baffled by your ability to put the most subtle things in speech and fail in writing. I repeat— you are a great artist—a great one!—but you are sometimes like one who has forgotten his medium.

A small thing: What I did sometimes, in changing your language, was to work for a more universal tone—thus cutting through those "femininities" I referred to in Louveciennes. Here I may have horribly distorted your meaning, but just regard it as a method of approach. Tear it all down, if you like, and build anew. But don't give up— because this is a test.

The one great reason why I cannot rewrite it perfectly for you is because I cannot put myself in your place, see and feel with you. I can make all the muscular gestures, but they remain gestures. I want *you* to develop a little muscle. . . .

Finally—so good does it seem to me, so immensely good—that I should be willing and happy to spend infinite time and pains on it. So don't get the idea that I am chafing at the bit. But it's the thought, the ideas, back of each sentence that I need so much to discuss with you. I have a peculiar, helpless feeling.

Let me know whether my draft seemed a terrible abortion or an advancement of some sort.

Henry

[Paris]
[April 24, 1933]

[Henry:]

I have been working over your corrections of "Alraune," which prove to me what a gorgeous poet and imaginist *you* are—*definitely.*

Listen: set yourself the date of *June first* to complete your Brochure, because I feel we will be able to be together then and I will attack the revisions of it. Read it all over yesterday and see it all so clearly. And if possible then we must be able to talk over the "June" book—work it out. I know I will be able to incite you. We will wrestle it out—as you created your attack of psychoanalysis out of the collision with my defense of it. You will find *in me* the June you want to come to grips with. I feel more than ever how much of her there is in me—I *feel* her lies, motives, *raison d'être,* reason for subterfuges, evasions etc.

A complete imaginative assimilation, similitudes. I don't know if I make this clear.

I expect you tomorrow as early as possible, because it is so warm here for work and talk. You don't need to telephone unless you cannot come because you want to work.

[Anaïs]

Café Richelieu
9, Boulevard des Italiens
[Thursday] April 27, 1933*

[Anaïs:]

Wrote some more pages on arriving home and then had to sneak out because Wambly Bald was coming & I couldn't bear any unproductive neuroticism.

After dictating to you all A.M. it seemed rather ironical to me. Asking you not only for wisdom but dictating to you your own wisdom. Do you see it?

If you get word from Bachman please let me know at once, as I want to forward his letter—it may contain important news.

What a session we had! Jesus, I left feeling like a blazing furnace. I thought, for a little while today, that I was really going nuts.

I say so little when with you of my real appreciation—all your efforts to please me, surprise me, etc. I want you to know that I don't ignore or forget them!

[Henry]

[Louveciennes]
[May 3, 1933]

[Henry:]

You ask me if I felt well after our holiday! Well! I exploded with joy, contentment, gratitude, worship etc. etc. in the journal. More pages for you to enjoy someday.

Bachman. Yes. The trait I did not like. References to me simply mean in English: "Since it is you who introduced me to Anaïs I can

*Dated in A. N.'s handwriting.

confess to you I am constantly preoccupied with thoughts of Anaïs. Trying to make out in myself what feelings it is she inspired in me." A half-confession which he began one day here, and if he mentions this it is because he does not know what feelings I inspire in you! O.K. A nice naïveté about this, that is likeable, or stupid, as you wish. The mandolin tones I mentioned once.

I'm so happy about Kahane. Tell him I will go to prison with you too, nail lacquer, false curls and all.

Bradley telephoned and asked if he could come here Monday, that he had a great deal to say to me.

I did not write you after you left because I had a lot to do Tuesday.

I retract what I said about [Louis-Ferdinand Céline's] *Voyage au Bout de la Nuit.* You will have to read it in June. There are affinities there with your earlier work. It's another form of absolute, and therefore valuable.

Got a beautiful letter from my father again, transports of un-French and even un-Spanish affection. I see where I get some of my Russianisms! The Spaniard does not give his mind and soul to the woman! The Spaniard is the man who associates with man only in the building of a world.

It's funny that one could overlook your committing a *crime* because you are so *big,* and a little shrewdness in Bachman looms and stains him all over.

Boussie [Hélène Boussinesq]* picked on the portrait of you to translate. She said that could not be *one* man but a composite of a hundred. *Voilà.* That's *you.*

Anaïs

Come Friday if you can.

If your notes are bound have it delivered Friday evening. I will have the money for it Friday. On second thought, enclosing check. *Please* get yourself the tie you want—I haven't a moment to go with you. Get something from me as good as possible . . . it will make me happy.

I sent Bachman money and *beg* you not to send him anything.

---

*A teacher of English literature and translator; friend of A. N.

[Louveciennes]
[May 8, 1933]

[Henry:]

Will hold this letter open to tell you what Bradley said. Spent Sunday reading *Voyage* and thinking of your work, making notes and comparisons all to your favor. Yet there are marvellous passages in the *Voyage*. I have enjoyed the *"amertume virile,"* the pessimism, the crapulousness. Some pages will make you homesick for the beauty of American women.

I don't know yet when I can see you. Tomorrow Artaud, and I can't put him off as I have already done so for ten days. Wednesday my father.* The weeks are too short. Thursday and Friday I must catch up with Allendy's work. But there is hope for a weekend together because Hugh may go to Switzerland. If not I will see you Thursday evening there. Hugh said yesterday that the conjunction of Neptune and Uranus gives me an "eventful and strange life." And you? Your holding back the essence and climax of your book excites me. I'm expecting a superb surprise.

You have many affinities with Céline. [Bernard] Steele† ought to like you immensely. He is coming next Tuesday—I can't see him before. You are much much greater on *women*. Céline is *arid*.

Mailing this immediately as you may need check.

Anaïs

[Clichy]
Tuesday [May 9, 1933]

[Anaïs:]

[. . .] Last night I finished reading [Dorothy Brett's] *Brett and Lawrence* in a café and the tears were running down my cheeks as I finished. Believe me, Lawrence was much finer, greater than I ever thought. I have seen so much of myself in him, and his battles with Frieda so keenly resemble my battles, and over similar issues, that it

---

*Through the intervention of Gustavo Duran, A. N. had agreed to see her father, from whom she had been separated since he left her mother in 1914 for another woman, and A. N. had been taken to the United States. The reconciliation is described in detail in *The Diary of Anaïs Nin*, 1931–1934. See Biographical Notes for Nin y Castellanos.
†A partner in the French publishing firm Denoël & Steele.

gets me. And then his traits of character, many of them are my own— the defects chiefly. The conclusion is that he created a great body of work—and that answers all claims against him. That is where I failed by comparison. Never mind how he failed or triumphed as a man. As artist—did he succeed? I say—magnificently!

Henry

[Louveciennes]
[May 9, 1933]

[Henry:]

Well, I *got* my talk with Bradley about you. He said fine things about you. When you are good you are *unsurpassable*. Believes *greatly* in you. That you are a *poet*. Likes humanly your generosity in regard to other writers (negligible ones like Fred). Wishes he had the means to give an income to *worthwhile* writers like you, so you wouldn't worry anymore and could work in peace. Said you needed to be finished with June episode to be able to write well about it, that you tried to do so too soon and now expects greater things, greater things (they are coming, they are coming!). I happened to say that if the public could accept *Voyage au Bout de la Nuit* it would accept your book, referring to the language, and so apropos of this he said: "Miller is a far more distinguished mind than Céline." Distinguished mind! Hurrah! Applauded my trying out Steele, although he says French public is not important. Says Kahane is not afraid of trouble but of not selling, and is holding back other books as well, because of general conditions, as he counts on tourists as readers. He also said there was not in *Voyage* anything like the *satanic Dantesque imagination you have*. Full marks for Bradley. I could have embraced him (but I didn't). He deserved it! We talked endlessly. He talked much about himself.

He wants the whole [childhood] journal. Complete. French & English. Will show it to [Alfred] Knopf next week. Suggested cutting out the religious part. O.K. The poems. O.K. Will do the cutting out himself. The secret of Bradley is that when he was young he wrote a book of poems (thought daring at the time)* and that behind his work lies a wistful interest in writing; he loves to help, direct, criticize,

---

Amicitia Amorque, privately printed, in an edition of 100 copies, in 1901, when he was twenty-three years old.

influence, sympathize etc. He is really fine. Dreams of playing the role X [Ford Madox Ford] played with [Joseph] Conrad. Supported and sustained Conrad. That is his vision of his role. He loves to handle and work on manuscripts and really participates in all that is done, with a great secret second-hand satisfaction. The type of man that every non-artist should aspire to become if he had enough humility and the power to abdicate and serve. I admire Bradley for that.

Said the [childhood] journal gave a very amusing picture of New York, enjoyed the sense of humor (my unflattering descriptions of myself and others), amusing picture of the child that is well brought up and *sage* (knitting, serving, obeying etc.) with that secret and overflowing emotional, intense, chaotic, dramatic life underneath. I am another who has benefited from your generosity! That, I have often noted in the journal, your generosity (your help of Osborn, patience with Bald etc.). Now it is you who presents my journal to the world. Bradley said it must be prefaced by some very *well-known* writer. Listen, Henry, this person can only be *you*. This *well-known* person is the *you* I saw the first day. Please impress my image of your greatness on the world—so that you can write the preface!!! I am going to wait for you. I am waiting for you. Believe me, at certain moments I may have seemed a little crazy, yet none of my extravagant statements about you were ever untrue. Other people will discover that later. I am too quick, you say, always too quick. That's my way. I was afraid to talk too much about you. Bradley was curious about my life. Imagines me sheltered, preciously unknown, discovered by him. His face fell when I said my life was eventful. He did not want it to be so! Nobody wants me to live, to get known. Like a guitar for chamber music only. You alone say: "Get out. Get a little tougher." You dare me. It's you who are right. I love you for that.

Insisted on seeing "Alraune." I gave it to him and told him what remained to be done. I had made the corrections of all you underlined in the last version. I was quaky about giving him that before you had fixed it, but he seems to understand work in progress, even to like it. Feels he takes a share in it. Anyway, I must stand or fall by my own writing. I have a terrible fear that he may say: only the journal is good. He is very curious to see if I am a writer, outside of the journal.

Just got your feverish letter on the "Crown" [by D. H. Lawrence]. I give you the "Crown," it belongs to you, since you discovered its meaning. I failed to get anything out of it. That shows you how deeply and how far you have gone. I'm terribly excited. Listen, as soon as there is a break call me up. I'll manage so as to see you somehow or other. I wish the month of June would come immediately.

I was vague about my life. Did not know how much I could tell Bradley. It will come. He saw your photo on my desk. "Alraune" will tell him everything, I suppose.

He was amazing. Concerned about my health because of references to it in the journal! The damn journal should end with Wednesday when my father comes to Louveciennes. But my life is only beginning now or at least since I met the well-known writer H.V.M. That was the beginning of the journal of H.V.M.!

I wish I could read what you are doing. I would give anything to be in Clichy tonight!

Anaïs

You can't image what I feel when I hear others praise you—such a joy it gives me. And at the same time I feel each one gets a fragment and that I alone know the *whole*.

I love the idea of anonymity for the journal. It fits my earliest desire to remain unknown. It's wonderful, that secrecy again and always.

[Louveciennes]
[May 15, 1933]

[Henry:]

There was no smash-up, but I feel that Hugh's confidence is permanently shaken. All that you said yesterday touched me, but I am determined never to become a *burden* to you. I want above everything else to preserve that security which enables you to work. Your *security* and your *independence* at all cost. Remember what I told you, my life is subject to your needs, primarily. It revolves around your needs. It isn't necessary to you that I should be in Clichy, but it is essential that you should go on getting only the perfect, the gifts, without responsibilities and without ties. No hindrances. Liberty for you always, Henry.

Can't write much today—so much shaken by everything. My father's fervent approval of my life is a wonderful pillar.

Hugh is going to London next weekend. I will have to wait until then to see you because I have so much work. The real trouble came from the gate being unlocked. Otherwise it would have been easy for you to disappear coat and all!

Bradley asks to see me Thursday P.M. Hasn't read "Alraune" but is satisfied with 2nd and 3rd volumes of journal. Knopf interested.

Anaïs

Wepler/Café-Restaurant
14, Place Clichy
Wednesday [May 17, 1933]

[Anaïs:]

The gate! Yes! Always there is a gate unlocked—it runs like a classic incident thru all romantic lives. It had to be sooner or later.

What you write sort of overwhelms me. I simply can't offer you anything—you always offer more! You just refuse to let me do anything for you. However, it's all *reasonable*—for the time being. No woman ever said these things to me before—so sincerely, honestly. I believe you implicitly and it makes me feel wonderful. (For when others spoke thus I felt it was only a gesture and I was supposed to protest, or something.)

With your attitude and mine—how can things go wrong? I am so thankful not to have to exert a *will* any longer. What belongs to me is mind and nothing can take it from me. This is so different from the struggle to hold, to preserve, etc. I think now we both have attained a wisdom that is not crippling—or merely comfortable. Something rooted in life and living. I was anxious about you. These must be trying days—I know from experience what the atmosphere is like afterwards—the heavy, choking, smothering spell like dry electricity accumulating.

But—the total absence of *fear!* God, what a relief that is. I was thinking afterwards that I might have been killed. And no pains or regrets over the prospect. I can take death as I have taken life. Reject nothing! Here is where Whitman rose superior to Lawrence—despite L.'s magnificent assault. (I must revert again to the perpetual theme: in the criticism of Melville & Whitman, and even Poe, Lawrence revealed a magnificent force, an understanding beyond all criticism heretofore known. The roughness & simplicity, the apparent laziness of it is disarming. Underneath tho' a terrible power & penetration.)

Today I got the *Magnus Case & Apocalypse* from the library.

(*Aaron's Rod* has been stolen—hurrah! I wish they would steal them all!)

And I saw yours again! Always gives me a thrill. A great thrill. I should like to pass the shop windows and see your Diary and your "Alraune" advertised. See your name in gilt letters everywhere.

I want to do for L. what he did for Melville and Whitman. (The Etruscan book would have been interesting, I now discover—he thought their life was as it should be for man. They were near his ideal!)

I only feel badly that you are smothered under another name— that you are on the defensive, expected to give an account of yourself— instead of the other way round. The irony of things! If tomorrow you decamped, how different the situation would become immediately. Then everything would be forgiven you. That we cannot rise equal to situations when we are in them—that is the tragedy of life. A Hugo! With his rock-bound geometric principles of life!

Somehow, Anaïs, I feel very insouciant. Should I!

When I reread that "Open Road" I almost wept with joy. How many know what that really means—the open road? And one of the greatest things Lawrence said, after paying his homage to Whitman (and he said big things about him!) was—"man has not even begun to bud yet. He is all roots and leaves."

Henry

P.S. The difference in tenor between L.'s grasp of *Moby Dick* is revelatory.

[Louveciennes]
[May 23, 1933]

Henry, when June said you were utterly selfish I never believed it. Today you shocked me deeply. I always knew you only loved me for what I could give you, and I was willing to understand and accept this because you were an artist. I made all the excuses for you. I never expected you to be human for a whole lifetime, even seven days a week. It didn't seem so very difficult to be so one day a week, or a day after ten days. Since you left me that Monday Hugh returned, I realized you didn't care a hang about what happened. You set out immediately to forget it all. You wrote me: I feel so insouciant. I didn't mind all that. You accepted my desire to leave you free, free of everything. You knew I meant it. But as soon as I freed you of all anxiety, you went back to your self-engrossed life. And I knew it. Friday I said to myself: I won't let Henry come. He loves me selfishly, only for the good things. He doesn't really care about *me*. And today you proved it. You felt well, healthy, carefree. You didn't care about my life. You saw me after ten days and were cold. You didn't even caress me. You didn't come into the house to be gentle, after your callousness. The truth is you are completely happy in Clichy, alone. I will see that you will continue to have your security, your independence. But that is all, Henry. All the rest is dead. You killed it.

Anaïs

You say I'm touchy. So are you. Only, I spend my life watching over your touchiness. It may be touchy to want to talk to you as I did today—confide in you—and get the response I got. The only time I leaned on you, needed you. I needed you, Henry!

[Clichy]
Wednesday [May 24, 1933]

Listen, Anaïs, it's shameful, this healthiness, this insouciance, this *real* gaiety, but are you going to hang me for that? Your letter doesn't crush me. I don't believe you want to crush me. I left yesterday rather confused, mystified, wondering what it was all about. But I didn't feel hurt, or callous, or angry, or indifferent. I just felt good all the time, so good that even seeing you in tears couldn't squelch it. That isn't being selfish, as you seem to think. Hell, am I so selfish as you pretend suddenly? Do you believe all that nonsense you write—"I always knew you only loved me for what I could give you . . . he loves me selfishly only for the good things . . ." Bah! If I thought you really felt that way about me I'd never see you again . . . never. Because that's a degradation of all that exists between us. When you talk that way I do have genuine sympathy for you—I know you must be in some kind of torture, but just what has induced it is beyond me. And I'm not even too curious. I'm aloof in some decent human way, *not inhumanly*. I leave you on a Monday and the next day you have a breakdown. But I still don't know the cause of it. And I don't think you have explained it to me.

You lie a little bit. All right. Why shouldn't you lie? You wanted to spare me something. Should I probe into that and make you uncomfortable? I did perhaps act a little callously talking about Joachim [Joaquin], but only because I don't like that brother-sister devotion, or I don't understand it. Or I understand it too well and I fear it. Or . . . Well, maybe it's plain jealousy. . . . As for your father, if you think I said cruel things, then you are for once quite blind and unsubtle. I am so much for your father that I could make sacrifices for him—even though I don't know him. I think your father, whether he be right or wrong, underwent a cruel deprivation. I see nothing wrong in his wanting you so fiercely for a little while. Nor that you should want him. You do need each other. You never had a proper relationship. And when I said he would soon be disillusioned, I meant it. In this sense— that a man of his age and his keen intelligence would gradually come to realize that he could never have the daughter whom he had forsaken. I've reconciled myself to that. If in a dream I could break down and sob so bitterly when I meet my daughter it is only because I know, even in the dream, that I cannot really have her. When one lets so many years intervene one gets only ghosts.

Here it is, Anaïs, about this callousness. I don't want to be bitter about life—about love and friendship and all the human, emotional entanglements. I've had more than my share of human disappointments, deprivations, disillusionment. I want to love people and life above all; I want to be able to say always, "if you feel bitter or disillusioned, there is something wrong with yourself, not with people, not with life." I won't reject love and friendship. I won't live alone on a frozen mountain peak.

But I say to you, nevertheless, there must be something tougher than you evince in your letter, in a relationship such as ours. You're not going to tell me, are you really, that however it was I failed you yesterday, it's the end, that I killed it? I should imagine that I ought to be able to fail you still more miserably, and yet not let it be the end. On Tuesday I may prove a failure. And on Thursday or Friday I may prove magnificent. People have calendars too. Or *are* calendars. To take a moment of incomprehension and erect a structure of misunderstanding on it is not worthy of you or me. I talk to you as if I were forgiving you for something. That must gall you. But look—who created this robust, healthy, insouciant, selfish individual whose callousness wounded you so yesterday? Weren't you rather proud and happy all along in seeing me bloom? Did you know that last week, while you were going through your pangs (of what . . . of *neuroticism?*), I felt that I had arrived at the peak of fitness? I was overwhelmed with joy that I should find myself in such superb health. And now you want to take the fruits from me. You want me to be unhappy, to squirm again, to torture myself.

No, Anaïs. It's either one thing or the other. Either you want me to be what I am and like it, or you are deceiving yourself about me. Health! I tell you, it's not indifference, not callousness. It's a very human condition which lifts you, temporarily at least, above so many useless problems and vexations. You just can't be made wretched, sorrowful, miserable. You live there for a while, at the apex of clarity, and you see things with the naked eye and everything looks good, *is* good. It's almost like getting religion—only so much better, so much more sane.

You gave me the bicycle and I have been enjoying it—only a wee bit. Believe me, I have done much less sun-bathing than my letters seem to convey. Only a little touch of sun and I am giddy. Only a little touch of happiness and I forget—all too quickly, you say—my human miseries. Fundamentally I am happy, gay, livable. I can get along with anybody. And at the summit of this well-being I can get along with just myself—and nature. I wouldn't call that inhuman, selfish—not so quickly. You were quick, you know. Ordinarily you wouldn't be hurt by my selfish enjoyment of life. You would relish it. But yesterday— well, yesterday was . . . something was rankling inside you. . . .

Let me go back a little bit. That day I called you up, remember that I called up to say I wouldn't come. I really was keen about working. And then suddenly you informed me you were ill. And I suppose you wanted me to come out. I would have come out too—at once—only you added, and I thought it was sincere, that you wanted to be alone and rest for a while. I thought it was good to do that. At bottom I hate all this pampering we give each other, the moment we learn that another is ill. Why shouldn't one enjoy his illness too? One gets ill sometimes just to be alone for a while. It's a way the body has of conquering the mind. Here are problems which the mind simply can- not solve. And we get tortured and helpless and we collapse. We get ill, we say. O.K. We go to bed and, lying there, just doing nothing, surrendering to the insolvable problems, we gradually get a new vision of things. We succumb to certain ineluctable things which we hadn't the courage to face while we stood up on our hind legs and used that bloody instrument, the mind. I respect that. There are times when nobody can help you, not even the one you love. You have to be alone. You have to be ill, and wallow in your illness. Your soul needs it.

And so I dismissed it promptly and I wrote that "insouciant" letter to Emil. If I had any genuine fears about you, do you think I would dismiss your illness so light-heartedly? Am I a monster? Hardly. I make a distinction between the illnesses we bring on, we *invite,* and the illnesses we succumb to. I wanted you to have your invited illness. And there is more than just this to it. I understood tacitly that something had brought on the illness which you would never reveal to me. It's in the diary, no doubt. Oh, I know that diary of yours, Anaïs, much much better than you can imagine. That's why I truly am not curious to see it all. You could leave me alone with it and feel quite safe. I wouldn't open it. I wouldn't because I know that there must be shadows around all those images of light you read to me. There must be cruel things in the diary, much more cruel than I could ever bring myself to admit.

I think this, Anaïs, to make it very simple—that when one makes the sacrifices for another, as you have for me, there will always be a margin of "ungratefulness," of "callousness," of "non-comprehension," from which you will suffer. I will never be able to make up for all that you have done. Never. And that produces a little secret resentment for which one is not responsible. One pays a penalty for the sacrifices one makes, ironical as that may sound. Whereas with June I came to detest that, to feel bitter and tortured about it, in your case I don't. I thought I was rising above that. Because I recognize *my* responsibility too—not to be slavishly grateful, not to humiliate you, not to destroy the fine thing in you which prompted you to make the sacrifices.

I think, as I started to say above, that the situation has gotten too complicated for you. All the mess seems somehow to gravitate about me. I am at the center, the cause of it all. Not truly, not entirely—for you too are partly responsible. We both wanted it. What I should like to say to you, Anaïs, without the least bitterness, without the least resentment, without the least feeling of injury is—do for yourself whatever it is you wish to do. If there is a struggle in you, of which you have only revealed to me certain aspects, decide what it is you want and do it. Because my real desire is only to help you. I should say just the opposite of what you wrote me. Do *not* continue to bother about my security, my independence. That is not enough for me, or for you. Forget that and let all the rest matter. Don't make the one dependent on the other, as you so cruelly pretended, because I don't believe it. I would despise you if I thought you meant all the things you said. I know you don't. But I am a burden to you. You are trying to do impossible things for me. And you don't want to admit that you cannot cope with them. I beg you to forget your self-imposed responsibilities. Forget all about the physical-economic side of me, that I could let myself be so comfortably protected. Well, try me out the other way. See if I fail you. Just say to me honestly—"I can't do any more for you, Henry . . . I can't!" And see what happens to me.

I am deeply, deeply regretful that I failed you yesterday. I tell you still, it is all confusing and mysterious to me. I came in high spirits, with intention of putting my arms around you immediately and loving you to death. And then, as always happens—it isn't a new thing!—I enter the house and I am conscious of being a guest, even though a very privileged one. It is not my house and you are not my wife. You stand there in the open door and I always see a princess who for some secret whim has condescended to offer me her love. I feel like nobody. I feel that I might be X. Everything is a gift. And a crazy delicacy comes over me and I stand there and shake your hand and talk about intermediate things and I say to myself it's so wonderful here and none of this is real, it's all a dream. I say it because, though I know I deserve a little of life, I do not merit all that you give me. And even when I talk so much about myself, which must be terribly boring to you, it's probably because I'm trying to talk myself into the reality of all this which you bring to me when you just stand by the open door and greet me. You don't know what a great moment that always is for me. Then I become so human that I grow delicate. And so it was yesterday. . . . My callousness was delicacy. I was hungry for you. I could have pulled your clothes off when you brought me back to the hammock; I could have devoured you. But I sit there opposite you and I talk. I made a detour and got lost so that I might be with you five minutes sooner. But you looked awfully frail yesterday; you looked as if you had been ill. And I felt that my devouring hunger might seem truly indelicate. I wanted you to have the best part of me. And so we talked and what really hurt you was that I did not put my arms around you. Well, it was a strange kind of callousness that prevented me. Not your imagined callousness. I thought that my "healthiness" would dissipate all the fumes of illness. I thought—and I guess that's romanticism—that I could just sit there and be with you and make you feel wonderful inside. What I really wanted was to lay you down in the grass and go with you. I'm still *naïf* and clumsy. I'm sorry. I wasn't in any mood for soul-pangs, but I certainly was not indifferent, nor callous. I don't know if you'll ever get the distinction.

Anyway, the devil with all this. I left you in a dazed way, a little pleased at your sending me off that way—because I like it too when you play the grand Spanish lady with me!—and I wanted to call you up and tell you I was sorry, but then I didn't know what I was supposed to be sorry for and feared you would be more hurt by my ignorance or insensitiveness or God knows what, than if I remained silent and "obeyed orders." You know damned well, I didn't need to obey orders. I could have turned around at the gate and grabbed you and said, "No, I won't go away, I'm going to stay here and love you and make you like it." But that seemed crudely romantic to me. You wanted to have the pleasure of chasing me away and I gave it to you. That's what I call delicacy. You wanted me to feel a little humiliated and so I went off, obediently, with my tail between my legs. On the way down the hill I felt very happy, because I imagined you going upstairs and *writing* some more "Alraune" pages. And if driving me away like that would help you to write some more "Alraune" then I am always at your service. You can always make a human doormat of me—for *your art.* That ought to please you a little, Anaïs Nin! (Because I think you're a great artist.)

And as for that personality of yours. Yes, you have that too. A great personality. Even if you had kept no diary. I don't appreciate so much what Nestor* said—it's a little over my head. I should only say that there are days, like yesterday, when you don't know what you are—artist, human being, personality, or self-portrait—and then you make others miserable. But that is all right. I approve of it. You *should* make others miserable once in a while. You have your bad moments, like all of us. You are not perfect. Maybe that's what I don't like about Nestor's compliment. That, and the fact that you said it just to irritate me—as you did about the letters your father writes you. Do you suppose I would want to rival those letters he writes you? Where does he come off then? Is he not to have his glory too? Should he not write even more ardently than me? You made him suffer. Do you want me to suffer too? So that I can write you these wonderful letters? Do you want "letters" or do you want the real live tangible imperfect and substantial me?

You don't want a monster, I know that. But it's very wrong of you, Anaïs, to hurl June's words at me. I don't deserve it. I forgive you

*A Russian painter.

immediately. Because you were weak to write that. You insult yourself when you write me that. I don't think of you as a being who is offering herself to me to be sapped dry. I don't want anything of you but you. Try me out. Don't write "all the rest is dead . . . you killed it." It sounds too melodramatic. It isn't you. (I like it, though. It tickles me. I laugh when I get such a letter. I laugh in a callous, delicate way. I see how things can go all haywire when we let ourselves grow too sensitive.)

Anaïs, Spring is here. I've been enjoying it. But in order to enjoy it I had to have you. Otherwise there wouldn't have been any spring for me. I've known other springs, black springs. And when I wrote that exultant letter to Emil, about being filled with the Holy Ghost, etc.—*et cetera*—I thought to myself how queer it is that we palm it off on the Holy Ghost. You are the Holy Ghost inside me. You make my spring. You make the Gare St. Lazare and my love for Paris. Do you know the way you sent me off yesterday? A little bit like I was your gardener. I took another detour after passing Bougival. I climbed up a tremendous hill—Jonchère, I think it was called. And there was a fine inn there, among the trees. A marvellous view. Out of the world completely. And I thought, forgetting all about my "discharge," that I would like to go there with you some afternoon toward twilight and have dinner there with you. I thought too of your remark once about showing you the streets—how we would think of that when it was too late. I thought of a lot of things as I climbed up the hill and then saw a most wonderful view. I saw the whole valley lying below and Louveciennes too. And I thought of you shutting yourself up in that then gloomy house and writing in your diary. And that really pained me. Because if you could have been with me on the hill everything would have been right again. It needed only a better perspective, a little altitude. Forgive me, I'm not trying to lord it over you. I'm stating it sincerely, as a fact, a spiritual fact. Yesterday I couldn't be crushed. Maybe today. Maybe tomorrow. You *can* crush a human being, if you try hard enough. But is that worthwhile?

As for causing you pain, that was furthest from my heart. Always will be. I could never deliberately, consciously, do you the least injury. You can walk over me, if you like—if that makes you feel better, stronger. But I won't walk over you. I get nothing from it. All the "good things" I got from you were intangible. They are the most lasting, imperishable. It would be utterly impossible for me to reject or deny them. One can't dispose of the great gifts . . . they remain with one.

Just as I write the above your telegram and money order arrive. I'm going out and telephone you, raise hell with you, and then I'm sending you this letter. I'm going to ask you to come here tonight, since you said Hugo was going away today. But when I get in the telephone booth I may get tongue-tied, and that's why I send you the letter. But please, Anaïs, don't rub it in—*"j'enverrai plus demain!"* That hurts. That puts me in a class with Bachman and all the rest. I don't want it. I won't have it. I'm going out now and telephone you and try to make you understand that it's you, only you yourself that I want. But you're angry now and you may not give me a chance. And it's hard for me to talk to you if you are grave and silent with me. It's so unnatural.

I want you to come to Clichy, if you can. *I want you.* You can keep the mystery. Only bring yourself. But if you send me more telegrams like that I'm going to give you the gate. *Je t'envois tout mon coeur et demain pas plus, rien que le coeur. Compris?*

HVM

[Louveciennes]
[May 29, 1933]

I'm full of you tonight, Henry, and sad because I would much much prefer to be going away with *you.* I realized today when you mentioned my trousseaux that everything I get I wonder whether *you* would like it. I do not ask myself if my father will. I am terribly far from my past and terribly close to you. It touched me that you should find the coffee doubly good. Everything will be doubly good on *our* vacation.

I'm really hungry for our vacation. Was it too *feminine* of me to want to see you every day because I felt your mood was greyish and I wanted you floating again. I don't want you tortured . . . even by a cold!

Saturday we'll go and choose records together, eh?

Send me my "Self-Portrait" letter which I left.*

Remember Lawrence's last words in the *Apocalypse*—something about being right with the Sun. What good will the Sun be to me? The Sun is O.K. for the man, the creator, the cosmic male etc. The woman

---

*The working title for *Black Spring,* which evolved from various segments of H. M.'s "Self-Portrait."

is so damned *personal* even the Sun must be incarnate in a man. In Henry for me.

A.

[Clichy]
[May 30, 1933]

[Anaïs:]

Just got your letter, this instant, and am answering at once. It must be I who make you feel sad. I felt that when I was leaving you yesterday. I wasn't all there exactly. I woke up in a fog and I remained in a fog. It isn't the cold. The cold is the result of something else. I must be tired out and showing it that way, I guess.

Anyway, yesterday when you were here, or was it day before?—and I was typing the remainder of those pages, suddenly I noticed that you had been stealing up alongside me and had put carbons in the paper for me. And when I noticed that, I was done for. *I was so touched.* Believe me, that is the height of self-abnegation. Nobody ever did *that* much for me. I was bowled over, I couldn't write any more, because I was thinking of that too deeply—and then I never mentioned a word to you of my feelings.

Nor did I even seem to be appreciative of your coming in and waking me up and all that. But I was. I would like you to come every day. Today I looked for you—I had got used to it. And then I remembered that you weren't free. Don't worry about buying records. That'll take care of itself gradually. Whether I want to or not, I suppose I'll be buying them. But I like getting them slowly, torturing myself a little, earning them, as it were. I feel I ought to write a hell of a lot before I go out and buy a record.

Today came a pathetic letter from Bachman detailing his miseries, his pilgrimage through a journey in the rain, without food, without soles on his shoes, etc. etc. I was not in the least affected. I laughed. I thought to myself—you are having a grand time and you don't know it. He threw away his overcoat, then his coat, he walks around in shirt and knickerbockers and begs food and lodging at night-lodgings and hospitals. Fine. Just the thing. A man ought to enjoy that, if he has any sense. So when he asks for 30 francs a month from Fred and myself each, I laugh. I won't send him any 30 francs. Not for postage, or toothpaste, or haircut, etc. He details all the necessary items of his existence. To hell with him. I am going to treat Bachman as I always said Lawrence should have had the courage to treat Magnus. I want to see him croak. Die in the gutter. It won't hurt a bit. I won't feel badly about his suicide. I think all the Bachmans of this world should come to an end. I'm going to help him put an end to himself. Because it wearies me to hear about his petty little miseries. And the itinerary he gave of his pilgrimage through Germany—a very pathetic account—I shall put in my next notebook. It looks interesting, authentic. Diary of a failure. A miserable one.

I wish I were going with you now to the Riviera. I feel the need of the vacation now. Need of the sunshine, indolence. I have come to some kind of a natural stop, I guess. It is only my will that keeps me on, keeps me *reading*, making notes. I really don't want to write. I'm a little fed up. But when the cold passes off I guess I will feel differently.

Anyway, here are the pages you spoke of, and some more—dream records.* I am indulging myself. I am going to the bookshop today and bind my manuscripts. I am buying little things for myself. That's how I feel. Shop your head off.

Henry

[Louveciennes]
[June 1, 1933]

[Henry:]

Putting carbons in your paper is not self-abnegation, it is merely sound and profound acknowledgement of value, a wise *critical* appreciation! It is the logical sequence of books about Lawrence etc., it's *intelligence*, not sacrifice! Don't be touched! Take it as such. Was thinking tonight of the tremendous expansion you make of small seeds, like the book on dreams. Here is a note I made about the dream quality: "The headlessness corresponds to what you described as absence of inhibition. Alraune deviated from the dream regions because I have so often the dream mood while awake and life has often that quality for me." You will do a bigger and less fictitious thing. I'm immensely fevered about it.

Thinking today of an amusing experiment: What would happen if instead of writing in the journal I should send you ten pages or so

---

*A. N. had suggested H. M. write down his dreams.

a day of "Self-Portrait"? Believe me, for a long time now I have written it for you. I feel that such a batch arriving on your loaded desk would be very bad. You need a woman, not a library! Henry, the real reason of the journal is always the feeling that people are too busy, are not interested in all I have to say and there is so damned much! Don't mind the journal. It is what makes me a person one can live with! What a joke if someday the world would read these pages that I have filled with what I thought uninteresting to others!

I like when I sit here in the evenings writing and Hugh turns on the radio and I say to myself: perhaps Henry is having music too. I see by your letter you do want to rest from writing. *Rest!* You've worked like a galley slave all winter. I give you absolution! Analysis says we need it, from somebody. I'll give it to you! For everything you do!

Anaïs

Bradley said you do far better "ejaculatory" writing than I—

[Clichy]
Sunday [June 18, 1933]

[Anaïs:]

I only realized when I got the telegram that you were really going. Sat down in a café at [the Métro station] La Fourche afterwards and went through strange emotions. When I see words like *"je pars"*—"good-bye" etc. it goes thru me like cold steel. I know it's only for a short while, but when one takes a voyage it always raises a question of other voyages—final voyages. It makes one inexpressibly and beautifully sad. I sat in the café and [. . .] scarcely realizing it, I was weeping. But that was momentary.

Everything's ok now and I'm looking forward to some interesting news from you. Those talks with your father! Tell me as much as possible, or rather as you feel free to divulge.

You remember when I left for Dijon? And how, immediately we started corresponding, it was Proust and Dostoevsky? Well, here it is again. Something about your departure impelled me to reread the [Samuel] Beckett book on Proust—with the result that today I copied some 28 pages. Am holding them up in the hope of annotating them generously. We started nebulously on Proust—now it seems crystal clear. But do you realize what a lot of mental work we have done this past year or so? I can see it now plain as day. These pages from Beckett form a fine supplement to the [Arnaud] Dandieu thesis.* He writes rather intricately at times—I think he will irritate you a bit. But the stuff is all there—well presented.

Did I tell you how good you looked in that new dress—with the Egyptian fandangles? You were dancing around me that day like the wind. I miss so much the fire and light you shed. Things seem to have gone dead since I left Louveciennes.

This must seem like a funny letter from me—the truth is I haven't a letter in me—for what reason I don't know. I feel rather blank. I don't find the name of your town in the *Larousse*. Is there such a place?

What did you mean by the *accident?* Did Hugo absent-mindedly try to kill you all off? You sounded upset.

Listen—this is all old stuff. Now you're somewhere in the sun, I suppose—tho' it's hard to believe, as the temperature has fallen here to almost winter. Tell me if it seems good there. Blow a little fresh air on me. And sunshine! Paris seems more gray than I have ever felt it.

Don't mind these drawings. I didn't do them. They look like Fred's.

When I see you I'll have started another Journal for you. Drink champagne! It's advertised in the *Tribune* as a "health" drink. Drink champagne while listening to Bach and Beethoven. It's a fine preventative.

I don't think I ever wrote such a dumb letter in my life. I can't help it. You'll have to excuse me. I'm defocalized.

Tomorrow! But love—lots of love. I miss you.

Henry

P.S. That's it—I miss you already so much. I'm absent. You said you were going away and I said "Sure, go!" but I didn't know what I was saying.

Don't let me make you miserable by this. Maybe it doesn't make you so miserable as I imagine. Have a good time—as you say to me so often. Really! Enjoy yourself. Drink in the sunshine. Don't let the buzzards back in Louveciennes worry you. What touched me—over the telephone—was your saying that your trunk wasn't packed. Imagine that! You who pack everybody's valise—and all those lazy bums

*Marcel Proust, Sa Révélation Psychologique (Paris: Firmon-Didot, 1930).

lying around and no one to pack your things. Things must have been sadly deregulated in Louveciennes.

Henry

Anaïs—

I'm in a frightfully temperamental mood. Can't do a thing. Can't even enjoy myself. Your letter, with check, which Theresa [the maid] mailed, only arrived today. Am waiting anxiously for a letter from the South—none has come so far.

What shall I do? I'm wretched. If the enclosed check had not been N.G. (because of discrepancy between written figure and numerical one, 300–350), I would have boarded a train and gone south today, to be somewhere near you. As I was pretty tight, I cashed the reserve check (dated June 4th)—I hope that's all right.

I'm all right as to funds, but I can't make a move unless I know how you stand. I hate telling you that I'm miserable, but it's the truth. Yesterday I couldn't even write you a letter. I just hate looking at words. Full up. Had I stayed in Louveciennes everything would doubtless have been all right. It was a crime being routed out suddenly like that.

Listen, do you want me to come down there—to St. Raphaël or St. Tropez? Is it beautiful, is it warm, inviting? To add to my depression let me say that the weather is at its worst here—rain, rain, rain. I could go mad.

Telegraph me what you think I should do. If you're low in funds, don't hesitate to say so. Maybe all I want is to hear from you. It seems so long ago since I left Louveciennes.

And perhaps if I just hear from you I can wait until the proper moment. I don't know what your plans are. But do write me at once. I'm in a sweat. Everything looks rotten to me. I *hate* Paris. Hate the whole world. Jesus, I don't know what's come over me.

This sounds childish and petulant. Forgive me. I love you— terribly. I wouldn't be able to do a damned thing without you. I've just realized that you're the whole world to me. And when I talked so glibly about my self-sufficiency I was just a braggart and a liar. So there you are.

Write quickly or telegraph. Is it going well with your father? I'm completely disoriented. *Love,*

Henry

[Clichy]
Thursday [June 22, 1933]

Anaïs—

This is after sending you the telegram. I am still here in Paris and I am going to stay here until it's time for me to meet you.

I have just had a warm bath and feel right again. Am going out on my bicycle for dinner. Just spent a good hour cleaning and oiling it. It sparkles.

So I figure I've had the trip! Been all over France again *in my imagination*—and feel quite sure that I had a better time of it *anticipating* my joys than realizing them. Anyway, I wasn't joyful—and I guess that's why I didn't go. It seemed like running away from something instead of going to something. And I can't do things in that state of mind. I can't hope to find peace etc. in traveling—*just traveling.* In fact, that makes one miserable.

It's very curious, my indecision. It's more like a phobia. And if I trace it back I think it started with my extradition from England. That, and partly too because when I pull out the maps and see myself riding the bike & stopping places—*in France*—I go all over the ride with June—which was so bitter. Just looking at the river Rhône, all those marvellous tours along the way, makes me sick at heart. I had thought of going to Carcassonne, had all the information—was going to take the 5 P.M. train this evening and get off at Orléans, ride to Augoulême and take the train again from there to Carcassonne. But again—the time is too short until the first, when you are free. I would be riding my head off just to cover ground—and what sense would there be in that?

So, I rest. And I'm quite content. I think I'll have a change of heart now and begin working again. After all, I didn't *earn* my vacation. Nothing was finished, as I had intended. I'm too boastful. And those last few days I've felt downright humble. I needed to be humbled. My vanity was getting too great.

You speak of meeting you in Marseilles (I haven't received your letter "express" yet). Must it be Marseilles? If not, and if a hundred or 2 hundred kilometers this way or that makes no difference I will suggest another place before you are ready to quit St. Raphaël. In fact, look up the fare to Carcassonne and see if that would be too much for you to lay out. You've sent me a pile and I ought to be able to get by until I see you, fare and all. Or maybe you have a place to suggest. I only say *not* Marseilles because really I don't think you would care for it either. It's a dirty thieves' den, full of bums, full of misery, full of wind. It has a semi-provincial air, too. There's only the Port, and that's for *men*—a place to knock around in.

It's funny. I have a hunch too that Hugo is going to drop in on you unexpectedly. Poor you! You must feel harassed—what with your father's gentle tyranny, Hugo's letters, my indecision, etc. It seems as though we all conspire to prevent your having a good time.

Don't think any more about my moods. I believe it's all over. My room looks like heaven. Can it be, by God, that I'm losing the taste for adventure, too? That would be terrible. A catastrophe. But I don't think it's so. Only, the thought of merely passing on from one town to the next, dragging my body along, as it were, seemed totally uninspiring. I'm a schizoid!

But every time this happens I appreciate still more that passage in *A Rebours*—that unfinished trip to London that ended in a restaurant.

Love—and keep your shirt on! Let your father devour you. It will give him dyspepsia. He has no idea what he's trying to bite off. More, shortly,

Henry

P.S. Is he disturbed by all these communications?

Grand Café Terminus,* Carcassonne
Maison la plus réputée de la région
Saturday [June 24, 1933]

[Anaïs:]

"*Vous croyez peut-être qu'on voyage pour son plaisir? Quelle erreur! Chacun de nous, dans son propre mesure, est victime de son imagination. Victime résignée, ou heureuse, ou pitoyable . . .*"

Thus commences *Mon Périple* of Elie Faure, which I started

*"This looks like a department store in Newark, N.J." reads a note by H. M. on the drawing of the hotel at the top of the stationery.

reading on the train. And it's devastatingly true. Carcassonne does not fit my preconceived image. Some cities strike one immediately, others exert their charms slowly, insidiously. But others again remain precisely what they appeared to be on first glance. I believe Carcassonne is one of them.

The great walled city *(la cité)* is fine in its way—one of the world's wonders maybe, but it is only a tiny part of the city of Carcassonne—situated about half an hour from the station. At the foot of the city are hovels, filled with the filthiest Spaniards imaginable. They cannot be the *real* Spaniards. They represent the evils of transplantation. And yet, I got a great kick being among Spaniards. I knew them at first glance—the bodies somewhat degenerated, somewhat scrungy, scavengy-looking, evil, suspicious, *malin. (First impressions!)* Three quarters of Carcassonne is of Spanish blood. Rich peasants. But no gaiety here. A very dead place—even now on a Saturday night! It would only disappoint you to come here. I must find another place—for us. Tomorrow I will ride about, explore, inquire. I have three tentative goals in mind—Toulouse, Perpignan or Avignon.

I don't mind a very small village being dead—that seems right. But when you have 30,000 inhabitants and on a Saturday night the streets are deserted, and not one café with music—there's something wrong. I wouldn't mind laying up with you in a fishing village. But no dead provincial towns! This is worse than Dijon—tho' the country roundabout is more pleasing.

The country has an appeal for me. I mean the Midi. Wherever these Catalonian people are. Wherever there are these low rolling hills, sombre trees, brown, reddish earth, old, old looking—so reminiscent of Caesar, Hannibal, of Druids, of early Greek settlements, of myth & folklore. The country is really sacred. . . .

And it's a crime to see large empty cafés with old duffers playing cards & billiards—and not a sound of music. It's wrong. I remember Arles. Same people, same tongue, same landscape. But a violence underneath.

In fact when day dawned this morning and I looked out of the train window, I had that same first sensation as when I first looked out on the Midi from the train in the neighborhood of Orange. It impressed me. Corresponded to some deep, inexplicable pre-vision. Something sad, classic, *Latin* about it. The Midi is the spiritual frontier of *all* the Latin peoples. It is French, Italian, Spanish. I have seen it in the Florentine paintings, and again in [Ignacio] Zuloaga & Velásquez. It goes very deep. It is touching.

The climate I like. Very hot mid-day—scorching—and then a cool night, almost shivery. And dry! They say it's been raining here for weeks—but one doesn't feel it in the air. The first burst of sun dissipates all the moisture. That's what I like.

I can see now, being this close, that I would surely like Spain. I can see why northern Spain is so different from Andalusia. It is part of this Midi country really. So is northern Italy—Tuscany. It is that sombre, heavy dark green, the brown earth, the huge clouds that hang threateningly over the landscape, the dull electric accumulation in the blood, waiting for a discharge, the hard rocky soil, the whole combination is like a prelude to the vernal Paradise of the tropics which is only a few miles distant. It is the last accumulated sadness of the northern soil & race—the prelude, as I say, to perpetual Spring—sun, flowers, heat. Jesus, I feel it all in the blood. This land is like a pleasant Purgatory, the vestibule to either Heaven or Hell.

A little thing like curtains in the doorway, these *beaded* curtains that tumble striped with violent colors, *à la Mexique,* impress me strongly. At last, the door removed! Imagine life without doors—just these tumbling beaded curtains with violent-colored stripes!

It is well to get out and travel, even if one is disillusioned. One needs to change the rhythm and the temperature and the food and the sky. Just for change itself. For refecundation. I was nervous & worried about going because I felt it would be a drain on your resources—but when I saw "telephone me, don't mind expense" etc. I got right up & packed my bag. That settled it. And that's what I really wanted to do—to go somewhere. Believe me, I look back on Paris and appreciate it even more. Paris is one of the real wonders of the world—a little universe in itself. One knows that immediately after one leaves it. And then too one realizes how truly gracious, intelligent, pleasing, gay, carefree are the Parisians.

Well—the food is excessive here. There are no restaurants under 11 frs. But what a meal for 11 frs.—*service compris.* Huge! Can't put it away. One course after another—and a *demi-bouteille* of wine always. Packed with onions and garlic. Result—fine, turgid languor. One walks around with *real physical* desire—not *mental* desire. It leaves you in a perpetual state of rut. Whereas everything in Paris combines to give you mental stimulation, imaginary desires, cerebral passion. Here it's food, sky, earth. The penis swells automatically, involuntarily. The air blows in on the naked body and electrifies the whole organism. (The walled city is secondary. You buy picture post-cards, souvenirs etc. Lapse back into literary dreams of the Middle

Ages.) When I rode this afternoon, on my wheel, to Trèves, the next town, I had again a distinct physical shock. Terribly fascinating village. Shockingly medieval. As if one were walking thru a fairy tale. And repulsive—and attractive. Filled me with a sense of the past which the great walled city failed to do. This town (Trèves) is unknown, unimportant *touristically*. But here is the real flavor. I walked thru narrow streets choked with dirty children (Spanish again), the mothers sitting outdoors nursing, a howling & screeching going on, music, shouts, curses, drunkards, violence, abrupt turns, filth everywhere, grim, stark, pullulating with life.

But I, an American, in my good clothes, couldn't live there. They'd murder me. They look out at you through heavy-lidded eyes, like snakes basking in the sun. I loved it. But I could never explain myself to them. In their eyes I'd always be just a "rich tourist."

Incidentally, the Elie Faure travel book has some splendid passages. I will show you. Especially about Mexico. He raves about it. Old Mexico. The old Maya country. *Quetzalcoatl*. You will be fascinated.

Think where you would like to go with me. You say you have no ideas. Is that possible? What causes that? My trouble is just the opposite, you know. I have too many places in mind usually—and that's what also brings about an indecision, a paralysis. Avignon is good—I know it a little bit. Maybe there are places west of Carcassonne in the general direction of Arcachon. *Think!*

Anyway, what I look forward to is a good tranquil spot where we can be quite alone and together, where we don't have to do things, and yet are not oppressed by the external scene. When I think of that little square near the Palais des Papes in Avignon, it seems just the place. Do you know it? I can see it very clearly. So quietly gay, so promising, and yet really nothing at all. A ferment in the air. Colored awnings. The grim battlements of the Palace yonder and the little Greek temple of a theatre.

Well, think . . . !

The telephone at the Hotel Bristol, which is just opposite the Gare, is F.24. You gave me a wrong number for your hotel phone. It's 0-37, I believe. That caused some of the delay this evening.

And listen, Anaïs—"tampis" is spelled *tant pis*—2 words.

I wish you were here now. The food, the soil, the sky, it's making my blood think.

Henry

The tariff is reduced one-half on phone calls after 7:30 p.m. If you should want to phone me, for any reason, why do it bet. 7:30 and 8 p.m. But I suppose you can't very well.

P.S. That note your father left for breakfast—swell! Jesus, he's courting you with a vengeance.

> Grand Café de France, Perpignan
> Tuesday [June 27, 1933]
> *En route*

Anaïs—

Writing this between trains. Just arrived a few hours ago and knew immediately it was not the place for me. Do you think me fickle? Believe me, very disappointing here. Nothing Spanish about it, except the names. A bastard region that is neither this nor that. So I am going to Avignon, of which I have pleasant memories and hope it will not prove disappointing. Will mail this from there, giving you my address and telephone number—between 7:30 and 8 p.m. I will stick around in case you can call.

Only got your letter after dispatching telegram from Carcassonne this morning. Very sorry to hear about your father. That just about ruins your vacation.

Do you expect him to remain ill for some time? Would you prefer that I came to St. Raphaël? I am assuming that you will be free about the first! But if not, if you have to be a nurse, then why shouldn't I go near you? But try to get away, if possible, without leaving him to die. What is his trouble?

I know you can't write, and it's all right. I'll write you. I look forward with a little more hope to Avignon. It's small, but there was something about it once intrigued me. Perhaps I am getting spoiled. Certainly I see no use staying in squalid provincial towns just to pass the time.

It is too bad we could not have gone to Spain. There I am sure it would have been grand—even Barcelona. But these imitation Parises are frightful. Morbid. It makes one realize that 9/10 of humanity is moronic—just beast and plant. If the earth is theirs, then let them have it.

I get in Avignon early in the morning. Will drop this off from there with full particulars on awaking.

9 A.M. Looks good to me here and I like the region. Bull fights (real ones) in Nîmes nearby. *Tarascon* next station. Small, lively. Cafés open all night. People on streets at 1 a.m. More this evening. *Hotel du Midi.*

Henry

P.S. I could have called you but since you are nursing your father I thought it best to let you call me when you are free.

Café de la Gare, Avignon
Thursday [June 29, 1933]

[Anaïs:]

After telephoning you. Find that there is a train leaving St. Raphaël at 11:03 a.m. and arriving *direct* at Avignon at 15:39 p.m. In the afternoon there is one at 14:20 p.m. leaving St. Raphaël, arriving here at 19:26 p.m. You can make it quicker on the second train if you change at Marseilles.

So let me know by which train you are coming and I will meet you at the station Sunday.*

I have a room at 15 frs. per day, but will change it for a slightly better one Sunday. It's hard to find anything very cheap. I'm wrong about it costing less or the same as Paris. It is only so if you take pension rates, which I haven't done, or couldn't do because I didn't know how long I would remain in any one place.

I'm getting short now and would like it if you could telegraph me something on receipt of this—Friday. The long jumps from Carcassonne to Perpignan and then here ate into my purse heavily. I owe here for my room, one meal (which I ate while waiting for your call) and a telephone call of 9 minutes. Still have about 80 frs. in my pocket. But if they should hand me the bill unexpectedly I wouldn't be able to pay it.

---

*After visiting her father in the South of France for nine days, A. N. joined H. M. in Avignon on July 2. From there they traveled together via Grenoble to Chamonix. Miller left the Hotel du Fin Bec on July 10, shortly before A. N.'s husband arrived for a vacation, and planned to do some traveling on his own.

I am going now to Tarascon on the wheel. Went to Orange yesterday. Fine old town with interesting Roman ruins. I think you will like it here. If not, we will go elsewhere. I didn't understand where you said you were to meet Hugo—only "the mountains."

I'm waiting anxiously for you. It seems like Purgatory in between. Being alone is not much fun.

You may still have time to drop me a line on receipt of this. If there is much news, do so. In any case, I will reserve a larger, quieter room for us for Sunday on. I am on the street and it is more noisy than Clichy. But in the rear it is o.k. And the little square is fine—I remember the place so well.

Maybe you will want to hire a bicycle and go places? We'll see. Anyway, hurry!

Henry

[Clichy]
Sunday [July 16, 1933]

Anaïs,

Suppose you were amazed to hear that I had returned so soon. I got as far as Tours with Fred and gave it up. Fed up with travelling. Fed up with little provincial towns, and with nature especially. I'm a man of the big cities, sorry to say. I realize it now only too well.

Whether it was my physical condition, or Fred, or state of mind, I don't know, but everything seemed flat and uninteresting to me. We left Thursday by train, got off at Orléans in the late afternoon and began to ride. In an hour or so I was completely exhausted. Could hardly push on to the next town—18 kilometers away. The principal reason was the wind. A steady and strong wind from the ocean that knocked me out. This all the way to Tours.

I started in a nervous condition. When I arrived at Clichy from my first trip I found a note from my uncle Dave Leonard saying he was in Paris. I had to search for him, as he had already moved from his hotel, his wife being in the hospital. Spent considerable of my little time with him, which wore me down. Left after a few hours' sleep.

And then, immediately I started, I realized I had made a mistake to go with Fred. We don't hit it off at all. Nothing to say to each other. He rides on a mile ahead of me and grumbles because I am all in. It wasn't merely fatigue—it was exhaustion. I don't understand it.

Consequently, the Valley of the Loire looked rotten to me. And the castles didn't attract me in the least. Nothing looked good. Add to that that we had hideous rooms, slept two in a bed, no running water etc. In Blois I slept in the dirtiest hotel room I ever saw. Filthy! That discouraged me a lot.

Finally arrived in Tours (I had to go by bus while Fred rode the wheel). I asked myself what was I doing there. Felt homesick for Paris, for the quiet of my room, my books, the music, work—mental activity. Felt that I had disintegrated into some form of vegetable matter.

When Fred arrived I had already bought my train ticket. I left him looking wistful and pathetic, which enraged me all the more. What claim has he on me?

Coming back in the train I felt fine. Began to think, to meditate. Read a letter of Bachman's which I had neglected to read for several days. Finally tore it up, without finishing it. Too many details. He said he wrote you too. I'd ignore it if I were you.

And so today, my first day back, I enjoyed my room, the bath, the victrola, the books. Just glad to be back again. To be alone. Not "making" tours!

Am writing you from the most interesting café I have seen in ages. Chez Boudin—right around the corner from that cheap theater I recommended you to. Most diverse clientele—chiefly negroid: trap drummers, dancers, ham actors, pimps, whores, gamblers, fairies. Like Harlem almost. The conversations are rich. Unimaginable! I find all this so much more appetizing than châteaus and churches. Human beings! Not relics.

I'm so fed up with the provinces, *French* provinces. I have no more curiosity about France. Should I ever travel again it will be to see something utterly different. I know France inside out now.

I'll write you more in detail by machine tomorrow. Today I couldn't type. Just felt too good to do nothing. But I feel serious. I know I can work again. I've had my fill.

This is just to let you know I'm alive. You must have wondered why I didn't write sooner. Somehow I postponed giving you an address because I felt I would return soon.

What was the high spot? Chamonix! That view out the window. The peace of it. The good mountains. *You.* Your indulgence. *You* are a marvellous travelling companion. I wonder a great deal how you are finding it now. Are you bicycling? Is the snow still on the mountain tops?

You know, the famous Touraine is unimpressive. Flat, fertile and dull. All healthy places are dull. I wanted so much always to visit Chinon, Rabelais' birthplace. But tho' I was only a few kilometers from it, I had no desire to see it. Between the "literature" of Rabelais and the countryside I find little affinity. Rabelais had a gigantic imagination. Touraine is empty. And her castles are empty. The life is departed.

Tonight I saw a touching picture. Recommend it to you if it should pass your way—*Je Vous Aimerai Toujours.* Very, very human. I wouldn't stay to see the rest of the program for fear of spoiling my mood.

Finally—in the letter Emil sent me I found some old souvenirs of my past. He enclosed a batch of letters from my first wife. I glanced over them, found them tediously stupid and practical, and destroyed them without a qualm.

My "Cinema Vanves" article is amateurish, but contains some interesting material and I feel almost tempted to do it over.* More tomorrow. Am wondering if you are still in Chamonix?

Henry

[Annecy]
[July 16, 1933]

[Henry:]

Strange feeling it gave me, to read [Georges Duhamel's] *Salavin* when you were gone—Salavin who resembles you when *"il contemplait le pauvre sire avec une intérêt poignant, et, dans son coeur, grandissait un indicible désir d'être aussi cet homme si seul et si bas qu'il ne redoute plus ni l'abandon ni la chute."* Who resembles you when you are joyless and springless. You have his moods. It is no wonder you were thoughtful, afterwards. It made me weep. Those bitter reproaches of Salavin, at the end. But you notice he resents that having given all his ideas to Edouard was like throwing them in an abyss. When you marked all the reproaches against Edouard's gifts, were you thinking of yourself and June? Have I at least been able to help you *without* weakening you? It seems to me that Salavin is *more* humiliated because Edouard serves

---

*First written in 1930. H. M. had intended to use some of the material in *Tropic of Cancer,* but eventually recast it as an article.

him without comprehension. *That* is important, not the fact that he put his strength at Salavin's service but that he enslaved Salavin to nothingness, to a friend who was inadequate.

The material is only a symbol of a deeper dissatisfaction—a dissatisfaction with *all* that the man represented—like yours against June. But tell me that between us there will never be those bitter and unjust feelings about *gifts.* For they are unjust—their aim is *beyond* strength and weakness—it's strength of being against strength of fact. Salavin ought to have reproached Edouard simply for being Edouard, and insufficient, not for anything else.

I crave a liberation from your material dependence—so that *you* may be free of all shackles, if they are shackles. But it seems to me that between us there is an interdependence which balances and ennobles— eradicates measurements. The day we reproach each other it will be not for either weakening or enslaving or encroaching on or deforming each other, but merely for failing to be what the other needs. And that will be even more serious—also more just.

[With Salavin and Edouard] it's the injustice, the unfocussed, the unessential, the blundering in [their] friendship which hurts—they don't know *what* they can reproach each other for. It's worse than what is stated. "I reproach you for being Edouard," *tout simplement,* for not satisfying me. Poor Edouard, giving what he alone could find to give— since he had no ideas!—knowing or sensing his inadequacy, his *other* poverty.

Et pour comble, it rained all day. So, like Salavin, I wanted to sleep until the Spring—so tired I was with pity, all kinds of pities . . .

Annecy. Sunday. We moved because the altitude kept Hugh awake all night. He is very tired and needs a lot of care.

Annecy is beautiful. Venice—Bruges—Holland. Canals, old houses, lake—a castle—boats—

I'm sorry I did not ask you to telegraph me immediately. It will be many days before I hear how you are.

I'm writing quickly—not knowing when Hugh will return. It was raining and so I excused myself. We have rented bicycles. We are changing hotels again. Too much noise for Hugh.

I'm tired of changing. I would like to be back in Louveciennes in our studio, talking with you. I thought afterwards *our* vacation had not been perfect. I shouldn't have been ill. We should have had more love, more palatial rooms, more of everything—more time, and no telephone with Paris! Mont Blanc is the highest mountain in Europe. That was definitely superlative!

If you should want to stay 3 weeks with Fred tell me, then I would stay here—not return until you do.

The 14th of July in Chamonix was colorful. Italian gypsies. Fairs. Dancing. A lot of dashing types arrived for the 14th. The Outa was full and elegant. Hugh got me the Russian picture frame I was in love with. I took him to the café and he enjoyed it. I was passing on to him the little joys I owe you. It was good I left Chamonix. I was all the time thinking: Here I came with Henry. Here I sat with Henry. Henry liked this etc.

I am cured of the love of autocars. We nearly lost our lives coming to Annecy. 3 hours on mountain roads, up 1,500 feet, always skirting precipices, [crossing] narrow bridges that trembled, passing other auto-cars and having to ride way over [to] the edge to pass—once we skidded slightly over—everybody screamed. It was raining too—slippery. Infernal. I wanted to get off and walk. Would have given anything to have been on my own feet. I arrived a wreck, as after a nightmare. Never again. And turns, turns like Coney Island [rides]—and at each turn a car facing you—another giant, on a road made for one car. And tunnels. And light wooden bridges over huge waterfalls.

Your letters will be forwarded here. Write me "Annecy, Poste Restante." Isn't it amazing about Bachman? He begs me to write him in such a tone that I will do so today. So happy his fate is settled. He tells me he gives you all the details. I told him we didn't answer his letters because you were travelling on your bicycle and I with my father and he had given us a temporary address. No use hurting his feelings. But *ouf,* I felt a load off my chest to think he didn't starve to death.

Monday. Leaving for Aix-les-Bains in an hour. Hugh doesn't like Annecy.

Got your telegram today. Waiting for your letter.

Miss you terribly, Henry, my love. Write me "Aix-les-Bains. Poste Restante."

A.

[Clichy]
Monday [July 17, 1933]

[Anaïs:]

No letter from you since Friday! Sent you a telegram at noon, fearing something was amiss—that you were ill or that I had offended you unwittingly. Perhaps you addressed the envelope absent-mindedly!

Anyway, I am sitting in the café at Muette [Métro station], where I used to meet you. Stumbled on it after exploring the neighborhood around Avenue Henri Martin—all those streets named after poets, musicians, generals and admirals. What a different Paris this is! So tony! Hard to believe there are still people in the world who can afford to live in these mansions.

I haven't written any more since the first instalment I sent you because Wambly Bald has been with me last two days. I have been helping him write his *last* column. He came back from his vacation determined to give up his column.* Also refused a better job upstairs on the editorial staff. Because I had once told him he was better off as a proofreader!

Fred returned yesterday, with a dose of clap! From a waitress in Angoulême who had given him a good time on the promise that he would pray for her at Lourdes. (Of course this is confidential. You're not to commiserate [with] him or mention it in any way. He would be mortified.)

I'm feeling quite all right again. The proof is I enjoy Paris again—just sauntering about carelessly. And that I have wet dreams. For a while I thought I had lost everything—writing, passion, curiosity—etc. But no! Only a temporary condition. I feel luxuriously lazy. Not tiredly so. Enjoying my laziness, as it were.

And I'm giving attention to my room. Having the bookcase installed, the lamp rack, a new desk (a big one with drawers!), a rattan curtain (such as you suggested)—*tout ce qu 'il fait.* I'm going to live and work and have my being there. If you get a press in Louveciennes† I'll ride to & fro on my wheel. Why not? I must live in Paris. I need the hum and roar, the excitement, life, change, diversion of a big city. I realize that it is for me what the sea is for a sailor. I swim in it.

---

*For a number of years Bald contributed a weekly column, "La Vie de Bohème," to the Paris edition of the Chicago *Tribune.*
†Plans to set up their own press did not materialize.

Discovering a new street in Paris, or a new café, is much more interesting to me than visiting an old château or cathedral in some godforsaken hamlet.

I look forward impatiently to seeing you, talking to you, and other things. I almost wish winter were here, with its artificial cerebral stimulation. Sunshine is only a restorative—not a stimulus to work. I would write more but I am ashamed to ask for more paper. *Love.*

Henry

P.S. I suppose you too are fed up with vacationing. Tho' if you are free in September & wish to go somewhere—*fine!* I'm with you.

[Clichy]
Tuesday [July 18, 1933]

[Anaïs:]

Just got your letter. Hope you get the one I sent to Chamonix.

You can't imagine how strange it seems to sit down and type. I'm so surprised that the machine doesn't make a louder noise. It's been a struggle to sit down and write. I came back, as I wrote you, feeling utterly exhausted. The feeling is wearing away, but I am far from being ebullient. And yet this is what I want—to be at the machine. The rest is a nightmare. As I said to you once, it is a marvel to see how Lawrence moved from place to place, always writing. And you do it too. The moment I get away from my accustomed place, see strange things, breathe different airs, I cease being for a while. I drink in and am suffocated by all the new sensations. The most real moments for me, during my trip, were the reading of Faure and Duhamel. Only then was I really myself. The rest of the time I was just a body, and the sensations never floated up to my brain. [. . .]

To love anything, to appreciate anything, one has to live with it. Otherwise it has no meaning, no beauty. I like Tarascon so much because there was nothing there to see. It was a deserted village, and the woman who sold me the postcards, she said it was always thus. Splendid. Just dead. Nothingness. That is a relief in a country of ruins and relics and monuments and châteaux and cathedrals. Nothing. An empty village. And wind-swept street, the dogs dozing in the sunshine, the tabletops dusty, the windows barred and shuttered. The hotel I wanted to stop at was like a morgue inside. I didn't tell you that. I was reserving that for you as a treat. [. . .]

About Salavin. Do you know the upshot of *Le Club de Lyonnais?* It is that Salavin goes off, deserts his wife, to live among men—not to reform them, but to assuage them, to drop a word of comfort here and there. [. . .]

Perhaps it is a realization of the futility of altering men or things. That ripe speculative attitude which accepts life for what it is, and demands nothing more. Only with full consciousness, not out of inertia, or indifference.

Anyway, the feeling in me is strong now—that it is the Lawrencian desire to alter men which causes more havoc than good. It is blindly egotistical and neurotic. I notice that the desire to reform moves man away from his neighbor, and not towards him. It leads to isolation. To concern for the self. When one has grown utterly weary of trying to aid men one returns to the flock and then one really aids—just by his presence, because then the sum of experiences, of suffering, of self-analysis and soul-struggle have mellowed the individual and he can aid because he speaks and moves out of a ripe, conscious wisdom—not through precepts, ideas, formulas. I'm thinking that perhaps the root of all dissension between "friends" (subject so engrossing to Lawrence and Duhamel) is the quality of idealism contained in it. It is again a too sacred, too private, too isolated thing. Pure love, pure friendship—these are ideals. These may exist now and then, and they are beautiful things to behold. But they are not goals. They are phenomenal and accidental. They should be regarded as one regards the phenomena of Nature—Mont Blanc, Niagara Falls, the great caves etc. One should go to them for rest or inspiration. Not to dwell there.

When two men, such as Edouard and Salavin, form an eternal pact they are alienating themselves from the rest of mankind. Which is a sin. You notice that the tie which held them together kept them aloof from the rest, made them contemptuous of the others, full of hatreds and resentments, of invidious comparisons, etc. If love of friendship does that, then it is no good. So I imagine, at any rate.

[Henry]

Helder Hotel, Rue Franklin
Aix-les-Bains
July 20, 1933

[Henry:]

I'm glad you are back where you want to be. I don't really believe the places you went to were bad—châteaux, Carcassonne etc. It was your mood. You were in a discontented mood, like some of Lawrence's. Strange for you who always finds something interesting everywhere. What a contrary and stifling mood.

I had thought you would feel worse to stay in Paris while I, Fred and everybody else were wandering. You had envied Bachman. At least don't have regrets for the places you didn't see! They, too, would have looked wrong to you. I believe you wanted something else, or perhaps didn't know what you wanted. But realize it wasn't the *place*, but the mood.

Faure and Duhamel, I have been living in both. I like what you say: ". . . the Lawrencian desire to alter men which causes more havoc than good. It is blindly egotistical and neurotic. I notice that the desire to reform moves man away from his neighbor, and not towards him. It leads to isolation" etc. I love all this. It is *very wise*, very wise and true.

And you add this: *"The* root of all dissention between friends is the quality of idealism contained in it." Very fine. The idealism which criticizes, demands, exacts, complains, enforces, drives, measures. Damn this idealism. Let people *be*—let them alone. You have a gift for that uncriticalness in general (not in particular! In particular you too are a fault-finding idealist!).

I believe, oh, I believe what you say about aloofness. "We are placed in the world to be part of it, to be nourished, and to nourish." All of us, Lawrence etc. seek the *eternal* friendship, the *eternal* love with which to *withdraw* from the world.

I didn't mean Duhamel should point out the inadequacy of his friend. No. Either accept him or leave him alone. I mean what you say: not seek that ideal two-beinged aloofness which is sterile. I meant that Duhamel's friend was "inadequate" because there *are* certain people it is worthwhile retiring from the world with, for a while, as a profound all-engulfing experience. Notice I said for a while! Duhamel's experience was not even that . . . poor man. Edouard had less to supply to that exchange and world-creating union.

Anyway, you are writing more pages on "Lawrence." They could apply to your reading of *Aaron's Rod* in the future! All that you wrote about friendship was really good. A fine sharp shaft at idealism, all that nonsense about the one and only love, the one life—long friendship etc. Splendid. A plea for "flow" in love as well as in friendship. For movement which nourishes. Anti-static. Bravo.

I read. I write in my Journal because I have to talk to somebody and even you snuffed me out in the Avignon terrace café. The Journal always resuscitates, receptive to the "uncalled for"!

Strange days which I am shortening by a passion for gambling. I feel in Dostoevsky's skin. Every evening, after dinner, I get feverish. I put on my watery black satin dress. I walk to the Casino. The green table. The ball rolling on a big round cup. Music from the dancing in the salons. Hugh gave me only 50 frs. the first night but I made 500 frs. with two shots. I was flushed. Everybody was watching me. (It's a small game—not like roulette—the highest sum made is 3,000 frs.) In the middle of that night I wake Hugh up to say to him: Tomorrow I will play on the 4. And I did. And I won 300 frs. first shot. And I'm playing tonight, on the 3. But Hugh takes all the money away from me because we are so short that we were planning to leave for home—and I was certainly willing, but then we received something from Hugh's sister for his birthday, and he wants to stay. However, he has promised to give it all back to me. In Annecy we were short already, and Hugh borrowed on his next salary. I'm a little anxious about your checks. I hope they are O.K. And on the 25th the salary will be deposited, so I am sure you will be safe. I have a feeling I will get the 3,000 frs.

The women are ugly and envious, skeletons choking in pearls. They seem to think I am too fortunate. Aix-les-Bains is too proper—too *ancien régime*. I'm out of place. I went out in my pajamas as they did in Chamonix and was almost jailed. Such fine pants, Henry, in black, with a red shirt. I look like an Apache.

It's raining, *Dieu merci,* so I can write. Otherwise we would be at the beach—the Lac Bourget inspired Lamartine. Oh Lac! etc. something about the passing of time. A sad poem. I want the time to pass—so eager to be in Louveciennes and at work. Will you see Bradley? And Rank?

Anaïs

Coirier's Grand Hotel*
Valescure-St. Raphaël
Sunday, July 2[3], 1933

[Henry:]

Yesterday on the road there was a man pushing a wheelbarrow. On the wheelbarrow a barrel full of turquoise liquid. With a sprayer, he sprays the insecticide over the vines. The vines turn a blue-mauve-green tone. Beautiful. He also sprays the faces of the houses, incidentally, when there are vines over the mouths of the houses. The spray falls back over him, so that his cap is turquoise colored, his shoulders, his neck, his hands. Turquoise! Can you imagine what pleasure to meet this turquoise-colored man, a barrel overflowing with this color, a wheelbarrow stained with it? The man who goes about painting the world! I have seen the world being painted, quietly, while the sun splashed. To paint the world, the vines, the houses, one's self. I would like to come immediately and spray your moods turquoise. I will come to you splashed with sun. The man with the turquoise cap walks through my dreams. If he can paint the vines we thought everlastingly fixed in green, I can paint your moods, your butcher-red Clichy away.

Why so much *distance* between us? Why do we not click on time? Why do you say you don't understand what I write you about? Above all, why do you force yourself to write me? Such forced letters don't make me happy. I am not a woman you should force yourself to write to. I would rather you slept. You are cross at everything, cross at yourself for wanting to sleep. I'm preparing a barrel full of joy, of drunkenness for you, of turquoise paint. I will splash it all over you, Monday night. I am coming alone. Hugh has to go to Geneva. Don't write me any more forced letters. They disillusion me. I [would] rather have none. I don't like your dragging yourself to your typewriter. I have done nothing to deserve your lack of enthusiasm. Moods, I forgive and understand moods. I let them pass. I don't attribute them to a period. It is the world before the man passed with a turquoise cap and a sprayer, spraying color and illusion. Don't offend the illusion by writing forced letters. Let things flow. I'm preparing a daring mixture. Caricatures of

---

*Though written on hotel stationery from St. Raphaël, where A. N. visited her father earlier, the context seems to indicate that it was written from Aix-les-Bains, probably July 23.

Aix, the casino, sunbathers, the American Apollo who followed us from Chamonix, stories, a feeling I have that from August on things will be sparklingly alive again. As I said before I am glad there is only one Seventh Day in the week—only one day of rest. This is my one day of rest. When I return we will drink to the sun—drink to your pages on Nudism which you wouldn't live up to, to your spittings on health, the sun, nature, to your contradictions and your perfect pages, to the man with turquoise paint on his hands, to this act of painting vines which are growing, painting leaves which are trembling, painting moods which are drooping, living, pushing a barrel, walking, drinking sun.

Anaïs

I can go on because the P.O. is closed. I had forgotten it was Sunday. Wanted to mail you this immediately. I get a strange, distressed feeling when we lose our closeness. Never mind.

I was very pleased with the books, although I have not had time to read them. They look and feel very savory. Will begin them soon. I have very little time for reading, and more in the mood for dreaming. Faure on Mexico, specially, affected me for days. A powerful impression. China too, but less. Mexico, his Mexico, is a splendor, and enough to last one a lifetime—images, symbols, philosophies. Wonder what your Mexico would be. And mine. I know quite definitely now that I will have to see the whole world for myself. Nobody else sees it as I do, nobody can tell me about it. I'm waiting for your "Tour de France."

It strikes me you are still hovering between an external and an internal world. You don't know whether or not to take *yourself* around. I'll make this clear when I see you. Faure takes his *vision* with him, but not his moods. I take my moods and all of myself. You sometimes describe things as the man of the street sees them—on the flat—and sometimes you prophesy and Spenglerize etc. And other times, like the last, you are a victim of a mood, a mood that does not quite know what to attack, what to kill.

If you can, see a movie called *Tuer pour Vivre.* Superb show of animals' cruelty. How the ant is eaten by the rat, the rat eaten by the snake, the porcupine swallows the rat and the snake, the lion eats the porcupine, and the alligator the frog etc. etc. Wonderful scenes of thirst in the jungle, fire in the forests, night owls, bats etc. We saw that in Annecy.

I sent you some P.L.M. [French Mediterranean Steamship Line] posters. Saw one in blue on Algérie which I loved. Man could not take it off show window but gave me another. I thought they would amuse you for a few days on the walls of your room.

My father is reading Lawrence in French and getting a false impression, of course, so now I am busy defending Lawrence in French, explaining him in French etc. That refreshes all I have to say—a new language, a new attitude. New formulas.

If you walked through Henri Martin explore rue Heinrich Heine where I will live next winter. House with colored-stone windows. I don't know the number.

I liked all you wrote about music. But what I think most about is all you wrote about isolation. Faure expands on this theme of synchronizations of nations beautifully, with his "spiritual synthesis" etc. Beautiful preface.

You don't really mean that Duhamel has done it all better than Lawrence—the friendship theme—where is your love of the stuttering man, the obscurities, the chaos—where your hatred of that *"café filtre"* quality of French literature? So beautifully *filtre*, sifted, that, like my own way of handling Lawrence, it leaves room for a German elephantine volume to be written?

You are not taking starving men home any more not because you're indifferent but because you have more important things to do. It was your work which crowded out Bachman—not your lack of sympathy. That is good—that you are preserving yourself for your work. I think Bachman is a little too vain & proud not to be able to appear before the notaries as he is. He does not know yet what real suffering is. He dodges it. Like the crab, he sinks into the sand and calls for help. I am sorry I wrote him—I'm not interested in him, but he seemed so desperate that I had stopped writing.

Then I get your telegram and I can't quite make out your state of mind. Did you think your letter would make me anxious etc. and did you want to reassure me? I don't know. I hate to see you in a *drab* country—relatives, hospitals etc. It is time I come and save you! Can't let you breathe drab air. Anything else, dirt, foulness, crime, yes, but no dullness.

A.

Helder Hotel, Rue Franklin
Aix-les-Bains
Monday A.M. [July 24, 1933]

[Henry:]

Is there such a word in English as "fabulation" or "confabulation"? I saw it in French and I liked it.

I could not get interested in [Gérard de] Nerval. *Trop léger.* Meringue. (When I return we will go and have a frosted chocolate together. And an orgy of records.)

I write you as in a journal. Whenever I have a moment I add a little. . . .

I have become a personage at the Casino. Known as the "lucky woman" who looks like a drug addict. The croupier, the cashier, the ball thrower, all greet me so excitedly. They like me because I bring excitement to the game. Immediately a group forms to watch me and to play on the numbers I choose. The "Apollo" (you saw him in Chamonix) and a gigolo who is off duty for the moment stand guard. They have not been able to talk to me yet! Hugh is amazingly watchful! Tonight I won 77 frs. but I lost all I won by continuing to play—lost my usual wisdom, became feverish.

Then we come "home" and turn on the radio Hugh bought. And I read Rank with profound delight.

Got a letter from the girl who will do the copy work in August. She is reasonable and I have engaged her.

Hugh will go to New York in October. If I can visit my father in September I may be able to be with you all October.

Monday. Just got your letter. "Cinema Vanves" is interesting— just a little bit "listless," but as you say, it is the beginning and your wheel is always slow in beginning, only to reach afterwards tremendous power—so it is O.K. I'm happy that you are writing. I understand your discontent better now. Your letter was alive.

I don't understand why you don't see me as a gambler—afraid of consequences etc. Nobody would know better than I what to do with 10,000 frs! Or a fortune.

Hugh is doing my father's horoscope. He is born under Libra, *comme moi et Oscar Wilde!*

No, I didn't read [the article in the *Psychoanalytical Review*] about Napoleon.

(On Napoleon: Since I read that he had a soft slushy female body I've lost interest in him. I dislike plump slushy bodies in men as you hate masculinity in women. *Trop mou.* Oscar Wilde too. *Trop mou.*)

Wondering today why—if we are all haunted by our first love—if it isn't only because we have not possessed it. We should all, at some time or other, live conjugally, sexually, etc. with our chosen first love and we would quickly be cured of our obsession. It's only the lure of the unattained. The illusion. Your mother is the only woman you will never know, sexually, as a woman. The fragments of her in other women (if you say so) only augment the halo of the unknown. I say, let us fuck our parents and thereby rid ourselves of them. Fucking shadows of them accomplishes nothing. Only why, if you are beginning to see this theme in your life, did you always say you couldn't understand what I was talking about that day in the garden when I sent you away?

I am going to have one roof-raising talk with Rank on the subject. I'm going clear, plumb to the bottom of it. I'm ready for a superb encounter with Rank—art will be dragged in, too—*tout.* I want a violent and thorough coming to grips with it. I don't think anybody has.

I see you, then Rank, immediately. I have a lot to say to him—but incognito.

I lie in my sunbath in the cabin next to Princess of Rumania— wife of Nicolas. Nicolas puts all his money on the same number as I do. He leaves when I leave. It's all very dime novel.

P.S. Just got your telegram and answered it immediately. Terribly sorry I worried you. You had said "writing again" and I was waiting for the second letter, feeling, as you guessed, a little discouraged by your letter. Then Sunday came in between, I kept the letter I was writing you until this morning. I had already begun this one. As you can see I was a bit off key myself, hurt by imaginary things therefore ironic. But it's all over.

Sending this off immediately.

A.

[Henry:]

Yes, I have been playing possum here—I'm no real *marmotte*. As soon as you write to me about the City I get a fever. When I hear a fragment of *"Chanson d'Amour,"* floating on the Lake, I get restless. Recuperation, renovation—I was repaired after three sunbaths. And now, as you guessed well, I am fed up with Golden Syrup skins, with standing my bicycle on its ear, with paying 30 centimes for certain letters which contain nothing. Not yours! Yours make me want to be in Clichy, Monday night. During my sunbath I open my legs and think of you.

I'm enjoying Chagall's *Ma Vie*. Pictorially strong—humanly savoury. Rank I cannot read here because I need continuity. Here we are moving constantly—climbing up the Solarium, climbing down, lunch, the café, Japanese billiards, short siestas, bicycle tours—I can do acrobatics on it now, sing. Explaining Lawrence to the Padre, writing down his horoscope at café tables at rest periods. I carry your letters about on the frontal basket of my bicycle, and Chagall and the Journal. How I like this and how it fits you: *"J'avais l'impression que nous rôdons encore sur la surface de la matière, que nous avons peur de plonger dans le chaos, de briser, de renverser sous nos pieds la surface habituelle."*
You have no *such* fears. I have already said this about you in other words but I also used breaking up—*briser*, you notice.

A.

[Henry:]

Rushing this off to you with the check.
Writing you only during the time it takes for Hugh to dress—may cut it off unexpectedly, like the letter I sent you the day before yesterday, so you would have news oftener.
Enjoyed your philosophical letter, and understand your pursuit of wisdom, in Duhamel, in Faure, in China.
I won't answer you on travelling. Neither will I defend monu-

ments. The love of monuments, relics, deeply understood, is *evocative*—I have lost all interest in them, except historically. I know the phase during which I loved them was a historical one, and right. I could stand in one of those castles and smell a whole period. And reading Spengler afterwards, who gave significance and the symbolical meaning of houses, cathedrals, gardens, mosques etc., augmented the power of this feeling. The imagination can be stirred by an Egyptian mummy, Indian spear, an arcade, a dress that is falling to dust, a broken vase, an armless statue. Instead of fuming against the tourist, the organized and effusive conscientiousness etc. I went about ruminating the past, eating it, digesting it, reflecting it, and then it was finished. As Spengler said, each man who evolves, traverses in himself all the different phases of history. I went through all that—an awe, a respect, a wistful reliving, retraversing of as many centuries as I knew something about . . . very few. It was beautiful, and it is dead now. Today I can agree with you. I was more interested in the whore street than in the Palais des Papes. I feel that reading Spengler is all we need to know of the past. But from this to a renunciation of voyages—No. You are a pessimist, Henry. It isn't Egypt I will go and see, but the wonderful things Egypt will do to me. It is I-the-novelty I carry about—and this I, I know, will respond to and see [more] things than a million travellers. I have no interest in monuments, but I have a lot of curiosity because I know even a monument, a dead monument, can give birth to something in me. In other words, I don't care whether things are dead or alive—while I know that a mummy can ignite me. The key word of your errors is *impersonal.* Why impersonal? Here is where again my deep desire to see your Self affirmed proves itself wise. Your Self—a synthesis—then your Self—wisdom—Self Vision. A vision. An attitude which serves as a vantage point.

The travelling ceases to be a distressing lurching about—it has, like Faure's *Périple,* a knitted quality. Why, if you were sure it was what you wanted, didn't you go with the whores in Avignon and come back rotting like Fred—if that is life to you? Why do you talk about not having travelled with a clear conscience? Who held you back? What kept you from doing all you wished? No anxiety, money in your pocket, no need of humiliations.

I must say, as you did, why all this? Perhaps it's only because it's the first time I don't understand what you are bitter about. It must be something else. Let's forget all this. Please get a bottle of champagne for Monday night. And wouldn't you like to come to Louveciennes?

There will be nobody there, not even Emilia. Somehow I don't like the idea of Clichy, with Fred rotting away there. On the other hand if it disappoints you that I shouldn't see your room all fixed up, why I'll come. And I beg you, Henry, Henry, my love, to take care of yourself living with Fred.

You never answer my letters in personal matters! Do you realize that whatever effort one makes in love to reestablish understanding is an effort to dissipate the isolation—and those efforts you overlook.

Par contre I liked all you wrote about Lawrence and isolation etc. Still writing your book on Lawrence! Was struck by these lines: "The man who is intoxicated with life does not pass judgment, does not seek to come to a conclusion, does not impose his message on the world. Art has and always will have these two poles—those who wish to alter life and those who wish to enjoy it, to praise it, or just to accept it." So coincidental with some thoughts I had about you the other day when I was trying to analyze your bitterness. I believe you are unhappy when you enter the world of ideas, opinions, judgments. I believe you are destined to *describe* life, to give only your intoxicated moods, your enjoyment. I believe Bradley was not so far wrong when he praised above all things your descriptions, your ecstasies. Your judgments, your opinions are not as great as your enjoyments and acceptances. When you write about the demented team and the girl in Tarascon, it is beautiful. On that ground even I feel impelled to question your judgments, because judgments must come from *a* philosophy, one unified attitude, to be effective. Enjoyment alone is multilateral, multiformed, varied, chaotic. You do not have *a* philosophy. You have feelings.

Your ideology woven in the Lawrence book is really a protest against ideology. Your whole discontent and windmill attacks are a protest against opinions, judgments, messages, prophecies, conclusions.

Your letters to me have been a protest against ideas, although they are full of ideas. You are at war with yourself, with the intellectual you. I say let the intellectual you alone, the savant, the philosopher. Enjoy life. Intoxicate yourself. Describe it. Don't comment [on] it. Don't frame it. I am sure of it now. You have had your cerebral winter—your mental fevers. You weren't happy. You rose to supreme heights of wisdom, of vision, but you were nervous and unhappy. The Season book [*Black Spring*] is a compromise. It will satisfy you. But after your book on Lawrence I beg you, give up cerebration. You took a cerebral trip.

I don't know why. Now you regret it. And you are full of inner, secret rebellion. You say things which hurt without meaning to hurt anyone. And at first I couldn't understand. Now I do, I do, Henry, and I want to help you, to clarify you.

Listen: "The highest expression of the Librian character is *devotion.*" That's me—for you.

A.

[Clichy]
Friday [July 28, 1933]

Dear Anaïs,

everything you write me is so true, so wise, and I feel badly that I should have given you any pain or anxiety, or misgivings or uneasiness. No, I have not been myself, but I am getting to be. Listen—somewhere in me is a strong feeling of guilt. I know it now by a thousand symptoms. Something that occurred last night (which I am doing my best to withhold from you now in order to give you a pleasant surprise when you arrive) confirms my ruminations. It settles a lot of things, but I don't know that it will remove the canker.

You are quite right—I have avoided responding to all the personal overtures. But not deliberately. Instinctively, for fear that in this mood I will say things that may hurt—not that I have reason to wish to injure you, but that I strike out, metaphorically, with intention to injure somebody, anybody. And the result of this actually is that one injures the one whom he would least wish to injure. Is that not so?

I tell you, and you may believe it or not, that one of the great troubles with me is, when travelling, that my imagination is too great. Everything fails to fit into my preconceived image of things. And just to prove this, in a silly but awful truthful way, I must confess to you that this morning, upon receiving another instalment of Osborn's major opus I was carried away, exalted, by his descriptions of the Loire, the châteaux, Venice, Capri, etc. He visited all these places, they burned deep into him, and he retained his image of them successfully until the moment he sat down to record them. I have never been able to do that. I confessed to myself that I have never gained anything imperishable from my travels. The letters I wrote to my friends, on these occasions, are banal, trivial, petulant, impersonal, lacking in vision, in tenderness, in sympathy, in everything. I see it all as a grand waste, relieved by momentary, episodic patches of whimsical and highly personal value. These, nobody is interested in, unless the man who writes them is already an accepted figure, and consequently everything happening to him is important. They will not tell the reader much about Venice, Carcassonne, etc., but they will reveal something about the author's state of mind, his soul condition. But all these revelations come afterwards, with me. They come involuntarily.

In my thrashing about I have hinted at a certain chagrin—that you and Lawrence could write so continuously, so personally, so wisely, so uninterruptedly, during your changes of time and place. Perhaps you give the clue in your last letter—you carry your vision, your philosophy of life with you, it is something solid, real, tangible, and vital all the time. I don't. I am amorphous, spiritually speaking. I suffer from my colorative adaptability, to use a Darwinian image. I take on the dullness of the landscape, the torpid heat of the day, the barren vista of rocks, the anonymous stream of humanity that sluices back and forth through city after city endlessly and ceaselessly. I am protean, to the point of disease.

You picture me as being unhappy for some thinly disguised reason. You think I have problems of some sort, which I am reluctant or ashamed to confess. No, unfortunately, no. Unlike you, I am not always aware of what it is I suffer from. Like Salavin again, whose lines I remember so vividly, I suffer because of myself. It is my own soul all the time that is bothering me. I am completely egocentric.

Here is a little paragraph about myself from Osborn's latest instalment. Not one of his best, but I denote it simply because it is repetitious, an obsessive factor in his memory of me:

"A curious and strange premonition of disaster hovers over me. I fear I shall be murdered in my bed. My relations with Barton (who is Wilke), the circumstances of our meeting, the peculiar mystifying character of the fellow, strange, unfathomable strange . . . Hueffer [Miller] too, but in a different way—for all his pretended (!) friendship, the fellow is treacherous, treacherous at the core, I feel it in my bones—the most dangerous sort of treachery since it is not the common man to man sort, but has behind it a philosophical compulsion, an egotistical creator's justification of itself, as if the life of no one was really important except his own, all other people's lives, even those of his most intimate friends but fodder for the unrolling of his own sanctified destiny, his own creative urges, a smiling German ruthlessness, a genial undermining, like mines sewn behind a smoke-screen—

yet good apart from this, good, only the treachery is part of his nature, he cannot help himself."

All this is devilishly true, insanely cunning and subtle. This man has accepted me, with the reservation of my innate treachery. A fact which raises him in my estimation. But as to the proof of my treachery? When has he ever had that? Never, I can assure. I have acted most honorably with him. He has nothing with which to reproach me, except perhaps omissions, things I may have done, words I may have offered and withheld. Overtly, nothing. Yet, he reads me right. (I am not overlooking the fact that my good friend [John] Nichols, whom he saw again recently, may have dropped a few drops of poison into his ear. Nichols would do that, partly for the fun of it, the drama, and partly out of injured vanity—because I, who was really his most cherished companion in Paris, did not even bother to say good-bye to him, or to run with the crowd to see him off, or to say, "write me a line when you get back." "So long," I said breezily, the last time we met, as though, well, if I never see you again, it was a pleasant time we had, but nothing to be conserved as a treasure.)

But to come back to Osborn's instinctive hunch. How remarkable it is that this passage greets me just when, in the last few weeks (during my depression) I have been planning the most diabolical outrage. I have been planning with a vindictiveness born of sheer indifference to bore into him on the subject of his insanity—for the sake of experiment! I have been intending to write him letter after letter, prying into his hallucinations, his fears, his obsessions, his persecutions. So that, he will either come to see it all as a delusion, or go definitely crazy. The only impeding thought thus far is that my letters might be held against me later. It might be said that I had deliberately driven him mad! The thought of the crime itself does not disturb me. Only the detection, the punishment.

But I forgot to conclude what I had begun previously. Reading his passages about the great cities of Europe—excellently done, by the way . . . truly!—I realized that for me it is only and always the "literary" appeal that people and places make. The reality is void of interest. Flat. Osborn's description of Chambord and of Amboise has life for me. The actual château had none. Spengler's great panoramic review of the past is again full of life and meaning for me. The actual events always left me cold.

I like what you said about your own absorption of the past. You stated it beautifully. And it also disturbs me a little, how you can dispatch things so beautifully. How you can know so definitely, so cleanly, so intelligently, when a thing is finished for you and when it is not. You have no grand blurs, in this respect. You are fortunate.

It is not important to come here Monday. The carpenter isn't quite finished yet, and won't be till the middle of the week. All that can wait. One thing I have already and enjoy—the rattan curtain which lets the light filter through softly. It always looks outside as if it were about to rain. A great, great relief on the eyes and nerves.

Be prepared to go with me to the Cinéma Ursulines just as soon as_possible, when you return. That is the surprise I am withholding from you. It takes all my willpower not to reveal the reasons for my pleasure. You are going there without any introduction, or warning. I am feverishly anticipating your reactions. The result of last night's visit has stirred me, stirred my mental processes, my imagination. If I were to reveal any more I would spoil it for you. So I desist.

About Fred. Don't fear. I did not lie or exaggerate. But everything has turned out miraculously for the best. It is a mystery. I saw with my own eyes—and yet now it is all over. Apparently. He offers no credible explanation. I can offer none. Complete mystery . . . In any case, I am one who takes supreme care in such things. He knows it too. I stand over him while he scrubs the tub. I am mortally afraid of these things. The one great horror—to me! Unclean! How I hate that! (Guilt again.)

I am assuming this will reach you before you leave. Wire me when to meet you and where. Believe me, everything is all right. You have a too vivid imagination. You used a curious expression that sticks in my crop all the time. You said "frontal basket." I say that is a vastly symbolic word. It's just a baggage carrier, you know. "Frontal basket" opens up such vistas of fancy. Somehow I always think first of a kangaroo in reverse. You carry my children before you, before the world, cleaving a way for them with your bicycle, even as you talk with the Padre. You carry them under everybody's nose, with a secret feline pleasure. You almost wish that they would spill out and cause disaster. Then you go to the gambling casino with your scarlet breeches of flaming indecency and the King of Norway flirts with you, and the innocent young gigolo from America, the Adonis whom I deliberately avoid mentioning, tracks you down. He saw you with another man. He knows and you know. A grand secret between you. And he interprets it one way, and you another. Kaleidoscopic collisions of thought. You throw up smoke screens, using the gigolo as a submarine. Everybody is agog, first about the King of Sweden, then about the gigolo. You blush about it. You grow confused. Admirable. Admirable prevaricator! Lying without ever opening your mouth. Creating a mountain of insinuations, implications, suspicions, jealousies, wars—over an "innocent" gigolo. And the best of it all is, nobody knows, and nobody will ever know, just wherein the charm of that gratuitous "innocence" lies. Perhaps even the journal knows nothing about it. But like a person who laughs hysterically at the wrong moment your gigolo appears persistently, ubiquitously, irrelevantly, in your letters. I succumb to the mystery of it. I don't question you. There he is, at your side, looking over your shoulder, turning round as you pass the corner. "Innocent" young man from America. Remarkable. Strange. Like a double who pursues you. Who is he? Why is he? Nobody knows.

Anaïs, I overlooked nothing. (This refers to your marginal note—not to the gigolo.) I am waiting feverishly for you to return. I shall only begin to breathe again when you come back.

I must end this in order to mail it in time. Your two letters only arrived this afternoon, together. I was waiting to hear from you, wondering if you had suddenly decided to return earlier. Make any plans you want. I am free. One thing—you write as if possibly I had some resentment against you, as if I checked myself on your account. Don't misunderstand. If I was miserable ever it was my own fault. I was not miserable with you.

You remember my impulse to write Anatole? Well, I looked him up when I got back. Had a beautiful session with him and Leon* in their stuffy hotel room. Just like out of Dostoevsky. Anatole is so terribly a nobody that he is fascinating to me. I find these nobodies so much more interesting than the celebrated people. Why is that?

Henry

[Aix-les-Bains]
[July 28, 1933]

[Henry:]

I wanted to sit and tell you what parts of your "Cinema Vanves" stayed in my memory, for those I judge as having come off grandly—

---

*Anatole and Leon Pachoutinsky, Russian brothers, whom H. M. writes about in *Tropic of Cancer*.

but I'm overwhelmed by the heat. I wonder if you are suffering from it.

But even though the heat mists, I single out the ring of this phrase as the first beautiful one. It seems to *begin* there: "I felt eternal and without knowledge of its meaning." And from there on, the mood is effective, moving . . . the walk through the streets etc. Up to the movies—Lil Dagover. Here it becomes too factual—listless. But in paragraph "We step across the street again to the office" there is a fine feeling—"triumph from the bottom"—good—human! On the whole I'm afraid you *forced* yourself to write it. When I think of those imaginative, amazing pages you wrote in Louveciennes for [*Black*] *Spring* I wonder why you should *ever* force yourself to write and feel conscience stricken. You could afford to sit back on those pages. It seems to me Eugene came off better in the novel and the streets, too, if I remember, and all your moods. In this there is nothing new or that you have not written better elsewhere. Am I right—someday you'll get *intoxicated* with that period again and then watch! But wait until you're drunk with your subject—with June too—always drunk!

Friday A.M. Nothing from you today. I hope that check reached you on time. If I had had the money I would have telegraphed it. Couldn't ask Hugh. Monday I'll bring you more.

You must be suffering with heat. No more thinking. Just feeling, and waiting for Monday.

A.

[Clichy]
Thursday [August 3, 1933]

Anaïs:

The enclosed letter to Bradley, which I leave to your discretion to send or not to send, states the case for your pages.* Sorry to cut short

---

*In nine typed pages, dated August 2, 1933, Miller made a strong plea for the unadulterated publication of A. N.'s diary. Bradley, who had seen some of the childhood volumes in their entirety, and some of the later volumes in an excised and somewhat disguised form, apparently had suggested an "adaptation" of some of the material to make it more palatable for commercial publication. "Can you be certain," Miller wrote, "that what you find uninteresting will not appeal to thousands, perhaps

your exciting labors, your hopes, etc. But this is my honest view. The pages were all right—neither good nor bad, neither fish nor fowl. As I read them I seemed to hear the original lines from which they were abstracted, saw the wavering handwriting, and the curious childlike drawings, the mistakes, the bad spelling, the ink spots, the greasy finger-prints, the cheap paper (which is so touching in itself—the cheapest for genius always!). I rebelled. It is a crime to tamper with the original document. It is almost a sacrilege to print it. It should be preserved, like the first copies of the Gutenberg Bible, under a glass case. There should be no exemplars. There should be four posts and a velvet rope around the glass case. Not even the air that people breathe, that they foul with their dirty lungs, should be allowed to contaminate it. That's what I personally think! I couldn't say that to Bradley. But I hope I said enough. I hope to Christ he gets sore and gives us all the slip. Let him get down on his knees and beg for it. They will yet—you mark my words. Just hold out! Keep on believing in yourself, and trust in Providence. I can see the world knocking at your door. And vacations with ample allowances. I see it all, because, damn it, had I never met you that Journal would have affected me precisely as it does now. It grows better and better in retrospect. It must not be aborted. You must not be brought down to the level of Luhan, Stein, Duncan, Bashkirtsev.

Henry

[Louveciennes]
[August 6, 1933]

[Henry:]

I was overwhelmed when I received your letter, and all the more so because I was at the very moment writing in my journal on the irony in our talk about what my faith and love had done to you. Ironic, I say,

---

millions of others? . . . I am thinking of the work as if it were actually launched. I am thinking of the Japanese reader, the Hindu reader, the Spanish reader, the Scandinavian reader. . . . I am thinking of the reader to come in the year 2,000 A.D. and later, when the original manuscript, with the correct names, is brought to light. . . ." This "Letter to William Bradley" was eventually published in the section "More About Anaïs Nin," in the collection *Sunday After the War* (Norfolk, CT: New Directions, August 1944). According to a note in A. N.'s unpublished diary, the letter was never sent, and it was made public only after Bradley's death.

because without your being conscious of it, you worked the same miracle on me. You came when I had nothing to live for, and gave me life and strength and inspiration, Henry. All the joys. And then your letter comes to confirm this faith of yours, this life-giving enthusiasm, this sustenance. I do not think the letter is for Bradley. It is for me, for the moment, and then greatly for the world. It is a marvellous piece of *loyalty!* So definite you are, and illuminating for me. Immediately I dreamed of your preface. I underlined this: "The fundamental note which she sounds is that of pain. The pain of isolation. The very keynote of the artist's eternal rack." I was humanly, terribly happy to see you combatting for me. Your letter was a bombshell. And fundamentally so right. Abortion. The word was good. The attitude (and you know it by our talk in the garden) a great clarifier for me, coinciding with my feelings. Big words you used for me . . . genius etc. I enjoyed it. What I enjoyed most was your protectiveness, your great literary protectiveness, which you gave "Alraune" too. I sat back and enjoyed myself. You will testify I am not a beauty without brains etc.? You were cutting, you know. And you did kill the dragon. I am saved. Yes, I am full of confidence, the confidence you give me. Do you know what I liked too? The reality of the journal for you, what you wrote on the stains, the bad paper etc. We'll put that in the preface too! And now to work. Maybe you need a woman behind you, as I need a *man* behind me. I said a *man!* Mars the warrior, with fire in his nostrils.

Anaïs

Important request. For the sake of the great spiritual order! Please *date* your letters!

[Louveciennes]
August 8, 1933

[Henry:]

Bradley said he had no definite statement from Kahane. Also that he might not see you before next week because he might be leaving this Friday for a few days' rest. Listen, Henry. I beg you to see Kahane yourself. I imagine Kahane and Bradley are none too intimate. If you put the question honestly to Kahane, he must answer you. Tell him your situation is desperate etc. I am afraid Bradley has the impression now that your situation is not desperate etc. For some foolish reason, that desperateness seems to act on him better than your *literary* needs (of communication etc.). It is the more obvious need, and other writers put that forward. I wish I could do this for you. I would like you to be able to keep on writing and have no bothers of any kind. If I were your wife I would keep all that damned business away from you. And if you want to, by god, I will see Kahane myself. I mean this. I am ready now to call on the Pope, on all the Kings and all the editors. I tell you, Henry, I am undaunted. I am stronger than I have ever been. You can count on me. I know my encouragement, my faith, is not enough. You need contact with the world now. But until you have that, believe *me*, to an unmeasurable degree! I told Bradley yesterday you had written your most *eternal* pages, your most magnificent work lately. He was interested. I said you had become cohesive, you had coalesced. He said that was the only quality lacking in you. He had been concerned over the diffuseness. He was impressed when I said this. *He knows a cohesive force is a supreme force.* Write on. I love you, I believe you the greatest writer on earth today. See Kahane immediately if you want to. If you don't want to, I will. I can talk to him. I can talk to anybody. Monday I see [Robert] Denoël,* but I would like to know about Kahane first. And don't wait, because everybody goes away for [the feast of the] Assumption, the fifteenth.

I myself am working like a Trojan. Never felt so full, or so sure or so strong. Obsessed with my work, and with you. With your work and you, and writing. I realize a tremendous spiritual thing has happened to me. I closed a big cycle of my life. I closed the main theme of my life when I found my father again. And just as you began to work after you closed your June cycle, and to reminisce etc. I turned away from life to work, to bring the work up to date. This is our time of peace, when one writes music.

Curious, that wine which did not go to one's head. Or were our heads impermeable to all but music and words? So it seems.

Bradley said he would be glad to read my journal because in life I was such an *enigmatic* character. But yesterday I was honest with him. I did not specify but I gave him to understand I had things to tell in the journal which were deadly. We had a very interesting talk about my *lies*. He was keen about that. I realized too I have entered a phase of honesty because I am through with a certain world, a certain illusion, a certain role. I am only an artist now. I have quit acting etc.

*French publisher (Denoël & Steele).

for the moment. I may embark on a new role, invent a new way of living. But one kind of living has come to an end. And necessarily so, since I am revealing all my tricks with the journal. I am in a fever of ruthless honesty.

Anaïs

You should be *here*. We should work together—read each other's work at night—fire each other, keep each other. This is a great crime, this separation.

I won't mail you any pages. Your head is full enough and you have too much to do. Will give them to you when I see you. But send me yours.

Café George V
120 Avenue des Champs-Elysées
Wednesday [August 23, 1933]

[Anaïs:]

This is one of these cafés where you get only one sheet of paper at a time. You say to write about myself. That means "no literature," eh? Well, there's damned little I have to say about myself. When you go away it isn't just to St. Raphaël or the Creuse—you go away.* It might be to China. Places don't mean a thing. In Louveciennes I can picture you. When you take the train it's all a blur. Hugo is right, you know. You have to devour a person to be sure you have him or her. I'm not unhappy. Nor am I happy. I'm just extended—between places. When you left I said to myself—what use is it to write if that means pushing the one you want away from you. I don't want to die in harness. I wish you were with me all the time—then one wouldn't have to make decisions, like the other day. I'm not jealous. I'm lonely. Chamonix was a marvellous sort of stupor—from which one could always recover. The main thing is to feel your presence—hear you humming or yawning, see your combs & brushes lying around, worry about which dress you should put on, etc. If I enjoyed [Georges Duhamel's] *Deux Hommes* so much it was because you were lying close to me. It's totally different when you do things alone. When I look at those wonderful pages I wrote in Louveciennes I know it's because you were there, waiting for

*A. N. went to see her father at Valescure and returned with him and his second wife, Maruca, to Paris by car. She returned to Louveciennes on August 30.

me to write them. I know you're always "there"—but being there in spirit isn't quite the same as being there in the flesh. Your father knows it and he's a very wise man to get taken down with lumbago the way he does. We should all be taken down with lumbago—permanently.

There—that's what I'm thinking. I don't send you any more pages because they're not finished. I'm searching for a phrase that will release everything that's pent up in me.

If you are not going to be in Evreux after Friday you'd better telegraph so that I don't send the pages to the post office.

How is your eternal lover? Is he resting comfortably? I miss you a hell of a lot. You shouldn't get permission so easily.

[Henry]

Le Grand Hotel
Evaux-les-Bains (Creuse)
Wednesday [August 23, 1933]

[Henry:]

I was happy to get your letter when I arrived—may not have time tonight to answer you on the writing—I want to read it carefully—and I'm still dizzy from four days of travelling. Yes, my father *is* a rogue! He was paralyzed and in bed the day before I arrived. He got up and met me at the station and has been walking about since, gaily. The day I arrived in Valescure Paderewski invited us to dinner. Beautiful personage—soft, gentle, *aware*, keen, at 65—nobility of bearing and *élan*. Reads through people with eyes shaped like yours. Feminine laughter inside of his Polish red-blond mustache. Culture. Terribly interesting confrontation with Padre—he the romantic, always overflowing, spilling over, playing without exactitude, not playing Chopin but playing always Paderewski—and Padre, the Greek, whose ideas are the very opposite (the impersonal, the form, the measure—all Classical) but who bows to the *man Paderewski*, the unique person. What matter what he does, how he does it. It is *he*—Paderewski. I liked Padre's capitulation. And what a duel they had, what a joy the old man had in his face. At the end he asked Padre if he could kiss him—all this with grace, noblesse [. . . .] Paderewski is very courtly—and *illumined*— glowing. He is writing his memoirs. He gives everything he has. He is superb, and like all strong men, gentle. He said to me: "You have a beauty of other ages."

Then we rushed away, Padre and I—through Nîmes, Tarascon,

les Cévennes. . . . Slept in Alès, in Issoire (a dirty hotel in whose reception book Padre wrote: *Merde!*). The car broke down. We were delayed . . . and Padre's talk was inspiring, I tell you—a *man*—a man such as you are, of other epochs—who hates impotency, neuroses, illness—who demands force, health, sex, vigor! Who says what *you* say: Let the failures drown. Let the flabby ones croak! Survival of the fit. Kill the deformed, the ugly and the mental *"détraquis."* Doctors shouldn't save those who can commit suicide (your very words!). Let the cripples die, die. I was thinking how you would enjoy this. It is wonderful, Henry, to have a father of stature. He is damned wise, and his wisdom doesn't interfere with his flowingness. Listen, if there are only two *men* in the world and *one* woman life is worth creating . . . there *is* life. The three of us can fight the tide of Spengler's asphyxiating gas—pessimism. To say we belong in other epochs doesn't embalm us. We are going to make the future.

I'm raving, but I have been the last month so full of certitudes— all kinds of certitudes!

No, it didn't hurt at all, our last hours. I understand too much. It only hurt in the yearning afterwards—like yours. Don't forget, I am in love with your work too. In love with it!

It looks doubtful whether I will be home Sunday. But Monday or Tuesday for sure. I will send you a definite telegram Saturday. I may not be able to write at length. Padre has to lie down most of the day. I read to him etc. It's a place where there is nothing but a hotel and a little village, so I must make up for everything lacking. (Paderewski loves the *movies*—just movies.)

Anaïs

I sent you a telegram which may have sounded sentimental. I meant I had really a dream of you which I will tell you when I see you.

Le Grand Hotel
Evaux-les-Bains (Creuse)
[August 25, 1933]

[Henry:]

I got two letters from you today—one at Poste Restante. That one gave me great joy to read—great *closeness*. I'm waiting for you to announce your lumbago! Meanwhile I have been reading your pages, and becoming more and more definitely Spanish because my father's talk arouses my racial consciousness.

Your pages, they are wonderful.* Wonderful the beginning where you describe the confusion in your mind while they are all talking around you. And your feelings when Cronstadt explains you. I am not so very sure about the dialogue . . . but that's not important. Beautiful at the end, the description of Cronstadt and his poetry. Not ashen at all. Marvellous writing. It's a *tour de force* to describe so clearly an obscure and very subtly mysterious condition of yours. *Real inspiration,* Henry.

And then again, the strange poetic and ironic literary injustices! I was laughing with tears in my eyes about it all—a few hours before Cronstadt explains you in a way that arouses your tremendous "double" feeling. I had said somewhat the same thing to Fraenkel—about your work. And much more of the same sort, other times explaining you to yourself. Yet Cronstadt gets the impetuous literary gratitude— you're bursting with joy. And by Poste Restante I get the human candle offering, reestablishing a strange balance which makes the woman-artist weep. *I* was there, you say so beautifully, while you wrote those exultant pages in Louveciennes, and I am there, too, while you write intoxicated praise of Lowenfels' poetry . . . and *understanding.* But *I understand,* Henry, and, after all, I prefer my letter at the Poste Restante!!!!!! But for that I shall have to run away periodically.

Music in the Park. Talk. Father and I discover we have both dug seeds out of the ground when 15 years old to study the miracle of growth, and watched for hours. We begin here and end in Lapland. Father says: No such thing possible as a universal literature. What will the Laplanders get out of words like "rutilant," "truculence," etc. Those are *Spanish* words—Spanish feelings. I, the nomad, sit listening and feel myself becoming Spanish all through. [Mosén Vacinto] Verdaguer, a great Catalonian poet, said to Father, who was young and anxious over great confusions in his head: "Confusion is a sign of vast embracing. Don't be anxious about it. Later, you will make the synthesis. First take in, understand, love everything. . . . It's good!"

*Apparently a manuscript version of what became the chapter "Jabberwhorl Cronstadt" in *Black Spring,* inspired by Walter Lowenfels and his family.

It is now 2 A.M. I'm falling asleep—wondering if I am writing you nonsense.

Anaïs

And the page on the "I" and "he"—the double motif—is really *superbly done.* "Have I invented him? Am *I* talking? Am I what he is saying?" And when he tells you to shut up because you are deforming your own thought. Very beautiful.

Le Grand Hotel
Evaux-les-Bains (Creuse)
[August 26, 1933]

[Henry:]

I prefer telling you about the last pages when I return. . . . I don't like them as well as the others—I can't tell why. They make me think of Gertrude Stein. The machine running loose, but ineffectually—a kind of madness that does not intoxicate. Henry, believe me, it's indiscriminate madness! Great difference between this one and the other— the other is sublime. I'm instinctively sure they are not so good. Don't like to dissect them while you are working. Continue, because when one writes as much as you do a few pages must fall out. It's nothing . . . nothing. The *mood* is grand. The material, the substance, trivial. It is a mood in which one should write either as you did before or just shout like [Cab] Calloway—ha-ha etc. This is Calloway gibberish, only not as *pure!*

We will talk Wednesday. I don't know yet whether I arrive Wednesday morning or Tuesday night but for you it's Wednesday. Will send you a message immediately. If I get more pages from you I will telegraph you. Don't mind these few pages falling out. Don't forget, the rest was *eternal*—most eternal.

Anaïs

The last page, on the odor from the Bay, is effective. So are many other lines.

Sometimes I have a feeling you write *on,* as I do in my journal, when you have already said what you wanted to say. It isn't that I miss the riotousness, the marvellous mood of nonsense, incongruities, far-fetchedness, etc. the irony too, like an American extravaganza—yet even there I don't like a certain degree of buffoonishness like *Beautiful, Marvellous* etc. No. It's like the great novelist on a rest cure!

Wednesday, Wednesday! Wednesday you can beat me up for this!

Anaïs

Le Grand Hotel
Evaux-les-Bains (Creuse)
9.30 P.M. [August 27, 1933]

[Henry:]

I'm beginning this hoping to add a P.S. tomorrow morning quickly if I get pages from you. Father is writing to his wife. [. . .] Was hearing now about Father's *flair* for discovering and putting forward talent. He took La Argentina out of the Olympia where she was making 800 frs. a month. He unearthed [Andrés] Segovia, and the Quartor Aguilar. I am continuing the tradition. You know *who* I mean. Unerring flair! I told him about the painters, posing, in N.Y., dress modelling etc. He was furious and hurt to think of a Nin woman having been within reach of those Jews with their tongues hanging out etc. But I told him it didn't hurt me—I wrote a novel! I would do it all over again.

Forgive me for the definiteness of my last letter, but the feeling persists and it must therefore be true.

Father's obsession has been to create a consistency between himself and his work. Creation and the self one and the same. He *means* what he writes and writes only what he *is* and can do, and Paderewski recognized this in one hour of talk: You are an *"homme complet."* That is why he is so intolerant of neurotic art and artists.

Monday morning. I just got your telegram. *Merci.* I'm arriving Tuesday night. Was so happy to know you are working and that more pages will greet me. It always seems a long time, Henry—too long.

Anaïs

Louveciennes
September 2, 1933*

[Henry:]

My intuition was right. I like Lowenfels personally. I like a certain mellowness and brightness, a charm, a talent. But his mental universe negates mine. When you talk with him, you and I are cleaved. You are again before June, playing with a confusion whose aim is not very difficult to transcend, but you like the atmosphere. You like feeling lost. You enjoy being baffled. It gives you a false sense of mental energy, activity. The other, mine, the moving forward in swift luminous strides you enjoyed perhaps, but you always fall back into the false mysteries. I was sad last night. You were back again into the old mysteries of the Jewish collective habit of thinking for *effect*, for protection of an amorphous, disunified ocean. Not thinking sincerely and taking upon itself the responsibility of an attitude. Always eluding. Lowenfels is your chaotic double, yes, and so I accept him. I like him, as I necessarily like those who are your friends. I will enjoy him. But seeing you seek out that artificially created confusion in preference to the structure of a Rank, for example, baffles me. I say this: The superb, enormous machine of your genius, with its great weight and power, needed the little touches of oiling my clarity gave [in order] to function. Lowenfels, like June, will seem to stimulate you and in the end will only throw spokes into the machinery. You will see. However, if it is true I now believe the Jewish mind is not creative but anarchistic, it is also true I feel we can all enjoy each other, and don't take my letter as in any way opposing anyone. I feel the need of being truthful about the danger I feared. Now that I have been truthful I am no longer anxious.

Anaïs

P.S. Telephone me Monday before 4—I may be free in the evening. I begin to do everything on earth to get money together for end of the year for your book. Help me. Don't buy any more records just for the moment. Afterwards we'll have record orgies etc!

*Dated on carbon in A. N.'s handwriting.

[Louveciennes]
[September 9, 1933]

Henry:

Just a little question stayed on my mind last night when I read that you thought June had sacrificed herself for your sake by entrusting you to my care. Henry, do you really believe I for instance would stop helping you and entrust you to the care of another woman while I had strength left in me to do it myself, while I loved you? And why had June ceased to take care of you before I appeared?

All this means nothing except that I cannot let you believe that June loved you in the way I loved you, and if you only recognize this sufficiently, at least [do] not pity her for the acts which were not guided by love. Believe in her all you want but not to the extent of attributing to love and self-sacrifice the one act, the only one, I hold against June.

[Anaïs]

[Louveciennes]
[September 14, 1933]

Henry:

Tonight I feel that it does not matter what I exposed to the world, because I reveal a you nobody knows. All the feelings I have had at certain moments against exposing you pale now when I realize the nature of the portrait. And if you should feel this then all is right. Take Lowenfels, damn it, he does not know you. What is the use of knowing you, as I do, Henry, know you so deeply, if I cannot reveal you better, more beautifully, more completely than I have revealed Lawrence? Tonight I am all in flames. Working. I am sorry I carried my disturbed mood to you. I don't like to do that, yet you dissolved it.

[Anaïs]

[Louveciennes]
Wednesday, Oct. 4, [19]33

Henry:

When you leave on the bicycle I am concerned about you all evening, conscious of you with feeling which would give you joy to realize.

My imagination is all aflame with that *real* journal for Hugh.* You don't know how I would love to write it all at once. I began it tonight. Five pages. All craft. It may turn out a marvellous piece of mystification, the two sides of an attitude, and it becomes so real to me while I write it, for example the determination [. . .] never to be possessed by you because men remember longest the women they have not had (Cora). I believe that if you read this journal I could almost persuade *you* you have never had me at all! To confront the two could easily drive a man insane. I would love to die and watch Hugh read them both. In it I will explain the origin of every *invention* relating to our story. How I got to know the aspect of a certain hotel room from your talk about it etc. etc. Will reconstruct the [sessions] with Allendy: he telling me to distinguish carefully between my *literary* adventures (you) and my truly human one (Hugh!). Ironies. Reversals of situations. When you read it you will regret *not* having had me. You won't know after a while whether you did or not. Depends on which journal you read. You will be offered a choice! To begin with, try and remember that the *real* journal is the *unreal* one. Wonderful. *This* is the journal of my true feelings. Which one? The *tone*, you say, but when a man is a real actor, you can't tell about the tone. I suppose I am sublimating a situation which, deep down, I feel too tragically. Enjoying it intellectually. Making it bearable. As you said. I was also able today to see all the humor in the Lowenfels-Cronstadt legend. It is the men who take the women to the circus, and they go to hear the men laugh!

Please read, Henry, read. I need your faith. And I have much to tell you in those pages, more in the ones which are coming. I need your faith to go on. My hands are tied for the job until I get my *permis de travail*, and that gives me time to write the June book in a month. And then that is all. After that I become *your* instrument. I love you a thousand times more than I do myself. You the "Thou"—that is why I asked you last night if you wanted me to stop writing. I want to be that girl you wished for in the dream, whom you could mould to use; as artist you need so many tools. I am very young, that way, Henry. I am also more than Hannah, I have much more to give you, and because there is so much more to be used as fuel, it is all a much more wonderful story. And I will do justice to you. I don't mind your *literary* unfaithfulness! I don't mind that you adore Kay Boyle. I understand. You wrote

*A. N. planned to write an imaginary journal, parallel to the authentic one, which, if it was ever read by her husband, would present all her relationships in a different light.

a wonderful preface to the 1920 journal, anticipating all the revelations of the horoscope. I will have to remind you of it. It was prophetic. Please read, read with patience. Wait for all the pages. And then write me a letter asking if you can meet me! I may answer you, from the country of Neptune. Write me, too, so I can be wistful but not jealous!

Anaïs

I have three slick black binders for you when you come. Write me amount of rent so I can send the check. June will not be unhappy says the astrologer—in spite of Neptune—Venus & Sun make her strong, undefeatable, impermeable.

[Louveciennes]
Friday. Oct. 6, [19]33

[Henry:]

I read twenty-eight pages of Kay Boyle* and I know I will love it, and I know why you love it. That subdued, intense, poignant tone. Yes, the best in the Anglo-Saxons, a quality which has haunted me the Latin, and which eludes me, me, with all my color and skyrockets! I always meant skyrockets when I talked about fireworks. But wait, oh wait for me, Henry. I will do better than that, in another way. I have had my more serene rhythm. It was finding you which made me lose it. I have been too happy. I will get quiet now and write my story. Turbulence. You and I have to tame ourselves, when it comes to writing. Discipline, damn it, discipline the fever for the form. How I like when she lies down and thinks over the past, leading up to the moment in bed with Martin—so we will know how she got there. It was a *trick*. One does not think over the past all at once, so clearly. I had always looked down on those tricks. Mr. Bradley saying: "How do we know Alraune is Rab's wife? You have not said it. And we don't know what Alan looks like yet." *She.* It will be a *she*, too. I am tired of that "I," the weak I, the over-audacious I, the aggressive I, the timid I, the I of the Chinese language signs. I swallowing all my letters.

*Apparently the novel *Year Before Last*, which retraces Boyle's relationship with Ernest Walsh (Martin), "The Man Who Was Marked for Death" in Ernest Hemingway's *A Moveable Feast*. A fragment of the novel had appeared in the Summer 1928 issue of *transition* under the title "Written for Royalty."

Swallowing some of the notes. *Trop rapide. Trop fiévreuse.* Uncontrolled. It [is] piling up my *faults* these days which made me act so much like a *woman* today. Forgive me. Low ebb. I chuck away the journal, my notes, my notes which gave me the illusion of having written something. I begin all clean. And after all, what does it matter? I get such a joy from your work. I am a good *reader*, eh, Henry? Yes, I am all ears, all eyes, all memory for you. All attentiveness. Give me, grant me that talent! And go to sleep. Kay Boyle is moving and beautiful. I am all right. We'll go to the movies Tuesday.

Anaïs

[Clichy]
Friday night [October 6, 1933]

Anaïs—

Everything hurts. [Harry] Harvey* was here and is gone. I am playing Bach. A little heavy with wine, yet not drunk. But terribly regretful that I should have let you go as you did. You don't know what your words did to me—"I feel lonely!" I don't ever want to hear you say them again. Rather than you should say this, we ought to brave everything. I want you and I to think it's a crime that we must keep putting things off indefinitely. No one book is going to settle it. I did a terrible thing, falling off to sleep on you, and yet not so terrible either—shows how natural I feel with you. But it hurts to hear you say you felt lonely. Hurts terribly. I can't bear to think of causing you the slightest pain. You are wonderful, wonderful—and I know it. And I don't just take it for granted. I feel like getting down on my knees to you and asking you to forgive me. Do you? This man Harvey was here and he talked wonderfully about his wife—21 years of marriage! That's how I feel about you—after 21 years I could still talk wonderfully about you.

It's a crime to live apart. I don't know what to do about it. I don't want you to come to grief. I'm helpless. But if you see a way, and whenever and however you want to arrange it, just do. I love you and I want you to be happy. I put myself like a child in your hands. Don't scold me if I fall asleep. It doesn't mean a thing, except that I'm tired. Do you understand?

Please let me know that you forgive me.

*Husband of Dorothy Dudley. See Biographical Notes.

I had a wonderful letter from Emil just after you left. He sends you his love. You must see the letter.

In real anguish.

Henry

[Louveciennes]
[October 8, 1933]

[Henry:]

Your letter was a beautiful gift to me. I was hoping you had realized that when I said I was lonely it was not because you had gone to sleep—it was a more immense loneliness which I felt at that moment, more unbearable. I wrote you when I came home that I was sad about writing etc. and that was not it. I didn't want to reveal the other cause. But you divined it. No, Henry, there is no way out and what is the use of my coming with my lapses of courage to you? That story of Martin [in Kay Boyle's novel] you don't know what it did to me. Martin was dying, but in the same way I am aware of days dying, of all I miss—and I lose my courage. But I have courage again today. If I accepted your gift—so many times now you have offered to brave everything—I would no longer be giving you only life, only strength. I want to be your south wind—bringing good and fruitful things only— and the most essential is the peace you work with now, the absence of problems and for that I must stay here where I am. Don't feel any anguish. I get joyous again as soon as I am with you, and it lasts me for days.

I'm coming Tuesday for breakfast and the night—to work with you, to be with you. Coming only as the south wind.

Anaïs

[Clichy]
Thursday [October 12, 1933]

[Anaïs:]

I have finished reading the pages for Bradley in the black folder.* I can understand a little better now Bradley's irritation, his fault-finding,

*In an effort to make some material from the diary publishable without revealing the actual persons involved, A. N., at various times, had "adapted" sections by changing

his exasperation. He forgot that it was a journal, and that it had been excised. The story interested him, as it will interest everybody in the world, I tell you, from China to Mexico. A marvellous story. *But a bad diary.* That is, if you judged from these pages alone. And the diary writing mars the story, strangles it. Before I go on to give you some detailed points of criticism, as I noted them *en passant* (and against my will, because I wanted to read straight through as you wished), I must say what I think is rather important, perhaps a new slant on the work. What you are trying to do is a piece of art that is perfect in itself as art and yet retains the imperfection, the *human* fragmented, chaotic characteristics of a diary written on the spot in white heat. I don't know whether it can be done. It's a problem. It's like soldering two kinds of metals which refuse to be fused. Seems to me, at this moment, that one or the other aspect of the work must be sacrificed. And it could be successfully done by the technical trick (a justifiable one!) of maintaining the illusion, for the reader, that he is perusing an intimate journal, but doing your story with infinite care, infinite pains. I think the story is the more important thing—not your diary. It is a big story too, with all manner of ramifications which naturally, in diary form, are often cursorily treated and cause damage.

Trying to read it as it now stands, for what there is of literature in it, was at first difficult for me—I shared all Bradley's pungent criticisms. But I know your aims, your desires. So it won't serve much purpose to restate these weaknesses—if you've very candidly, wholeheartedly admitted the truth of them to yourself—and I think you did more through comparing your writing with Kay Boyle's than through Bradley's direct and withering attack. Only, at risk of causing you more pain—but feeling it absolutely necessary—I must add this: that there are two kinds of mistakes, or rather defects . . . the one which everybody makes through haste, inattention, etc. . . . . the other through a sort of incompetence, a more ingrained, more tenacious, more serious kind of defect. This latter is what Bradley no doubt was aiming at. The difference is perceptible or sensed through one's taste, and, of course, with malice behind it this can be exaggerated to crushing dimensions. But the importance, the seriousness of it must be recognized and dealt with

---

names (H. M. became "Rab" or "Hans," June Miller "Alraune," Dr. Allendy "Auriol") or by recasting diary material as fiction. At the same time, she had also worked on a number of manuscripts involving June, Henry, and her father, which eventually were incorporated to some extent in *House of Incest* and *Winter of Artifice.*

squarely. Without the most humble and sedulous grappling with the inner defects there can never be any real mastery—and the most beautiful efforts will come to nought.

I was reading critically for perhaps a third of the volume. Couldn't help it. But then I got vitally interested and despite occasional lapses I could not be interrupted to make notes. That indicates the power of your narrative. I think, for instance, that with the arrival of Alraune to the very end there is a gripping, a moving eloquence, a fine passion and much splendid writing. The gaps that had irritated me in the earlier pages (even though I know they are filled in elsewhere, in other volumes and that you would have the sense to insert them) these gaps became much more rare, hardly noticeable. You see, back of this story, implicit in the telling of it, lies the other stories you have written into your journal, and no outsider reading these isolated pages can possibly smell them out or reconstruct them for himself if he did smell them out. (In short, it was a mistake to have shown Bradley these pages—even though he was impatient enough to demand them.)

Here's what I think about the work as [a] possibility for [a] book: first, make devilishly clear to yourself what are the main themes; chart them out. Make sure how much of your own background, your past problems you feel it necessary to reveal in order to tell this particular narrative. Find the most salient, the most revelatory features of the story and expand them to the utmost, wring the last drop of juice from them. It needn't have an ending, in the conventional sense of novel ending, but it should have its own inherent close—not, for example, that pseudo-psychological disquisition such as you have at the end, which is very fine in itself—I marked it especially—but which is enfeebling from a literary, an artistic standpoint because it should come out through implication in the telling of the story.

Incidentally, this is one of the worst defects in all the journal writing—this *tacking on* of recently digested syntheses. No syntheses, please! And in the finished work, no slippery escapes, no short, pithy, ambiguous lines or sentences. Full out, or else nothing.

Before I go on with detailed criticisms remember this—that I insist on your showing me what you are writing as you go along. You must let me help you. You must toughen up for criticism. I won't bludgeon just for the fun of destroying—you know that. I almost wish to implore you to stop writing any more in your journal and concentrate all your energies on the task ahead of you. The hours that go to the journal are an evasion, fundamentally, of the imminent, the ever-impending problem—that of mastering your medium, of becoming the artist you are. That is absolutely clear to me. You need to write much much less and sweat more, go through agonies of torture in acquiring that craft which people less gifted than you or me have acquired earlier in their career. I think we will aid each other this way—we both need this medicine. And we are both inclined to be too tender with ourselves on this subject. It is the only subject which we should allow to bother us. The rest is easy and natural and god-given. So when you begin on a definite task you should be writing me about trifles, the merest trifles being important where they concern style, form, technique. Let's discuss only the technical aspects of things—which is what artists usually do, if you will observe. And I must apologize profusely for having let you run along alone so long. Believe me, I want you to unload these problems on me—there is no sacrifice involved at all. We shall both profit from it.

As to what I tell you now, it is perhaps hardly necessary, since Bradley gave it to you, but I add it to show you how I look at it more critically. . . . And I am giving it to you briefly. I can expand when I see you—maybe tomorrow, Friday—I'll call you up.

In general there is too staccato, too jerky, too hectic and hysterical a use of the sentence. Too dramatic, all highlights, and little or no relief. Too much use of abstract terms, of abstract emotions. Often culminating in slightly ridiculous hyperboles . . . "I was stirred in my very womb" . . . "I am light!" Etc. etc. Avoid mentioning "Rab" and "Alraune" so much—use "he" and "her" as much as possible. The reason often that things get a false, melodramatic flavor which Bradley could pierce and caricature is that there is no expansion in between—it is all shrieks, all abstracts. The very moment you settle down to concretize a scene, a passion, a thought you are splendid and no one could find fault with your writing. I felt that perhaps this is one of the great failings of writing a diary instantly after a thing happens—it frustrates the needed accumulation of drag and slag, of flesh and blood, of obscurities and obstacles and obfuscations, which because they must be tackled and offer one resistance produce inevitably the quality of art. I think this is quite important—the business of overcoming resistance! The resistance is the material, the events, the enigmas, the obscure motivations of the characters. Avoid grappling with these and you have a surface affair—a linear pattern, a solo melody in one key and monotonous and eventually exasperating. I ask myself, isn't it this precisely which gives a diary its essential character? Is it not like the sketch which an artist employs for the final architecture? Is it not the thin melody on which the composer sets to work, and from this slender, given clue, spins his luxurious, compact web? You see, I am aiming seriously at the destruction of this diary. It is good only if you recognize it for what it's worth—otherwise it is dangerous, poisonous, inclined to make one lazy, facile, self-contented. "Peacock feathers," as you would say. Perhaps another clue is this—that the impulse to put everything down immediately is a weakness—a neurotic fear of losing something. You should know by now that the memory is an immense steel reservoir—nothing escapes it. Write immediately, yes! But as artist! Write with the task in mind—always trying to say the thing in the best way you can. The how! Not the what! (I apply this to myself, also!) [. . .]

No need to despair. Need to work, that's all. And I'm going to help you. Jesus, believe me. Ask me, make me! Don't get a *permis de travail*. Cut me down to the bone and let me help you write these two or three books which you have right in your hands. You will go over big, I'm sure of it. They are still bigger stories than Kay Boyle's—I honestly believe that. I wrote her a letter last night, after finishing the book in a café. I did not send it yet—want to show it to you first. Don't send it now because it would seem like an indelicacy. Wrote about 25 pages yesterday—on the tailor shop.* Bringing them along too.

Just read this now and don't weep. Exult! What impresses me is that you have so much accomplished already. We need only to sharpen up the implements. I can see you giving birth to books in rapid succession. I believe in you enormously—I was genuinely stirred—also exasperated.

Henry

[Louveciennes]
[October 14, 1933]

Henry:

Working this morning and looking over the corrections. Feel you are going a bit too far, letting loose the over-critical and fault-finding you. You have it in for the diary, you know. I am referring to part where I say that when they fucked they became sincere and human etc. It

---

*These reminiscences of his father's business on 31st Street in Manhattan eventually became a chapter, under the title "The Tailor Shop," in *Black Spring*.

is neither teary nor sentimental at all. You ought to know how many times you have fucked without becoming yourself, or yielding yourself, or departing from the influence of your imagination and your literary curiosity. There is no false accent here, only a truth about the difference between wholeness and fragmented living such as artists do so often. Watch yourself a bit now, Henry, you're enjoying this dissection, you know, and you're getting heavy-handed. You're also getting too astringent. This may be the wrong word but it says what I mean.

As it happens, I unconsciously deceived you when I said the pages you described as a good full portrait were written fresh. All but the very last, and this last page is half out of the diary, belongs to the diary, I see now. A certain rewriting of another's writing can be dangerous and go beyond criticism. You're writing now as *you* would, changing things which are not wrong but different, sometimes. You're ironizing [sic], enjoying yourself. That does not do any good. What you say in that mood can be easily debated. I don't like that mood, and believe me, anyone can find such material for ridicule in the other. For the moment, I won't send you any more pages. You're not serious, and you yourself could not write if I were ready to ridicule your smallest error. [. . .] Amuse yourself with something else. A prize fighter, for instance.

Do you know what I think of your criticism? That it is good for a Bradley, for an outsider, for the world. That coming from you it is wrong. You read coolly, and without sympathy, without the initial responsiveness. I can prove to you that the responsiveness is lacking. A page you once thought wonderful, which made you gasp when you read it in "Alraune," which you praised highly one afternoon right on the couch here, today you say is very badly written. Also, why worry about the intrusion of the "ego" when your ego permeates your whole work. Do I worry about the assertions of your ego—why must you immediately jump on this when I do it on a minor scale? Do you know what I think of people who mind the intrusion of the ego? That they have something against the ego. You are angry in all this. There is nothing to be exasperated about. The defects do not win out. Besides, the trouble with such criticisms is that when they come to an honest writer they come long after he knows all about them. I know my defects. I don't need you to take that stand-offish and unsympathetic tone. I get enough of that from the men who can't bully me into loving them, or obeying them (Bradley, Steele, etc. etc.). You were very cruel, you know, Henry. When you returned from Bradley and he had hurt you in some way, I did not take his side as you did that day and point to, at the same moment, a book I thought better written than yours. You did that to me. You did not defend me. And you offered me Kay Boyle. It may have been just, but it was not very human. That is what I mean when I say you have no loyalty. One can love many people and admire a thousand, but give one the feeling that it changes nothing. I do that to you. I have admired Artaud and his writing without ever making you feel that I thought he had been more subtle than you, etc.

What you should have done if you had not been standing on the outside, like a stranger, is, having heard all about Bradley's criticisms, knowing I took them in, weighed them, and was sufficiently candid and clear-minded, to have given me what I give you, that is, response and an appreciation of what *is* good, with the emphasis on the good. That is my way with you. I know perfectly well you get all the technical examinations and exaggerations of your faults from the others. What you need from me is understanding. You don't need me to repeat what Bradley said and agree with it. You always fail me in that. You are just absent, that's all. Uncreative, in that way, as the mood takes you. Too indifferent really.

I take all you send me and read it for the understanding of it. This time you read me like a Bradley, and that's of no use to me. (That is, you read me as Bradley read me before his personal feelings came into play. *Before*, I was wonderful. What cowardice!)

You know, Henry, your understanding works on and off, very waveringly. When your own enthusiasm is wandering somewhere else, it's off. Mine has a funny quality of being always on, no matter where I am wandering. I don't mean by loyalty what other people mean. I mean just that quality of continuity. There is a break in it, just now. Just let it be. That is the way you are. I will not take this letter seriously. I take it as the letter of a man who is not at home. Just not there. Let me know when you are ready to accompany me again, to come along with me. Otherwise, leave me alone. Don't pretend. Just say: "Not at home." What hurts is the falseness, that's all. This is only an eclipse of your understanding. I am not going to weep over an eclipse.

You may think I have not been treated roughly enough—that I need toughening, as you say. Should I have said that to you the day you told me about Bradley's visit and your saying to him: "What I need is faith," and that is what you don't give me. When you tell me these things you count on my taking your side, always, deep down; even when you know your faults, I don't notice them, they are not important. You may think we have pampered each other, but then you forget that we agreed that the world would give us plenty of beatings and that what we needed was the *support* of each other. That, you have failed to give me. At the moment I most needed you, you let my manuscript lie there and you read Kay Boyle. Why aren't you more honest and say what is really true: at this moment you aren't interested in what I am doing. Your new enthusiasm always displaces the old. Always. You cannot keep all things going at once as I do. You don't care enough, really, to hold on to one thing at the same time as you experience and enjoy another. That is the difference between us. Artaud etc. does not alter you in my mind one second. But you can only give sympathy to one thing at a time, understanding only whatever it is you find new, and for that new thing you have all the tolerance, all the faith, as for Lowenfels and Kay Boyle. I carry you along with me in my wanderings, as I carry myself along. You carry nothing along. You take up the new thing and it is the all powerful. There is such a difference in this last letter of yours and others you wrote me about the 1920 journal, which was such an inferior piece of work—but which you read with sympathy, you read with *feeling*. No feeling this time. Just an artificial task. I have ceased believing in people's objectivity. I know what is behind Bradley's bad humor. I wonder what is behind yours. From now on, then, you too will remain outside. I don't quite trust all you say.

There are human eyes, and visionary eyes. [. . .]

Sometimes I have a feeling that I am too honest, that I give away to my enemies the very instrument by which they can touch me. Too noble, I say, to have given Bradley confessions of my faults etc. and then expect him not to make use of this to ridicule me. It's cowardly. I am too honest, I admit in the journal that my analysis is bad, I say in the journal things against the journal, then why the devil must these things be repeated to me like a discovery? My honesty should have made certain criticisms superfluous. But Bradley likes to put the dots on the i. And now you too. "I believe in you enormously. I was genuinely stirred—also exasperated." That is so false, so false. You have not been sincere about all this for one moment. You have taken some sort of a pose. You didn't know which to take. I suppose you wanted to be objective. Objective with Bradley's influence written all over you. Never once Henry Miller. Just a man fulfilling a duty. You are very honest, Henry, but not honest enough. Not honest enough to say: "For the moment this doesn't interest me." Don't you think there is a bit of cruelty in your writing that letter to Kay Boyle just at this moment— bringing the contrast to light? Why do you do it? Is it to punish me for the unburnt photograph [of John Erskine], or some line in the journal you did not like? A cold letter. Thanks. And a cold response from me. That's good. That leaves me alone again, and as you read in the journal, I am strong when I am alone.

[Anaïs]

[Clichy]
Tuesday [October 17, 1933]

[Anaïs:]

Criticism is always a thankless task. Unless one is going to do a piece of aesthetic creation, which amounts to a piece of creation. What I'm trying to do for your manuscript is very much like what a maestro does in an academy of art—and that's an important distinction. When the latter sits down to write a book on art, say a critique of a contemporary, or a study of a period, or anything you choose, he calls into play more subtle faculties. In the studio, the classroom, he may often seem brutal, pitiless. He does not say to the student—this is wrong, this is bad, but I appreciate all you are striving to say, etc. He harps on the faults, with an occasional word of praise for a good stroke—like salt and pepper, a seasoning of the spicy sauce of criticism.

That's what I'm trying to do with you. No doubt it is wrong of me to get behind the actual technique occasionally, as I do, and criticize the thought, the tendency. I notice that when all is right between us you say—hit me hard, say the worst, etc.! As you did Monday morning. But if you sense the slightest injustice you retract, you grow sensitive, you shut me off from your work. You must make allowances for me, too—as a teacher. Teaching isn't a profession with me, or I would have ironed out these faults, no doubt. When you grow despairing you must remind yourself of what I have said again and again, and which stands: one, that I accept your diary in toto! Two, that I say it is a great human document, with all its faults, and perhaps just because of its faults, because they are as revelatory of your personality as the perfections! Three, that I want you to drop your god-damned diary someday, and that in helping you to perfect yourself as an artist I am aiding you in the accomplishment of this. Fourth, that whatever you present to me as art I must view as art, not as diary, not as intention— but as the thing-in-itself, the work of art. Fifth, that you will make no progress as artist unless you constantly regard your writing from that angle—and no other! Unless it cause you pain and annoyance, unless you be thinking constantly and forever of technique, which if it isn't ninety percent is certainly fifty percent of the story.

Sixth, that as an artist, you have more handicaps than the usual worker, than even a cheap, hack writer, for example. You *are* artist through and through, as Rank quickly perceived, but you are working with bad implements, with the worst materials. The goal is to become unconscious of the medium—or as much so as possible. But this can never happen until you are master of your medium—and even then one is never wholly unconscious. I mean, specifically, that when a da Vinci or a Dante or a Michelangelo seems, to the ordinary observer, to the average artist even, to be quite sure of himself, only the private documents, the personal statements, the private admissions of these men later reveal to us how tremendously they were concerned about things which apparently gave them no thought. That is why I keep saying that Lowenfels has a big idea behind his general thesis. He is terribly one-sided, terribly fanatical, but he has a big truth in his hands. He would say that the form of expression *is* the poem—always. Only what is there! The possibilities that lay unexpressed, the ideas that did not quite come off, they exist, to be sure, and may be the basis of other poems, other paintings, other music. There is no ideal, no perfect work of art. All is approximation, compromise, an *is* rather than an *ought* or a *could be*. Credit only for what comes off. Etc. Etc.

All of us know, when we do a thing, how much we left out, how greatly we failed, and we carry around inside us an image of the perfect thing that failed to materialize, and *that* we regard as the poem, *that* is what we demand credit for. This is our pride, our ego, demanding its full recognition. And it is difficult to separate the work of art from the man or woman who produced it. We tend to confuse the two. After all, I suppose, the story of the struggle that the artist went through to give birth to his idea is so patent, so intense that even though we wish to remain critical—at times—we find it almost impossible to do so. But just because art is *not* life, just because art is a creation that is inextricably bound up with life, we need to make great efforts to isolate the art element rather than the life element. Sometimes it seems almost ridiculous to me that we say this man is more human than that, reveals more of life, etc., in his work. How can one really say that—if one pursues this to the very limit? Because the least stroke of the pen is revelatory—it is *all* revelation. It is all a clear record—to him who can read—of the struggle of the individual with life. Exactitude and authenticity—

these are words to express the degree of vital relation between the two, art and life, the degree of measuring the struggle. (Badly stated—but you get what I'm driving at.)

So if I have the temerity to say "this sounds weak and sentimental," consider it rather as too true than the reverse. Because *I* am reading your work, prejudiced in your favor, not against. If therefore a thing strikes me, your ardent reader, as false or weak, watch out. Don't get angry with me too easily. I may be unjust. You may be able to convince me that I was wrong. I hope you can—I would like you to. But don't evade the conflict by retreating into your shell—for that is why you wrote the diary—to evade the problem of writing, the problem of art, which is an expression of the personality, a symbol of the struggle, and a challenge for further struggle. When you employed the image of the "prize-fighter"—saying, "amuse yourself with a prize-fighter"—I say, "Good! You *are* the prize-fighter!" The servitude of art is, in a way, like one long training bout for a fight that never comes off. You have to take it on the chin occasionally, you have to be knocked out, you have to be defeated over and over, in order to acquire the necessary ring tactics, the strategy, the art of fighting—and the real fight is always indefinitely postponed. But training for a fight is different from shadow-boxing in your room. The one is actual preparation for combat; the other is exercise, pure and simple. You could learn to do the most fantastic, the most wonderful things in the privacy of your room—as a shadow-boxer—and you might not last two minutes when you step into the ring.

Anyway, your three pages were good. Only one mistake, from a technical standpoint. There is no such word as "ironizing." It is "to be ironical." Naturally, I resort to irony—to all sorts of devices for working up your combative instinct. It is because you are not combative enough with your work that I tap you on the chin now and then. It hurts? Good. Better that I tap you lightly on the chin, before the bout commences, than that you enter the ring unprepared and get all your teeth knocked down your throat! Am I right? I'm toughening you for the final bout. If I always used twelve-ounce gloves you'd never know what it was to receive a hard blow. I'm giving you the blows as a training master, not to defeat you publicly.

I'll make a little digression. With [Hilaire] Hiler* and [Frederick] Kann I'm between two fires, two opposite poles of thought. Hiler

*See Biographical Notes.

looked at my things [watercolors] the other night and seemed to be quite astonished—said he felt like returning my money. Said I could draw well enough to express what I wanted, that I had a variety of technique, and, above all, that I had plenty of *"s'en foutisme"*—a *masculine* attitude, guts—which, he said, is more than your friend Kann ever shows. More guts in your things than in all Kann's work put together. Says Kann has an anal-something-or-other complex—over careful, tight, cautious, conscientious, timid etc. He says: why should I worry about drawing in a third dimension, about showing perspective, about representing things as they are in nature. *Art is not nature.* Hiler is a "Neo-Naturist," a word he coined, and which he explained to me. Anyway, says he, we cannot get away from nature, no matter how hard we try. We *can't* deny space, volume, distance, dimensions, etc. Accept these then as the conditions, but don't let us therefore become slaves to them. What *is* reality? Not something out there—something *inside* one, etc. etc.

I go to Kann. He says: naturally your work will be interesting. Childish things are always interesting. But you are doing what every child does. If that satisfies you, then don't come to me. Do you want to express yourself as a child? Is that sufficient? We must learn to look at objects in nature so as to be able to see what we do *not* see. All great art is built upon sound knowledge, knowledge of form and structure, knowledge of light and color, etc. [. . .]

There are two distinct attitudes, and at bottom they fuse into one. That art is long and painful and never-ending. That you need not become an artist to give yourself great pleasure, or even to express yourself. [. . .] Does this say anything?

Henry

[Louveciennes]
[November 1, 1933]

[Henry:]

It is very clear to me today that [many] pages can be taken out of the fantastic "Alraune" without hurting the dream-like book, because they belong in the *human* book. The language is different. The mood is human, not hallucinated. There is more reality in them. I separated them today and I feel it is right. You will see it as soon as you read them. I will refer from now on to "Alraune One" [*House of Incest*] as the fantasy, and "Alraune Two" [*Winter of Artifice*] as the human book. I have plans for "Alraune One." No longer the birth of the three women and the Man, but separated and unrelated personages (June, Louise, Artaud, and Eduardo) related only to Mandra (me), like distant tales of distinct maladies. The liar, the mad ascetic, the Heliogabalus madness, the paralytic. I forgot the Astrologer [Allendy]. Will dramatize and accentuate each one with all the manifestations of their obsessions etc. Naturally you don't belong there any more. That last part about you was always weak. I can tone down a bit the fantasy in these extracted pages so they will fit better in the human book. But at first glance they are more human than fantastic, even in language. What you and I need is to sit and write all day and have someone next to us filing each page into the proper cover. And our books are done! I got a letter from Charles Henri Ford's friends telling me he is starving and to please help. My father sent something. And I with typical female loyalty send you the hundred [francs] instead! Indifference to the cosmos!

[Anaïs]

[Louveciennes]
11/11/33*

Henry:

Enclosing a picture which I thought would please you for your note book.

When I came home I had a conference with my Manager and Press Agent. I said to him: Well, what is the program for the week?

My husband and Director answered: Well, your father called up while you were away and said he would come in his Chrysler on Wednesday afternoon. Joaquin telephoned that you had to come in Monday sometime to say good-bye because he is leaving for Madrid. On Monday you must also see Mr. Steele, who called up about a manuscript he said you wanted. There is also Ethel [Guiler]'s disconsolate ex-lover who needs to talk to you. He expects you if possible Tuesday at the Colisée. On Wednesday night we have to attend a musical evening at the Frasers' house. Very important, because I want Mr. X to like you. He may be a trust prospect. On Thursday night we are invited to have dinner with the Prince Bourbon of Spain. Will you have to get yourself a dress for that? Friday we are to see *Emperor Jones*

*Dated subsequently, apparently, in A. N.'s handwriting.

with Mr. and Mrs. [. . .] Can't put them off any longer. Very important. On Saturday Louise [de Vilmorin] is coming to see you while I ride with Henry Hunt. She is hurt because she says you haven't seen her for two weeks.

O.K. I answered breezily. But on Monday next I am leaving for an uncharted route. For some country not on the map. For a week. No questions to be asked, and I will telephone you every day. Is that fair?

O.K. answered the Head of the Trust Department. Will you be back for the weekend?

[Anaïs]

4, Ave. Anatole France
Clichy (Seine)
[December 6, 1933]

Dear Anaïs:

It isn't to frighten you that I am writing this. Only, a feeling of fatality hangs over me, which I can't shake off, a premonition of imminent death. The enclosed is my will and testament, which if it lacks legality through signature of witnesses, we can arrange, should I not die in the next forty-eight hours. I make you the sole inheritor of my estate (such as it is!). It is only because I have a feeling that immediately I die my work may be worth something that I take these steps to insure the proper distribution of the proceeds. Naturally I would like to take care of a number of people—principally my parents and sister, June, my child [Barbara]. I have a faint recollection that before leaving for Europe one of my friends (A. M. Elkus) induced me to draw up a will leaving everything to June. I now withdraw that, not that I would deny June her due, but that I fear she would be unable to use it wisely; it is for her own interest, therefore, that I leave everything to you, knowing that you would deal wisely and justly in everything. [. . .]

Naturally it all depends on how much my books earn, after my demise, as to how far you might carry out my idea in proportioning the earnings. To begin with, any manuscripts left unfinished you have my permission to complete in any way you wish, under any title or signature you wish. My letters alone might be worth something should my personality create attention. Many of my letters, together with old manuscripts (which are for *you*, and not for June), will be found in my wooden file-case now supposedly in the possession of June's mother,

Mrs. William Smith. Emil Schnellock, George C. Buzby, A. M. Elkus, Harolde O. Ross, my first wife, Beatrice Wickens, and also Stanley J. Borowski (my oldest friend)—all these people have my best letters and would know where others are to be found.

Now then, assuming there is much money to be earned from my books—here is what I would like done with it, in so far as possible.

[Here follows a list of some thirty names, with varying sums specified, ranging from $25.00 to $350.00, including some former employees of the Western Union Telegraph Company and Monsieur Ellis, of whom Miller writes: "(concierge in [Edward] Titus' building, Rue Delambre—father was Russian Admiral on Battleship Potemkin, now works as handyman at Café Dôme, I believe)—owe him nothing, actually, but would like him to have much as possible, out of friendship and gratitude for his kindness, his great heart."]

To Emil Schnellock and Fred Perlès money would be an insult. Let them share what there is of personal value, sentimental things etc.

As for debts to tradespeople, hotels etc. I refuse to pay them. With the exception of a hundred francs I owe to Monsieur Paul on the Rue Lamartine (Fred knows the address). Pay with interest and blow him to a stiff drink. He was good to me. [. . .]

There is one other who never asked me for help, whom I saw little of in later life, but whom I regard as a jewel of a man—my cousin, Henry Baumann, the person who most resembles me, in heart, of all my relatives. I would like to have helped him sometime, but how? He should at least have copies of all my books. [. . .]

These are all I can think of from memory. There may be many more whom I have unintentionally omitted; my friends Emil Schnellock and Joe O'Regan would certainly know the truth if any claims were made.

Henry V. Miller

[Louveciennes]
Jan. 10, 1934*

[Henry:]

What a gorgeous holiday you gave me! Found Rank sick, with such a bad grippe he had almost no voice, so that it is doubtful if he will be able to come Friday. If you want to we'll go to the movies

*Dated subsequently, apparently, in A. N.'s handwriting.

together, if we have deserved it and paid for it with twenty pages or so! I'm expecting the dream wind-up and if you have a moment's leisure then call me up to see where you will move. I will see some things this afternoon between three and five, and then I am invited to see the German Joos ballets which are supposed to be ironic, ugly and powerful, satirical, grotesque etc. Maybe you will go too and will be looking up at the balcony? We are going with a bank ménage.

Enclosing two pages on lies. Can't number them because I don't know where they fit yet.

The artist (HVM) saw more in the dream than the analyst (Otto Rank). The poet *invented* a meaning (that about the turning horoscope, which struck me so). That is how it should be. The vision of the artist. The artist is the hero. But I am not convinced yet about there being Incidents. Nothing but Destiny. Olympian dramas and no Montparnasse. Maybe I'm elevating everything. Just a habit; maybe I should acquire the Philosophy of Triviality in place of the Sacred. Hiler asked to be made no drunkard. I asked Rank to make me a drunkard to please you.*

[Anaïs]

[Paris]
[March 26, 1934]

[Anaïs:]

I saw Kahane, after the third attempt, and finally had a good chat with him. Nothing is wrong, except that the world is out of joint—his buying public has temporarily vanished, he is not publishing a thing until something definite is done about the pound, the franc, the dollar. He was very reasonable, sympathetic and sincere, so I thought. Wants to publish but says it is just ruining both our chances at this critical period. We understood each other quite well. My belief in his integrity and good intentions is improved. He's intelligent, alert and direct. No

---

*On November 7, 1933, A. N. had begun her analysis with Dr. Otto Rank and upon his advice she moved temporarily into a residential hotel in Auteuil, on Rue des Marroniers, near his offices on Boulevard Suchet. For a while, H. M. occupied an adjoining room, before he moved to the Hotel Havana in Montmartre, where he worked on the final rewrite of *Tropic of Cancer*. Little correspondence for this period seems to have survived.

need on either side for equivocation. I told him of my plans—and all the details of our conversation and the net result I'll tell you more fully when I see you. For the present, the crisis stops everything! [. . .]*

They are closing up here. Must close.

Henry

[Paris]
Thursday [April 26, 1934]

Anaïs—

This is just a whiff, in between the time I await your letter and the Madame telephones the *propriétaire* to start the heat going, to let you know that I saw Sylvia Beach—who is a *little* "subglacial," abstract, retroussé etc.—and that it's alright, but between ourselves I don't think it is necessary to invite her—just a politeness. She's got snow in her veins. [. . .]

I'm writing from a café because the cold drives me out of the room. Am going over the *Tropic of Cancer* with a fine comb. A little dull, here and there, but on the whole good. If anybody had written a preface for it they might have explained that the book was written on the wing, as it were, between my 25 addresses. It gives that sensation of constant change of address, environment, etc. Like a bad dream. And for that it is good. Hectic. Kaleidoscopic. Here and there a bit sentimental—sententious even. But I'll try to weed this out.

Your infallible taste, of course, is right. It is not on the level of *Black Spring.* But, if this is not soon published it will never be! It will be outdated. There's a time for everything—and this is the time!

Now the sun is shining. In a minute it will be black again. Foul, miserable weather. I do hope London looks more cheerful to you. . . .†

Henry

*To overcome Kahane's reluctance, A. N., in June 1934, decided to underwrite the publication of *Tropic of Cancer* and paid 5,000 francs down. She also wrote a brief preface for the book, which was finally published in September, at the same time H. M. moved into a studio at 18 Villa Seurat, which had previously been occupied by Antonin Artaud.
†A. N. had gone to England to interest Rebecca West and other literary figures in H. M.'s work, i.e., the manuscript of *Black Spring* and a section of the work on D. H. Lawrence, but there was little response.

Royal Louvre Tuileries
Brasserie/Restaurant/Café
194 Rue de Rivoli
[October 1934]

[Henry:]

You didn't understand why I jumped this morning. Henry, I'm so tired, so tired to death of *needing* things, wanting things, and this morning Hugh gave me 200 frs. to get underwear and stockings. I bring them to you. Meanwhile you give Lowenfels the checks you get, the first checks you got. Never occurred to you to think of me. No. Never thought you might get me something—that you might do something with it for me. I'm very *tired*. If I go to N.Y. it's with a desperate idea of doing *anything*, anything to get out of my ever narrowing financial life. I beg you not to have that book bound— that's a luxury. There are other things I really need, like a coat. You have done this a hundred times. Will always do it. Always. I'm so tired of your lack of everything thoughtful, wise about you. You act like a child, a child that just asks and asks and asks and never thinks and sucks one to death, and I'm sitting here just crying because it's so hopeless to ever expect you to be otherwise. Don't bind a book for me. Don't make empty gestures. I want plain things, warm things. I'm just tired of denying myself every little thing for you to go on like a man with a hole in his pocket. Above all, I'm sad, because it is always the same. June's feelings too. Everything hopelessly the same. And rebellion. And a desire to run away from it all to some real human love. At the bottom it's because it's only *yourself* that counts, your friends, your mood, your need of generosity for the public, your impulses . . . but all like a child's, irresponsible, meaningless, without any depths.

[Anaïs]

United States Lines
On Board S.S............................
Monday [November 26, 1934]*

[Henry:]

Bottles are breaking, chairs are sliding, walls are cracking, the portholes are closed. Would not write you a diary of life on board because it is only this:

Oatmeal for breakfast.
Swimming in the pool.
Invitation for cocktail.
Walk with So and So.
Lunch with Mr. & Mrs. Nobody.
Movies with Mr. Connecticut Yankee.
Tea with Count Z.
Cocktails with rich Jewish merchant.
Dinner with X.
Dancing until midnight.

I was so blue the day I sailed, in spite of the sunshine, that I let myself become, two hours later, the center of attention & invitations. Did not want to be alone.

When I have time, I note down all the "dates" I won't keep in N.Y., and the proposals. At the gala dinner I was given a big bottle of perfume. Prize for Popularity. That's America. They tell me I have personality! Already I know I will not feel at home. But it's all breezy and innocuous. Their talk is all very graphic. One young man says to me: "After heavy drinking my mouth feels like the bottom of a bird-cage."

We had two days of rough sailing. I was sick one day only.

In the train I took flight from the world and spent two hours working on "Alraune." One hour weeping preceded the work.

I'm sending you check for Brassai.† 100 frs. for him, 100 frs. for you, which I won betting.

I forgot to tell you you won't get the radio right away. Mother and Joaquin want it for a while until he sails Dec. 4. Tell me if Emilia

*In an effort to achieve a measure of economic independence, A. N. went to New York, but her plans to resume modeling or dancing did not materialize. Instead, she joined Dr. Rank, with whom she had established an intimate relationship during the summer of 1934, in his psychotherapeutic practice.
†See Biographical Notes.

brought you the white sheets and whether she sewed the bottom of the curtains. She will be working for Mother until she goes to Spain.

I give away the prospectus to people and tell them to ask for *Tropic of Cancer* at the Gotham Book Market. [*sic*]

Tuesday. We had to be tied to the tables for dinner! When I sat in the bar I often slid over into the Grand Salon. Played craps all night. We may land Wednesday night. Yes, a foolish trip, Henry, but as soon as you approach America it is better to start skidding and sliding along, like their stairways, because their life Principle is Surface. If you submerge, you are alone, with Alraune, neurosis, memories of deeper worlds left behind.

All the introductory elements are here: toughness (the woman who washed my hair handled me like a football), crude ways, pragmatism. It makes me bristle. If I don't *dance* along with them, on light feet, then I would hate them. But I have decided to go to the big American party. I have already accepted tomato juice cocktails!

No time to read, but I know D. D. [Dorothy Dudley]* has said all I could say about America.

Are you alright? Good mood? Work? Not cold in the studio? Don't worry about *big* letters, if you're working, but write often.

A.

[Villa Seurat]
Nov. 29th [1934]

Anaïs—

More interesting news. Another letter from Hiler, this time from Mexico City, saying that he had shown the book [*Tropic of Cancer*], while in Hollywood, to a man who deals in "private" editions, and he thought this man wanted to print my book in America—and pay me for it. Said the man would *have* to pay because he could put the Federal authorities on his trail, if he didn't. [. . .] Anyway, I'm writing him now to inquire what he has to propose.

Last night I met the Pickering family [. . . .] This is the family whose mother Halasz [Brassaï] spoke of as liking my book so much.

*See Biographical Notes.

[. . .] We had a fine conversation in a quiet café where [Aleister] Crowley* used to sit.

Somehow the subject got around to Spain, where they have lived for some time. And then I discovered that the mother was entirely Spanish, tho raised in England. She told me a lot of interesting things about the *liberation* of the Spanish woman since the new regime. She talks very directly, hard, straight out—almost fiercely at times. She's the whole family, I can see. Has character. And in typical Spanish fashion the evening ended by *her* paying [for] the drinks and promising to give me a bunch of records—as they have more than enuf! I was quite delighted—but even more pleased by the way she insisted on paying for everything. You would have liked that.

Told me also that when Eugene O'Neill was living in Budapest they became good friends and that she herself did a lot of work for him—correcting, criticizing, encouraging. Seems he was a bit scared then of saying too much—and she used to egg him on. What a queer sidelight that throws on the great American sex artist, eh? And they helped him out with dough too when he was up against it. Not that she bragged about it. No, very casual like.†

Anyway, she says that the first trip they make to England she is going to bring over a batch of my books. She says they're still the same old hypocritical bastards they always were—and that it ought to go like wildfire.

You know I just dispatched copies to Aldous Huxley & Ezra Pound—finally heard from them. And to Blaise Cendrars.‡ Also wrote a good letter to Emma Goldman. I expect her to step to the bat too. Also had an order from the negro elevator runner in my father's building. Said he was "desirious of securing a copy."

In the [Dorothy] Dudley letter about the book, copy of which I enclose, she said that Marcel Duchamp was up to see them recently and expressed unprovoked & unstinted admiration for the book, had great pleasure in reading it, etc. I think thru him, and [Raymond] Queneau & Jacques Baron, I may finally get the attention of the Surrealist gang—and possibly the South American colony, which seems

---

*English writer, painter, occultist (1875–1947), who authored numerous books, among them *Magick in Theory and Practice* and his multivolumed *Confessions.*
†There is no evidence that the American playwright Eugene O'Neill ever visited Hungary. The reference may be to a writer with the same name.
‡See Biographical Notes.

to pivot around Dali & his wife, Gala. (Buñuel is in Andalusia, did I tell you, making a long *documentaire* of a small isolated colony of "defectives" where incest & cruelty abound. How like him!)*

I notice now that there won't be any mail for about a week after you get this. That'll give you time to finish the section I am working on—"the tailor shop." You already have the first pages, as originally written. The changes were subtle—not important. I am working successfully every day now—active in every way. So much so that I can scarcely sleep. Wake up thinking aloud. Which is fine!

By the way, if Kahane is willing to mail out the books, a few at a time, to all my friends in N.Y. where do you want them delivered? To Kay Bryant's address? *Let me know immediately.*

I wait most impatiently to hear the results of your first interviews—*about yourself*, I mean. With George Bye, Mrs. [Blanche] Knopf, etc. Show them the Lawrence book, by all means. (By the way, the Spanish woman (Mrs. Pickering) remarked about your preface— said it was powerfully done. Was glad to hear it had been written by a *Spanish* woman!)

I gave you the address of that publisher in Hollywood for yourself too. In case you don't make headway with the legitimate guys, try him. You forgot to leave Kahane's copy with me. But that's okay for the present. Put both copies of your MS. into use. Work on all four cylinders. By the way, will you be going to Hollywood? Today you land there—Thanksgiving Eve. Suppose you will have a big feast in a swell hotel! I visualize you sitting in a Roman bath like the Pennsylvania Station and waving a fan of ostrich plumes languidly.

I can't get over the difference between Jung and Rank. Jung shows strong cohesion, a lofty simplicity. You can see that *he's got it.* Sure, certain, easy & large in his doubts & apprehensions. Rank is the intellectual. Still fog bound. Everything he says Jung says also—but without reservations—and in language that anyone can understand. He strikes you finally as a very *human* fellow—not afraid to make mistakes. And his chapter on the "duties of the analyst" is swell. It ends on a pessimistic note. As for Freud—he simply wipes him off the board with a sweep of the hand. Puts his finger on the Jewishness. If you don't see a copy in N.Y. I'll mail you mine. Maybe you don't want to hear another word about psychology. (But *ASTROLOGY??* Oh la la!!)

---

*Apparently *Las Hurdes (Land Without Bread)*, a film about the plight of a poor Spanish village, which Buñuel finished in 1932, and which was the last film he did for some time.

Anyway, I'm jealous about that guy Otto. Yes, *Otto*. I know he'll be there at all hours waiting for you with his limousine and his soft German words. He must be in Heaven now. A fine Thanksgiving for him! Over here—*Der TOTE TAG. Versteht? TOTE TAG.* At Harry's Bar free turkey sandwiches. The lieutenant just borrowed 35 frs. to get his wife's evening gown out of the cleaners. Must wear formal dress. Benno [Greenstein] borrowed 40 frs. to make a photo of his paintings for D[orothy] D[udley]'s article.* But everything's OK. In fact, swell. I am husbanding my resources, cooking & cleaning every day with the phono going full blast. "Sweet and Lovely," "Body & Soul." When I hear this music I see you dancing at the Ritz, at Tony's, at the Waldorf, at Reisenweber's. And finally at the Ballet Russe. Oi, oi! You certainly have carte blanche now. A free hand and no apron strings attached. Woman, I must have a lot of faith in you to let you loose among the wolves & hyaenas.

Now I know that the boat has arrived I breathe a little easier. I kept worrying about a safe voyage. Thinking of floating icebergs, etc. How did the immigration officials treat you this time? I hope you can rush that naturalization through. It's important.

If you ever see a copy of the magazine *Esquire* let me know if you think they would take a story or article by me. Ask George Bye about it. I have two things in mind—short, snappy, *très Parisien*, which I think might suit them. Or even *Vanity Fair*—if my name were big enough for them. (They took old Wambly once.) And they pay *money*. Enough for your passage back—or the rent—or coal & wood.

Just remember once the [Katherine Anne] Porter woman asked if I would like her to place those things from *Black Spring*—"The Horse," & "Jabberwocky Cronstadt." I don't know what reviews she had in mind, but keep it in the back of your head. The old editor of *Harper's* (who knows Lowenfels well) might be just the guy, if he were met casually enough. I have the right, you know, to sell any of these things in advance of book publication.

I'm only suggesting this because I am thinking about the rent and don't want you to worry too much about it, or "save on health"! I'm not a bit worried. I don't need anything in excess of those checks you left. *Honestly.* And I *would* like to *earn* the rent, by fair means or foul.

---

*See also "Benno, the Wild Man from Borneo," by H. M., which first appeared in *The Booster* (September 1937) and was included in *The Wisdom of the Heart* (Norfolk, CT: New Directions, 1941).

I have a hunch more orders are coming in. Lots more. And I'll write anything for anybody—if only they'll promise to take it. *I'm active now.*

So you please slow up and enjoy yourself. See New York! I want you to talk to me about it for months & months when you are back. Are you happy? Relatively so, I mean! Keep away from the dangerous guys. I LOVE YOU.

Henry

[New York City]
Nov. 30 [1934]

[Henry:]

Rushing this off to you by [S.S.] *Europa*. Swamped and drowned in work for Psychological Center for the moment. Did not see the [contact] at the pier at all.* I asked for him. Perhaps because I arrived Wednesday night. Have not settled anywhere definitely yet because the hotel we came to is too expensive. I'm in love with New York. When you bring your own riches to it, it is like drinking from a Venetian glass. It is beautiful, vital, and magical. When I walked into a restaurant the door opened by itself, magically. You have to know *how* to use the magic of New York, how to swim in its Babylonian proportions. I love it. It's made for great swoops and daring and for hope in life. It is full of hope. Full of beauty and dancing and lights, and polish, and a lovely thing to play with one's own self, to color with one's own mood. I tell you it is a beautiful material. Worked so feverishly, so frantically, I did not write you more, but I will tonight.

A.

Barbizon Plaza Hotel
6th Ave. & 58th St.
Dec. 3, 1934

[Henry:]

I rushed you a note the other day and have not been able to write a line for myself since. Have let things take their course and since

---

*A friend had arranged to bring in some copies of *Tropic of Cancer*, which, due to censorship, could not be legally mailed to the United States.

making money for the rent was the first item on the list I accepted the enormous amount of work required by the [Psychological] Center. Next weekend I see about the dancing.* Meanwhile, I'm busy all day, like a big business woman, and then every night somebody says: "Let us show you New York." Americans are like Spaniards. So I have seen shows, Broadway, lunch on top of the Empire State, a dance hall in Harlem, movies at Radio City. I'm in love with N.Y. It matches my mood. I'm not overwhelmed. It is the suitable scene for my ever ever heightened life. I love the proportions, the amplitude, the brilliance, the polish, the solidity. I look up at Radio City insolently and love it. It is all great, and Babylonian. Broadway at night. Cellophane. The newness. The vitality. True, it is only physical. But it's inspiring. Just bring your own contents, and you create a sparkle of the highest power. I'm not moved, not speechless. I stand straight, tough, and I meet the impact. I feel the glow and the dancing in everything. The radio music in the taxis, scientific magic, which can all be used lyrically. That's my last word. Give New York to a poet. He can use it. It can be poetized. Or maybe that's a mania of mine, to poetize. I live lightly, smoothly, actively, ears and eyes wide open, alert, oiled! I feel a kind of exhilaration and the tempo is like that of my blood. I'm at once beyond, over and in New York, tasting it fully.

I don't know if I am telling you enough. I write you between telephone calls, visitors, letters etc. I don't hear myself writing. The only missing element is time. It is rare! We are flying. One goes for the weekend to Washington. One flies to Chicago in four hours. Rank has to go for lectures all over, and leaves me in charge. A ship "scalp" gave me Frieda's book on Lawrence [*Not I, But the Wind . . .*]. I can't read it. Saving it for you. But here is the rent check. Are you happy?

The telephone is at my elbow. Any day I may be idle, then I call up Emil [Schnellock] or I walk through Brooklyn.

Write me at the Barbizon. They never send up the mail. I call for it. It is quite safe.

A.

---

*A. N. apparently had sought interviews with George Balanchine and others.

CABLE

DEC 8 '34

NLT KAY BRYANT CARE POWERS 220 EAST 42 ST NY
ANAÏS BE CAREFUL HUGO RECEIVED FIRST LETTER [of November 26]
WITH CHECK ENVELOPES INTERCHANGED DISREGARD BREMEN LETTER
OKAY NOW

HENRY

[Villa Seurat]
(Friday night) Dec. 7th. [1934]

Anaïs—

A horrible blunder has been made. You mailed me the letter to Hugo, the day you arrived, and you sent mine to him. Hugo has been trying frantically to get in touch with me. Sent Amelia here who left the enclosed note under the door. She was here in the morning and again this evening. I thought in the morning it was Hugo himself and that he was here to "get" me—so I didn't answer the door. Since I already had *his* letter the night before (your letter to him) I had a presentiment that the letters were put in wrong envelopes and I was wary. Tonight I mailed his letter to him at 18 bis Ave. de Versailles without giving my own address. I can't say in this letter yet whether I will get the one intended for me. I hope so. I suppose he knows everything now. But I am avoiding him because I don't want to make either an admission or a denial. He must be furious and at the same time in a terrible state. I am myself almost exhausted with apprehension. Have brought Fred in here with me because until Hugo leaves I shall be on pins & needles. I know if he killed me he would not be without reason.

Fortunately you are out of reach—for the moment. No doubt he has cabled you already. I shall probably cable myself over the week-end—when I know something more definite. Especially when I have your letter. Don't do anything rash. Stay there and if it looks threatening don't give your address. Let him deal with Rank.

I understand very well how it all happened and at bottom I feel really glad. Now something drastic will have to happen. A divorce, most likely. Christ, I hope so! This couldn't go on forever.

For the moment I'm in a quandary. I suppose he'll stop all checks going through the bank. I'm going to try to cash one tomorrow through a third person. Will write again immediately on receiving your letter, which I expect he will mail me. I sent his letter directly to him, not to Amelia, of course. Amelia was good. Saved my life again I guess.

Owing to the fact that I have to cable you *c/o of Bryant c/o Powers* I can't say much. Will probably ask for your address & cable full dope in second cable.

This is undoubtedly the *Scandal* which your magician predicted. If he predicted other things which you withheld from me, better take thought. Too bad you didn't tell me you went alone.* I imagine I know why, but just the same I felt badly. But what does all that matter now? Keep cool and do whatever you think best. *But,* do keep me truly advised now of what Hugo is doing—when he sails, etc. It's important. You can imagine my state of mind at present.

One thing you must bear in mind. You are a free woman—you can do as you please. I wouldn't try to squirm out of it. To me it seems as though the worst should turn out for the best. Deep down you wanted this. Well, here it is!

I may have to leave town until Hugo goes. That depends on his behavior. For the present I am staying here, behind locked doors.

What a strange situation! This exchange of letters—comparisons—etc. Fortunately again, you wrote him a fine letter. I'm wondering what mine is like. I got a previous one, a short note of *Nov. 30th*—rushed with work etc. Must have been the first. Maybe now I ought to go see the mind-reader. What a woman you are! If we only knew you 24 hours out of the day! However, I believe in you. That's just it! *We all do.* No, but seriously—I hope this will mean the end of all double-dealing, that we take a chance and embark together, absolutely with and for each other alone.

Do you believe in me absolutely? Do you know that I want only you? Believe that. I can't say much more now—I'm exhausted with nervousness. I hope you understand. This is a blow. A real one!

Send letters or cables here until further notice, because even if I do go away a few days Fred will watch the mail for me. Be calm. You're 3000 miles away. But don't meet Hugo alone the first time—if you must meet him. *Take care!!*

Love, Henry

---

*H. M. initially assumed that Hugh Guiler would accompany his wife on the boat trip to New York.

Barbizon Plaza Hotel [New York]
December 7, 1934

[Henry:]

Got your second letter yesterday from Kay. Rejoicing over all the activity. To answer your questions: Lyons did not meet me at the boat for the reason that it broke the speed record, being my own chartered boat, you know, and I arrived Wednesday evening. Which provided me with a view of New York which made me instantaneously drunk—perhaps permanently. The buildings were twinkling and seemed not to have feet, rising out of the Thousand-and-One-Nights midnight mauve. No. I don't want to write about it. It makes my head turn. No Lyons. But what an arrival, with the band playing and a Southern gentleman making love to me saying: "Listen, honey, listen honey, honey I love you, honey, listen. Isn't it wonderful, coming in New York being made love to, honey?" I pretended not to hear because the band was playing but I think that is what made me fall in love with New York and not the Southerner, the music, and the boat sliding in, and the American voice saying: "Listen, honey," and the buildings twinkling, and now when he calls up I am not in town, because he was only a symbol!

I wish to introduce you to the cellophane symphony. I have mentioned cellophane before. The sum of American transcendentalism, and that shine over things which appeals to my eternal playing spirit. I'm playing, Henry, as I have never played. The setting is right. It's all cellophane. No real texture, but the glow, the brittleness, the glamour! I am poetizing New York to a frenzy.

I think it was very good for me to leave you. It awakened my own activity.

Let me know about the smuggled books as soon as possible. I can't do anything without copies of the book.

Very glad you let Bradley do the manipulations.

I am interested in seeing [Emil] Conason. Will look him up as soon as I get a breathing spell.

The dancing resolved itself into another sleeping proposition. Probably the Hollywood will too. At least all this is in suspense for the moment.

How are you coming out financially? It may be tight for the moment because I borrowed on my future salary for the rent and am more closely watched here.

Beautiful idea, sending me copies of my [Lawrence] book. Very delicately thought out. I asked in Scribner's and Brentano's [bookstores] one day and they said they had none. I need one at least.

Liked the Vlaminck sketch. Whenever a rock falls, it is good to go forward and meet it. That's the adventure. The motion, with all the feelings crowded in the moment of meeting both disaster and bliss. Motion. Motion and humor are now my obsession. Only I prefer his talk to his painting. His painting is monotonous. Maybe he bores himself and is glad of a war.

I have not time to read. Oscillating in my dreams at night between dancing and analyzing, between writing letters to you or seeing Emil [Schnellock], Conason etc. Will do them all, in the end. Rank says I work *magically*. Magic is another word which goes well here, not in speech, but when you look at Radio City at twilight.

[Anaïs]

[Villa Seurat]
Saturday night [December 8, 1934]
Next day!

[Anaïs:]

Luck is with you—with us! Eduardo brought your letter to me (the one meant for me with 200 frs check for Brassai & self) this afternoon. *Marvellous* that there was not one word out of the way!!! Even Eduardo commented on it. I had to read it over in his presence to make sure it was true. Too good to believe! And I had imagined that *everything* was in that letter—that you spilled the beans. A great relief—the first time in three days I drew an easy breath.

But now—immediately after the shock—am I so pleased? Would it not have been better to write a few rash words? This time it is the husband who must be congratulating himself. A clean bill of love.

And now all my wonderful psychologizing goes by the board. To unravel the *real* reason for the mistake, this peculiar mistake in which you whitewash yourself so completely—that takes time for a dull oaf like me. It's as tho' you had wanted to give the husband a most convincing proof of your loyalty & fidelity. Couldn't have been better had it been calculated cold-bloodedly. Even down to the program on board the boat—never a slip. Perfection! I congratulate you.

You see, I had been thinking—"what must he be thinking now

of his wife when in the same mail, written at the very same time, he sees her breathing love and devotion to two men at once." Yes, that's what I was thinking. And I didn't know how I would answer when he confronted me with your letter (to me). And I was thinking where can I hide so as to avoid this question. And what will I do with myself when I get there? I was so sure of what you must have said. And then when I read your letter I nearly fell over. It was incredible. And now I wonder a great deal.

The only line that meant anything to me was the one wherein you say you wept. Yes, I was really glad.

Interval. Just sent you cable c/o Kay Bryant. Had to leave it for her to read as I saw no other way out—too long to wait for answer, etc. My main fear is that you may do it a second time. I won't rest comfortable until I know Hugo has gone. *Is he ever going?* Or is that a myth? I couldn't ask Eduardo. He's too cold-blooded. And I felt too humiliated.

The mystery deepens. I don't know why I feel hurt but I do, nor why I feel distrustful but I do, nor why jealous, but I do. And why I detest Rank, but I do. (Despite the little you told me that was assuring from the magician's forecast.) One little lie, even tho' given with the best intentions, sometimes causes terrible havoc. I feel the ground unsteady. And I hate to ask for reassurances. I hate to believe there are things you'd want so much to conceal from me. And yet, common sense tells me there are, must be. If between *us* there can't be honesty, then what? Then where, how, o crazy world! What ballast? What rock? It's frightful. I can say to myself, you're a woman and all women are liars, incorrigible liars, the best of them. But the strange thing about your behavior is the underlying note of sincerity—profound sincerity. It's like a queen dressing in rags because she's certain of her charms, and to test them is amusing. And yet it's much more than that.

If I reproach myself it's for the man's fault of never being delicate or attentive enough—not giving the woman he loves the little bon-bons which any gigolo is only too ready to shower her with. That one forgets what a woman is, of what stuff composed, of her vital feminine needs. All that compounds a list which begins with Messrs. Allendy & Rank, down to Turner* and the hundred or so I never met—the Messrs. X, Y, Z, met here, there & everywhere.

---

*An American acquaintance of the Guilers in Paris who was apparently infatuated with A. N.

So I'm sad. I throw my vanity aside. I'm questioning myself. If the day on which you happen to read this letter proves to be one in which you're depressed, I know I'll get one kind of answer. Another day another.

Don't misunderstand. I read Hugo's letter very attentively. I can't ever forget it. If all you told me is so, I can understand that letter. If there were omissions in your recital (for whatever reason), and if in my discouragement I attempt to fill in those missing links, then I understand even better—but feel much worse.

Perhaps a letter like this makes you happy. Be happy, then! I know only that I am miserable. Forgive me for saying so, but it almost seems as tho' you *wouldn't* put in a little word about love until you were certain that I missed you—that I *confessed* it. Well, if you have been waiting—and not found it hitherto—then here it is. Must we all be reduced to puppies before you're satisfied? That's demoralizing, and you know it.

In the letter I tore up (fortunately) when I received the wrong letter I said that between absolute faith and absolute disillusionment there is only a hairline. But that hairline is strong enough to hold apart heaven & hell.

I reproach myself at this point once again—for disturbing you—with my jealous misgivings. I can say, just as Hugo does, "I believe in you absolutely." But I am not capable any longer of blinding myself to facts. Herein perhaps I only prove that I am less of a poet—not "the grand poet." Do you want a "blind" poet? I am not even sure now that as you read this letter the kind Otto will not be reading it over your shoulder. I am not sure of a thing.

When you write "the hotel *we* stopped at was too expensive"— that could be one of those truthful lies we have so often discussed.

I hate myself for even harboring such thoughts. I feel reduced. Somehow I had imagined that you would take the first opportunity to go for one of those walks I recommended. It would have meant a great deal to me. And perhaps you have! Perhaps you have! Only how will I know?

Anaïs, there is so little, if anything, that I have ever had to reproach you for, that this trifle must seem unforgivably exaggerated. Take that as a measure of my feelings. Put the best construction you can on it. I feel I merit nothing—nothing. I'm all muddled.

I'm going back home now because by this time Fred & his Etienette have probably *"tiré un coup."* I have permission to return now—the time is up.

I didn't thank you for sending the 100 frs. But I do. I liked so much what you said about inviting the whole gang to a farewell dinner. And I don't believe at all you *won* the money. I believe, yes, you may have won 50 frs. but you spend 500 frs. out of enthusiasm. Only, did you stop to think—how could this money you won already have been deposited in the Chase bank? I thought that good too. Higher book-keeping. Astrology's.

Fred has been to the magician by [Louis] Andard's* *orders*—and got a superb reading. *Excellent future!* He wants me to go. He's quite convinced now because—well, no matter. Will I go? No! More than ever I think it absurd. Both to try to read the future, or to build it on a preconceived plan, however grandiose. The future, or the seeds of it, lie in today and yesterday. "A man is what he does every day," said Emerson. A man is not what he hopes or fears every day. The future ought to be a fruit, and not a miracle. One can't shut his eyes and put his hand in a grab-bag. If he does he may pull out a booby prize—or a diamond. And in either case he'll only *retain* what truly belongs to him, what suits him. I am not uneasy about my future and I don't want any Arab even tho' he's a French Arab to be fingering my future. It belongs to me solely. My guess, *if I choose to guess,* is as good as his. What is called "psychic" may be inexplicable, but not more true therefore.

But drat all this! When I referred to the magician in a previous letter, it was not so much to emphasize his divinatory powers, as to throw into relief the things you omitted to tell me and which, alas, I see now must have strongly activated you. And if we accept your very clever interpretation of this phenomenon—"mind-reading"—then how much more important still becomes this lacuna that you so thoughtfully forgot to fill out for me.

One goes to the magician, as one goes to the analyst, or any quack—to reaffirm one's own secret volitions. Not to be cured, not to be warned, not to be saved, but to become what one wants to be. Yes, I am working—or was up until the shock. Will probably resume—savagely. Must. Even without hope.

And after all I can't stop here on this note. Can't be bitter, rancorous—with you. God-damn it, *I love you*—that's what's the matter. You've drawn blood. Go show it to Otto! Dance around the magnificent ballrooms in that dazzling atmosphere you love to describe. Shout it to everybody. Full conquest. *I love you.* Full stop.

*French politician for whom Perlès worked for a time.

That means that everything preceding needs a new interpretation. That you don't even have to calm me, lie to me, soothe me, etc. etc. *Salute!*

Henry

P.S. In the grand excitement of last few days the remarkable thing is I didn't have or couldn't find telephone number of *18 bis.* JASMIN 01-34.* Hello—Amelia? *What???*

P.P.S. And if there is any man in the world I could kill in cold blood it's Eduardo Sanchez. Ugh!

[Villa Seurat]
Midi, Dec. 11, 1934

[Anaïs:]

No cable, no mail since that first two of November 30th, "will write tonight" etc. Mail due this evening, or tomorrow morning however. Still *un peu d'espoir.* My letters are probably reaching you all out of time. After that *Bremen* letter of Dec. 7th, giving you the first intimation of the blunder, I sent another, a long one, in pen and ink, from a café. Night of Dec. 8th. Dropped it absent-mindedly in a letter box, instead of at *gare.* May have caught the S.S. *Ilsenstein,* due to reach New York only on December 22nd. This ought to reach you on the 20th, or maybe the 18th. Via the S.S. *Olympic.* I may yet send you another cable. If so, it will read like this: "Disregard Bremen letter only as concerns danger. Not otherwise."

Wish I had your hotel address. Hate cabling through another person. Wish you had had enough confidence in me to say what you were doing. I am sitting tight until the 15th, not knowing what results you have had, and fearing the worst. If I get by that date all right I will probably cable. I don't care about lack of eats, but I don't like to squander rent money on cables.

I've got to give you some other kind of news now, so please remember that the important letter was the one of the 8th arriving on the slow boat. There will be more like that betweenwhiles, don't worry.

---

*The apartment at 18 bis Avenue de Versailles where Hugh Guiler was staying was the apartment used by A. N.'s mother and brother. The Guilers had moved in October to 41 Avenue de Versailles and sublet the house in Louveciennes for the winter.

Only now let me say—I hope you are happy to know the state of my emotions. If there is a little grief attached, forgive that! I don't want to hurt you. I want you to know how much you mean to me, that's all. There is a crazy letter which I started last night, and abandoned. I may send it, and I may not. Not till later. Anyway, I send you in another envelope the little book which came. And the porno stuff is for Emil, if you see him. *Un rasoir et un témoignage* is for you. The letter written in Fred's hand is a little testimonial from the night of the shock. Spent two days running up and down the ladder to the terrace every time there was a knock at the door. Have a beautiful cold as a result. What I detest about these books of maxims is that they are so platitudinously true. A la Molière, Aesop, La Rochefoucauld—Shakespeare. They apply to *all* women, and that must include you too. But somehow it doesn't ring true to me. But it's disquieting.

I saw Kahane yesterday and had a good talk with him, and got along much better than ever. Signed the option, as Bradley had said the terms could not be better. He wants to act as agent still, and so I am to hand him the *Black Spring* to give to Kahane when I am ready. The dope is this. At present everything is dull in the book trade—frightfully dull. It will be so until the Spring. Kahane asked me to have confidence in him, in his judgment as a business man, as one who had as much interest in making the book a success as I have myself. *Alors,* wait a bit, take it easy, he said. In the Spring we'll get it rolling properly. And no use bringing out another book until this one gets properly launched. It would be fatal, it would spoil the sales of *T. of C.* He got out his accounts again to show me how things stood. In the last ten days they sold only 9 books, 6 of which were mine. It is trickling along, Eve Adams* still selling a few now and then. Much réclame in Montparnasse. Have to keep away from [Café] Dôme and other places because I am constantly being introduced to jackasses who read the book and whom I don't care to know. [. . .]

A little more pleasant news is the letter enclosed from Blaise Cendrars. I shall certainly go to meet him, as I understand he is a fine fellow. I enclose two more sections, retyped and revised, from *Black Spring*. These are perhaps less acceptable then the first two. (Note changes in Epilogue!) [Frank] Dobo has already returned the first two, saying no use, no magazine in England would print them. Have a little more hope, however, in America. It all depends on how they are

*An American expatriate who sold magazines and books in Paris cafés.

presented, to whom and by whom. (I am waiting for news from Ezra Pound and from Kay Boyle, to whom I sent carbons. They may make valuable suggestions.) So, take it easy about shooting them out. And when you do, I forgot to warn you, be sure to enclose an addressed and stamped envelope for the return. Give an address which you are sure is bona fide—a month or two hence. Or two addresses, for different dates. I can't attach stamps because I have no American postage.

Anyway, I am going on with these short stories—revamping other material, anything I think suitable. I want to make a last desperate attempt now while you are there and can do something, to put myself over. I hope you don't think it a waste of time. It may mean at least one good fat check—and I am deeply worried about finances. I feel I have no right here at all. It's too luxurious. There will be no receipts from _T. of C._, unless a miracle occurs, for some time. And I am not sending you any copies through the mail, as Lyons advised, because I had a letter just the other day again from Harolde Ross saying that the censor had held up his copy too. They are wise to me, I fear, and it is useless to waste money on stamps. I must wait and see if Osborn's friend, the sailor, will take any over with him. (Had a cordial note from Dos Passos, in Key West, Fla., saying he would be delighted to receive a copy—but I'm not sending him one, for the reason given.) Also received a letter from Benno's sister saying whom to send copies to for review in Russia, and expressing a belief that it would be printed there. But she had not yet received her copy, and she adds—"I doubt that I ever will." However, I am writing George Reavey, of the European Literary Bureau, who deals with Russia, to see what he thinks.

Anaïs, I have written one god-awful pile of letters—more than I dared tell you, and I have walked my legs off seeing people and badgering them, and so on. I felt I had to. I can't see the thing die like that in childbirth. Someday it will fall into the right hands. Some man, I hope, will rise up and do something about it. That's my firm belief. And so I must bide my time.

I am progressing all right with the part I set out to finish in _Black Spring_. Have over forty pages done now. But it is in fits and starts, with these blasted interruptions and setbacks. I long for a profound tranquillity, something deep as death. I _can_ write above the melee, as it were, but I don't like the forced effort. It doesn't ring the way I want it to. I get off-key. I feel now, after my talk with Kahane, that I can work calmly and leisurely, to do all that I planned to do, with fullness and vigor. I want it large, opulent. Fraenkel says—"Go on with the book,

I mean the one you sent me." Slick remark, but he's right, after all.

I am so impatient to get a real letter from you. Not that I expect you have accomplished anything startling already—it's much too soon. But a letter from *you*, telling about yourself, about how you feel. *Our* plans.

It seems more than ever imperative that I find a way to earn money. "Money *as* destiny," says Pound. I disliked that. Yet, what prospects are there for us, if I don't find a means of becoming responsible? I feel so rotten that Rank refused to help us in the only way possible. If you could get your citizenship and remain in America, get divorced, free yourself of Hugo and the whole damned family, could we do something over there? I would go anywhere you say. I don't believe much that America shows any improvement. I discount the glittering Babylonian description you give—first effects. Shake it down. What remains? And yet, if I had you, and if I were sure you would be content over there, if there were something we could do together, I would say let's try. My literary efforts will earn me nothing, I am afraid. I think even if they liked my stuff they would oppose it now because I am still and have been an exile. I received more clippings from over there, which reveals their feelings strongly. I don't belong there, I know it. But I would do anything you advocate if there is some solid basis to it. Not money, not security exactly. But something solid for us. I don't like veering around from one thing to another—one day the analyst, the next day the dancer, the next day the movies, and so on. I know it's sheer desperation that provokes this. And I know it's because I am ineffective that causes it. So it's no reproach. *I'm responsible.* But what to do? What, what, what? It drives me nuts.

Once it would have been possible for me to work for and with Rank. Now I am afraid it is out of the question. I really hate him. And he feels the same, no doubt. He will offer you the whole world, and sincerely, but not to help *us*. He *Rankles* me. But it's human, I suppose.

Fred and I are sleeping together. He has to go to bed by midnight in order to get up at 7 o'clock. *Alors,* I have to accompany him. All this as a result of the wrong envelopes. As usual, he acted the faithful dog. Would have done anything to get me out of harm's way. And that very day his term was up at the hotel and he had no money and no place to go and so I said come over until you find a place.

Andard hasn't paid him a cent yet because he thinks he still has part of his salary from the *Tribune.* Fred is going to talk to him however. I am not shelling out anything for him, believe me. Not because I wouldn't, but because I don't feel I have a right to. I am getting along all right with the checks you left. Quite all right. If the rent isn't all there I'll hand over all the checks and what cash I have too, and take a chance on something coming in for eats. That's the least worry. (Lowenfels' check went through on the second trial and so I could hand that over again to Plancher as partial payment for the gas & electricity.) Maybe all this isn't clear—you must read the crazy letter which I am not yet sending. My greatest outlay has been for postage—heavy mails, Mss., letters, etc. That eats in heavily. Otherwise I am absolutely spendthrifty.

One thing about American liberality, obscenity, etc. Just saw a book of Hemingway's—short stories—*Winner Takes Nothing*. He says out most anything and everything. For "fuck" they print "f- - -." "Whore" goes, "Christ" goes, "shit" goes, etc. And yet somehow there is not the same ring behind his dirty words as with mine. Sincere enough, frank, honest, but not so raw. Almost seems justifiable. Mine seems flagrant and wanton.

I'm holding this up now to see if there is anything to add upon receipt of mail tonight. Waiting. Waiting. In a fever and sweat. Why aren't you in the Tyrol? America is horribly far away. I am going to burn the cables. . . .

[Henry]

P.S. Didn't receive the radio, naturally! *He* (?) mustn't have sailed yet. But I did receive another copy of *The Holy Grail.*

[Villa Seurat]
[December 11, 1934]
Midnight. (Fuck Fred! I'm love-sick.)

[Anaïs:]

Since writing preceding, your letter of Dec. 3rd from the Barbizon arrived. With the check! I am not happy. I am flabbergasted. In four days one can't really earn all that dough! Unless you're getting the rates of an analyst. What the hell *are* you doing? From the very first note it sounds incredible & preposterous to me. It's true I never saw N.Y. from the top floor. I couldn't stand up so tough & straight & insolent as you appear to do.

Since you say at the end of your letter to address you at the hotel—because "it is safe" etc.—I take it Hugo is not going to America at all. Because, to translate a phrase like "they never send the mail up ... I go down for it," simply means that you are still hornswoggling me. True, you're very gentle. You don't even lie overtly. Undoubtedly you *do* go down for the mail—and maybe that's why you pay no attention to my cable & letters addressed to Kay Bryant. You forgot probably that you gave me that address. And she probably doesn't know that you're in New York!

Anaïs—all this must sound rotten to you if what you've done was only to please me, help me, etc. But *why* the deception??? Why? *That is driving me crazy.* Must you deceive me too?

Maybe while I am writing this you are walking thru the streets of Williamsburg. How must I feel not knowing what you are doing? Everything you have written me is tinsel. Don't try to dazzle me, Anaïs. Put on the rubber apron and wash the lettuce leaves. Fry the *raie* with black butter sauce. Tell me you like simple people, simple meals. I weep when you become "a big business woman" & rake in all that dough. And step out every night to the pasteboard places. Did I expect you to sit in a room and mope? *No!* But I didn't expect you to *love* N.Y. or glorify it, or say it requires a poet. Why that sounds American—the worst kind of Americanism.

All this is my fault, I fear. Perhaps because I said once that I hated to leave this studio you are bending heaven & earth to hold it for me. But it's not for *me*—just *me*, Anaïs. *For us.* What good is this beautiful place if you are going out into the world to change your very soul? The person I want is not the one who writes these letters—in champagne foam & embossed print, with a golden-tipped pen etc. The "you" that I love is the one who said the last night—"Don't invite Halasz to dinner. I want to be with you alone."

I know you have a chameleon nature, but I know too the steady immutable core of you. That's what I want. Don't dance around me with jewel dust & klieg lights. Like we talked in Louveciennes—like it was when the window was open on the garden. That! That! That's *you*—and that's me.

Louveciennes isn't there in the Dept. of Seine et Oise. It's in you. You've got to keep it there. We can build a palace around us if everything is right between us.

I want it to be right! I may never be a worldly success but I may bring you other riches.

Never before have I offered myself to you so wholly and sincerely and devotedly. If you do not understand that all this is because I love you than I can say nothing more.

I do not know whether I shall write another letter after this—until I hear from you deeply and convincingly.

This letter & the one of the 8th addressed to Kay Bryant. That means practically till Christmas. If I ever do write to the Barbizon Hotel you may be sure there will be nothing "embarrassing" in the letter. I know the whole history of the Barbizon address. The grand poet must be truly pleased. *If* and *when* he comes.

H.

P.S. All this hurts me more, much more, a thousand times more than it can ever hurt you.

Men have their periods too, but the blood doesn't stop flowing automatically. There is a wild raging river flowing inside of me. I can't dam it. I'm hurt so badly. Believe me—oh shit! *Believe, believe—* what's there to believe any more?

CABLE
1934 DEC 12

ANAIS GUILER BARBIZON PLAZA HOTEL SIXTH AVENUE FIFTY EIGHT STREET
DISREGARD LETTERS DATED SEVENTH TO TWELFTH CARE BRYANT EXCEPT FOR TE AMO STOP IS CHECK NEGOTIABLE FIFTEENTH MAD AS HATTER

HENRY

Barbizon Plaza Hotel
101 West 58th Street, New York
[December 13, 1934]

[Henry:]

Got your letter finally. Kay had not been at her office. I thought I had asked you to write to the Barbizon. Why did you cable me so excitedly twice to disregard your letter except for *"te amo"*? I thought you were giving me hell. There is nothing in your letter to worry me!

No hell, I mean, for the lies! You seem just vaguely puzzled. The cables had alarmed me. Anyway, here is the explanation.

I don't know how, but Hugh did find out you were at the studio, thinks you stayed there when I left it. I hope he got his own letter by now. That is all he seemed to be worried about; having discovered there was nothing, he forgave me for the other trickeries. So today I got a cable from him for Christmas.

Have been too upset to write you about the high moments. Meeting Emil [Schnellock] was one of the very highest. I liked him instantly, as I knew I would, for his softness, understanding, responsiveness. He came up to my room. We were shy at first, but admitted it. But we had so much to talk about that it soon wore away. I told him about my troubles, the reason I had done this etc., we laughed about it after a while, talked our heads off about you, the past, your book, my novels, his life etc. Had dinner together down [in] the Village; planned to make the pilgrimage together; I showed him I had taken your list of places to see, of your own history, and put [it in] an envelope [marked] "Walks with Emil." He began by showing me the cellar on Henry Street. It hurt me to see it. Wished I had not. It's too real. And all that was so fantastic to me. I don't know that I want it concretized. It's another cellar, not the one you created in my mind. It's yours I liked. Emil and I talked marvellously, smoothly, almost interrupting each other with the rush of things to say. He is a part of you, he *is* in fact the soft, scrupulous, responsive you—that I prefer to whatever it is Lowenfels represents of another side. There is the southern, relaxed, seeing-you in him. It was a very exciting and swimming kind of evening, though we did nothing but have dinner and walk a while—it was too cold for me to walk much. We looked in through the window of some coffee house where the expatriates meet. Emil was disappointed I could not live down there, he naturally did not like the Barbizon. I explained how I still had my social ties. People from the Bank call for me there. (I had to go out with Mrs. Perkins, who is delightful.) Otherwise I would have liked staying [in] the Village. I also have to be near the Center etc.

Will write you more about the meeting with Emil. How aware he is of everything, intuitively, fine perceptions, immune to "ideas." He quotes you and me freely and aptly. His appreciativeness is very warming. Your mellow self is all there. He will never disappoint you, or disillusion you.

Have wasted some time being sick, due to overheated apartments—awful, like Turkish baths, and then going out in icy cold weather. Had to postpone seeing Harrison Smith* though I had a date with him etc. Shaking with fever from the violent changes. The illusion of N.Y. is wearing off. Once you get behind or inside the buildings, the externals, the minds are terrible, the newspapers, the movies, the conversations, the mentality, the parties, the wisecracks—I can't tell you how ugly, or how brutal, or how imbecilic. Loathsome. There is so much of it. I believe one could not find or be one's self here without a strong preparation, having lived in Paris first, I would say, to create this integrity, and then one may live here with what one has amassed. But creating the self here is herculean, and I see why I ran away, why you ran away, and stayed away. One has to be terribly whole to stand it, to be indifferent, to nourish one's self and live only with a few people. More coming—like a Diary! Love,

A.

Write me here. Cable: *Guiler Barbplaza* if necessary.

[Villa Seurat]
Friday night, the 14th [December 1934]

[Anaïs:]

Your two letters on cellophane just arrived—of the 7th. Don't even sign your name now. No mention of my name. Not a word of love. If I hadn't received your cable I would be stark crazy by now. What a punishment you are meting out to me! And for what? For what? Well, it's something to know that you're happy. Something to know that Radio City makes somebody glad. It's all just as you say. You're in another world. I'm here and the best I can do to grip you is to see *Amok*, because you said you liked it. And when I saw the opening, the lianas, the tangled trees, the thick dense tropical jungle I said to myself—Why this is just like "Alraune." A perfect match to Anaïs' writing. It was very impressive that opening. Very wonderful of you to have caught all that in writing. And now your life is all cellophane—"I love you, honey," etc. It's too bad that when I say these things there are no bands around, no sky line, no new world on the horizon.

---

*American publisher (1888–1971), owner of the firm Smith & Haas, which was merged with Random House in 1936. From 1938 to 1966 he edited the *Saturday Review of Literature*.

Anaïs, forgive me, but I am sad, wretchedly, abominably miserable. Nothing will help me until I see the words you have so willfully, stubbornly omitted from all your letters. Your letters tell me nothing. It's like that kiss Andard blew into the nape of your neck—makes a big smacking noise and you laugh about it afterwards. Only one thing I thank you for—you don't invent any unnecessary lies. You don't even lie—you just keep silent. I don't want to break the magical mood. If the blunder hadn't occurred perhaps I would have been happy with these cellophane letters. Out of the cable I squeeze two words which once you left on a little sheet of paper in the early morning and I never forget them. In that little room I was very happy. I had *you*. Now I have this big cheerless studio and I am the saddest man in the world. Everybody says: "What a wonderful place!" But for me it is hell. Hell de luxe, do you get me?

What did I want? *I wanted a life with you!* And I get instead Radio City, the lights going up, "honey I love you," dancing all night, crap shooting, cellophane magic, chrome and black marble. In the letter I have not sent is a list of all the blasted things which now acquire significance. I am raving mad, I am hungry, and I am frantic because I don't know which way to turn. Believe me, if I had the money I would take the very next boat. You can't ever know what a temptation it was to take the rent check and cash it and leave the god-damned studio. Maybe that's what I should have done! But I can do that still, it's necessary. I'll cable to everybody I know and I'll get there somehow if I don't get a letter with some real consolation, something deep and sincere and heartfelt, something that means something to me. I'll try to wait another few days. I don't know when that letter is due—the one you say "explains." Drat it, I don't want the explanations. I want something beyond that, bigger than that. Explanations are for husbands, for people you don't care about any more. I want something which only you can give me. I want it badly. You congratulate me on my activity. Well, all that's gone to sand. I'm still working, but it's like a ghost. I live only in anticipation of that letter. And if that letter falls short then God help us!

Anaïs, I wish you could see through this paper, these words—see me face to face. You know what I look like. Look into me deeply, read what is there. While everything is wrapped in cellophane over there, here it is still Paris, still the Villa Seurat, a dark, quiet street, and tonight it is raining cats and dogs. Figure to yourself what it is like, with this terrible distance between us, with your going weeks ahead of time, with the date of your return uncertain, with these bright, scintillating letters that are unsigned. I don't envy the good time you are having, please believe that! I am glad that you are enjoying yourself. Truly glad. But now that is unimportant. I have something much more important to say to you. Are you listening? Are you all there? This letter will reach you via the *Europa*, sailing on the 16th. I send it care of Bryant, because I don't know when Hugo arrives and I don't want to put you in danger. I expect you to burn this letter after you read it—for your own sake. If you love me you won't forget what it contains.

This is it. When you get this letter, and after you have thought it over carefully, I want you to send me a cable, and a letter too, if you will. I want to know if you will give up everything and live your life with me—not part time, not furtively, but twenty-four hours of the day and for good. I will come over there if it is best to come there, and I suppose it is. That depends on what you think best. You would have to become a citizen in order to do that. As an American citizen you can live here too if you wish. You can live anywhere. When I say America, it's because your letters make me feel that perhaps there is something I might find to do over there. To make a living here seems practically hopeless. *But*—remember this above all! First of all I am a human being, and as human being the most important thing on earth for me is to hold you. For that I would give up writing, would do anything, anything that would enable me to keep you by my side. I think sometimes that perhaps I have been unfair to put my writing above everything else. I am a man and I want my woman. If writing interferes then to hell with writing. If I am a truly great man, as I hope I am, then I shall be able to do both—to work for you and hold you, and to keep on writing. I must not be mollycoddled.

Heretofore I have had some consideration for others—for the peculiar situation in which you have been placed. Now I regard all this as secondary. I can't stop to think about your mother, about Hugo, about Joachim. I won't relinquish you no matter who stands in the way. Is that clear? It is time you had a right to your own life. I will make any sacrifice necessary to protect the others, except surrendering you.

Donc, I want a cable saying what you think. I don't care how much it costs. Charge it up to the Psychological Center! But don't be equivocal with me, else I'll hop the boat immediately. When the time comes to go I'll find the means, don't worry. And maybe the band will play for me too when I enter the harbor! The very thought makes me sick to the guts. You don't know what a wild, crazy longing I have, what an ache there is inside me. I won't roam up and down Mexico as Lawrence did. That's not my tactics. I'll go straight to your room and knock at the door. And if there's no answer I'll go to the Psychological Center. I'll find you even if you are buried away in Radio City. But there better not be anybody with you when I arrive—no creamy lemon voices, no southern drawl, no honey business.

But very seriously, Anaïs . . . what I propose is in deadly earnest. I don't know what plan of action to pursue. I hesitate to suggest because I don't want anything to happen to you. I know that Hugo is capable of anything when his anger is aroused. It would be better to get out of reach and then let him know. But you need to get your papers straightened out first. I'm afraid this way you have very little rights, very little freedom of movement.

In any case, what I want *immediately* is a definite answer. That ought to be before Christmas. Make it my Christmas present! Or my birthday present, which is the next day. If you think I should come, say so and I will begin cabling to my friends immediately. I am on tenterhooks, I tell you. A fever in my bones. Each day is a fresh torture, an agony. Tomorrow Blaise Cendrars is coming here. God knows how I will receive him. I'm like a blabbering idiot. I'm already praying that he won't stay long.

There's another thing I must warn you about. You will see from the enclosed letters sent me by Harolde Ross how things stand with the Federal authorities. Whether they would clamp the lid on me immediately on landing, I don't know. I daren't show it to Kahane because he would probably be scared to death. Perhaps you could consult a lawyer in N.Y. and find out if I am likely to be apprehended and clapped in jail. Some of those packages [with copies of *Tropic of Cancer*] must have been signed by me as the dispatcher. And maybe one or two by you! What a mess! So, in any case, lay low on all activity about the book. Don't get yourself in trouble! I'm not sending out any more, naturally. And I haven't seen or heard of Osborn's friend yet. I doubt if he will ever show up.

Before Cendrars comes . . . Please read over the enclosed letters and then send them on to Ross—his address is on his letterhead. If you can see a good lawyer discreetly do so. If not, the hell with it. Don't be too alarmed. Nothing has happened to Ford and he's back in America *(The Young and Evil)*.* But keep your name out of this

---

*In 1933, the Obelisk Press had published Charles Henri Ford's "underground" novel of homosexual life. He was then twenty years old.

thing—don't write letters about it to people and don't use your Nin name on back of envelopes because these Federal people are the damndest sleuths. Get your citizenship first! After that, fuck them! I'm in a mood to fight if that's what they want of me. I've lain awake nights making speeches on the witness stand. But I detest all that. I don't want to be plastered all over the newspapers. Nor hounded to death by all sorts of wrong people, particularly those who might rush to defend me. *Comprenez-vous?* If they ever bring me to court it will be dramatic because I will refuse to adapt myself to the procedure. Either they will let me talk as I choose and refuse to talk when I choose or I give them the choice to clap me into jail immediately. I'll not swear on any Bible, nor even promise on my word of honor to tell the truth etc. I'll stand on my rights as a human being, and that's all—and to hell with all their rigmarole.*

Two A.M. Boat train leaves 9:30 A.M. Cendrars came at three P.M. and I have just gotten away from him, had to run away. As a man I must have sorely disappointed him. I was almost taciturn. *A cause de toi!* And yet, what a day! What a night! [. . .] He's a real man I tell you, and I feel bad that I let him down. Perhaps he is that one man I wrote about recently, the man I expected to come forward and hail me. And how I fucked myself! *A cause de toi, ma chérie. Oui! Mais je ne le regrette pas.* This letter is more important to me than that champion I thought a few days ago was so terribly necessary. You're my champion! With you I'll get anywhere I want. I want you to realize that. I'm not laying it on thick. Nothing is exaggerated in all I have recounted. It was all like receiving the Prix Goncourt—and then throwing it down the toilet. (He said Hamsun never budged from his seat to go for his Nobel Prize. "Too late," he said. "You should have offered it to me thirty years ago when I had a future ahead of me.")

Well, that's that! Enclosed is a letter from Pound, the latest. Kahane was elated to know that the famous T. S. Eliot might print Pound's review [of *Tropic of Cancer*] in his fucking magazine [*The Criterion*]. I'm not. *Je m'en fous de tout ca! Je travaille. Plus que jamais!* Another letter in today's mail, from James Laughlin IV, dated Rapallo,

---

*H. M. never had to testify personally in the censorship battles that surrounded his work, but *Tropic of Cancer* and *Tropic of Capricorn*, as well as some of his other works, did not get published openly in the United States until the early 1960s, when his publisher, Grove Press, fought a series of court cases and won.

also. "May I tell you that I think the *T. of C.* is a great book? Hell, you wrote it. I don't need to tell you. I shall spread the word, of course." O.K. *Tout ça ne m'intéresse pas maintenant. Trop tard. Moi je m'occupe d'une Espagnole. Oui, c'est ça. Exactement. Ou ça m'amenera je ne sais pas. Mais je t'aime. Follement. Je suis devenu fou. Et tu parles de la cellophane. Raconte-moi ça encore et je te donne un beau gifle. Tu entends? Un gifle, dans ta geule! Compris? Moi, je ne suis pas matelot, ni aventurier, ni rien que un homme, un homme au bout de ses nerfs. Je m'emmerde ici. A cause de toi. Je me couche maintenant—tout seul. Je me couche avec des cauchemares. Chaque nuit des cauchemares. Pour toi. Pour Noël. Alors, je t'embrasse. Pour Noël. Pour l'avenir. Pour toi-même parce que tu es devenue la femme, la seule. Je n'aurais aucune vie sans toi, compris? Si, tu comprends très bien. Mais tu es maline, rusée. Tu te moques de moi. Si, je le sais. Tu as tout le pouvoir dans ta main. Tu as moi, le tout de moi.*

[Henry]

[Villa Seurat]
Dec. 17th, 1934.

[Anaïs:]

The last sheet of the paper you gave me some months ago, in the hope, no doubt, of inspiring me to work! Enclosing some more MSS. The last from *Black Spring.* If I send any more, it will be the new stuff, a triplicate copy. The carbons you can read and throw away afterwards. The telegram, if I send it today, will read: *"Sur la fleuve amour avec les anges de première qualité.* Signed: *H. Fauxbidet."*

What keeps singing in my ears is—*"Puisque mon amour ne pendra jamais fin, que cette musique reste inachevée à jamais."*

You might say whether you get all the MSS. I send you. I don't know what gets through any more. All the letters except one, with MSS. enclosed, went to Kay Bryant. This will go there too.

Your "letter" can't arrive before the 20th. Until then it's black spring, and how! Because even though it was for the best it was a breach of confidence, of trust, and how that hurts and hurts. I am crying inside all the time. That worst letter you wrote me was nothing compared to this shock. If you had only said to me—"Henry, you've got to under-stand why I'm doing this . . ." I would grant you anything. But no. And the worst is that I have nothing to reproach you for. *Nothing.* It's because the scale weighs so heavily against me that I am overwhelmed. Because it was my fault.

Saw your letter to Kahane—"most cordially yours, Anaïs Nin."

P.S. Forgot to say that Cendrars' reference to "Preface" was also my fault—and I told him so, without giving the cat away. Said it was my idea—those names, which is true. I hope you didn't feel too badly about it.

Henry

TELEGRAM
1934 DEC 18

ANAIS GUILER CARE THE BARBIZON PLAZA 58TH STREET AND 6TH AVE NEW YORK
LETTERS MUST ARRIVE SOON YOU WILL BE HAPPY LOVE

[HENRY]

[Villa Seurat]
Dec. 18th, 1934

My dear, lovely Anaïs,

this is supposed to be a secret but I can't keep it, it's so good, and I want so much for you to be happy. I have just dispatched a cable in answer to yours. I said you would be happy when you finally got all the letters, and I know you will, even though there may be a bit of grief and anguish mixed up with it. Because at the bottom of all the letters lies one big word—LOVE. That you may be sure of—always.

But I am getting off. This noon, coming back from the cable office, I met Fred and we had lunch together. He is very busy now, absent most of the day, working for Andard, and going often to the Chambre des Députés, and writing for deputies, etc. He is getting along famously. And he will leave as soon as Andard gives him his first month's salary, which will be soon. Everything's all right on that score. (How bad it is that my letters come so late!) Anyway, during the lunch he told me that Andard is likely to take over the Baudinière concern. Baudinière is badly in debt and must be squeezed out. Andard has *"la galette." "J'ai la galette, moi!"* We shout this at intervals during the day. One of Andard's favorite phrases. But wait. The best is this: Andard said that if he took over the business he would like to publish your book! In French!

When I heard that I jumped. "Tell Andard, I said to send Anaïs a cable immediately. Send a night letter, it only costs 50 frs. Tell him that! I will give you the cable address—it will be still cheaper." Now this isn't all. Things have happened here. Never happened so fast and furiously. And good things. As though all your astrological divinations were coming true. About myself I don't care. I know I am in the lap of the gods and that destiny is with me. That's why I don't get too excited—about myself, I mean. I can bide my time. *But you!* I am weeping with joy to think that you are going to get a break. All this is supposed to be a secret. You must not tell a soul about Andard's projects. Nothing is definitely arranged yet, but I am sure it will happen. He has *"la galette." Quoi!* [. . .]

And that is why I want Andard to send you a cable. Perhaps you can show that cable to an editor and secure your American rights. But you must not say that Andard is taking over the Baudinière business. That's a secret.

It may also surprise you to know that Andard finished my book and admired it extremely when he had gotten through with it. Said there were passages in it that beat anything he had ever read. Said I was "a man, *quoi!*" Which is very decent of him considering that he's my rival and tries to fuck me behind my back. *N'est ce pas?* [. . .]

So people are going to do things for you. That's what makes me wild with joy. You have been doing things for people all your life. And now at last they are going to do something for you. I am delirious about it!

And I too am doing something for you. Before Christmas or Christmas day, I shall probably cable you again, saying that "Alraune" is on its way, and that it's my Christmas present for you. And I am signing your name to it, and I want you to leave it there—providing you agree with the worthiness of the MS. It *is your* book, your *"Scenario."* That I wrote it is nothing. I only rewrote what you had done. I only lived out the inspiration you received and which you bequeathed to me.*

---

*Inspired by A. N.'s "Alraune," which eventually became *House of Incest*, H. M. wrote a *Scenario* for "a film with sound," which was published in a limited edition of 200 copies, with a frontispiece by Abraham Rattner, by the Obelisk Press, Paris, in 1937.

And all this you will only get about the 28th of December. Anaïs, my dear Anaïs, if I were at all wealthy I would cable the whole *Scenario* to you. It gripes me not to be able to send more cables. I would cable every day. *Sur la fleuve Amour, avec les anges,* etc. *Puisque mon amour ne prendra jamais fin,* etc. I would cable you my heart, if it could be done.

True, I have been very miserable, terribly miserable. But at the bottom was hope, confidence, above all, a love such as I have never had for another human being. Not one. Believe that, Anaïs. *You are my woman and I must have you all to myself and I shall never surrender you.* I made the great mistake of letting you mother me. But now I am strong and confident of my own powers. I will make a way for the both of us.

It's true that the *Scenario* will not be a commercial venture. I don't expect you to sell it, even to a deluxe pornographer. But it will bring fame, that I believe. And what I want you to do is ask Rank if he will lend the money to have it published here in France, in a deluxe edition, a limited number—say 100 copies. And let him write a preface to it! (Now I know of 3 cheap and good publishers.) Let him sign his name to something, since it is yours. I won't let you tell him that I did it! Understand? It's yours, all yours, and I want you to lie to him. This time I will approve your lies! Because it's not a lie. . . .

The lies! When I write this word the blood starts flowing. Dear Anaïs, you must forgive me if I sometimes hurt you by a cruel word. You must realize that more than any man you know I have suffered because of these lies. Not yours, but the ones before you, the lies June told me. You must realize that the little deception, honest and good as it was, which I believe without ever seeing your letter of explanation, nevertheless threw me completely off balance. Threw me back on to the old treadmill of pain and jealousy, of utter disillusionment. Everything you had so preciously built up for me toppled. Everything was spinning and I was like a madman roaming about in search of that word which had fallen from my mouth and which no letter of yours seemed to bring. Now that is gone—at least temporarily. Gone because I have swamped myself completely in my joy of bringing you perhaps a little pleasure by the good news I recount. Joy that I may be of service to

It was later included in *The Cosmological Eye,* the first book by Miller to be published in the United States (Norfolk, CT: New Directions, 1939). *Scenario* was produced on French radio in 1952, introduced by Blaise Cendrars.

you, just a little service. Cry if you like. I am crying myself as I write this. All was for the best. You know how much I care—and that is worth any pain.

This ought to go via the *Hamburg*. I wish I were bringing it to you myself. I wish I were there with you. How I have eaten my words, the little, thoughtless words that wounded you one day when I said I would like to go to America alone. Now I am alone and I am paying for my thoughtlessness. I count the days. I hate to ask when exactly, because I know it is too far off. But the thought that you went ahead of time—Christ, that stabs and stabs. And *I* made you go ahead of time! I know all that you're going to tell me in that letter which will not arrive until long, long after I have written this. I know it all. I'm the cause. My weakness. Woe, woe! Everything that happens to us we deserve. We make our own destinies. That's a certainty. But over and above the pain is the rainbow. Nothing is lost. Out of suffering comes joy, or holiness. That's true too.

After what I have been through these days to read in the cable that you were "upset" gave me no pleasure. Even though I felt that you deserved to be just a little upset. And I had to laugh, a little bitterly, it is true, that you waited for the *Bremen* letter before writing your letter! How wiley! How feminine! Yes, that hurt too. That was like June's cables. "Letter following" and then no letter. Waiting to see what I would say, how I would react. But no, I can't believe that of you. I can't believe that you would play such a game with me. And yet that is how it looks—from the cables. But I wait. Now it's the 18th. I must wait until the 28th most likely. That's ten days. Try to conceive what ten days of suspense means to a man who's dying to know the truth from the woman he loves! Try it, Anaïs. Today the *Albert Ballin* doesn't even appear on the boat lists. It's too soon. Frantically searching the papers for a sign of the *Albert Ballin*. Walking to the cable office with head down—*Albert Ballin. Albert Ballin.* Ah yes, what do you know of all this? You are "upset." Dear God, I hope you're not *very* upset. I hope you have not suffered as I have. I wouldn't wish it on my worst enemy.

I must stop. I must conserve myself a bit. For the last ten days it has been a steady outgive, a drain, a drive without let [up]. Back and forth to the Gare, to the cable office, here, there, everywhere, writing you, dreaming of you, tossing about all night, smoking during the night, meeting people, smiling at them, not hearing them, playing the clown, laughing, crying secretly, working, hoping, despairing, praying, and always waiting and waiting and waiting for the letters, for something, for one word even that would make me happy. (And you sent me Cellophane! Was I mad? I was so furious I tore it off and chewed it to bits. I blew down all the fucking skyscrapers and radios and chrome and marble baths and swinging doors. I *hate* your god-damned N.Y.!) But I am calm now. It is getting dark. I can barely see here. I wonder where you are, whom you are talking to, what street you are walking, what invitation for dinner, what legs you rub up against, *who* gets an erection dancing with you, who says "Honey isn't it grand, etc." I wonder if you ever saw my friend Emil Schnellock, if you ever sat and talked about me, just for five minutes. I wonder if the thought ever came to wander down those streets I mentioned, to look up that little house on "the street of early sorrows." I wonder and wonder. You have been terribly good to me and you have been terribly cruel too. I forgive everything, certainly! How could I not? It's love, and love is anguish. Does that make you happy, as you said when you sent the check? *Does that make you happy?* Oh, then be happy! I am happy too in my sad way.

[Henry]

Barbizon Plaza Hotel
December 19, 1934

Oh Henry, Henry. I'm upset. No letter off the *Bremen*. No knowledge of what you feel or think. Just those cables. I couldn't write you. It's really very simple, terribly simple, Henry—I don't know how far back I have to go. The cut in Hugh's salary, or his discovery of my check-drawing, anyway, I saw I couldn't get the rent money, that I couldn't keep you going, it seemed as if all my protection was crumbling, and I owe Rank the money for your book—not Hugh. Rank promised me that if I came to New York I would get independent from Hugh, and could take care of as many people as I wanted to. I couldn't tell you because you might not have let me come—without Hugh, especially. I used Hugh's furlough as a justification. He *is* coming over, but later. I told Hugh I not only wanted to pay him back, but make a new start, break with the past, find myself etc. He thought I was going away from *you*, that is why he permitted it. He was so overwhelmingly generous, and helped me so much, that I wrote him wonderful love letters, dictated by gratitude and guilt. I think *that* you could see through.

My plan was: to see what Rank would do. If really I was to make money then I could stay here until the Spring and send for you. But meanwhile you would be working and not anxious. Then all the cables came. What I don't understand is that I got a letter from Hugh on this last Saturday. Nothing from you. With him everything is O.K. I did not write *you* any love letters. I enclosed a check—not for you but for Brassai for the photos. Hugh writes: "This error you made proved to me there was nothing between you and Henry. About letting him occupy your studio while you're away—I forgive you!"

My plans *did* work out. You got the rent money. I am building up an independence from Hugh. The rest will develop later. Later on, I can send for you. You can stay as long as you want to there. Work. Give notice for the studio for March 15th. Unless I can get Eduardo to take it over. Will discuss this later. There's plenty of time.

I have so much to do that I write you on trains, in subways, wherever I can sit down. I'm a bit tired. Not in the mood to tell you about the beautiful events, outstanding one meeting with Emil. Will see Erskine, Harrison Smith, Dreiser, Bye, Simpson etc. this week.

March would be a tentative date for your coming over.

Your cable today, just arrived, did me good. Can't understand the *Bremen* mystery. Nor why you were "mad as hatter." Because of the lies?

[Anaïs]

P.S. What was the date on the last check I gave you?

[Villa Seurat]
December 19, 1934

[Anaïs:]

And now it's midnight again—next day—and until that letter comes I won't be myself. *Albert Ballin.* When? How? Expect cables. Listen for footsteps. In starting the "Alraune" I found some notes you made on back of telegram. Never noticed telegram before. Now I read: "Madrid—Everything fine. Love." No name to it so I suppose that's you. And then I remember that when you developed the sinus trouble and missed the boat—you were going even earlier than you did!—you said that Hugo threatened to carry you onto the boat even if you were ill. Yes, he was so bent on getting away! Jesus, that was a fine gratuitous lie! Superb! And so for finally bundling you off (against your will) you write and thank him.

Well, *par contre*, as I sit down to the "Alraune" I say to myself—what a writer! I doubt now that I can even bring the *Scenario* up to the imaginative level you reached. *Jamais!* There are things you have written, pages & pages, which still baffle me—I mean the grasp, the conception, the execution.

And curiously enough it all gibes marvellously with your horoscope—which I reread and with the most attention. Read it again if you have it! And then wrap a little cellophane around it.

In my present state I hesitate meeting Blaise Cendrars again. He had asked to see me again, *very soon,* and I promised to invite him for dinner. But I haven't the gusto for it. I may feel sad when he comes—and that would spoil things. I can't even write him a letter tho' I've tried to several times. He must have a strange opinion of me.

Only now it occurs to me, on reading your cable over for the twentieth time, that perhaps you doubted whether I ever sent a letter via the *Bremen.* But surely you must have received it by now. I went with Fred to the *gare* myself that day of the 7th, an early morning, and tho' I didn't go inside the *gare*, for fear of meeting Hugo at the letter-box (thinking he would be doing exactly what I was doing), I waited outside and I'm sure it was properly posted for I cross-examined Fred several times. The only thing I can possibly imagine is that we were *too early* and instead of catching the special mail bag which is posted just before train leaves we put it in the one near the P.O. where it is marked with boat, and as I explained in one of my letters, the very next letter, mailed next day, caught a boat which wouldn't arrive until almost 2 weeks later. That was *my* fault—because I was out of my head at the moment. But by now you must have all these letters & you can see from the date & hour of posting that I am not lying.

I am in a terribly nervous condition, which alternates with moments of great peace and calm when I believe that you must surely know me and understand me. I would have cabled you every day, but I just couldn't. I mean the money wouldn't stretch that far. I only paid Halasz today, for example. No extravagance, I assure you. But forget this. It's just to let you know that I have really cabled as often as possible.

I am still mailing letters to Kay Bryant because I think it safer for you. I don't know anything about Hugo—even whether he has left or not. That's the only reason why I may not sign my name to the cables—not because of the extra word. You can imagine to what point I got when I tried persuading Fred to borrow some dough for me of Andard. I wanted it for cables, cables. (There are three rates, you know—a deferred day rate, a night letter of 30 words, and a straight fast message day or night transmitted in a half-hour—delivery??—*par les Français, ou par les* half-wits *de* Western Union at N.Y.)

And now this goes by the *Hamburg* & it takes 7 days! And I say, "Go boat, go! Speed on! Full *vitesse!*" But only your boats, your special chartered boats, break the record. It's that way in "Alraune" and it's that way in the horoscope. Full speed ahead! Maybe I'm just a brake for you(?). But I'm a good *"break"* too. Look that up in your dictionary of slang.

Anyway, I'm wondering now if the reason Hugo was so mad about Turner's sailing was because *you* had planned to take the same boat? And was the sinus trouble an unconscious desire to be faithful—*and to whom?* [Aleister] Crowley said the other night that Jung confesses to being almost incapable where women are concerned. Says men's minds are easy enough to read. But women's . . . ? Too many centuries of enforced cunning and deceit! (Swell thing to tell me out of a clear sky. I said nothing about my worries at all. I wouldn't want that guy tampering with me. No sir! But I must say he gave me a marvellous clarification on the "anima-animus" business. Remind me sometime of the goddess Athena and what the Greeks did.)

I have got to simplify all these things even if I am thoroughly in the wrong. There is no living with a brain divided in two. No peace that way. Better to be wrong, behind time, ignorant, and to *roll,* than get stuck in this vast bog of erudition. "The food for the soul is light and space." Aye! Aye! And amen!

Jealousy renders one impotent and fouls one too, at the same time. To keep me in such a state would be tantamount to destroying me. Be glad, yes, that I can suffer, but don't use it as a weapon. In the end it only acts as a boomerang. For if you destroy me you destroy yourself. I am sure you know all this, without my telling you. But now and then a woman likes not only to *feel* her power, but to use it.

What threw me into consternation was the evident enjoyment with which you swam in a sea of flattery. As tho' no one in all your life had ever paid you a compliment. That's *your* weakness. *That* weakness I can't play up to. It's not my nature. I've never withheld saying a good and beautiful thing to you, but to say them constantly, just to pamper you, no, I can't do it. It's false. You ought not to expect to be fed that every day. I don't like even writing you this way, even telling you such things. Because together it was never necessary. You never did anything that could be criticized. I found a perfection in you. And that perfection which is yours can't be altered. It's you. I want you to keep it, keep your essential self. When I think of you it's of a woman who dances into the room—everything at once radiant and luminous. That's why you're always in the prow of the boat, singing. You light the mariner on his way.

Stop! Full stop! If I were to halt here the picture would be only half-true. I don't see you as a beacon-light merely. (Tho' for most men, and especially artists, that would be sufficient.) I see you *as a woman.* That light is only the effulgence of your spirit. But your body claims me too—just as much. Your body burns in me. I don't want a searchlight with me, however powerful. I want the whole apparatus. And I'm not just content with the radiant aura you throw about everything. I want the whole apparatus. And want it uniquely, for myself alone. That is the mistake I made—to share you. That made the woman less, I fear. Now it's got to be you altogether, seven days in the week, and voyages included. (And no understudying for psychoanalysts, no parts in the ballet, no Paramount tests, "no sleeping propositions.") To hear you rattle off all these things in your letters, to know the endless pressing, the clamor, the sweating that goes on about you just drives me nuts. If you think I've become a Puritan, think so. I don't care. *I won't share you!!!* You're mine and I'm going to keep you. I have become fiercely possessive. But I'm not a tyrant. I ask only justice—justice in the name of love.

Henry

P.S. You ought to be over your period now and riding the waves again. With woman the psychological moment is often the biological moment.

[Barbizon Plaza Hotel, New York]
Thursday Night—Dec. 20 [1934]

Henry, Henry—

don't ever regret the letters you wrote me—they made everything right! I didn't know my own feelings when I wrote you yesterday. I think if you see *through* my last letter everything was revealed in a cold phrase about my evading "sentimental considerations because you always do . . ." and separateness. I didn't know myself why I couldn't go down to *your* streets. You yourself explained everything when you say something in your last letters—"I know it's because I'm ineffective that causes it. I'm responsible."

This weakness about life—which I *don't reproach you for;* but in spite of myself, when I'm doing things, or subjected to Hugh etc. I feel rebellious, not against you, but whatever it is in you that obliges me to do those things. Then I probably try to hurt you in other ways, though I don't want to. I don't love N.Y. I don't love glitter, but I want my material liberty from *one* man, and if it isn't Hugh, it's another. I want to stand on my own feet, because you can't. You are weak, Henry. Don't tell me, for example, Fred's coming to the studio was to protect *you* against Hugh. No. You were too weak to protest, that's all, and I know it means interruptions, and why did you sleep on the porch? Etienette has moved in too. As soon as I leave, you are helpless. You can't defend even the space you write in, work in. That made me angry. And that, as I told you one day almost weeping, will never change. And for that you'll have to pay the penalty of my becoming a business woman, and as I can't do it with bitterness, I must do it gaily and humorously, as I was doing it until the letters got mixed up, and that is why I didn't go down to your streets—not to awaken any feeling. Then you write me about losing my soul etc.

I don't want to hurt you. You know why I came. I borrowed the rent money on my month's salary. I am working. It doesn't do me any harm. The deception, you know, was necessary. You wouldn't have let me come without Hugh. And if you had resisted me the slightest bit I wouldn't have had the courage to come. You want to know what I do—I leave the Barbizon at 8:30. I go to the Center's office, the room where I analyze, write letters, & conferences for Rank etc. Sometimes I eat lunch alone at the cafeteria on 7th Avenue when I need the time for myself, but I try not to be alone—have nothing much to dream about, and then if I do I break down, I get lonely and yearning.

I like simple people and simple meals. But I'm passive. I let everybody take me out. I don't like to be alone. And I take an interest, not in the people but in what my imagination is constructing out of N.Y. Out of what I hear and see.

Never before, Henry, did I offer myself so wholly, sincerely and devotedly, but that's why I'm doing mad things for you.

Why do you think you can't write to the Barbizon? Who is "the grand poet" who will be pleased. Oh, Henry, Henry, let's get close to each other again. Two things you said in Paris stuck in my head—that about seeing N.Y. alone, which comes out in yesterday's letter together with a glorification of *toys*, of the American toys—radio etc. *because* one replaces real things that way. And another day saying ours was an almost cold-blooded relationship . . .

But now it's all over. Don't be hurt any more. You can come whenever you want to—as soon as I make the money—sooner than I said in the other letters, perhaps to hurt you.

Emil saw my room at the Barbizon. It's like a shoe box.

In these letters—when you talk about I being Louveciennes and "we can build a palace around us if everything is right between us," you write and talk as you never did before, more as I wrote and talked—these things seem to have become real and absolute for you only when I leave them for a cruder realization, because I was in greater danger of losing my strength [through] the conflict of my life with Hugh than I am of losing my soul in N.Y. Never fear that. But I was happy to be free and for a while that happiness took the form of exultant love of N.Y. It's not N.Y. I love, my Henry, my little Henry, my Henry. Can't write any more.

[Anaïs]

Tomorrow I'll cable you money. This is only for emergencies. You can use it if you need it. I can explain to Hugh.

TELEGRAM
1934 DEC 23

ANAIS GUILER BARBPLAZA NEWYORK
MAILING ALRAUNE FOR YOUR XMAS AWAIT REPLY EUROPA LETTER.

[HENRY]

[Henry:]

The finest thing which happened to me on X-mas Day was getting your cable that you were sending "Alraune," by which I take it you have been working on it.

Everything stopped when I got your three letters one almost right after the other. With one thing and another, work or strain or misery, or the loss of my gaiety, etc., anyway, I broke down and got real sick. Fortunately I had told everybody I was going away for X-mas. I hate all the fuss they make over it here. I did not want to go to the [Maxwell] Perkins' house, in Greenwich, did not want to go to the Guilers, etc. I accepted a long ride through Connecticut with some people from the [Psychological] Center to see the country just over the weekend. So I saw Hartford, New Haven, Litchfield etc., and other places on the road. White wood houses, white wood churches, bare laceless trees, precise roads, geometric-looking people, shoe-box towns, drabness, or so it seemed to be, like a page of arithmetic. The towny places were like factories. Good food. No drinking—hard, I mean. Reminded me of Richmond Hill* and made me more ill inside than ever. The white curtains etc. Somehow it feels like starvation [starvation of the imagination]. It's too clean, too healthy, too I don't know what. You would hate it. It's no use, I cannot tell what you will feel when you come. [Some days] I love it, I love its surface, rhythm etc. All that I wrote you about is true. Spiritually, an ashy core; the mind—that is definitely lacking. Amused to enter a small antique and book shop in a small place, Litchfield, I think, and find on a shelf of reduced-price books at one dollar the [anthology] *Americans Abroad.* They could not sell it! Oh, Henry, I will never finish answering the other letters. I better follow instructions in the cable which said: Disregard everything except *"te amo."* I did try to answer them. I don't know whether the cable was sent because something I said in the letters you got after the mixed ones revealed something to you, or what. I don't want to go into details. What you call my astrological calculations. Do you really want to know why if I win something betting on the boat I send it to you by check?

---

*A. N. had lived in Richmond Hill, Queens, New York, with her mother and brothers before her marriage in 1923, and she and her husband lived there prior to their move to France in December 1924.

[. . .] Must I explain that I reduce that check by whatever Hugh has given me the right to draw for my allowance and tell him so, etc.? I sent you by cable 20 dollars the other day, thinking you might be short. And for Christmas.

I mentioned quite casually the leaving of the studio in my other letters. Trying not to be sentimental. But I don't see any other way, Henry. I don't want to get you out of your groove as long as you wish to stay in it. I said "come in March" because I don't see how I can get the money for your trip before that. But I leave that to you. For myself, I would like you to come in February, before Hugh arrives, so that we may have some time together. [. . .]

I want to know: your state of mind about coming over. Ultimately you will want to come, because if Hugh comes in March he will stay at least a month. That means I cannot return to Paris until April. For the sake of your work, the studio (which symbolically you gave up anyway the day you gave it over to Fred and his girl—that was so discouraging, to make sacrifices *for your having the studio*, and then that is how you use it. Henry, please try to understand me, all those efforts wasted, so often wasted, destroyed by you). Symbolically, I don't see any use in my straining to keep you in a groove which you already gave up. Then you don't know what you do want, anyway. Emil says he detects homesickness in your letters. One day it's hate, another, yearning. Since you discarded the studio, as it were, do you think that means you want to come over? You see, I don't want to say: come over, because otherwise we will be separated five months. I want you to do what you want, Henry, what you need. I have been trapped by the financial problem here. I'm accepting it like everything, as something to be transformed into pleasure. I was full of humor and gaiety about it. Everything is interesting, everything can be created and invented, whatever emptiness there is in New York I don't feel because I live in my own world, with my own love, with you, with the riches you give, with all I possess, and Louveciennes can be made anywhere, it all comes from one's self anyway.

New York, really, has only this defect: that it does not permit the birth of the individual. It is too crushing, too brutal, too enormous, too great a machine, one gets ground to bits, *but* after the individual is born (in Paris, in Italy, anywhere but here) then New York lies in the palm of one's hand as an instrument to be used. Then one masters it, enjoys it, laughs at it. [. . .]

When you come, the good of that will be that you will find out what you want. You'll know if you want Europe. There will be no more pulling, tugging, contradictions. [. . .]

Don't take seriously the talk of orchids etc. I did like being a bit spoiled, Henry; so do you. That is human. But it's not the spoiling I like best. And you know it. You were only trying to give me hell, *for something else,* and not for the loss of my soul! I haven't lost anything. I'm only adding, adding to myself, to us, to our world, to our work! Always adding.

[Anaïs]

[Barbizon Plaza Hotel, New York]
December 27, 1934

What made me ill, Henry my love, was to have hurt you. But it is all over now, surely, all over. You must have my love letter, and my cables, and you must understand what the hardness was all about, and that maybe I needed it not to break down, because now when I look back on it I am amazed that I could have taken such a step at all, and I only did it by a tremendous blind leap into space, which required toughening. About your last letters—I don't know what to say. You seem to be so full of me for the first time, yes, Henry. The first year you were still full of June, and then after that the writing, and [there was a] contrast not only between how full I was of you against how full you were of things other than me, but between how little space I seemed to occupy in you as against what everyone else gave me—not the gifts, no, but that fullness with me which I craved. And everything is always askew; that comes to you after I leaped so far away that I almost leaped out of your life, when in the effort to be less sentimental, and tougher, I almost changed my whole nature. If, in a sense, I was almost trying to forget you, it was again only *for* our love and not against it. I felt I was not alone enough to withstand the attacks of others' love. When you speak of feeling sad and thinking of the bon-bons women want, etc. It was not that you meant. I don't want bonbons. It was something very essential I was given by others and less so by you. Anyway, it is all over, isn't it, we have to make plans, we have to work for some kind of happiness.

I will answer your last letter separately. I mean the business in it. [. . .]

About Blaise Cendrars: I don't believe you "fucked yourself." You were just bewildered. I'm sure he did not mind. Tell me more of what he said. It was wonderful, the whole evening, quite crazy and touching and overwhelming, and comical. I'm afraid, though, that it was again that throwing away of whatever you have wanted for a long time—that instinct you have for non-realization, for evading anything that crystallizes, evading pleasure and content, because you have a passion for difficulties, as I have, a love of raising obstacles in order to have them to tear down, a love of complicating for the fun of unravelling, a love of tangling and botching to exert your spirit, your mind, your imagination, your emotions. Whatever you finally grasp, whatever finally comes your way, whatever materializes, is a kind of danger. It's too simple, too joyful, it might make you happy, in an ordinary way. You won't have it. You must have the game. I understand you, Henry. I do it in other ways. My life is full of such games, chess games of all kinds, roles, etc. And you know it. You know why it is I leap over things, I don't go step by step like the French woman, you know why it is I believe in a kind of magic, in the impossible which does happen, why "Alraune" is real to me. That is why, when you don't know any more whether I'm playing, inventing, acting, pretending, you like to remember when I cooked the *raie au beurre noir*, and the red cabbage . . . *that*, you are sure of, that I love you humanly, and now you say you are, above everything else, a man, and you want, above everything else, your woman. Strange new talk, Henry, oh, strange, after all these years. Strange creativity in us, which flourishes and expands at the expense of our human contentment. Maybe I did not need to get you that studio and make life approximate the fairytale so closely. I got you the studio, I reached for the ultimate, the most dream-like, then I had to pay so dearly for it. I had to come here, break away, be alone, fight, and we might still be in the Hotel Havana, which you thought beautiful! Yet all the while, horizon[s] are bursting, and everything grows deep and *"merveilleux,"* even when we are both so hurt, as we are. . . . Yours

Anaïs

[Anaïs:]

Just got your letter. It's hard to write you because I'm stunned. I've waited almost two weeks now for this letter. If it had been ten times as long and ten times as explicit it couldn't make up for the pain I've endured. "Vaguely puzzled," you say. Like a sleepy bear, eh? Well, perhaps it would be better for you to believe that than know the truth. You seem to expect me to beat you up—physically or mentally. I can't do that. It's not my way. "Mad as a hatter" does not mean angry, but crazy. The cables I sent you excitedly at the beginning were to allay your fears. I thought Hugo would be going any day and I was afraid he would do you harm. And I felt sorry too that I had said the least thing that might be considered a reproach, because I tried my best to believe that it was all done for a worthy purpose. But you seem not to be satisfied. You wanted to be punished, I suppose.

Anaïs, listen to me—so long as I love you as I do now I can never squabble with you, or punish you, nor berate you, nor lie to you. It hurts me to think that the terrible scenes you have with Hugo do afford you some satisfaction after all. I won't go through that with you ever, I can promise you that. I think too much of you to sully our relationship that way. It's degrading to you—and to me. All this talk of "guilt" and "gratitude," of writing half-false love letters, half true, half false, sickens me. I want to ask you a very simple question. What have you to fear if you declare your mind openly? Haven't you the right, as a human being, to lead your own life, make your own choices? I don't say to cruelly, wantonly hurt Hugo, but it's time now to make a stand, to be firm. If I were you I wouldn't tell the truth—not after all the lies. It would be too horrible. But there are other ways out. You can sincerely desire to be free. If he won't give you a divorce, he must at least permit you to be free. Nobody on God's earth can prevent that, if you want it.

I may cable you before you get this letter, telling you that I want to come quickly. March, or even February, is too far off. I can't wait that long. Realize this, that ever since that little error I have not slept properly one night, that I have a constant pain in the guts. I am just finishing your "Alraune"—it will go in the same mail as this. How I did it I don't know. Perhaps those *"intermittences du coeur"* produced by your cables. Yes, they did lift me up. I was elated. But I couldn't sustain it. I have felt, and I still do, that there is something *louche,* as they say. Mostly in the Rank quarter. You don't know how miserable I felt when I read your letter and realized that the money came from him. I thought of many things simultaneously—of the return from La Havre particularly. I thought of the look on your face when I left you at the door of your house early in the morning. It reminded me of your description of Alraune's face swimming in the taxi. It haunted me for a long time. I felt profoundly uneasy.

You see, Anaïs, I understand everything and forgive, if forgiveness there must be, with a whole heart. But what saddens me is that when it comes to a choice you prefer to protect me by a lie rather than confide in me as a man, as an equal, as your partner in life and death. Don't you know that you can tell me *everything?* How small I feel when I think of all you've had to do—*to protect me.* No man wants protection at such a price—you must own to that. And as I said once before, my whole life has been darkened by the fact that it was just this false attitude which brought about the tragic situation with June.

You know, I believed you so implicitly that when I opened that wrong letter I was dazed. Not "vaguely puzzled," but the ground opened beneath my feet. Even before the letter came I had had a warning which I refused to take. I was standing at the sink washing the dishes, Fred drying them. He said: "Guiler is still in town, did you know that?" I said: "You're crazy." "Well," he said, "Andard was talking to him yesterday." "Impossible," I said, laughing at him. "Must have talked to someone else—someone must have answered for him." That passed. I saw a quizzical smile on Fred's face, but I forgot about it for the moment. When the letter came he said—"I didn't want to tell you the other day, but Andard was talking to Guiler face to face—he met him on the Champs Elysées." Recall for a moment the passage I marked in *Albertine Disparue.* That's all.

To go back a few days, soon after I commenced working on the "Alraune" I got news from Fred that Andard might publish your book. Tremendous elation. I wrote you immediately—would have cabled had I not been broke. Finally I did cable about the "Alraune." Thought it would be a pleasant surprise for you. At the same time I thought I would have an answer to my *Europa* letter, at least in the form of a Christmas greeting. Christmas Eve no cable. Christmas day no cable. The two days a constant coming and going here—everybody dropping in to say hello. Christmas night Fred brings Etienette,

Neoshil's daughter, her fiancé, and Roger [Klein]* was here of his own accord. I got so hysterical with impatience that I yelled at them, *"Je m'en fous de vous, je suis triste, je suis triste!"* I ran downstairs and invited the lieutenant and his wife to come up. It was the weakest moment of my life since I have been in Paris. I said to the lieutenant—"You've got to come upstairs. I need to talk to an American. I'm sad, I'm homesick, I'm lonesome. I can't stand the sound of French voices." (It was almost like the Osborn crisis, funny enough.) When they had all gone I lay in bed and wept.

I could not understand how you would forget to think of me. And I woke the next day to face another day of anguish. All day long waiting for the hands to go round, hoping against hope you would cable— because I had asked you to. I had asked you to be good to me. Late that night I went downstairs with the garbage pail and seeing the uncalled-for letters on the radiator I swept them up and threw them in the pail—enraged because there was nothing for me from you. And then just as I was dumping them I had an impulse to glance over them a second time. I noticed my name on the blue-faced envelope enclosed. I tore it open—it was dated the 22nd. I felt crushed. You see, I scarcely ever look at those colored open-face envelopes because they are always filled with bills for people who don't live here any more. [. . .]

Perhaps this occurred Christmas night, I'm not sure any more, the days are still topsy-turvy. Anyway, I cabled again—to Emil this time because I feared that Hugo was now at the hotel with you and might intercept the message. In fact, I thought that possibly he had intercepted the others and that that was why I hadn't heard from you. Then I became absolutely panic-stricken, desolate. I thought you were ill, and several times I thought you were dead. I wanted to call your father, but then I thought he would not want to hear from me, especially if anything had happened to you. I started to hunt for Mrs. Rank's address, thinking that at least Rank would be decent enough to tell me the truth. I don't know what prevented me from carrying that out— pride, humiliation, fear, anguish, fear of messing up other people's lives too? I walked around in a sweat. [. . .] I walked home like a drunken man [. . .]. I fell on the bed about three A.M. and lay wide awake, listening for footsteps. [. . .] During the night—I sleep in the studio now—the light of the moon suddenly shone full on the bed. At that moment the tension broke and I fell asleep, mumbling to myself—now

*French writer.

I know it's all right. Everything is all right. She will cable. She will cable. [. . .]

Only now it hits me—how you must have felt leaving this place and knowing that you would never come back to it. How you could do that without breaking down beats me. You have courage. What an actress! What a terrible role! Now I understand better the look in the doorway, the tears in the train before writing "Alraune." Anaïs, all this drives me nuts. You say "stay as long as you want and work." That's impossible. I want to get out of here as quickly as possible. I've got to be beside you and I'll never let you get away from me. [. . .]

It's important, Anaïs, that you tell me the whole truth about Hugo. When does he arrive and is he supposed to remain over there for good, or was he planning to return in the spring? I don't want to send letters or cables to the Barbizon and have him intercept them. Also, why did you say February or March? Aside from the money question is there any other reason for delaying? Be honest. I'll never say anything to you again about "lies," take my word for it, but I'm going to assume that hereafter you will be absolutely truthful with me. If you can't it will be disastrous. I was never one to nag you, to worry things out of you. In fact, you have often accused me of being indifferent, which was never so—it was just a sublime confidence in you. That confidence has to be restored, and I will help you. But this is a pact. I want your word. [. . .]

A few odds and ends before I close this. Roger is sending a copy [of *Tropic of Cancer*], which he bought, to Andre Gide's nephew [Marc Allégret] in Cambodia, who is a good friend of Roger's and a writer too. The Grand Hotel on the Rue Scribe has ordered a dozen copies already. It's selling there.

[. . .] Are we divorced, June and I? You will see from the "Alraune" manuscript that I killed her off. A piece out of the Unconscious.*

In fact, I must add a little about the MS. It is different from what we originally planned. Less rigid, less determined. I think myself it is more artistic this way. I followed your story quite faithfully, but not always consecutively. I put the beginning at the end, where I think it truly belongs—don't you? I hope you like it. I worked at it with a vim during the few good spurts I had—and with love. Some of the scenes, such as the Neptunian-Atlantis one, or the hotel room, seem at the moment quite well done. I re-read your horoscope carefully and allowed

*On December 20, H. M. was divorced, by proxy, in Mexico City.

that to penetrate me too. In short, I did everything I could that seemed to represent you. I wanted to put a blue folder about it, but haven't the time. I may or may not write a short foreword. I have an idea written out on a paper napkin. But that's not important. I'll be there soon after it arrives anyway. We'll celebrate it—you and I and Emil. That made me very very happy, that you did look him up, and also that you struck it off so well. I wept a bit as I read that part of your letter. Sorry you went to Henry Street. Naturally it's all changed—how could you ever recognize my picture of it? But had you seen the kitchen in the back, the thin pole that supports the roof, and had you remembered all I told you and what I wrote, too, you could have visualized me marching around that like a drunken bear while Alraune and her consort sang their crazy songs through the back window, the fire out, the candles burning, the chairs broken, me going nuts.

But look, I must stop. I want to read this over with you when I get there. I feel that I have a few friends left back there, and that things won't be too rough in the beginning. I will take a long chance. My time is up here. Almost five years to the month! Five years of exile. But I never thought it would be under such circumstances that I would sail back. You must be good to me, tender, loving. I need you so much. I give you everything I possess. I want nothing but your love.

Henry

Exhausted—can't add another word. This is next day. Determined to come. Have already cabled you. May write more tomorrow for next boat mail. Do get your citizenship! Important now!

CABLE
1934 DEC 28 AM 9:42

GUILER BARBPLAZA NEWYORK
SAILING NEXT WEEK DO NOT ADVISE EDUARDO HAS EMILIA KEY FOR LOUVECIENNES

HENRY

CABLE
DEC 29 1934

GUILER HOTEL BARBIZON PLAZA NY
CONTINUE MAIL PARIS UNTIL FURTHER ADVICE MONEY OKEH HAPPY NEW
YEAR FAMILY AND RANK ETERNAL LOVE YOURSELF

[HENRY]

[Villa Seurat]
Dec. 29th. [1934]

[Anaïs:]

Since the long letter, received several letters from you, the check, and finally your cable. So you *are* happy? You wanted me to come! Your letters come one after the other and they cut through the heavy atmosphere surrounding me like flashing swords. I feel that you are helping me to hack my way out of the entangled net. I walk the streets answering your letters, eat and don't know what I have eaten, get out the subway at the wrong stations, bump into people, fall down the steps—all the little things I never did before.

You say to wait for more letters—that I will be happy. I would, Anaïs, if it were not that I am already happy and so impatient to hold you in my arms that not even your beautiful letters can hold me back. I am hoping to leave on the *Champlain*, sailing the 3rd. I am waiting for responses to the cables I sent out. I feel confident I will get what I need in time. Confident.

Everything fell into whack the moment I took my resolution and decided to act. All along I have had impulses, intuitions, which stifled. A woman obeys her impulses. Men are often ashamed of them. Perhaps because men are more childish. They continue to believe even when they have the visible evidence before them. You say in the last letter, which made me break down completely, that if I had only put up the least resistance you might have stayed. You say I don't know how, or can't or won't stand on my own feet—and that's why everything happens as it does. You say I am weak. In every letter there is some cruel, telling thrust which makes me wince, which allows no time for the wounds to heal. Your letter ends in a sob. Mine ended in a state of collapse. We have tortured each other. I wrote you the last letter with my last ounce of energy, of hope, of faith, of courage. I don't know what's in it—I couldn't even re-read it. I only know that I am coming and that things are going to be different. No fixed program but a very serious, earnest resolution. I should be on the water when this reaches you. I hope the last few days, the last letters, will bring me closer to you than I have ever been before, that when I see you I shan't have to say a word, but just look at you and know, know that it's all right. Don't let's talk of forgiveness, nor of right or wrong. Just let's *be* together, as we always were.

The last cable made me terribly happy especially when you said "our return." Why? That tells me that you don't care about New York, as does your last letter too. If New York had claimed you I should have been bitterly disappointed in you. I come to New York with open eyes, with a full realization of its lure and of its emptiness, its ugliness. I see no . . .

Interrupted here for an hour by an unexpected visit from Dobo, over [from England] for the holidays. Turned down invitation "to do Montmartre" with him. Want to write you, write you, until the boat leaves and maybe on the boat too. So expect more letters right up until I come, maybe even after I arrive. [. . .]

I will tell you this now, since you are aware that I did not have the money to come, that I had cabled Emil the same time as you, asking him to raise some money among my friends. That too I feel I have a perfect right to do. Why shouldn't I appeal to my friends—or does your cable mean that Emil got in touch with you and that I have no friends left—except poor old Lowenfels. I knew Emil had nothing. I expressly worded my cable so he would understand that. I did add that he should look after you—because I am anxious about you, but I didn't think he would be indiscreet enough to tell you that I needed money. The whole point is this—I wanted to come without you helping me. I wanted to show you that I could do it on my own. You shouldn't question my tactics—after all, that's my affair, isn't it so? The main thing is that I wanted to reach you and as soon as possible, and to do that I would do far worse things than this, if I am to infer that you are angry again or disappointed. I was not sure I could get the money. I spent 400 francs in cables and telegrams. Yes, like a millionaire. But I'm a poet, not a businessman. If I could have *earned* the money I would have, don't doubt that for a minute. That's why, for instance, I went through all that foolish labor of retyping sections of *Black Spring*. I was hoping and hoping to accomplish something that way—honestly, by my own efforts, as it were. I know, without you telling me now, that nothing came of this. Kahane, who was going to send them to a friend in England, a Lovat Dickson, refused to send these sections on. Said they were "monotonous," "too much of a tropical garden," "not what people want to read," "not a high-brow and not a low-brow." Dobo just now told me that I must have been crazy to send him the MSS. Not a magazine in England would consider them. Alors, I blink my eyes. It's the truth. Facts are facts. Whatever I attempt to do, as a writer, counts for nothing. I'm not wanted. No doors open anywhere.

And the writer, who is terribly human, who feels like a rat in a cage, who sees walls going up around him everywhere and no exit, the writer and the human being make one frantic desperate individual who would stop at nothing to attain his end. Christ, if you reproach me for this I don't know what I shall answer. Anyway, you will not have to give Lowenfels that money he lends you. I expect to cable you beforehand saying that I will return it myself. I expect to raise that money by myself, and it's my affair, do you understand? So is the 35 dollars he *gives* me. I don't want him to give me a cent! Though if I were in his boots I would do so willingly. I remember so well that day you flared up over the six-dollar check I loaned him. And shortly afterwards, turning to my friends here and saying—"that's just like him, he gives everything away." Yes, I give away things, and I take things. I demand a lot and I give a lot, or at least I hope I do. If I seem only to take, as you wrote in that terrible letter, then I am no damned good, not worth a son-of-a-bitch, and you should throw me over right now, for good. I'm worthless. But I don't see myself that way. I notice that I do have friends (I had supposed so until now—your cable makes me doubt even that a bit), and surely I couldn't build up friendships purely on a basis of blood-sucking. Or am I a peculiar specimen, just that?

So many things you have revealed to me about my shortcomings recently. I take everything humbly. My mouth is stopped. As I said to you many many times I owe you everything. I'm deeply aware of that.

I'm trying to drive back to where I started, when Dobo interrupted me. I had such a long letter to write you. I wanted to tell you of my attitude, of how I approach New York, of what I want to do with you, do *for* you.

FLASH—do you suppose for one minute that had I known what you were doing I would have paid another month's rent here? The money you sweated for. My whole passage money gone for nothing! Every one of these errors costs blood and pain. *But I didn't know!*

Christ, don't hold that against me. Try to see me here, my uncertainty, my perplexity, my anguish—because, as I hinted above, I *did* know something was wrong all the while. But I was an idiot. I was blunt, obtuse. I had the wrong kind of confidence. I remember so well when I caught you around the waist the last evening, and asked you point-blank if you were telling me the truth, if you were really coming back, etc. I didn't know how to ask the question—it was humiliating to even think you might betray me. And you answered with a "why would I do a thing like that?" Yes, I remember that vividly. I thought it weak, the answer beginning with a "why would I . . . ?" That's always an admission or a denial or a suppression of the real thing. The real truth always pops out differently. I should have trusted my intuition, but I didn't. But again, that was only because I trusted you implicitly. And I want to trust you implicitly again. Always. I don't want to be a man of hunches and intuitions and vagaries and what-not. I don't talk of absolute truths. In human relations there is no absolute. We are flesh and blood. The blood says one thing, sentiment another, intelligence another. We make mistakes. We do injuries we never meant. It can't be absolute—or else it's sterile.

On the other hand, there is an absolute, and that must be in the heart. We must all meet, everyone who has something in common with another, in this domain where there is absolute trust, confidence, loyalty, integrity. If not, everything crumbles away. And so, when you let yourself be swayed by pride, by wounded vanity, by all the surface errors, you really do me an injustice. Because I have been absolutely loyal to you always in my heart. I have never been so utterly faithful with another individual, man or woman. You say: "Henry, we must get close together again." And I weep when I read that. I want that. I want to be always face to face with you, open, honest, carefree, happy. But if I am not there to convince you are you going to doubt me? Can you only be convinced by my voice, my eyes, or whatever it is that touches you in the vital spot? Must I reassure you, reassure you always? Won't you take me once and all for what I am, for the man who puts love above all, who has found in you his perfect mate?

Soon, soon, soon I will be there. I took this chance of coming ahead of time, because I am confident of making my own way. It's not to cripple you further, to make you pay for love in this horrible way. I am coming straight to you, and when I have seen you and talked to you, I go directly to Rank and I talk to him straight out—but decently, I assure you. I am going to appeal to him as a man to do something for me, to make a place for me, if not your job then another. I can do him a lot of good—and also a lot of harm if he crosses me. But I will give him a fair chance. It would be better for me, with my temperament, to work for him than to work like Lowenfels, for instance. I shall try to convince him of that, and convince him besides of my earnestness. He doesn't know my capabilities at all. He knows me scarcely at all, and then mostly as an irresponsible artist, as a kept man, as a leech, I suppose. But I am capable of doing anything under the sun. I don't need to lie in bed until noon. I don't need to be paid a magnificent wage. I don't need to be instructed like the ordinary American. I'm just as big a man as he is, every inch, though my life and my training has been utterly different. I chose to live—but that does not make me worthless, or irresponsible, or incapable or inefficient. He should give me a chance, at least.*

And he *must* prove to me that his generosity is unselfish. He *must* prove to me that he can worship you without having you. I will not tolerate him around as a love-sick dog, nor a rival and competitor just because he holds the whip in his hand, the dough-bag, as it were. That's Jewish and that stinks, to my way of thinking. He's got to rise above that. Otherwise he's going to regret it. I'm going to make him miserable. I can't help saying it, my blood's up. I am going to wipe them all off the face of the map, every one of them. That's a frightful thing, you say—"if not Hugh, then another." Frightful. *For me?* I'll tell you something. . . . If I fail, if I can't make all that unnecessary, then I will blow my brains out. But there's a big effort I'm going to make before entertaining such a contingency.

You break down in the last letter saying "my little Henry." You make me break down too. Let's be done with the kingdom of fathers and mothers. Let's talk frankly to one another, *you* even more than me. Let's not pretend that things are so and so when they're not. Let's be honest. Then perhaps I can solve things. I'm really not a half-wit. And I'm really not so weak as you imagine. My life as a writer is menaced. Good. I'll make another life. And I'll write too, just the same, more desperately perhaps, more sincerely too. Let people hammer at me, let them turn me down, let them do what they like. Only let me see their real faces, their real souls. Nothing can kill me. I'm a realist. I have as

*There is no evidence that Dr. Rank let H. M. work for him, though both A. N. and H. M. subsequently took on some "patients" while in New York in 1935 and again early in 1936.

many levels as you. I can't compromise on the writing—I mean, tone it down to suit the feeble appetites. That would be a betrayal of my own self. No, I can adapt myself to the world, take up the cudgels, fight and curse and swindle and barter and keep the other private self clean and trust that someday it will be recognized. It would have been better not to. But the world makes its demands. Love makes its demands. I'll do anything *for you*—because my whole life is centered in you.

A telegram just came from Crowley. "Cheque on way," he says. Waiting still for word from Ross and from Emil. Ross and Crowley I promised to repay. *I-I-I.* Do you understand? I will get out on the street at night and beg for it, if necessary. I did it before, I can do it again. Fuck my pride. Fuck everything. I'm so desperately hungry for you, so desperately eager to prove to you that what I say and write is not a sham, a hoax, a lie, that I will kill, *kill* do you understand? I'm coming back like a raving maniac. I loathe New York. I loathe America. I come back to lift you out of a horrible mess, to wash you all over, cleanse you, love you as no man has ever loved a woman. I rush to get there ahead of Hugo. I won't let him touch you. Where was I, who was I, ever to permit all this? I get down on my knees to you and I beg you to forgive me. I have been a crazy dreamer. I have been everything you said, and worse perhaps. The whole thing hits me between the eyes. Just wait for me, Anaïs. Just don't let anything disturb you. If possible find a room where we can be together, unmolested, for a few days. Give me a few days of peace in your arms—I need it terribly. I'm ragged, worn, exhausted. After that I can face the world. Don't tell Lowenfels or anybody what boat I am coming on—I haven't. Be there on the dock, if you can. I'll come third class, naturally. And I ought to have a little dough with me—enough for a few days. Then I'll fend for myself.

I leave here with all sorts of strings dangling. Something may break unexpectedly. Read that long letter from the Filipino girl without prejudice. It's naïve, silly, and yet charming. I felt awfully good to get it. Why? Because it had Spanish blood in it. Just like the photographs made me feel good, those heavy, doll-like Spanish faces, the goodness of them, the blood, the warmth. And I responded with alacrity, writing as though I were writing to one of Pierre Loti's Turkish women. I was hoping that we might go there should everything prove disappointing in New York. Go there with you in the sunshine, among simple, friendly, joyous people. I know they would warm to you—and perhaps to me too. Don't let the flirty quality of the letter disturb you. Sure,

I'd like to be among them, those pretty little women, because they're like flowers, and so grave and so ornate and so deep at the same time. It's soothing. My head is not turned. The Filipino girls won't run after *me!* But the Filipino men may run after *you!* Yes, I've been thinking of other places, other climes, other occupations. Warm places, where your hair would wave as it did in Louveciennes when the window was wide open and you ran around in that dress with holes in it, like the goddess Indra. The dress with a thousand eyes. I thought so much of the eyes [while] writing the *Scenario*. Of the water, oh, of everything that seemed the real you, the you I adore. Don't please accuse me of being slow, of not grasping the high moments, the precious hours. Don't! Don't! I am aware of everything, just as quick as you, but I don't like to sit over it as it happens, or even to feel sad afterwards. Life flows on. One thing fades out, another comes. It's in us, in us solely that everything takes place, and we can and will always create the golden moments. Even when I talk about misery, poverty, the strife and struggle, the curses, the fight, all that—don't forget that in that too are precious things. One can't be protected against these dire things and have full realization of the other blessed moments. The two together. But I'd rather it be me than you. I can take everything. I'm really strong, and brave. But I get lulled. Maybe I'm lazy, indolent. I must be, I suppose. And I love, love, love all that goes with it, all that stops the clock, kills duty, etc. That is why Rank rankles me, and all the other blasted professional idiots with their talk of adaptation. Get it, the adaptation, and what have you in your hands—a fine, smooth piece of machinery. No pain, no joy, nothing but perfect functioning—work. Is that life? Is that the goal?

No, you get a room, Anaïs. I don't know how things work back there, whether you have to pretend to be married or what. Say any damned thing, but a warm room and cosy for a few days at least. I want to see you walk around naked, I want to examine you all over. Let's shut out the world and lie together in that white house with the white down walls, the hammock, the endless ecstasy and orgasm. "Break down the walls of idealism." Yes, I sat up when I read that in your script. And so many other things which, due to my keen emotions, my heartbreak, my longing, I interpreted with the keenest imagination. In your book lies a vast epic. We must do it over and do it over until it comes out perfect. And not show it to publishers! But print it ourselves. If only we two believe in it, that's sufficient. Time will do the rest.

I believe I know that work now almost as well as you. I don't say the Scenario proves that. No. I don't know how well I succeeded. Some things may touch you. But I'm too close, and I was too wrought up, too stabbed by a thousand passing things to realize completely what I was doing. But I was saturated with you. I should like to see it printed in Mayenne, Mayenne, where there is an honest, intelligent French publisher. And we must write something together as a foreword perhaps. Forget what I said about Rank and the money. That was before I knew about his giving you the money for T. of C. But if he knew, if he understood, if he were half the artist that he is the scholar and the business man, he should be glad to append his name to your work.*
You and I, we are a little previous. And the analyst is a little behind time always. And the world, the big public which pays Joe Schrank 48,000 dollars and 750 dollars a week royalties and God knows what— well, about them the less said the better. We belong to the future. That is why I am unruffled about criticism, why I persist doggedly in my own fashion. It may be that I can write only one great book—but that is better than a hundred little ones. It's not my fault if the times are out of joint. We are oppressed by the age. Born in the wrong time. I am human enough to accept the times—any times. But not be seduced by the times.

Oh, I am saying a lot of things, eh? Are you laughing at me? I feel so much better, so much! I can really smile now. I don't look into the mirror and see two round black holes where my eyes should be. I was frightened recently. My eyes looked mad. I thought I was going mad. And when I coughed in the Métro people moved away, looked at me suspiciously, as though I had the con. But I haven't! I'm healing up rapidly. And if you would send me a radio[gram] out to sea when you get this letter I will heal up completely. This should come January 6th, on the Cherbourg. And I will come on the 10th probably, via the Champlain. [. . .] I had a boat offered me at $64.00, but it was a cargo boat, sailing only on Jan. 12th and not due for ten days. And I want to get there instantly. The fastest boat.

Finally—don't worry about what I said in the last letter. I shall come without any books, except yours, the one I had bound, if it is ready. I am not giving up the place, because I don't know what may

---

*Rank, in fact, wrote an introduction to a manuscript version of "Alraune" (See Anaïs: An International Journal, Vol. 3, 1985, pp. 49–54), which was never used and was rediscovered only in the early 1970s.

happen and I can always write to the *gérant.* Fred will hold it down until March 15. I am giving him full instructions, in case we want the things, how to proceed. I leave most of the things behind. Perhaps I will bring the scarlet couch cover, as a symbol of Louveciennes. But the books and other paraphernalia, no.

And just this about Fred. You got angry about it. You don't know the whole situation. Etienette is not staying here. I wouldn't permit that. I couldn't, of course, refuse to let them sleep together occasionally. But Fred has not been in my way, because he has been busy working for Andard. Very busy. Away most of the day. And at night I don't see him either. I go my own way. I have even less connection with him then when in Clichy. On the other hand, I could not refuse to take him in—and he *was* a protection, though not *physically.* I had to use him as a buffer during those days I waited anxiously for Hugo to come and pull a gun on me. And how could I not ask Fred to share this place? Was he not the one who had rescued me when I was utterly alone and adrift? Can I forget that? Would you ask me to? Maybe he didn't perform miracles, but he did everything he could, and in such moments it's what a man *tries* to do for you that counts. *Please* get that straight. I felt like a con when I wrote him telling him not to come. And I felt worse than a con when I said all right, come if you like, because then it was evident that my words were dictated by selfish reasons. There you are! But it worked out quite all right. Nobody can stop you from doing what you want—only yourself. I did work as you should know by now. How I did it is beyond me. Never a tranquil, easy moment. Waiting for letters, cables, footsteps. Trying to read the stars, trying to close my eyes and see you there in New York. Trying to forget what you so cruelly wrote—the tinsel, the gaiety, the luxury, the attention of others, all those things you knew would gall me and wound me. Trying to clutch *you.*

And another last trifle . . . You say in the cable not to worry about the manuscripts in Louveciennes. But, dear God, that's not it! *It's the letters.* Or did you take them out? That's why I urged you not to advise Eduardo of my leaving. Now you still have time to write Emilia, or whoever has the key, and tell them what to do. If they are safe there, all right. You speak of our returning here together. What had you in mind? Remember, a new life. No more double life. No more Hugo. I don't want you to go through an ordeal with him. You are clever, but whether you are clever enough, strong enough, resolute enough, I don't know yet. I will try to work out a plan with you. And let you tell me this—that if you think it better, wiser, safer, for me to face Hugo I will do it. I have no fear of him, as long as I am not caught in a compromising position. Because then my sense of justice gets the upper hand. I know he has a right to act violently. I don't want to be shot, Anaïs. I want to live. I've got everything to live for now.

Henry

See—I sign my name! Damn you—why don't you sign your name? It means so much!

[Barbizon Plaza Hotel, New York]
Jan. 1, 1935

Henry, my love, my love, I don't know if this letter will reach you. I don't know when you are arriving. I've lived dark days, feeling that you were suffering and that nothing I could write or cable could help you. It isn't only I who have hurt you. You're going through some deep struggle, on account of the shock, because it reminded you of other shocks, and after resting in my love peacefully, you have suddenly been pushed into reality. I didn't want to hurt you, god knows. Just before I left I begged you for activity. I may have felt our love too was becoming unreal. I wanted to give birth to Henry Miller, and the last effort of that birth was to leave you alone, not to help you, to let you be born into your own strength. Facing America was a test, and *fighting* for me was another. Your love was unreal and not human for me. My *presence* was hardly necessary. Your arms didn't even tighten around me when I left you. You lived in a dream and loved me thus, and that was killing me . . . it was negative and inert. You loved other things much more. Your peace, for instance. No struggle. And my going away was all in a dream. I felt that you didn't *feel* it. And suddenly now you're *awake*, you suffer. I can't bear this, yet it may save you, and save us! Forgive me, yet it may be one of those many darkly instinctive things I did *for you*, for your birth as artist, as man. If this shock makes you whole, the man in fragments of *Black Spring* and the man who loved me in [a] fragmented dream way may both become whole.

If this gets to you, when you're preparing to come over, understand, Henry, that there will be no more suffering when you come over. I will be meeting you, alone.

Hugh is arriving tomorrow, on the *Europa,* came suddenly too, I don't know why. Full of fears and doubts of me, like yours. We are to stay [with relatives] in Forest Hills, to save money, but I paid my room at the Barbizon until Feb. 1. You can use it. I need it only for patients occasionally. On Feb. 1 Hugh has to leave *for three weeks* and we will be together then, Henry.

Until you come I'll be busy with *Tropic of Cancer,* doing all I can do. Tonight I'm putting all the MS. in those folders you liked with the punched holes. I'm thinking of you constantly. I thought of you at midnight. I'm desperately anxious over you, about your mood, it makes me sad that you are coming without joy. I wanted this trip to be an adventure for you. I sent you a cable not to let anybody know date of your arrival. After you and I have found our own world again, our Louveciennes world, our studio world, our togetherness, then everything will be joyous again. You know it. We'll work for the book. You'll explore America, maybe. Emil lost his woman through self-love and inertia. You won't do that, Henry. If you do get this letter in time cable me something that will tell me you won't be making this voyage in any black mood. Please.

I kiss you with my whole being, as always. I was yours as nobody was ever yours, come and take me all back again, Henry, Henry!

Anaïs

The Adams
Eighty-Six Street at Fifth Avenue, New York
[February 1, 1935]

[Henry:]

Will be at the Barbizon with my valises at 3.—So that we can enter our home together. I'm terribly happy today, Henry, to be coming to you, to be with you.

A.

The extra $20 is for you. Get wine, get everything you want. Get a new suit if you want to.

Barbizon Plaza Hotel [New York]
[February 1935]

Anaïs—

Three A.M. and I'm wide awake and trying to smother a terrific erection. The air, the women, the music—it makes you want to fuck, nothing but fuck.

I went to the burlesque alone and it was marvellous—erotic, dirty, low, vulgar—good as ever and more daring. Went to a dance hall afterwards and had to shake the girls off. Want to come home with you immediately. Just as open and daring as Paris—and better-looking cunts.

Your "George" called up—nice Southern voice, and Simpson and Hoffman and one or two who didn't leave any names. You must have cut a wide swath.

I'm nuts about you and wondering what the hell you're doing—if it's just as innocuous as you pretend. Or if Otto went along—or some other guy.*

Jesus, what a sexy place this is! It's in the air. How can I trust you out of my sight?

And every phone call is a different name. All hungry, all burning the wires to get at you. You've got to fight to go to bed alone in this town. It's wild. No Puritanism.

I saw a dance at the burlesque that knocked the African stuff last night into a cocked hat. Electric, spasms, orgasmic. Girl pulls her dress up swiftly, one jerk, and pushes her twat forward. Just a piece of black tape over her cunt—like an eye cap. Almost could see the hairs. Women with busts exposed. Ass bare—cracks showing. Beautiful women. It makes you crazy. Guys soliciting me on the street. Two bucks and you can have anything. Open brothels. Full swing. The lid's off.

My balls are aching. I want you. I want to fuck you silly. What we had was only an hors d'oeuvre. Come back here and let me shove it into you—from the rear. I want to do everything with you. We haven't begun to fuck yet.

[Henry]

---

*A. N. seems to have broken off her relationship with Otto Rank in February, though she continued the practice of psychotherapy, which she had begun in October 1934 at the Villa Seurat. Until her return to Paris in May 1935 she devoted herself to her patients in New York and during this period H. M. apparently took on some therapeutical work in collaboration with her.

[New York]
[February 1935]*

Anaïs—

I was terribly wrong to have mentioned what I did. But I am in
real anguish now—because of you. What I was going to say you would
have understood and even liked, because it concerned you and me,
what had happened to me because of you. It was not of June I wanted
to speak—that's dead and will stay dead. It was of myself I caught a
true glimpse and that terrified me a bit.

If you had only seen me last night, heard what I said—"about the
past"—you would never have hung up on me, you would never doubt
me. I have made everything over into you—completely. Everybody can
see it—can see the change in me. How can I tell you, assure you that
the past is dead? It's your own doubts of me, of yourself, that make you
act this way.

But Anaïs, I can't and won't let anything get between us. That's
final. You *must* come tonight. Whom else do I want to see? What am
I here for? Aren't you certain of me yet?

If I have wounded you then I get down on my knees and beg your
forgiveness. Yes, come here, and I will prove it to you.

Even if you were to leave me I would never go back to June, or
to my past. I couldn't. Seeing my old friends last night I realized the
void between myself & them. I realized that I had escaped a horrible fate. I came home late, exhausted with talk, but so happy to
have found you, to know that my life is bound up with yours *forever.*
There is nothing else in life I want. Can't you believe that?

I hurt you again. I curse myself. I tell you I am in terrible agony.
I can't stand this. I will call you again to say that I am bringing this
letter to your office. I don't care what you say to me over the phone.
Read this. *Believe this!*

Never, never, will I ever again refer to anything in the past, except
where it is *our* past. That's a sincere promise.

But don't be cruel now, don't hurt me. I need you so much. I don't

---

*H. M. moved from the Barbizon Plaza Hotel to the Roger Williams Apartments at
28 East 31st Street. The Guilers had rented an apartment at Park Avenue and 34th
Street for the remainder of Hugh's stay in New York. By late April, H. M. had finished
the revisions of *Black Spring,* and he, too, returned to the Villa Seurat by early summer.
Little correspondence, apparently, has been preserved from this period.

want you to mother me, protect me—*just be with me*. I have only found you—don't push me away. I could forgive you anything. Can't you forgive me a little?

Nothing else matters but you. I will stand outside your office at 6 o'clock and wait for you. I may not be back here again. I am in such a torment I must walk—alone. Nobody I want to see. I wait for you. I'm hungry for you.

Henry

[New York]
[March 1935]

[Anaïs:]

If only you are with me twenty-four hours of the day, watch me in every gesture, sleep with me, eat with me, work with me, these things can never happen. When I am away from you I am thinking of you constantly, it colors every thing I say and do. And if you only knew how faithful I am to you! Not just physically, but mentally, morally, spiritually. There is no temptation here for me, none at all. I am immune to New York, to my old friends, to the past, to everything. For the first time in my life I am completely centered in another being, in you. I can give everything without fear of being exhausted or being lost. When I wrote in my article yesterday "Had I never gone to Europe etc." it was not Europe I had in mind, but you. But I can't tell that to the world in an article. Europe is *you*. You took me, a broken man and you made me whole. And I am not going to fall apart—there isn't the slightest danger of that. But I am more sensitive now, more responsive to every note of danger. If I chase after you madly, implore you to listen, stand outside your door and wait for you, it is not that I am trying to humiliate myself. There is no humiliation for me in this struggle to keep you. This is only the proof that I am intensely aware, intensely alert, eager, profoundly eager and desperate to make you realize that my great love for you is a terribly real and beautiful thing. Once I would have paid the woman back for any suffering I had to endure. But I know now that this suffering is the result of my own behavior. I know that the moment something happens, something amiss, it must be *my* fault. It's not guilt I feel, but a profound humility in the face of your love. I don't doubt you, Anaïs—not in any way. You have given me all the proofs a woman could give a man. It is I who must learn how to accept and guard this love. I have made so many blunders. I will make more blunders, doubtless. But I am not slipping backwards. Each day seems to bring me to a higher level. You have raised me to the heights—keep me there, I beg you.

I thought to say to you over the phone, but then I get so rattled— "Anaïs, I can't walk the streets in anguish. It's not right. I have so much to do and I don't want to destroy myself, not even the least part of myself. Everything I have is precious and I have been trying to guard it, to make a gift of it to you."

I don't walk the streets here as I used to. The streets have nothing to say to me. That too was a putting of my self out into the world, instead of drawing the world within. Now I think of my little room, the room you saved for me, and I long to be back in it, to consecrate it by work. The whole world seems to have incorporated itself in you—why should I go out to seek it?

I feel in talking to people that there is something terribly beautiful inside me. I feel the distance between myself and others. I guard that distance. I do know now *who* I am. There are no doubts any more. But when you move away from me, even just the least bit, a blackness descends upon me, I feel engulfed. To hold to this which we have at last created between us, and in us, we must move perilously and swiftly, in full consciousness. We have reached to something that few people have ever known. We must be true to ourselves, to the best we know and feel. If you slip, I must hold you up. If I slip, you must do the same. Otherwise the world rocks and we are lost.

Don't think, Anaïs, that it's a fear of losing you that makes me act desperately. It's not fear, but a *desire* to hold you. The me who feared is dead. That me was passive, negligent, unconscious. The man I am now is awake and active, he leaps, he fights, he won't relinquish his grip. There's a difference, do you see? The old self would have pined away on the bed, or gotten drunk, or walked the streets, or looked up an old friend. These things I can never do again. All these things were buffers, they enabled me to wallow in pain and suffering, which probably then I wanted. I want no self-imposed torture. I will put myself before you always, face to face, quickly, directly. I won't allow a mistake, an accident to quicken into a misunderstanding. I won't let one weed grow up in this garden we are making. Life is too frightfully short for all that we wish to enjoy together. We must take time and wring its neck. We must live into each other.

When I called you I was not sure of getting you in. I called twice in the meantime and was told you were out. I was in a sweat. I walked up and down your street and around the block, and looked in restaurants, and came back and stood in front of your door. Had I not gotten you on the phone I was going to send you a telegram, and then come back to write you a special delivery letter. I looked in the phone book for the name Guiler, thinking I might catch you at your home—*their* home. Couldn't find the address. And had I waited for you this evening and not found you I would have hunted up Rank and I would have tried to get it out of him, by force if necessary. I couldn't imagine where you could be, what you were doing. I couldn't believe that you were still angry with me, only that you were moving away from me, hurt, bewildered, despairing of my love. Then it is that New York seems monstrous—the size of it, the endless crannies, the hopelessness of finding the one you search for frantically. One becomes a straw, a wisp blown about by the wind, torn by every memory, cursed, lost, broken, flung to the winds. You say you were weeping. And I was weeping, walking the streets with the tears rolling down my face. Oh, why, why? Why must we suffer? Are we so tender, so exposed to every dart? This is beautiful and terrible. But it is like twins trying to pull apart. Let us knit together, absolutely. Move into me, Anaïs, stay there, don't ever move away from me, not in a single thought.

You and I have had such terrible experiences, harrowing experiences. Can't we drown all that in our love? You know now that I have no false ideas about you, that I have accepted you as woman, *my woman*. Don't punish me for being tardy. Rather thank the stars that we have wrestled through successfully. I told you once in a letter how thoroughly certain I was about one's destiny being inside one—not out there in the stars. I feel that more and more. Do you? Do you? You must, because your letter says as much. The daring leap you made, how could that be anything but the response to an inner dictate. You had to leap for me, to show me the way. You proved what I once told you was a marvellous saying—do you remember it? "No daring is fatal." You saw it in the notes on my table at the Villa Seurat. Everything you ever noticed I remember well. I can see the light in your face, your eager hands, your airy, bird-like gestures. You are like the light itself for me—wherever you pass there is a blinding illumination.

Will you forgive me for writing all this, instead of working? Is not this, our life, more important than work? Work! Work! What am I working for? It must have been originally that I had a frightfully exaggerated opinion of myself, love of self, I made a fetich of work and tried to excuse it by various lies and delusions. I was erecting a monument to past sorrows. All that's finished. My face is turned towards the future, joyfully. The work will be more natural, it will not be an end in itself. I *was* becoming inhuman. You have saved me.

Now I realize that I am a complete human being and as a human being I must be worth more to you than as the greatest artist imaginable. Nothing is lost by this change. On the contrary, everything is gained. You are not a rival to my work. You are not the Muse who is sacrificed. How keenly aware I am, and grateful to you, for having accomplished this miracle. It is *your* creation, and a thoroughly human one, attained by the bitterest struggle. What you have done is no less than heroic. If you were merely a woman you would have failed. You are an artist—in life—and what greater compliment could I pay you? I was only the artist in words, and in life a bitter failure. Words, words—how they strangle the soul of one! Give me the woman and the words take their proper place. I was a slave to words. Now I shall *use* them.

I think sometimes that my coming here should have this one definite result, that my personality will be felt and recognized. I think, if I may expect a due reward, that once I have convinced people of my integrity anything I do or say, anything I write, will find its acclaim. People cannot ignore me when they know who I am, when they know my sincerity, my earnestness. I have no desire any longer to play the buffoon, the injured one, the neglected one. I long now to get hold of people, stand before them and talk to them, convince them. It isn't a question of literature any more, it's a question of my life, *of my life with you.* I feel that so strongly that I am sure it must make itself felt. Perhaps I will get to be much much more simple. Each word ought to burn. The words are filled with my blood, with my passion for you, my hunger for life, more life, eternal life. You have given me life, Anaïs. You are the flame that burns within me. And I am the keeper of the flame. I too have a holy task.

Oh, don't you see and know and believe all I write you? Is it not clear and true and just? Will you not stay with me, inside me always? I have come up from such depths to find you. To say that I love you isn't enough. It's more, more. Probe around inside me, unearth everything that's in me. I feel inexhaustibly rich.

Henry

[Villa Seurat]
Friday [October, 1935]*

Anaïs—

If you're closing Louveciennes up tight and no thought of going back there during the three months I thought I would remind you of some things to remove—if it's not inconvenient. For instance, the book of Lawrence Letters (which I didn't finish excerpts of), *Voyage au Bout de la Nuit,* the Malaisie book of Fred's—and, if you are not using them, what about the oil paints and oil brushes of Eduardo's—*not* the easel, but one of the light drawing boards. But if it is inconvenient, just forget about them.

I noticed that *Pancrace* (the wrestling picture) is playing in this neighborhood now—if you want to see it, remind me of it.

Once again, I say about [Cecil B. De Mille's] *Le Signe de la Croix* that the scenes of brutality in the amphitheater were done on a large scale—truly spectacular. Might appeal to you.

Notice too that the Lener Quartet comes Monday night to the Salle Gaveau. Do you expect to be free Monday? They are playing Ravel, César Franck & Debussy.

Was I very groggy? Sorry you had to get up and go out like that—without even coffee.

I have a feeling I may do something on the *Scenario* over the weekend.

The dough just arrived now—you're a brick.

Notice clipping enclosed. That looks bad!

Henry

---

*A. N. and her husband had returned to Paris from New York in May, and H. M., after finishing the manuscript of *Black Spring,* was back at the Villa Seurat, where plans were made for the publication of several books under the Siana Press imprint. In the fall, A. N. had rented Louise de Vilmorin's apartment, and Louveciennes was sublet for the winter months. Little correspondence seems to have survived from this period.

Norddeutscher Lloyd,* Bremen
[Paris]
[April 10, 1936]

Dear Henry:

Haven't been able to get away. Seeing Laura, shopping for a few little things. The trip will be marvellous. If you telephone tomorrow at lunch and if my book is there I'll come over and get it. If I have a chance I'll run over tomorrow even if only a few moments. But I'm enclosing the checks, to be sure. And please give Michael [Fraenkel] Rebecca [West]'s address: 15 Orchard Court, Portman Square W.

My address at Fez: *Palais Jamai, Fez—Maroc.*

Will be there a week after April 15—I will see Marrakesh—will be staying at the Chief's Palace—an Arab—Wish you could see all this.

A.

Cie Gle Transatlantique
French Line
15 April, 1936 Wednesday

[Henry:]

Marseilles at 8 A.M. in the sun. Paris *plus déshabillé, Paris en pantoufles, Paris en bonne humeur.* Stranger smells, more *urinoirs,* and many streets like that unique one in Avignon. One yard wide. Men and women sitting in the dark like rats. Dampness. *Ordures. Pelures.* Whores like monsters, old, fat, with leprous faces. Then sun. Beauty. *Le Vieux Parc.* Very romantic. Beautiful sailors mending their nets. A mixture of people. You would love it. Spent two hours walking around, then got on the little ship. But don't feel like writing. Dreaming. The Mayor to vote for in Marseilles was called Tasso—"Vote for Tasso." A man shouted as we passed: "Come and visit the cathedral up there." "And here is the chapel," he said, pointing to the café. It is six o'clock

---

*On January 18, 1936, A. N. and H. M. had sailed together on the S.S. *Bremen* for New York, though Miller was unhappy about returning to America. They returned on the same boat on April 5. While in New York, they attended her brother Joaquin's Town Hall debut, and worked with a number of old and new "patients" as psychotherapists. Before leaving, A. N. had a brief interview with Otto Rank at his Riverside Drive apartment, which was the last time she saw him. For a while, she continued to use S.S. *Bremen* stationery.

and the sky has the Algerian blue you see on advertisements. You expect an Arab to appear on a white horse. Strange to be on the sea again. Distance growing, clock distance, a long night and then a day and then a night, and another day and another night, that is how far I am from you. But then that's reality distance. We cover that, we annihiliate that. We dream. Distance & nearness are illusions. America seems very far, blotted out. Paris is nearer. I think of Emerson in Marseilles, sitting at the café table, about the idiots and imbeciles necessary to lend an air of reality to life.

The sky everywhere is of an intense, legendary blue. Africa. Purple sea.

On the train to Fez

Changed from ship to train at Algiers. Brief impression. Saw first woman with face covered. All is pale blue—only eyes showing. Very stirring, the mystery. Hats. Red fez. Turbans. Colonial African hat. Stop at little stations. Rapacious people. No tip is ever enough. Long Jewish arguments with hands. Algerian wine delicious. Land rolling and soft like Southern France. But at every stop groups of Arabs in costume—Biblical scenes. Women on small donkeys. Perfumed air. Burnooses are not only in white bath towel material but in rug material, dark browns, blues, tapestry effects. Turbans of all colors. No color depiction of this land is exaggerated.

7.30 A.M.

Arrived Fez at 6 A.M. Desert wind blowing. Rain. But no fools' paradise. Everything more beautiful than I expected or imagined. I can't write any more, nonchalantly. The Arabs are *noble* looking. Our maid's face is uncovered. She looks like these pictures, only her face is all tattooed, color of this ink, five starry spots. They all speak French. Going out to see Fez . . .

Anaïs

Palais Jamai, Fez
April 17, [1936]

[Henry:]

Lost again in the labyrinth. The predominant smell is like that of Spain—the olive oil with which they cook. And the smell of wet rags

like baby's diapers. Mysterious city. The Pasha's son's palace—was all
the time in the heart of it and we didn't know it until today when we
were led to it by way of the darkest and foulest little passageways—and
there it was, hidden away within walls right next to a stable, next to
a place where men in sackcloths were washing lamb skins from blood
and mud. And so we step into a palace of mosaic and lace work,
furnished with nothing but divans and low tables and pillows. Nothing
else. Where do they keep their clothes? Books? Mystery. We meet the
Pasha's son, who is taller than Hugh, handsome as they all are except
when they have leprosy, syphilis, or pockmarks, or diseases of the eyes,
or a nose missing. We sit on the divans in this manner, looking out of
the door at the garden and fountains—Pasha's son—his son, his
brother-in-law, his cousins, his brothers. It is Friday, that means their
Sunday, so the brother is holding on to his beads and praying. This
saves him from having to talk French. The Pasha's son's wives are at
the Haman. He is sorry. I won't see them. His wife, from which he has
3 children—he talks about. I ask him what does she look like? He
answers, "like you, and my daughter looks like you too." His son assents
and acknowledges the resemblance. We drink *thé à la menthe* and eat
cakes made by the wives. The air is perfumed with sandalwood. I feel
an immense, deep peace. Peace and simplicity. Peace. I have just come
from the Mosque where I heard the "big prayer." I'm not allowed in
but the tall gates are open and I saw them all praying. And I saw them
come out, rich and poor together. The blind and leprous wait for
money, chanting . . . chanting.

I saw oil being pressed out in cellars under a big wooden wheel
pushed by a puny, weary Arab.

The poor are dressed in sackcloths. The semi-poor in sheets and
bath towels. The well-to-do women in muslin and silk. The Jews wear
black and their noses are longer than anywhere else.

The atmosphere is so clear you feel you can see the whole world,
as clearly as you see Fez. I'm lying in bed now after walking five
hours up and down hill . . . the city lies there in the sun. The birds
don't just chat as they do in Paris, they chant and *gargarise* with
tropical fervor.

Our bedroom is exactly the color of my dining room in Louveciennes. Orange.

The children, Henry. They're beautiful. They work terribly hard,
carrying jugs, bread, wood, holding the weavers' silk spools. . . .

It seems to me like an inexhaustible city. One could live here and never entirely know it. What you would like is the *entassement*—terribly real, near, like the smells.

We leave here the 23rd. One day at Cadiz—two days at Madrid—*International Banking Corporation, Madrid,* is a sufficient address from 24th to 26th or 27th. Letters from here take 4 days—so I hope you were able to send yours by air, as I am sending mine.

Well, Professor Hemingway, are you glad I came without the Diary?

I'm eager to hear from you . . . are you all right? I dreamed the first night here that my valise was full of birds and that I was told each bird contained a pair of stockings, but had to be killed, of course, to get the stockings. I said I preferred to do without them and opened the valise and let them all fly.

Such a violent contrast between New York and this. Opposite poles! The place without a machine in it! Everything hand made. No drinking . . . such contentment they don't even smoke. They are at peace.

Good night, Henry . . . in a personal way!

A.

Palais Jamai, Fez
[April 19, 1936]

[Henry:]

Alone for the first time and able to write you directly, so I can begin by telling you I had a dream in which you paid me a most intimate and oriental visit—so vivid I feel as if you had been here for the night. It all began by your kissing me in the street before everybody and saying you were tired of mystery. Then we sat at a big banquet and I got up to get something and you got up with me and walked as if we were soldered like twins. You seemed very happy and in one of your soft moods. I hope you enjoyed it as much as I did! [. . .]

It is a drug, all this. It enmeshes you. Those palaces, a life of pleasure, of the body. It made me passionate, to sit there on pillows, with the sun, the birds, the infinite beauty of the mosaic, the tea kettle singing, the many trays shining, the twelve bottles of perfume in the center, the sandalwood smoking. The Caïd who received us yesterday had a white beard, and white eyebrows, black laughing eyes and a laughter from the stomach which was wonderful to hear.

Hugh will soon be back. I want to go down and send you this. We're leaving here Wednesday for Cadiz. If there is trouble in Spain Hugh may send me home alone from there. If so I'll telegraph you. I hope you sent me news. Have received none so far.

Je t'embrasse . . . comme tu m'a embrassé hier soir!

Anaïs

[Villa Seurat]
Tuesday, 20th [April 1936]

Dear Anaïs:

Your two letters from Casablanca and Fez just arrived. [. . .]

When I read your wonderful descriptions I realize that nothing is happening here. The most amazing thing to me is how you can stand the smell! This is the first time your delicate nostrils don't rebel. Is it because the eyes are so delighted?

What did you mean when you said the Arab's wife and daughters resembled you? I thought they were all fat and black-eyed and greasy. You seem to find your type everywhere, except in America. [. . .]

I say nothing's happened, and yet a few things have. For one thing Kahane has started the printing of *Black Spring*. I saw him twice and he seems full of pep, plans, ideas. At any rate, as far as finances go, we're all right. The 2,000 is wiped out by the earnings. As the account stood at the end of the year I owed him about 700-odd francs, mostly on account of the printing of *Aller Retour*.* But this too has been wiped out in the meantime, through sales of *Tropic* for the current year (he's sold close to a hundred so far this year). When June comes there will be a check for royalties. [. . .]

I hope you won't bother to bring things for me. Just bring me the descriptions, and a little of the smell of Araby. You don't mention the musk and the spices. There must be some of that along with the manure and whatnot.

It's hard to say much "personal" now. I'm saving it up until you

---

*H. M.'s account of his trip to New York from which he returned in May 1935, *Aller Retour New York*, was published in a limited edition of 150 copies in October 1935 by the Obelisk Press, Paris, and reprinted in Paris in the magazine *Europe* (Vol. 43, No. 172, April 15, 1937).

return. In fact, your being away seems very unreal. I have the feeling, despite the letters, that you're still in Paris. It was too sudden. *I love you.*

Henry.

Atelier Saint-Georges
51 Rue Saint-Georges, Paris (9)
Thursday [April 23, 1936]

Anaïs—

The second letter from Morocco just arrived. Read with increasing astonishment! *Quelle vie! Et la Fatima, quoi!*

Meanwhile things have happened here. Fraenkel flew the coop—to London. Cleared all the furniture out in the early hours of the morning and left without paying the fisc [local French tax collector]—or the landlady, Mrs. Ginsbourg. Typical stunt. Little debts everywhere—for gas, for typing, for newspaper ads, etc. Anathema everywhere. No one has a kind word to say about him.

I feel relieved. In fact, it was due to a talk we gave him, Fred and I, that he blew. We told him he was just a *mouse*—and it must have penetrated. He gave us one of those sinking, despairing looks that tell the story. And finally, as he was giving us his last "instructions" about this and that, he said—"Maybe you'll never see me again!" And we laughed and said—"That's O.K. too!" Which quite finished our task. He said he will be gone only a few weeks probably and then return to Louveciennes for the summer. Now I suggest that you tell Hugo to tell him that you've already rented the place. *Keep him out of France!* [. . .] Incidentally, I warned Fraenkel *not* to write you from London—as I am using his name on my envelopes to you. So don't tell Hugo anything about his going yet.

Eduardo was here one night when [Robert] Swasey came. I fell asleep on them—unfortunately. I hope he wasn't offended. [. . .]

Roger [Klein] just popped in a moment ago. He is working extra, at night, on a newspaper for the concierges—*Paris-Paris.* Earns about a 1,000 francs a month thereby and seems happy to have crawled out of the womb. He's very anxious to see you, of course.

Otherwise nothing new. When Fred goes things will return to normal again. I must say I am amazed by the way he responds to the "treatment." Not at all stupid and very *receptive.* Sees things quite clearly, especially when I dwell on his faults. Seems to have a most genuine desire to do something about it. And, to be sure, is quite impressed by the way I go about it. Apparently he had never imagined it was so sane.

Undoubtedly you must have received my letter to Fez—I made sure of the time of delivery.

I don't feel so damned good. Stomach seems to be out of order. But nothing serious. Just nervous. As I say, I'm glad now that Fraenkel's gone—and will be more glad when Fred goes too. I'm going to arrange something with him, so don't you worry about it. [. . .]

Well, I am waiting for your next letter to know when you think you will be back. Let me know in advance so that I can dispose of Fred. It's been cold and rainy here—but we have heat again. *Je t'embrasse*—with "tropical fervor."

Henry

Postcard
[Cadiz]
[April 23, 1936]

[Henry:]

This is the Jewish quarter. The Jews in Fez were given the task of salting the heads of the killed so they could be hung on the ramparts. We saw a dead Arab—all wrapped in narrow white linen bandages like the Egyptian mummies. Carried to cemetery on plain stretcher and buried thus, not in a coffin. Arabs go to cemetery for walks and to talk together. Carry prayer rug and bird cage (remember China reportage on bird cage?). Familiarity with death encouraged. Tonight I'll be in Cadiz. Everything wonderful except that I didn't hear from you and won't now for the rest of the trip. Will trust my dreams in which you are all right. I'm coming back fat and peaceful, psychically speaking! Very gay and contented. Enriched by all I have seen. New York wiped out, as if I had bathed in the Mosque fountains.

Hugh worried me unexpectedly when he told me he had withdrawn everything from bank but he sent money to Eduardo and I wrote immediately to Eduardo to give you whatever you needed—by air mail. I hope he fixed it all.

[Anaïs]

Postcard
Thursday, April 23, [1936]

[Henry:]

Cadiz, you may remember, is the city I describe in child[hood] diary. I didn't want to live there, I said, because women could not leave the house, or go out except on holidays. I enumerated its products and described the people on donkeys and the palm trees. Am writing you from the boat while I look at Gibraltar. We cut our stay short in Fez to see Granada and Seville on the way. I wanted so much to see these with *you!*

Anaïs

[30 Quai de Passy, Paris]
[March 1937]*

I want to try and explain to you, Henry, how it is you make things so inhuman and unreal that after a while I feel myself drifting away from you, seeking reality and warmth somewhere. You repeat over and over again that you need nobody, that you feel fine alone, that you enjoy yourself better without me, that you are independent and self-sufficient. You not only keep saying it regardless of the effect on me, but you never once make a gesture or a sign like a human being. I can walk in and out, I can stay away a week or a year, you never so much [as] telephone, or extend a hand to hold me, detain me. Everything in you pushed me away, your collective life, your constant life with others, your incapacity to create nearness or relationship with a person, always with a crowd. I seek, on the contrary, to keep you at the center of my life, but you make me feel the very opposite: that you are at the center of your life, with your work, and then you marvel why it is woman drifts away. My trip alone to New York was due entirely to this feeling you create in me, to this perverse thing in you which makes all your loves so negative and so destructive.

---

*A. N. returned to Louveciennes in May 1936 and subsequently took an apartment in Paris. From September 1936 to July 1937 she also rented a houseboat on the Seine, to which her friend Gonzalo More gave the name Nanankepichu, meaning "not at home" in the old Inca language Quechua. H. M. remained at Villa Seurat during this period, from which little correspondence seems to have survived.

What a twisted, ingrown, negative love you have. When I read what you write about June now, I feel almost like laughing. You spent your life storming at her, criticizing her, denying her self, her value, all she represented (and then you say you "love"—what is love but acceptance of the other, whatever he is). You could have made me yield with a sign, and this sign you never make. Remember this; it was never vanity which made me seek to be loved by others, but the need of reality, of humanness. The need of expression [. . .] one can put a finger on and say: there it is, it's a heart beating; if I move, this person feels it; if I leave, this person knows it; if I drop away, [this person] feels fear. I exist in him. That is life, there is something happening there. But when I walk into your place, I see the most expressionless face, the most vague, negative gestures, the most complete ghostliness. It is not enough just to take a woman in bed, you know. Human beings were given other forms of expression. I express what I feel, you go out of your way to deny, to blur and efface all manifestations of attachments of any sort. You harp on the collective, on the principle of friendship rather than the friend, the general "cunt world." I glanced over what you were writing in *Capricorn*, and there it was, the great anonymous, depersonalized fucking world. Instead of investing each woman with a different face, you take pleasure in reducing all women to an aperture, to a biological sameness. That is not very interesting, I say, nor very much of an addition. It's a disease. The man who begins to see all the world as a sex is really diseased. He is like a dog in heat. People get in rut, that is understood, and right. But man does not live in a state of rut. Your depersonalization is leading you so far, you are disintegrating so much that it all becomes sex, and sex is a hole, and after that death. Oblivion. My god, Henry, the only personal, individual thing that ever happened to you was June, because she tortured you and so she finally was able to distinguish herself from the sea you make. I am against what you are doing. I see you becoming [an] animal like Nijinsky, and then insane; the way you focus on sex is a death obsession. I have pulled you out of this many times; you once had such a primitive attitude towards lesbianism, for instance. Did she or did she not sleep with? That is all you knew. I gave you another conception of lesbianism, the "whether she slept" was not the millionth parcel of all that happened, or was meant by lesbianism. And now you are at it again— sleeping with what, with whom, how [. . .] And you think you are writing and living an apotheosis, and it is exactly the contrary, it's a downfall, it's the disease. That is where collectivity leads you. You are simply this: an Ego in a crowd. You are in the same danger of being an Ego in a crowd (the ego can only perceive the crowd, he cannot perceive an equal; that is the sign of the ego, because a crowd is a malleable thing he can identify himself with, or dominate, or dazzle, etc. It is the opposite of relationship). I use your attitude to me as an example. I am not making a personal plea. I am beyond that. Whatever that insufficiency in you is that cannot keep alive a relationship, I have got beyond lamenting. I made another life to supplement that. I have nothing to ask. Because I do not believe asking can change one. That is your way. Your destiny.

But while I am next to you I will continue to shout for the ego and his equal, not for myself, as I say, but because I can see through that god, ego, self, alone-man principle, and I will write about it, and fight against it, and every time I can awake you for one day to the consciousness of another, I will be glad for your life as a human being, as a man. One's life as a man is not in the collective principle, the crowd; it is in the friend, in the woman, in the inside of himself. That, you never acknowledge, never. You never make your gesture as a man, a simple, direct man who is losing something, unless you are driven by a violent situation. That is why I was so happy that time in New York and wanted to return there [. . .]. It was the only time you became Henry Miller a man, a human being [. . .]. After that, again began this vague, floating art world. And the key to that is FEAR. You made an illuminating statement once when I was saying that I brought all philosophy into you, and you said: But that is dangerous because you could lose me. It's tragic to put Laotse in me, it's dangerous. There you are: fear, fear of the immediate, possibly tragic, personal relationship, which I am not afraid of. But that is also why you evade tragedy, that is why you attain joy. You make the whole world the simple thing which we feel with acquaintances. We always say: we have a good time with certain people who don't mean much to us, but all of us agree that this "good time" is not what nourishes our life, and those who have only this kind of ephemeral, light contact with people, who have a continuous good time, soon find out they feel their life empty, they get sick of it, they feel empty and without deep joy. Fear. I see that in you now, when you sleep, elude, evade, slide away, seek the café, the crowd. With you and me, I don't understand because there was no reason for our relationship to be tragic. None, as far as I am concerned. But it has become so for me because you do nothing to make it real, all you do evaporates, dissolves, decomposes it. You volatilize.

[Anaïs]

[Villa Seurat]
Sunday [March 1937]

Anaïs—

I've waited this long to answer your letter because I wanted to reflect. I don't make much headway, frankly. I don't want to deny whatever is true, but is the truth a thing of black or white, as you represent it!

What you say is devastating. If this is what I really am like then I shouldn't be able to hold my head up—I'd want to run away and never see or hear from you again. I'd loathe myself.

I have a few suggestions to offer if you will come and talk it over. I want to do only what will make you happy. If you don't believe that then you don't know me at all.

The whole thing makes me sad and miserable. I don't want to be sad and miserable, nor repentant, nor anything else which is dark and negative. What I am now I shall probably always be. You know that I'm not struggling to become something different. If I do change it will only be quietly and unnoticeably, as I have already changed since [I've known] you.

I never dreamed that I was causing you so much pain. That's what makes it difficult to respond, because pain is something real and has roots. But how blind have I been then!

One thing I feel pretty sure of—and that's what makes it worse—that the cause of the explosion has nothing to do with the real situation. Admitting as much as you have you ought to go the whole hog and let me know everything. Only absolute honesty can bring us to a real understanding.

Henry

[Hotel Majestic, Bordeaux]
Sunday, A.M. [September 25, 1938]

Anaïs—

Got all the letters this morning. If there is no war I'll be coming back to Paris. But I'll wait a few days to make sure. I still think there is a chance to patch things up. Hitler has given a few days grace, it seems—like God Almighty.*

About my things—if there is still time—why do like this: the two cases with my name on and marked 1 and 2—you might give to Kahane. The tin trunk and the valise take to the American Express. *But don't do any of this if time is precious!* I can lose everything they contain. See that you get *yourself out safely*—and don't hesitate, if it's more possible, to go to London or any other place. I'll stay here because now I'll have to. If there is going to be aerial war this place isn't so safe either—it's within reach. But from here I can easily go to the country or get a boat to somewhere. Frankly, I'd rather be back in Paris. I almost left last night—but something held me back. This morning again I walked around for an hour trying to decide whether to return there or stay here. Then at 10 A.M. I came back to see if there was mail and found your letter.

I am writing a note to Kahane now to see if he would advance me any money on royalties. If you take the cases there perhaps you can add a word or two. I am dubious of him, naturally.

I don't do any work. I walk around or go to sleep, absolutely automatic. I haven't done anything but walk around in a trance since I left. I must have looked at thousands of pairs of shoes, at ties, socks, umbrellas, nightshirts etc.—as you would if you were mesmerized. I haven't talked to a soul either—and that's bad. All I can do is read the papers, sit down, get up, walk about. If I thought they weren't going to evacuate Paris I'd go back immediately. I'd rather be there during the air raids than in a strange place where you know nobody and can do nothing.

However, maybe now I'll look at the book again. I'll stay here and wait either for you to come or for things to clear up. That's a bit of progress. If I had had money I wouldn't be in such a funk. I could

*The "Munich Pact" of September 29/30 between Germany, France, Britain and Italy postponed the outbreak of the war for another year, and H. M. eventually returned to Paris.

decide easily enough to go somewhere out of all this. That's why I always fear the "trap." I have had plenty of such experiences. But since everybody is now more or less in the same boat perhaps it will be different. And finally there may be an American gun-boat! That's why I think that if Hugo urges you to go to London you should do it—you might get to America or some other place easier and quicker.

I give you the telephone number of this hotel in case you have to phone me: Urbain 80.530 and Inter 2.52. I think the latter is the one you want. I will be here until 9 A.M. always, and back again at 12 noon till 12.30, again from 7 to 7.30 P.M.

Don't worry about my things at Villa Seurat! That's a luxury, if the world is going to crack up. I still think something will be arranged—it's a perilous game, but I still think they're playing a chess game.

Anyway, I will sit tight for the time being. *Tout s'arrangera!* With love,

Henry

[Bordeaux]
Tuesday, 4 P.M. [September 27, 1938]
(2nd letter)

Anaïs—

After writing you this morning I dispatched a letter at noon to Kahane, which I think he will receive today yet, asking him to send cablegrams for me (I gave him the texts) to six people, asking for funds to help cover passage money. Only after mailing the letter did I think to go to the steamship lines here. To my surprise I find there are absolutely no boats leaving Bordeaux for America—only for South America. One would have to go to Le Havre or Cherbourg or Boulogne.

I'm telling you this so that you don't start down this way. If you leave Paris go to Le Havre if possible. I must stay here now three or four more days and wait for the answers to my cables. If the replies come quickly I'll get out of here and start for Le Havre *before October 1st.* I have a notion that Hitler will declare war midnight September 30th—and you may well expect that within two hours after that every large city in France will be bombed. If I smell that this is going to happen I won't take the train—if it means passing the night and going thru Paris, which one has to do. In that case, with what money arrives, I'll take a train for some small place, maybe Biarritz or even Arcachon, which is nearby, and wait. I will also be watching to see if an American gun-boat will stop off here at Bordeaux. I don't count on that too much. In short, I'm trying to impress on you that you would be safer off going to Le Havre—and you should try to go by the 29th the latest. The 30th will be a grand exodus—you'll see. Even if one can't get a boat right away one can wait there with relative safety. Or you could hop most any big boat and go to Cobh or Cork, Ireland. If these people respond to my cables I'll feel a lot better no matter where I am temporarily. Don't get panicky and feel you must wait and telephone—just send telegram advising what you do. I'll answer with a telegram immediately. I'll also notify you before leaving here—in time to wait for a reply, should it be necessary.

I told Kahane he could send cables to America deferred. Perhaps you might call him up and make sure he sends them—and let him send them first rate no matter what the expense. I told him to pay for me—it's the least he can do. The cables went to Fraenkel, c/o [James] Cooney, Durrell, Huntington Cairns,* Carl Holty, Laughlin and Eliot. I didn't ask for full fare—just what they could spare towards passage money. I thought it best to do this so that you would have as much for yourself—and Joachim and your mother—as possible. If I have a hundred or so American dollars in my pocket I won't be in any sweat—bombs or no bombs. My chief dread is to be stranded here in France, to be an able-bodied non-combatant—and further, to be an American—you'll see, they will turn against the Americans for not coming to the rescue immediately. I have already overheard plenty of caustic comments about our "neutrality." I know what I'm talking about.

At the very worst, I can get a boat from here to Lisbon—that's definite. I might have to wait a few days, that's all. But I believe one leaves any Saturday. But I don't want to stay—that's definite. I've thought it all out, from every possible angle. If one had been allowed to stay in Paris I wouldn't mind—but elsewhere, no. One feels like a rat hiding away. I can't stand being passive and watching things happen, and I am sure now I don't want to take any part in it. If it had been my private problem I could have settled it in a half-hour. But I am not going to be the victim of the stupidity and stubbornness of governments in which I have no interest. I feel clear-headed now and capable—I want action. No more waiting around. Remember, you go to Le Havre, if possible and I will try to join you there. If for any reason you have to hang on there, don't pass the night in Paris on the 30th—

*See Biographical Notes.

unless, of course, you read that everything looks to be settled. But if they are still *negotiating,* clear out. Hitler means business.

I'm O.K. now, I tell you. With love,

Henry

Peniche la Belle Aurore
Quai des Tuileries, Paris Ier
[December, 1938]*

Henry:

Sent you some mail yesterday care of [W. T.] Symons. Hope all the novelty is resting you.

Will you be seeing the *Seven* [magazine] people? Or [Edward] O'Brien?†

Saw [Jean Renoir's film] *La Bête Humaine* of Zola at the movies—an inflated newspaper item—no good.

[Jean] Carteret writes interesting things from Lapland. His is the best evasion of all. [Laplanders use] heated huts for Turkish baths [in] which they are born and die. Mothers are shut in the steaming place to give birth, and old Laplanders go there and die alone in the same heat. The *renne* will not eat anything touched by man's hand. Laplanders [handle their] food with gloves.

To chase away the hungry wolves who follow the pulka, throw a lighted box of matches behind you—and speed up.

He will hear X-mas mass in Byzantine. The priest throws a cross into an icy lake and fanatics plunge to find it.

The snowflakes‡ I got don't come from there.

Anaïs

Sending you stamp money.

---

*At their invitation and with their assistance, H. M. had gone to London to visit Nancy and Lawrence Durrell, whom he had met during their two visits to Paris in 1937 and 1938. In March 1938 A. N. had rented another houseboat, *La Belle Aurore,* which, after the loss of Louveciennes, had become her second home. Early in 1939, A. N. left the apartment at Quai de Passy and moved to 12 Rue Cassini, since her husband's work kept him in London most of the time.
†Editor of the annual *Best Short Stories.*
‡Paper snowflakes pasted above her letterhead.

[Anaïs:]

In the beginning was the word, but for the Word to come forth there had first to be a separation of some kind. To detach itself from the bosom of creation there had to be a need, a human need. The word is always the reminder of a more perfect state, of a union or unity which is ineffable and undescribable. Creation is always difficult because it is an attempt to recover what is lost. To regain we must first feel abandoned.

You know all the joys and terrors of creation. You have been playing God ever since you were able to talk. In that Neptunian atlas which you are consecrating to posterity you have recorded the protean metamorphoses of your unions and separations. It is the ark and the covenant of the lost. You began the construction of your vessel, like a true mariner, on the face of the waters. You consign it to the waters of oblivion. You carve your own image in the prow of the boat. You remain fixed there, cutting the waters endlessly. Whichever way the wind blows you point the way.

To me the Diary is like the moving needle of the compass. Though it is always pointing north, it moves nevertheless with the ship and with those who are sailing it and with the current that directs the ship's course. If we imagine your ship to sail endlessly on, as it undoubtedly will, the destination will change as the stars themselves change their course. The direction will always be due north, but the voyage will be eliptical, changes of climate rather than changes of latitude and longitude. In your interminable log only the handwriting remains unalterable. The signature will always be your own, always swift, precise and legible . . . you are writing from a point beyond change. You are recording the constancy of change, the eternality of metamorphoses. You have chosen not to create but to record creation. . . .

You are always striving to fill the empty vessel of life. At first literally, by giving things—the food and substance of life—later, realizing that it is a futile task, that you cannot possibly hope to cope with all the needs of those who come to you, transforming the loaves and fishes into the wine of life, giving from the endless fountain of wisdom which alone can give life.

And finally you will realize that even that is not sufficient, not effective enough [. . .].

While one sits in the body of the whale recording the changing temperature, mapping and charting the inner dynamism, the great whale itself is plowing through the deep. We must drop the pen, the pencil, the brush and become the great whale itself. The real experience lies yonder, in the deep waters through which the whale is swimming. You think you are nourishing the world—but you are only nourishing the whale [. . .].

When I say, as I often do, that my life since twenty-one up until recently was but a detour I mean that a large part of my efforts were wasted in an unacknowledged struggle to adapt myself to the world, the final adaptation masking itself as an effort to conquer or seduce the world through my creative powers as a writer. I should have been adapting myself to myself [. . .].

By an unflinching regard for one's self one gradually becomes so in harmony with the world that he no longer has to think about his duty toward others. One ceases to think about causing the other pain or sorrow or disillusionment because one's acts and speech become so transparent that the heart's intention always registers. Fear vanishes when one is convinced that he can do no evil, when he does as he pleases because it is the only thing to do. We often think we may cause harm by our behavior but we think so only because we have not enough faith in the other's intelligence and sympathy. We imagine that those who admire or love us do so because of our good qualities only. But more often than not the other person is fully aware of our frailties and is more prepared for our misbehavior than we ourselves are [. . .].

Henry

[Villa Seurat]
Monday night [May 22, 1939]

Dear Anaïs—

Just spent the evening with Eduardo. Going to the hotel at Porte d'Orléans, as the man moved me out early this morning. Very tired—but finished with packing at last. Waiting now for the money to arrive. Expect to find a letter with it at Kahane's tomorrow, or if not, Wednesday.

Will let you know soon as I get it. Think now to go first to Rocamadour, at the other end of the Valley of the Dordogne—then further south. Not rushing to Greece. Am too dead tired to take long jumps.

Saw [Conrad] Moricand* last night and had a fine talk with him. *"Le ciel encore chargé,"* he says—but *"il y augura les gains spirituels."* Also very definitely—*money*, some time in June. Says I'm doing the right thing.

Listen, I left a big valise in your place, together with Nancy [Durrell]'s things, also a blanket & some towels. The valise is full of my things. I am not leaving any with American Express. Have taken two small valises instead.

Will be reading your MS. tomorrow only and then will bring it along with me so as to talk it over with you.

I just missed you by a few minutes the other day.

Dead tired—more tomorrow.

HVM

[Porte d'Orléans, Paris]
Thursday [May 25, 1939]

[Anaïs:]

Still rushing about—thin as a rail. But everything executed. The check from the Gotham B[ook] M[art] arrived yesterday, but it's on a N.Y. bank and I'm waiting for Kahane to find someone to cash it—he says he hasn't that much in the bank himself. I'll need it. Am nearly finished with the other money and still have things to pay. Soon as I cash it I'll send you an American Express check for 2 or 3 thousand francs. Just sold the lamp now—6:30 P.M.—after 8 visits to the electrician—150 francs. Such a running around—never did so much in my life. Glad to get out of Villa Seurat—what a swamp of details! I even enjoy the idea of being in a hotel for a few days here in Paris. [. . .]

I'm not even getting visa for Greece yet. Will do that in Marseilles. Why shouldn't I pass leisurely through Italy? I'd like to see Florence, Ravenna, Naples, Rome, Taormina. Corfu is always there. Last thing I had to do was to mail the three blankets to the Durrells. Taking your MS. along with me. Just got [Jean Giraudoux's] *Ondine* too—and an English version of *Louis Lambert* from N.Y. Incidentally, Miss [Frances] Steloff of Gotham B.M. is a Theosophist—and pretty

*See Biographical Notes.

decent too. She didn't have the $200.00 when she sent check. That's why she made it out on a N.Y. bank—to gain time. I'm getting the *Secret Doctrine* [by Helena Petrovna Blavatsky] from her—the one book I have looked forward to so long.

Well, all this sounds hectic and is just the way I feel. I'll certainly meet you somewhere in the South, before going on to Corfu.* Why should I hurry to go anywhere? I'm fed up with activity. It's crazy. Maybe I'll see you in Monaco or Nice. Then to Marseilles. But I'll surely see the Vallée de la Dordogne now, with the prehistoric drawings of the Cro-Magnon men. And I'll go to Toulouse again! I still expect something wonderful of that place. Strange, eh? Give me an idea *when* I am to see you.

I'll write more in a day or two—before leaving Paris. If the check isn't cashable I'll stay on here till it is cashed in N.Y. But I hope Kahane will do something. He was amazed to see it—his mouth watered. More soon.

Henry

Zeyer/ Brasserie-Café-Tabac
230 à 234 Avenue du Maine
Thursday, 5.00 P.M. June 1st [1939]

Anaïs—

Just got the money cashed a few minutes ago and now to P.O. to get it off to you. After paying off debts, hotel, food, train etc. I should have about 3,000 francs when I reach Rocamadour. I will leave tomorrow night or Sat. night 9 P.M., depending on how quick I can get my glasses after seeing oculist. I am at Hotel L'Acropole, 199 Blvd. Brune (XIV). Phone—*Vaugirard* 64-1 7, in case you need to wire me. Won't see Kahane again for mail after tomorrow, Friday, as he's closed Saturday.

Your book [*Winter of Artifice*] will be out next week, he says. No chance to change blurb as it was already in hands of printer. I am paying him 375 frs. for the extra work on your book. He makes a point

---

*A. N. planned to leave on May 24 for the Riviera, where she spent the next three months on vacation, joined on several occasions by her husband, with whom she went back to London at the end of August. She returned to Paris late in September. H. M. sailed for Greece on July 14 for a prolonged visit with the Durrells.

of it always. He's doing big business though. *Tropic of Cancer* is now the biggest seller of all his books.

Won't write more now as I want to get this off to you by air mail. Wire hotel if you will stay at St. Raphaël yet awhile so that when I get to Rocamadour I will know what's what.

Henry

Maison Vaylet
12, rue des Capucines
Friday [June 2, 1939]

Anaïs—

No word from you since the postcard some days ago. This morning I sent a second telegram saying I would not leave till Wednesday night—there's a train for Rocamadour around 9 P.M. This because this morning I went to the oculist and he gave me an entirely new prescription for new glasses. I'm getting a bifocal pair now, and one dark pair—both expensive—cost me 200 frs. for examination and 600 for the glasses—and they can't be done until Wednesday. However, I don't mind too much. I'm now thru with all the jobs I had to do and think in the intervening days I'll make little trips by autobus to places I always intended to visit, like the Valley of the Chevreuse etc. I am only now beginning to feel normal. I am nursing myself along. I think it is only now too that all the injections are beginning to wear off.

I'm wondering whether you'd want to risk going to Rocamadour. I could go to St. Raphaël or Monte Carlo first, if necessary, but it would mean doubling back on my tracks. I won't miss seeing the Dordogne this time! The lottery is tonight. Maybe I'll have luck! This is my lucky month for money, according to Moricand. You know, I haven't yet spent a cent on myself. Paying out all obligations. I may get a bathrobe & a light hat or cap today if I feel I can afford it.

Another letter from Bessie Breuer this morning saying that Ben Hecht and perhaps Dos Passos may send me some money—she says they are great admirers of my work! The Castiglione shop is doing well. By the way, I am *not* paying Kahane the 375 frs. for now. Why not let him wait a while? He keeps us waiting for everything. He had the photo of the window taken—complained because it cost him 400 frs.

Well, I wait to hear from you now. Tell me what you'd like to do. There's time to arrange things. I sent the money order in a letter *recommandé*—was too late for the air mail. Hope you got it O.K. Still expecting some small checks. I'd like to be able to get *you* cleared up for once on your debts. I'm going to try.

Hurrying with this to catch the air mail.

HVM

P.S. I'm certainly cleaned up and in perfect order. It's a wonderful feeling.

Oriental/Hotel Tout le Confort Café
1 Avenue d'Orléans
Saturday [June 3, 1939]

Anaïs—

Got two letters hand-running this morning. This morning I stopped into the Bureau du Tourisme on the Champs Elysées and got a lot of information. Enclose a folder on Rocamadour, giving names of hotels. Even at full-pension rates they are not expensive, you see. And I think in a small place like this (not even a thousand inhabitants) it's better to take meals at the hotel. From there we could make excursions to the interesting places—if Rocamadour isn't insufferable.

How would you like to go there in advance, soon as you're free, and take a place—then wire me which one. I can't leave before Wednesday night. If the glasses are not ready then (tho he promised me solemnly!) then it will be Thursday. The night train arrives towards 5 in the morning. No need to get up to meet me. I'll have breakfast early at the *gare* and walk around the town first.

Tomorrow I'm going to Provins (the place I've wanted to see since I first came to Paris) and then the Valleé de Chevreuse on Monday. Feel sorry I never availed myself of the cheap Sunday fares to go to all these places. It was stupid of me.

I wanted to go to Rouen too, but it's too expensive. No reduced rates for Rouen.

You know, I think when I finally come back to Paris I'll get a good hotel room at full-pension rate. It's wonderful to have service and to know you'll eat well and regularly. And I think it's cheaper too—especially by the month or three or six months. Now I'm raring to go and see places. France looks good to me from the pamphlets of the Syndicate d'Initiative. Especially the little old towns on hills in rambling country—

that's what I like—with plenty of ancient ruins and good food. I'm not going to leave France till I've seen all I want of it.

I had a letter from a Frenchwoman Fred sent me from London—friend of the Symons. She is staying in the Pyrénées (Barcelonette) with a Javanese couple—dancers. They claim to know what is the matter with Nijinsky—I'll show you the letter. I have a hunch I could get some reliable information before writing my essay on him. The woman (Javanese dancer) says she had gone mad, like Nijinsky, and her husband cured her. Seems they know about this ailment in Java. Sounds good to me. Somewhere near Toulouse there's an Albigensian grotto from Rosecrucian—Knights Templar times, which I'd like to see. And so on . . .

I got shoes, hat, bathrobe and straw slippers. Feel ever so much better. Saw [Dr.] Danase again yesterday about my vaccination. Contrary to all *principles, it took!* O.K. I'll wait now to hear from you in answer to my suggestion.

HVM

Grand Café Glacier
La Canebière, Marseille
Sunday [July 9, 1939]

Anaïs—

Glad to hear you got the book! Haven't received any copies yet, nor any mail or *mandat* for my check from Kahane. But suppose I will Monday or Tuesday—by which time I may need some money. The hotel here asks me to pay up every two days. It's a very clean, new place and I picked a good room—at 45 frs! Had gone to a cheaper hotel recommended to me by the man in Nice—and couldn't stand it.

Yes, I am supposed to take the boat on the 14th. But I will have to wait for the money—I must get a visa for Greece too. If I can't make the boat I'll go by train.

Expect to go with [Henri] Fluchère to see [Jean] Giono on Tuesday—and maybe that night there will be a dinner given me and Fluchère's friends by a man who is a great admirer of mine here. I have already enjoyed my stay—cordial greetings everywhere.

Been swimming too—but the beaches are very poor here and the water rather dirty. It's hot as blazes here too and noisy—can hardly sleep nights.

I take it I should write you *"Boîte Postale"*—or telegraph that way too, if necessary.

Am going back to hotel now for a nap, if I can get one. It's difficult to sleep here. Frightful din.

I'll be looking for you on the 12th. The hotel is right near the station—on the street which the big steps lead down to.

More later.

HVM

Athens
July 19th [1939]

[Anaïs:]

Arrived this morning 8 A.M. in blistering heat. Climbed up the Acropolis. No Durrell in sight, no telegram from him. Going to take boat for Corfu tomorrow. Heat here would drive me crazy. It's expensive here, it seems to me. You get a lot of drachmas in exchange, but they count in 50 and 100 at a time almost. Can't say much now except that I must get out of here before being sunstruck. More from Corfu. Worse than the Sahara, this heat. New York is *nothing* compared to it.

Henry

[Corfu]
Sunday, August 6th [1939]

Anaïs—

Just got back from the camping trip, which I enjoyed immensely, except for minor discomfits such as sand in the food, ants, *flies*, etc. But feel great and am well burned now. Also have grown a beard, which is pepper and salt color. The peasants thought I was Larry's father! A bald head and a beard here is a sign of age. They guess me to be 60! But I feel like 30 now [. . .].

The spirit here seems very Spanish, or Moorish to me. I'm crazy about the olives, the olive oil for inside and out, the wonderful home-made bread, the luscious fruits and vegetables. It's a good healthy diet, I must say—for this kind of life even better than French cooking would be.

So you see I really like it. It doesn't pale a bit. I did have the right hunch after all. Everything in due season, I suppose. Whether I shall ever write anything here or not, I don't know. I feel I may. It's not improbable. But I am not trying to do anything [. . .].

Haven't heard anything from Kahane—I don't write him either. Know nothing about the fate of *Capricorn** and care nothing.

Durrell is strumming the guitar. Both he and Nancy send their love [. . .].

HVM

Aboard the *Exochorda* †
Jan. 12, 1940

[Anaïs:]

Two weeks at sea, and it seems as though a curtain had fallen over the recent past. Greece has fallen back into the well of experience. Something happened to me there, but what it was I can't formulate now. I am not on the high seas—I am in America already. America began at Piraeus, the moment I set foot on the boat. Greece is fading out rapidly, dying right before my eyes. The last thing to disappear is the light, the light over the hills, that light which I never saw before, which I could not possibly imagine if I had not seen it with my own eyes. The incredible light of Attica! If I retain no more than the memory of this it will do. That light represents for me the consummation of my own desires and experiences. I saw in it the flame of my own life consumed by the flame of the world. Everything seemed to burn to ash, and this ash itself was distilled and dispersed through the airs. I don't see what more any country, any landscape, could offer than this experience. Not only does one feel integrated, harmonious, at one with all life, but—*one is silenced.* That is perhaps the highest experience I know of. It is a death, but a death which puts life to shame. And now, on the boat, in the midst of the American scene, I feel as though I am living with people who are not yet born, with monsters who escaped from the womb before their time. I am no longer in communication

---

*The first edition of *Tropic of Capricorn* had been published by the Obelisk Press, in Paris, in February 1939.
†Following the outbreak of war in September 1939, A. N. had left Paris and returned to New York via Spain and Portugal. H. M. also had been forced to return to the United States, with A. N.'s help.

with anything. . . . Dimly I seem to remember that but a short time ago I was alive, alive in full sunlight. There is another light which envelops me now. It is like the illumination from a cold mechanical reflector. The house is dark. Only the stage is lit up. The curtain is rising.

Henry

Orange, Va.
Sunday, Feb. 11th [1940]

Anaïs—

Since I left Fredericksburg Wednesday night I've been staying here at the home of [the] Grays on the Montibello Estate and have really enjoyed myself this time. I've gotten around the country in autos quite a bit, seen some marvellous estates, had big dinners in huge baronial halls and been well received everywhere. I begin to see some virtue in the lives here—the quiet, serene, intimate side of their existence. Tomorrow, Leslie, the son, is driving me to Richmond, the capital of Va., where I think I'll stay a couple of days and then go to Washington for a couple of days. That means probably for the coming weekend. [Huntington] Cairns writes that he will put me up in his place. I am holding out fine—expenses low because of all the hospitality. I see I got a review in last Sunday's Richmond paper—not bad.*

Yesterday about 20 of us went in cars to Charlottesville to see *Gone With the Wind*. I found it overwhelming—the first half, that is. Perhaps I enjoyed it so much more because I have been listening to Civil War tales every day. I almost collapsed with emotion at the end of the first half.

I also saw Jefferson's wonderful home at Monticello, and the beautiful grounds of the University of Virginia—just a mile or so from where [David] Edgar† was raised. Really "civilized" places, I must say—full of great simple dignity.

I think we must go South. And Spring is almost here—it will be marvellous now. Wonder even whether I should come back to N.Y.

---

*A review, apparently, of *The Cosmological Eye*, which had been published by New Directions in 1939. The book was a collection of material drawn from the Obelisk Press editions of *Black Spring* (1936) and *Max and the White Phagocites* (1938), and was the first book by H. M. published in the United States.
†A friend of H. M. in Paris.

first. Am thinking about Charleston, S.C. and Savannah, Ga.—both wonderful atmospheres. What do you think? [. . .] I'd probably need my valise & laundry at Hotel Albert—and my little bag at [Abraham] Rattner's. But could come back to N.Y. first too, if you like. The fare from Wash. is only about 3 or 3.50 dollars. Getting fat from the idleness and good food. Hope you are feeling all right. Love.

Henry

Washington, D.C.
Monday [February 19, 1940]

Anaïs—

I'll probably be back now Thursday or Friday of this week. Will telephone as soon as I arrive. Am leaving here tomorrow morning either to go back to Fredericksburg or the same hotel in Washington—or maybe to Baltimore for a couple of days, just to be quiet and alone. The Cairns have been very kind and hospitable, but in their enthusiasm they have introduced me to so many people I am dizzy. It seems that Cairns is determined to have me recognized *and* published (if only in a private edition) here—and thinks I must have the favor first of influential people. [. . .]

I have some ideas about our trip,* but prefer to discuss things with you before going off again. It will be just the right time then—Spring is coming. I think you will enjoy it, if you can move about freely. I don't know if I've accomplished anything worthwhile—Cairns thinks I have—but I am certainly fed up with meeting people. I hope you feel all right now. You must be fed up with it too. I'll telephone as soon as I get in. May have to cash the last check now. But O.K. Love,

Henry

---

*Since H. M., after a brief visit to his family in Brooklyn, did not want to stay in New York, he conceived various plans to travel with A. N. through the United States, but when she could not get away, he eventually started on a trip to the West Coast, in October 1940, with the painter Abraham Rattner in a 1932 Buick. He gathered material for *The Air-Conditioned Nightmare*, a book originally commissioned with a $500 advance but rejected by the publisher and not published until 1945. During the summer, at Caresse Crosby's house in Virginia and in a room in New York, H. M. completed his memoir of Greece, *The Colossus of Maroussi*, and wrote *The World of Sex*.

New Iberia, Louisiana
[January 1941]

[Anaïs:]

At the first opportunity I have to sit down and write that Don Juan thing for [the Collector]. Then I'll feel done with him. I don't want to do that work any more for anything. I feel sorry you're involved—and urge you not to do a stroke more than you feel like. It's devastating. I feel as tho' I were getting rid of an incubus.*

Am hoping, in my explorations around here, to find a good place and tell you to come down for a while. Can't say yet—it's all new to me. When I go back to New Orleans I may come out here in the country on my own & look around. Train fare back to N.Y. is over $20.00 from here—one way. (With sleeper $50.00 or more!!) Wouldn't want to return to N.Y. just yet. Want to feel things out first. It's *hot* here now—like mid-summer. You can write me at New Orleans safely—will surely stay there a week. The red-light district is gone! But the houses are there yet. It must have been a great city once.

HVM

Albuquerque, N. Mex.
Saturday the 19th [April 1941]

Anaïs—

Got two more letters from you today. [. . .] I think I'll stay here for all next week. Can work in peace here. [. . .] This place in itself is nil. They tell me Taos is fine. Later I'll go up there. I'm testing the car out now to see if she's really going to make the grade. [. . .]

I look excellent now—good color etc. Feel normal, too. And if I get some more work finished I'll feel more wonderful. Maybe by then the miracle will happen. One lucky break now and you should be able to make it. Living out here is not expensive—especially in these comfortable tourist courts, which are most everywhere.

So I'll proceed slowly—hoping you'll be able to join me somewhere

---

*In an effort to earn some money from their writing, H. M. and A. N. had begun to write some erotic material for a private "collector" who offered to pay one dollar per page. See H. M.'s *The World of Sex;* and A. N.'s *Delta of Venus* and *Little Birds,* which became international best sellers after A. N.'s death in 1977.

out there in the vast, dry, arid, sterile, magnificent Indian country. I cough like hell again. So much dust in the atmosphere, they say. Cures or kills you, I guess.

Anyway, everything looks much more promising. I didn't send a telegram because the P.O. said you would get my letter of yesterday this morning.

Wish I could see those films you describe.

HVM

Grand Canyon, Arizona
Saturday, May 3rd [1941]

Anaïs—

[. . .] Amazing how you go on with the [Collector] stuff. Beats me. I haven't the least doubt you've developed a great technique. I want to read all [the erotica] when I see you.

So, if you're not going to join me soon I'll speed it up. Hollywood, Reno, San Francisco. Then either I get enuf to send for you or I return. How's that? But let's get to Mexico then without much delay. Do you think you can? N.Y. now seems farther away than ever. I'd rather live out here in the desert somewhere, if we had to stay in America. At least I think so now.

Please don't think I am dreaming. I hate extravagances. I've had everything a man could ask for. When I get back I'm ready for anything—a job if needs be. No matter what turn world events take I have nothing to lose. I'm a beggar now. When it gets bad for others it usually gets good for me. Let me hear from you as quickly as possible. If you send something I'll move on pronto. But give me the low-down—I'll feel better to know the truth.

HVM

Hotel Wilcox
6504 Selma Avenue, Hollywood, California
Thursday [June] 12th [1941]

Anaïs—

Decided to return here and do another big batch of pages for the American book. Found this hotel across the street from old one, at about ½ the rate—by the week! Will be able now to hold out till the 25th all right. Everything is cheap here, and the atmosphere is congenial. I can go bathing too. Anyway, I've taken this place for a week—may move to a beach later. Can't continue travelling and make any headway with the book. San Francisco left me cold—it's too big and not really distinctive in any way—and no matter which way you walk you have to climb steep hills which just knocks you out. Also, here I may make contacts to sell your MSS if the Satyr [Book] Shop falls down. I got the express package before leaving. Isn't it the original or the carbon? I'm checking up on it today.

That partner of [William] Roth's is an hysterical woman. Doubt if she's going to like your *Winter of Artifice.* Better talk it over with Roth.*

Had a letter from Fraenkel recently saying a Mexican book dealer in Mexico City would like to bring out a Mexican edition of my books. Lafe [Lafayette Young] is there too now. Maybe I'll get another break. Also, maybe there you can get *W. o. A.* done, or a condensed version of the Diary. Misrachi is the man's name. I might (or *you* might) take up the question of the "Erotica" with him—for publication under an assumed name.

I think by staying here a few weeks, economizing and working, we might get somewhere. Now there are still several sources of money open—any one of them should pay your fare out. I mean the Souchon article, Greek book, D[orothy] Norman,† *Atlantic Monthly,* Mexican man etc.‡

The Pacific ocean is not *warm!* The Japanese current is icy. But it's very hot by day—nights it cools off rapidly—by 7 o'clock it's almost chilly. Ideal climate. I have no doubt you would make a hit here. There *are* all sorts of people to meet.

Let me know how prospects are at your end.

---

*The publisher of the Colt Press in San Francisco, who had agreed to publish H. M.'s Greek book, *The Colossus of Maroussi,* which had been turned down by various larger publishing houses. He was visiting New York at this time. H. M. had suggested that Colt Press publish some of A. N.'s work.
†See Biographical Notes.
‡Apparently none of these possibilities was realized at the time, though H. M. eventually received an advance of $80 for *The Colossus of Maroussi.* A. N. depended for her support of H. M. on funds provided by her husband, who seems to have been uninformed of Miller's whereabouts. Her only income from writing then was the one-dollar-per-page fee from the collector of erotica.

By the way, won't Ethel [Guiler] tell Hugo I was coming to see [Robinson] Jeffers? You see, a friend of his (Lawrence Powell)* wrote him I was coming. Better find out about it.

HVM

[Hollywood]
June 14th [1941]

Anaïs—

Give you the above safe address [c/o Gilbert Neiman] in case I change my lodging. Have two invitations to stay at private homes—beautiful ones too. May accept in order to work better and economize more. Would get free meals, too, you see, and be driven around in a Packard. Don't get jealous—there's no mythical countess in the offing. People out here are very generous and hospitable. Everybody. There's such plenty and ease here—it's the lap of God. And that makes people good-natured. I have wonderful luncheons for 35 cents. The hotel here is eight dollars a week—plus $2.00 extra for car. One can find rooms in L.A.—in the poor quarter—for $2.50 a week! It's fantastic. [. . .]

Last night I was at a big dinner party given to Sir Victor Sassoon of China (the opium king). I sneaked out in the midst of it—bored to death. Though all the big shots were there. Am writing again and like it better than roaming about. Will send you a book shortly on Jeffers by my friend Larry Powell. There are interesting things in it. [. . .]

Look's like there is steady improvement, as far as worldly success goes. Funny, your reading nothing but French books now. You're perverse! In France you railed against them. But I admit, there are no American authors of any value.

H.

I am getting some photos of Shangri-la (the real one) for my big notebook. The story which they went to Tibet to film sounds like it might have been Otto Rank's "The Demon of the Mask," I think it was called—a German story.

*See Biographical Notes.

[New York]
[June 15, 1941]*

[Henry:]

The confusion was only caused by the impossibility of joining you. And in my confusion there is a perfectly accurate intuition which deals with the truth that your desire to live in the West has nothing to do at all with the necessities of your book, that it merely answers your own personal liking, and that this liking is over and beyond any consideration for us. As you can well understand, I am not going to beg you to come back, nor to live in New York if you do not like it. But your choice will be made, for a place to live in, alone, as you know that it is more and more impossible for me to travel out so far because when we planned this we were childishly ignorant of the cost. You write me: "One can live very cheaply, as I told you. I could find a decent shack near L.A. for twenty-five or thirty dollars. Somehow I dread the idea of returning to New York. It seems more than futile now that I've put so much distance between it and me. There are things to see all thru the West, grand country."

One thing is how much ground you have yet to cover to do your book, and this I have never questioned. Another is your desire to live in Hollywood. You confuse them. I do not. You wrote me that since I was not coming, you were slowly starting back. Today you write that you have a lot to see yet in the West. All right. You really expect me to believe that it is for your books that you have lived in Hollywood for over a month. I do not believe it, Henry. I think your book is now merely an excuse for your doing whatever pleases you. You can do whatever pleases you, but your letters now sound exactly like the letters you sent me from Greece, which almost estranged us for good. They are cold, egotistical, and concerned purely with your pleasure. All you can answer to my emotional attitude when I think I can leave and then cannot leave is thoroughly inhuman and mechanical: it is lack of self-confidence. That is not the truth at all. Mine is merely a human reaction. Yours, each day less human. Do not misunderstand me. I am not asking you to return. It would be meaningless to me if you did, because you would only be doing it at my asking, and that's useless. You have your book to do, your life to live, and the summer in New York

*The typed original of the letter bears a date in ink, "June 1942," which may have been added later. Miller arrived in Hollywood first on May 11, 1941.

would be awful. I would not want you to come back now. Everything would be all right if you wrote the right kind of letters. But you write the worst letters, letters bad enough to estrange anyone. I have never seen more expressionless, pan-faced letters, in regard to whether I come or do not come etc. More self-centered letters either. That's what creates distance, not time or a trip. The real distance and separation were always created by your letters.

You say such chaotic things: "Back there what little one earns is eaten up immediately." In New York! You do not seem to realize then that your trip has eaten infinitely more, plus the fact that I can't visit you. But never mind. You have effectively cured me of all emotional reactions. For good. I shall spend the summer quietly and pleasurably in Provincetown. When you are finished with your book on Hollywood, it will be time enough for you to decide where you want to live. By that time, if you can't write more humanly, I shall decide where I want to live too, and it may be China or South Africa.

I sent you fifty [dollars] care of Neiman.* You said that was the surest address. That is all I have saved for the moment but after the 25th I can send you more when you say the word.

After the second [of July] write me: General Delivery, Province-town.

I don't blame you at all for not liking New York. Nor wanting to come back. *Mais il y a la manière.*

Anaïs

[Hollywood]
[June 21, 1941]

Anaïs,

Just got your letter of the 15th, addressed to the Hotel Wilcox, which I left Saturday last. You certainly rub it into me. I don't know what to say. What can one say to such accusations? If that's the way you see me it's pretty sad. I know better than anyone that you can't live without money—I didn't say to live on nothing, I spoke of living as simply as possible, that's all. Is that crazy? With all that's being published now you know very well that I will have some small income—

*See Biographical Notes.

or do you believe that's a dream too? You seem to have become incorrigibly pessimistic. But I'll tell you—if it's to be a choice between doing work one doesn't believe in and sleeping on people's floors I choose the latter. I wouldn't mind doing menial work, not connected with writing, if I were obliged to, but after all the struggle to preserve integrity—not only on my part, *but on yours*—I would consider myself a traitor to act otherwise.

Yes, I see clearly that you're disturbed. I'm sorry about it. What do you wish me to do? I can't deliberately do anything that would cause you pain. If you mean it that you think it better for me to stay here till the end of August, why good, then I will stay. I will have the major part of the book done by then, I feel sure. And if you didn't mean it, if you want something else, why say so. I am going to do just as you wish. I hate it when you tell me that I'm selfish and thoughtless and irresponsible, that I never think of you, etc. etc. I think of you all the time, I talk about you to everybody. My whole life is made with you. It's true, I don't think of expanding my life, in a physical way. I think of narrowing it down. That seems to rub you the wrong way. You make me confused because you seem to twist my words around, and even my attitudes. But I won't argue with you. It's bad enough that I make you think the way you do.

I'm delighted to hear about Luise Rainer.* I hoped for just that. That was my strongest impression when I met her—that you were twins of some sort. You ought to have a glorious friendship. By the way, she gave me [her] date of birth, etc. in the hope I could get a better reading for her, but naturally I couldn't do anything about it with [Dane] Rudhyar†—it would cost money. Now, however, between Eduardo and Hugo you should be able to give her a more satisfactory horoscope. I wish I could see her too. I liked her immensely—and, as I told you, felt, above all, a great pity for her (which I am afraid I said out loud rather tactlessly). But I know she's in for more suffering— mostly because of her extreme gentleness, her sensitivity, the fact that she doesn't belong in this world—any more than you do. She looks as if she had liver trouble. But when she laughs it's quite wonderful—it's

---

*German-born actress, best known for her Oscar-winning role in the film *The Good Earth* (1937). H. M. had met her in Hollywood.
†Pseudonym of Daniel Chennevière, born in Paris in 1895, composer, painter, lecturer, who came to the U.S. in 1916 and became known for his writings on paraphysics and astrology. He eventually settled in Palo Alto, CA.

tinkling, mischievous, roguish. She's one of those unkillable neurotics, a gay heart overlarded with sorrow. [. . .]

Well, damn it, I wish you would get over these recriminations. I am not going to argue back and forth with you. You win. But the very strange part of it is that you heap these things on me just when I feel the least irresponsible. When you withdraw you say you're being wise in a French way. When I do it you say it's "childish renunciation." I insist, I feel very free at heart. I haven't any more terrors, if that means anything. Now then, what is it, Miss Nin? Should I roll up my sleeves and take a job? Should I become a script writer? What the devil is the use of freedom, what good in it, if it's to relapse into that kind of responsible individual? I tell you I'm not going to have to starve again—not unless the whole world starves, and then it wouldn't matter. I tell you that I want very little, less and less. Do my actions prove the contrary? How? What have I got that is extraneous? What am I asking for? Am I begging you to send me more money, or am I not doing my utmost to keep you from sending me money? You puzzle me.

And finally, and I never want to speak about it again—you talk of *protection*—of the attitude being important. I've protected, or tried to, the best in you. I never could promise to protect you body and soul—nobody can promise another that. The day I offend you deeply you won't protect me either—you know that. We can only make one another strong, help each other to believe in ourselves. There is no other genuine protection. Hugo does not protect you—he makes you a slave. You get befuddled. You need him and he needs you—and it's not true, it's a lie, and you know it, and that's the root of all your unhappiness. I don't lie to you. Nor do I try to hurt you when I am honest with you. I really get furious with you when you write this way. I've tried to make you stand alone, by realizing yourself as a writer. Yes, on the other hand, I prevented you, by making myself dependent on you. That was my weakness. But I don't think in terms of perpetual dependence. I try in my own way to free myself. And when I get earnest about it you balk and bring up the past. That's unfair, really. You should honor the moment, believe it to be genuine. Now if you're going to take this badly I'm going to blush for you.

H

Hotel Wilcox
Hollywood, California
July 9th [1941]

Anaïs,

I got the two letters this morning and telegram yesterday. Don't understand about this mail, but write me here at hotel hereafter, that's safe. So you've got to stay there all summer. You don't seem to believe that I wanted you to join me—I kept looking forward to it all the time. I wanted to show you some of the wonderful things in America—in the West. Now that's out, I guess. I'm trying to sell the car. Have to find a private individual—the dealers won't give me more than $50.00 for it, though they admit it's worth $200.00. I'm jittery now about driving—have seen too many accidents and wrecks out here. Besides, it's no pleasure to drive in a city.

You say I don't want to make sacrifices. I do, but not in the way you mention—via [the Collector] etc. I'd rather live more simply. Cut down on food and rent etc. Out here that is possible. I admit there is no life—no cultural, intellectual life. But in times like these, when everything is roped off, one has to fall back on oneself. I always feel good when I am alone. Solitude isn't frightening—it's strengthening.

What puzzles and depresses me at times is the realization that there is no end in sight, seemingly, to the hide and seek life. I am able to live almost anywhere, I think. I don't expect anything any more of the environment or of the people—not in this country, at least. But to be moved around by outside forces is inwardly disturbing. I seem to act as though I were free, but in reality you know that neither of us is free. Hugo pulls the strings, determines our movements.

Sometimes I think your resentment against America is more a resentment against my desire to see the country. Everything you say about the country I endorse a hundred times over. Now however there is only America—and Mexico perhaps. I prefer to adapt myself temporarily, that's all. This war may go on interminably—long after we're dead. I don't want to live with regrets and false hopes. The root of all the trouble, I really think, is that we are not free. Now, financially speaking, I could find a relative freedom—based on a very simple life. It's you, I feel, who thinks I need things which I can really do without. When I see a good spot I always feel like returning to a very primitive condition. There are loads of such places in the West. What does one need, after all? A little shack with a bed, a table, two chairs and a few dishes. You don't need clothes. To pay for this requires very little money. Instead of people, books, art, etc. you have to fall back on yourself and on nature. I know from my experience in Greece how beautiful that can be. Isn't that the truth? You give me innuendos about the delectable Hollywood, the beautiful women, etc. That's just your uneasiness. I have confidence in you—if I didn't it would be perpetual torture.

I know from your letters that you're unhappy. What do you really wish me to do? You say I can't return to Provincetown. But I feel you don't wish me to stay here either. You're not really resigned—you're forcing yourself to it. Now I tell you honestly, emotionally I am free. I can do anything, go anywhere you please. It's not sacrifice. I want you to be happy. When I tell you the truth, that I like a place, feel content, am enjoying myself, you jump to conclusions. I have had another vacation, that's all. And maybe nourished a dream that things could be different.

We've had so many unsatisfactory talks about our problem that I give up urging you to do things which evidently are impossible for you to do. And you, in defense, talk to me about my irresponsibility. Time is going on. And we're being cheated of a lot of things—we have only a partial existence together. Why blame one another? If you really can't do otherwise I have to accept. But any time you are ready to make a break, I am. Is that clear? I won't push you into doing something which will make you miserable. If we are ever to have a real life together it will probably be much more difficult than what we've known. But that's as it should be. We're paying dearly for our protection—*you* most of all. I see it all clearly and I tell you again that it's up to you. I have no problems any more—I'm free. The only bugaboo I see is poverty and that is no longer a bugaboo to me. That's easier than the deceit and lying and illusory freedom.

Well, I'm expecting about $80.00 this week from [my agent, Henry] V[olkening]—for the Greek book. Roth sent him the money yesterday. So you won't need to send anything. They say now they hope to have the book out by August 20th. And if I succeed in getting a price for the car I will have another round sum—I hope for a hundred at least.

I must tell you that the other night I was at the home of a Hazel McKinley (formerly Jean Farlow), who knows Hugo very well, from London or Paris—London, I think. Said she gave you a dinner once at her home. She's one of the Guggenheims. Seemed charmed with

Hugo—thought him a most interesting person. Wanted to know where to reach him—I said the bank, probably. Said very little to her because she seemed like a gossip. So Hugo may find out that I'm out here, if he doesn't know it already. It's impossible now to conceal my whereabouts. I find more and more that I'm talked about everywhere—and so are you. We're almost legendary.

Incidentally, in a footnote to his letter, Roth said he hoped later to do something of yours. I feel pretty confident I can persuade him. He is celebrated for his fine workmanship—all his books are collector's items, they tell me. The Greek book will probably be handsome. (Ben Abramson* did a good job too of *The World of Sex.*)

I was going to send you a telegram but because of the general delivery I thought it might be bad for you—delivered at the wrong time. Have been all at sea—that's why I didn't write sooner. So I'll stay here tranquilly for the time being. You tell me what you think. Don't rub it into me about America—I'm not defending it. And I don't have to live in Hollywood. The world is shrinking but if one feels free inside everything is fine. You made me free, liberated—now free yourself. I have no attachments. And no concubines either. Please believe in yourself, in your own powers. There is no need to be uneasy or depressed. Doubts and misgivings are destructive—and self-generated. It isn't Europe or America or the war or Hugo that causes your unhappiness—it's something in yourself. Nobody can cure that but yourself. I'll write soon again.

H.

[Provincetown]
[July 12, 1941]

[Henry:]

This is not *doubts*—it is an intuition. I believe that you only spoke of being free from Hugo because you misunderstood the cause of my sadness. I believe that you are beyond all need of me in any sense—that you can live alone—I believe this happened when you left for Greece. You were contented and complete alone. That is your new cycle. This is no reason for reproaching each other, I believe. I do not doubt that

---

*Chicago book dealer, owner of the Argus Book Shop, who issued limited editions of some of H. M.'s work and sold some of his manuscripts.

you wanted me to join you—no. But neither do I doubt that your reluctance to return to New York will still be there when I leave Provincetown. I only came here because of your obvious reluctance—to give you time. Your return to N.Y. after your resistance can never have any meaning for me. You allow two minor things—the book, your mother—to stand in the way of returning to me.

If I had given such minor excuses for not joining you, you would also have felt quietly that the time has come to separate.

Wouldn't it be better to be aware of this and not put it all down to moonstorms!

We understand each other perfectly.
[Letter incomplete]

[Anaïs]

1835 Camino Palmero, Hollywood
c/o David Commons
July 15th [1941]

Anaïs—

Just moved to the new address above—a private place, two rooms and bath, over a garage—seven dollars a week. Wonderful place to work in and a beautiful part of Hollywood, on a street lined with fat, gigantic palms.

I feel a lot better in this joint. Have to walk a mile or so to the restaurant three times a day—just what I want. I also have an invitation to use a fellow's bungalow at the beach—Santa Monica—about 15 miles away.

Well, I'm waiting to get a letter from you. Tell me more about Provincetown. Must be somewhat like Marin's watercolors, no? A bare rocky coast? And how is the town itself—isn't it full of Portuguese fishermen?

Yesterday was exactly two years ago that I left France—at Marseilles, you remember? [. . .]

HVM

P.S. Gilbert Neiman said you must be the most "aware" person imaginable—got it all from *The House of Incest.* Said amazing things about it. Spoke of your "mask"—your "dualities," etc.

[Provincetown]
[July 1941]

Henry:

Got your cheerful and serene letter from Camino Palmero so I see that my "suggestion" was the right one and that was what you most wanted to do.

Yes, this is like a Marin, but it is also a Frigidaire. I had to send for my winter coat and woolen dresses. I came dressed for Cuba and the tropical dream which haunts me and which I can never fulfill, came to a country of tight-lipped New Englanders who denounced me to the police because I took off my brassiere on the beach about five miles from human eyes!

Robert [Duncan] came but he could not stay. Virginia [Admiral] threw him out, and as he had nowhere to sleep but a parked car and I could not take him in, he has returned to New York. He is now a perfect young Moricand, non-human, removed and impersonal. Any human emotion unknown to him. He is somnambulistic, talks incoherently and beautifully and poetically, and rootlessly.

I am reading *Count Bruga* [by Ben Hecht]. I like it. It is imaginative and artificial.

After a bit of nausea, and resistance, I am starting to write for [the Collector] again slowly, so as to be ready for the time when you need something again. I am quite sure you are not going to put to a test your statement that I invent your needs and that you can do without all this . . . quite sure.

Anaïs

Luise [Rainer] and I slipped out one evening—she took me in her car to see the ocean which would take us to Europe. We stood on the shore and all we said was: Europe. And then: if we could we would return immediately.

[Hollywood]
Wednesday [July 23, 1941]

Anaïs—

Your letter must have crossed my last one. You're wrong—I *am* coming back, whenever you're ready. You said I couldn't stay in Provincetown—to stay here till the end of August. If I can't sell the car at a decent figure I'll return with it. I'm not afraid of the transcontinental journey—only of city traffic here. They're madmen. It's worse than Paris by far.

I wish there were some place outside of N.Y. City (not too far away) to live. I do hate the thought of N.Y. City. And it's expensive there. Do you have any ideas—not Woodstock! That's what lets me down—the dreary, empty life back there with the phoney artists or the sad-looking countryside, or the Jewish streets. That's all. It's the trap—to me. And you take it personally. But I'm coming back—and I may leave before the end of August, if I have to come by car. It's a good two to three week trip that way.

[The Collector] again. That gripes me. No, I'd rather live in a hut, cook, wash, launder, etc. than have you do that.

Had a warm, cordial letter from Frieda Lawrence (whom the Neimans know well) writing me to stay at a little house which I could have to myself near her place in New Mexico. I get a fine picture of her from everyone who knows her—different from the Lawrence portrait. Very simple peasant type—almost illiterate, it strikes me. But a "natural." I've had invitations from people (including critics and professors) from all over the country. I could just mosey along from place to place. But I don't really want to. It's all sterile—or I'm getting sterile. Nothing deeply excites me. And I repeat, I always did hope and believe you would join me somewhere. The trip is a grand abortion. Half the time I'm writing of recollections of Europe. I had to destroy a big batch of work—no good. I don't give a damn about the book—it's just a job—and it will probably be bad. Though I'm doing my best with it.

Count Bruga! What a strange book for you to read. Jean Kronski used to rave about it. You remember the puppet June carried around? I don't remember a damned thing about the book any more—complete blank.

You know, when you talk about Symmes [Robert Duncan] you fail to recognize that it's all for his good, this experience. It's marvellous—he needs it. It won't kill him. And I don't think it will dehumanize him either. He's just shell-shocked for the moment.

I'm now taking Spanish lessons—exchanging—with a Spanish poet from Madrid, a communist and playwright—Humberto Rivas. A man about 45—very gentle, cultured, idealistic etc. Typical Spaniard, I think. (He lived in Paris at time of Picasso, Jacob, Apollinaire etc.—knew them all intimately.) Has lived in Mexico ten years—likes the country but not the people. When I come back you'll have to help me on with the Spanish—I've got to learn it. The first word that sinks into my head—from constant repetition—is *"momismo."* I understand quite a little of what he says when he's talking to Gilbert Neiman. So many words are like French.

Glad again to hear about Luise Rainer. She ought to be a wonderful friend for you. A worthy one, at last. My friends are never any good. It must be *me.* If you want to see a good *bad* picture—a tear jerker in the Grade B. human vein—see *Penny Serenade,* with Irene Dunne & Cary Grant. You won't like it—but see it anyway.

HVM

Hollywood
Wednesday, PM [July 30, 1941]

Anaïs—

By August 6th, according to the astrological chart for the year which I was glancing at the other night, all our disputations will be over. Amazing how accurate the Capricorn diagnosis has been—along broad lines. I always consult it after my inner resolutions are made—and always find corroborations. Went to a fake astrologer—25 cents a reading—here one day and after the first few remarks I opened my mouth and had him tongue-tied. He said he never met a Capricorn of my type. Naturally.

But this is what I was thinking of after getting your letter today—about America and your literary problems. You make a mistake to have any illusions about the American attitude. You will be accepted all right, and royally, when your magnum opus appears. That is the Diary. All your other writings throw people off the track. Don't put up a fight for your minor efforts. Concentrate all your efforts on the big thing. I have been saying this over and over. I know I am right.

I repeat, if you were giving all your energy to the sole task of having the Diary published, even if it comes out piecemeal, fragment after fragment, you would feel better—and you would see a real response. Up till now you have had the excuse of not having the money for printing. But that hardly holds any more. I am your only burden—at least, I suppose that to be so. What you used to reserve for me, couldn't you put into the publication of the Diary? What's to hinder you? I am all for doing it thoroughly from the beginning, a few volumes at a time, and in the original language—no changes or cuts whatever. You've got to believe in the work—in the value of the whole. And if you don't, who will?

Again you speak of [the Collector]—and of my coming needs. Listen, please stop thinking that way. I am doing everything to avoid that—why not encourage me? I am quite sure that when the time comes I will find the means to return without calling on you for aid. Try to give yourself a break.

What you need now is the opportunity which you so magnanimously gave me. I want to help you. I believe that your Diary is really more important than all my work put together. And if not, certainly *as* important.

If [Kenneth] Patchen could sell his book [*The Journal of Albion Moonlight*] on subscription you certainly can. We could have the essay ["Une Etre Etoilique"] reprinted with a subscription blank and a few additional words of explanation. It could be done in Mexico—paper covered, if you wish. It is not utopian. By the time we reach the volumes which may be embarrassing for you to print, lots of things can happen. But it is futile and devastating to keep putting it off. It will eat into you more and more. You've made the most difficult sacrifice one can make—to squelch your own work. It's like trying to hide a natural child.

I would stop thinking of editors and publishers. We must do it ourselves. They will come to you later, you'll see. But they are so damned insignificant it's really foolish to care whether they like your work or not. I get no kick whatever from their praise. And the reviews mean nothing either. Only one thing counts, I find, and that is the esteem of one's equals. [. . .]

If we have the faith and the will the others will too eventually. You must admit there have been other reasons besides the financial one for your hesitancy. But your whole life has gone into the making of this—and whether you agree or don't you can't evade bringing it out indefinitely.

And as for America—this hypersensitivity, etc., well I have it too, but conquer it more and more. We are right to evaluate, but wrong—or unwise—to let it affect us deeply. If people like us can't hold our heads above water, then who is to? I can't say I am disillusioned—I'm merely disgusted.

By the way, there's a moon flower out here which is marvellous, opens up towards dark—like a sexual plant. Is pure white and seems made of satin rather than flower-like. Dies shortly after it opens. Has a five-pointed star in the petal. And outside my door is honeysuckle and jasmine—as in Louveciennes.

[Henry]

Should I address letter to General Delivery—or to the street address?

Hollywood
Tuesday [August 19, 1941]

Anaïs—

I'm hoping to get away the end of this week. May telegraph you for a small sum if I don't raise quite enough to get to Chicago. Don't know yet whether I will have to stop off at San Frisco to sign the pages [of *Colossus of Maroussi*]—but if I do, it won't hold me long. I'm pretty short now but expecting to sell my notebook on America, a script I'm not using and perhaps a few copies of *The World of Sex* which I have on hand.

The proofs of the new book [*The Wisdom of the Heart*] I expect today—they are at the American Express—I was out when they called on Saturday. I can leave here without difficulty now as the fellow & his wife went to N.Y. for a couple of weeks—by train. If they had gone by car I would have gone along. In fact, I may still hear of someone leaving by car and join up.

So it won't be long now. Whither then—after N.Y.? By the way, Fraenkel is apt to go to N.Y. soon—I just want to warn you. You must be looking marvellous. I'm in good shape too. We both found wonderful places. Next time let's find one together—yes? I'll write again before leaving.

HVM

Hollywood
Wednesday the 9th [September 1942]

Anaïs,

I just finished the Kerkhoven book a night or two ago. Effect tremendous, perhaps even more than the other book, because more intimately related to our problems, yours, mine, mother's analyst's, etc. I was amazed and happy that he should have ended it on the Mother's note. I saw some correlation here with my own psychology. The innate fanaticism born out of lack of parental affection. When I gave myself to my father that helped me greatly.*

I want to cite just a passage or two, to refresh your memory. Speaking of Marie's affection for Etzel, when at last they become involved as lovers, he says:

"As though in secret compensation, in inward justification, for having fettered all his youth to herself, she assumed, deliberately, and in response to some mystic impulse, the role of mother with that of lover and thus entered into *telepathic* relationship with that distant, unknown woman who was his real mother and who, as such, was remote and strange to him also. She could not speak to him of this except with the utmost caution, for the slightest hint of the maternal element in her love filled him with nothing short of horror."

And Etzel's response to this? Here it is, next page:

"All that Marie gave him, all that she was to him, was too little. The dream he lived, boundless as it was in its fulfillment, was a mere nothing to the dream whose fulfillment he desired. With unyielding demands he stood before her, before his fate, before his life, and stretched out open hands for more, for the immense, the impossible." [. . .]

And now, on this same page, comes an appraisal of Marie's attitude, which embraces her duality and duplicity, that made me open my eyes wide—because it is precisely your own attitude and the one thing in you I have never been utterly convinced about. I wonder if you observed it?

*Jacob Wassermann (1873–1934), German writer who achieved international recognition with his novels *Caspar Hauser* (1908) and *Christian Wahnschaffe (The World of Illusion)*, created a series of interconnected novels based on a famous criminal trial, *The Maurizius Case*. It included *Dr. Kerkhoven* (*Etzel Andergast* in the German original) and *Kerkhoven's Third Existence*. Miller apparently was deeply affected by them. He tried to write a screenplay and subsequently dealt with the subject in *Maurizius Forever* (San Francisco: The Colt Press, 1946) and in *Reflections on the Maurizius Case* (Santa Barbara: Capra Press, 1974). "It is one of those books," he wrote on October 31, 1959, to Lawrence Durrell, "which seem to have been written just for you. Every page has been annotated and underlined. Kerkhoven is as close to me as my skin." (*A Private Correspondence*, George Wickes, editor. New York: E. P. Dutton, 1963.) Miller reported that he was rereading the book for the third or fourth time, and that the character of Dr. Kerkhoven was supposedly based in part on C. G. Jung.

"It had been tacitly agreed between them from the beginning that Marie should not deny herself to her husband. Why should she? What had that to do with love? [. . .] If you free yourself from the chains of tradition, you fall into the morass of selfrighteousness. Yet it was not her nature brutally to burst the sacred ties that bound her, on the pretext of courageous truthfulness. She believed that hers was the higher courage, that it demanded of her more tact, more discretion, more consideration, more presence of mind and more self-sacrifice than were called for by instinctive frankness, *which is the courage of the weak.* . . ."

Could anyone have put it more completely and succinctly? I sat bolt upright. I had to admit that it was unanswerable.

And if I am still not altogether convinced, it is only—now I see it clearly—because something is lacking in me, something which complicates still further the original complication. Instinctively I have been trying to wean myself of irresponsibility, for one thing. It was a sort of last desperate effort, coming out here and searching for work in the movies.* I could no longer stand and watch you make all those sacrifices. (You are still worrying about me, I notice from the last letter.) That is where *you* are wrong, if I may say so. You must help me not to let you worry, don't you see? I get along all right. I always have a roof over my head, cigarettes, and food. With those fundamentals secured, there is not much to worry about. I don't like what I am doing—sponging on these poor people, but I repay in my own coin, and I know they do not suffer because of me. I eat out often, with other friends, clean up my own mess, and in general make myself inconspicuous as possible. If I only made twenty or twenty-five dollars a week everything would be O.K.—*here.* It's true I seldom have any money in my pocket, but then I don't need money, really. I have nothing to complain about. Only a slight feeling of guilt that in reality I have not solved the problem, only transferred my own problems to other hands. That can't go on indefinitely, I know. Now you wonder whether to send the usual sum or a bigger one. Please, please, don't let it disturb you.

---

*H. M. had returned to New York in October 1941, after a trip of some 25,000 miles, and by December he had written some 500 pages of *The Air-Conditioned Nightmare.* But he felt that after the Japanese attack on Pearl Harbor nobody would want a book critical of the United States. In 1941, he had earned about $450.00 from all his writing. For the first six months of 1942, he returned to work once more on the story of June (*The Rosy Crucifixion*), but when the Neimans offered him a room, he went back to the West Coast in the hope of finding employment as a scriptwriter.

Send me only what you can spare. I feel terrible every time I get it. And that you worry about it between times makes it worse. Let's stop worrying about whether the other is worrying too much. (It begins to sound like the Nijinsky dance!)

Anyway, nothing much has been accomplished so far. If I have to return to N.Y. (because I may be a failure here) what then? Will I find something to do in N.Y.? Or will I sink back into irresponsibility?

And underneath it all lies the fact that we are only living out a partial life together. We were meeting like railroad trains. That's no good, Anaïs. I know it, and you know it. Something is being destroyed. I don't accuse you. Far from it. I blame myself. But, in saying this, I'm no nearer a solution. I only feel we are making a mistake by living this way. [. . .]

Last night I was to see [Lion] Feuchtwanger, but went to the movies instead. So it goes. . . .

H.

Hollywood
Saturday [September 19, 1942]

Anaïs,

Just got your long letter. It's unanswerable. You're absolutely right. That's why I sent you the Wassermann excerpt—to show you that I realized, through Marie's reactions, how just was your attitude. The reference to Etzel's attitude (which I included) is not *my* attitude—it was once, when I was much younger. I could see when I read it how horrible it was. No, as for all this, the interesting thing is Kerkhoven's awakening. Apparently it did not end tragically; one knows that he and Marie resumed life together, that perhaps he gave up his larger role as healer and decided to live a simpler, more human life—with her.

There probably is very little correspondence between myself and Kerkhoven. I was much more interested in Marie than him or Etzel. There is only this superficial resemblance—that I am at the point where I am questioning my role, of writer. I have doubts about its importance. It begins to look more and more like a luxury. The only justification for continuing would be that I earn a living by some other work. As for the movies—you're wrong when you think I didn't want to do it. I really did. But I'm congenitally incapable of writing anything

I don't believe in. This may be an excuse, but I don't honestly think so. I have tried. It never works.

Then a worse thing happens. When I do nothing I find I like it immensely. One can do nothing here because the surroundings are in themselves sufficient. That was what I discovered in Greece. So now, instead of thinking how to make the most money in the shortest time, I get to thinking just the contrary—how to do the least without being too uncomfortable. This means either of two things, I suppose—one, that I am living in a dream world, completely cut off from life, or, that I have discovered real wisdom. It almost sounds mad to be engaging in such thoughts when the rest of the world is agonizing over the mere question of existence. But what they are fighting about doesn't interest me in the least.

You say that you doubt if I know what I want. That is understandable. Maybe I don't know—but I do know more clearly each day what I do not want. And perhaps that is the first step towards knowing what you do want. I know it sounds terribly negative. But what am I to do—invent a decision? Lately I have realized what I spoke to you of even in Paris—that I am coming back more and more to the position I found myself in as a young man, when I first had to go out into the world and earn a living. I don't see anything that I really care to engage in. I haven't any ambition. I see nothing but futility in struggle. I don't think I have accomplished anything thus far. I don't know that I want to accomplish anything.

This sounds like a plea for a vegetative existence. And I don't mean that either. I may be deceiving myself, of course, but the best way I can put it to you is like this—all these things that people are fighting for, hoping for, praying for, I have already realized in myself. I am ripe to lead the life which men will only begin to lead thousands of years hence. I am out of place, out of time. That might sound a bit mad—or terribly pretentious—but I am sincere in saying it. I am not competitive or warlike or envious or greedy or ambitious—I was going to add "nor selfish." But then I ask myself—maybe this is the highest form of selfishness? Do you see what a quandary I am in? Naturally, if I were not in the luxurious position of being free from the ordinary problems of life, I could not indulge in such speculations. But to put myself in that position—which I look upon as regressive—is no way of answering these questions. That's why I think of doing anything to earn a bare subsistence—it doesn't matter what I do to earn a living. Earning a living is not *living*. I have had more life when I didn't do a thing. I am ripe to do nothing—that's what it comes to, absurdly.

And of course, as life goes, that's impossible. I suppose I won't do anything until I am pushed to it. And that's defeatism. And there I am. . . . It's the height of contradictoriness. It may all be due to the fact that what it pleases me to do is of no interest to the world. Wisdom would dictate some kind of adaptation, no doubt—finding a way to do what you like and make the world like it. But I seem to have lost even the desire to make the world like what I want to do. What does it matter, I say to myself, whether they like or don't like? What difference does it make, in the ultimate, whether I put it down on paper and force them to read it, or keep it to myself and live with it, enjoy it for myself alone? There is so little real communication. Maybe a half dozen people in the world really appreciate what you think and do. What then does it matter about the rest? And as for that half dozen—is there any need to convince them? If they are your sort they accept you without the proofs.

This problem resembles that of the teacher's and healer's. In the midst of one's work, in the midst of the best intentions, in the midst of doing good for the world, or making the world happy, etc., one begins to have the gravest doubts. One has to find out whether one is acting because he wishes to do good or bring happiness or spread truth, etc., or whether it is out of egotism or compulsion or auto-therapy that one is acting. In other words, the ground gives way under your feet. That is where I am. That is why I give way to inertia. I'd rather not act than act for false reasons.

If this is being neurotic, then I am the worst kind of neurotic. What puzzles me is that I don't feel unsocial or inhibited or depressed. Nor would I fall into a panic if I were forced to do something I disliked. I can meet any outer persuasion or coercion. I mean by that I can understand and forgive others—I know what makes them interfere, invade your peace and privacy. I understand so damn much that without wanting it to be so I have become a spectator instead of a participator. The ideal thing would be to inspire others—but that again seems like an intrusive thing—an interference. Inspire them how? To see the world as I see it? So that everything will go smoothly? For me—or for them? Even the most rudimentary problems remain unsolved.

Another letter has just come. . . . It's marvellous to see how free you are of all this. You sound like the personification of action. You've cleared the ground. You're a worker.

If only I could believe in work. I hate work. Creation is not work—it's play. But who believes in that? I know it's true, but now it's one of those distant truths—as remote as the stars. It's treasonable even to think this way.

You speak of the "outer destruction." Perhaps that is the cause of the inner corrosion. And yet I am unconcerned about the war—totally indifferent to it. As far as my desires go, and I mean by this the real desire to create, the declaration of peace will not alter things much. There will be more work to do—when the war is over. People will have to rebuild what has been destroyed. That doesn't interest me either—this work of reconstruction. For twenty or fifty years, maybe, the only important work to occupy people's minds will be rehabilitation. We will have to deal with sick and damaged souls. Is that to be our audience? What a poverty-stricken world! When they are not killing one another they are licking their wounds. When they are not destroying they are repairing the ravages they have made. And this is almost the whole of life. On the fringe is the realm of art. A luxury which almost no one takes seriously. If one believes in the joy of creation one must then be willing to live like a dog. Or, if you are lucky, just about the time you are ready to kick off, you are accepted and rewarded.

I know as well as anyone that in spite of the cold truths which I have just expressed one has to go on acting—or rot. The flaw is not in the reasoning perhaps, but in the questioning. Something's happened to the mainspring. The impulses are broken. I've got to find new ground to stand on. The war isn't the worst thing. All around me people are doing meaningless things. When I am offered the chance to do something it is something repugnant, something false, something merely to make money. I had an offer to do ghost writing for an old actor the other day. Write his "biography." A beautiful home, good food, etc. But what an idiot! Why should I write *his* biography? If I collaborate with [Marcel] Friedman what happens to the script [of *The Maurizius Case*] is unthinkable. I have met the agents and producers and directors. Nobody gives a damn what he does—if only he be permitted to go on living. To me it's insanity. I loathe it. [. . .]

Always I have the forlorn wish that there might be a way of living here with you. It's terrible to think that you have the right place and the right person, but can never bring them together. And underneath it all is the question of the right life. I suppose it is utterly childish. But children often have good ideas. We needn't always be so proud of our ability to make adjustments. I'll write again soon. I'm sending this to you care of the Browns, as I am not sure if you want me to send the letters direct to the house. Maybe I'll think something through now. Anyway, don't you become discouraged or pessimistic because of me. I'm glad you are in such good humor. Someone has to keep hold of the helm.

H.

Beverly Glen
Tuesday [September 1942]

[Anaïs:]

[. . .] [Dr.] Friedman is still looking around for someone to collaborate on *The Maurizius Case*—the perfect screen writer. This can go on for months. There's an awful lot of vagueness, dubiety and procrastination here.* I suppose nobody knows what will happen tomorrow. Anyway, I think it's useless to stick around. [. . .]

Believe me, I am surrounded by well-wishing friends. Nobody wants to see me go under. I am ready for anything. I'll have more concrete news for you in a day or so. But things are going well. So please, please, relieve yourself of all concern about me. It sounds horrible when you say—"what good would my death do you?" As though that were what I wanted, what I hoped to accomplish. You don't realize it, perhaps, but you are turning these delusions and illusions of the past into criminal things. I am not a sufferer, Anaïs. Whatever I am guilty of was due to ignorance, blindness. Relinquish everything. Stay in bed, as Goethe did, until you feel so shock full of energy, hope, courage, that you bounce out of bed. You can only aid the world—if you still believe the world needs our individual aid—by retaining your faith in life. Your body may be weak, but I know you still have wings. You will fly again, once you believe there is a goal to fly towards.

I'm glad you are sending the [Isak] Dinesen book [*Seven Gothic Tales*]—I tried several places, but it's in great demand. I am very, very curious to read about "The Dreamers." [. . .]

Listen, please have a little more faith, won't you? I know that only deeds will prove my words true. It's not for my sake I ask it, but for yours. All you dreamed has come true. Dreams are never untrue. The poets are still the uncrowned legislators of the world, whether it looks

---

*Apparently, Marcel Friedman was unable to interest anybody in the project, and H. M. eventually received $100 as a fee for the work he had done for him.

that way or not. The Soviets are doing fine—in the trenches. But we belong on the heights. I don't want to usher in the New World with fixed bayonets. Bayonets get rusty. The spirit never does. More soon. Remember, Saturn is passing over Neptune. But you were a mighty bridge-builder—O Neptune! You are not going to cave in. More light, more light! Don't turn your face to the wall now. Stop the presses. Let God take them over for a while. Do you hear me?

HVM

[Beverly Glen]
Thursday [October 1942]

Anaïs,

You're writing me just as if I didn't answer your letters. You're punishing me cruelly too, by telling me all these terrible things I've done to you, though I know you don't mean to. You talk entirely from the standpoint of the past. You still don't realize that I've changed my attitude about work and many things. Why do you constantly bring up the question of "failing me," of not doing anything to hurt me. Haven't I told you over and over that all this is out of the question. Have I ever reproached you? You seem to *want* me to be insensitive and inhuman. Do you think I am not moved, profoundly moved, by all you write? You beg me again to help remove the strain. I thought this was all understood, agreed upon.

You tell me how you are killing yourself at the press.* My God, why do you continue? *Who* is pushing you to it? Why can't you give it all up, lie back, rest until you are well again? I am making no demands on you now. No matter what happens, I will never, never ask you to do another thing for me. Won't you please believe me—just for once? Why must you take it upon yourself to see me through? It is not *your* responsibility. You are not failing me. One only fails oneself. If you don't immediately declare yourself free of all responsibility you will never conquer this weakness.

I repeat what I said in another letter. Your efforts were not

---

*In late 1941, A. N. had established the Gemor Press, at 144 MacDougal Street in New York's Greenwich Village, where she began to handset and print, in small editions, some of her own work and books of her friends. Her *Winter of Artifice* appeared in May 1942 in an edition of 500 copies. During the winter of 1942, she was working on two books for Caresse Crosby.

without fruit. If they were, I would not be writing you as I am. It is only because you are in such a weak condition, physically, that you see things so darkly. You've lost faith—above all, in yourself. But I haven't lost faith in you. Nor in myself. Even if everything you say is true, even if one's whole life were a mistake, there is always time to change. Do you know what repentance really means—it is one of those mistranslated words: it means "changing one's thoughts." We are both doing that. You look upon it ruefully. I do not. I am happy that you are going to live for yourself. You have gone to the limits of self-sacrifice. Yes, it is a death, in a way. But after each death follows a re-birth. And even when those who commit the greatest sacrifices themselves begin to doubt, those who were saved know that it was not in vain. And I am one who was saved. I believe in you more than ever. There will be a great change, and you will reap all the rewards which you have sown. You are not casting an infant adrift and leaving him to the tender mercies of the world. You gave me the blood transfusion—it worked. You will recover, you'll see.

Just after I wrote you that I expected a miracle, that a man would come along, the right one, etc., I found a telegram at my door from a friend of Cairns. [. . .] He is helping me now, with introductions to his friends out here. I think something good will come of it. I am also promised part-time work in a library, if I want it. And—that publisher to whom I gave the Emil [Schnellock] letters is deeply interested. It looks quite certain that he will accept them.*

Just received a book by Alfred Kazin, called *On Native Grounds*, a critical work, in which I find myself sandwiched in between Faulkner and Wolfe.

Henceforth I am sticking to the major opus. It's foolish to do other things in the hope of this and that. I've got to get reconciled to poverty, grin and bear it. By the way, I think there's a possibility of my having the use of a little cottage on Long Island, which belongs to the Greek woman [Melpomene Niarchos] I spoke of. I don't remember exactly where it was—about 30 miles out, I believe. I wonder if that would be any solution to the rent problem. When I think of those N.Y. rents I freeze up. Here any comfortable place is from 20 to 35 a month, furnished, with garden, garage, dishes etc. What a difference!

[. . .] Well, I must buy myself a chop now. A long walk to the

---

*A selection of the letters, *Semblance of a Devoted Past*, was published by Bern Porter in 1944.

grocer up the canyon. Have stopped using the car, as I have no license—and that would mean a heavy fine, if I were caught. I think, when I leave, I might borrow an overcoat from Gilbert's wardrobe, and ship it back to him when I get to N.Y. He didn't take any to go to Sacramento. I'm still wearing summer clothes, with a sweater at night. I have my winter suit now.

Am waiting for a letter. Hope you didn't have a relapse.

HVM

The stars now are more brilliant than ever. Like Greece. Just unbelievably bright. Almost frightening. I stand out in the yard and look & look. A feast for the eyes.

[Beverly Glen]
Later, *Monday*
Nov. 9, 1942*

[Anaïs:]

Just received your letter about taking a job, on returning from Satyr [Book] Shop. This sounds fantastic. You mean that you're doing this because of me? I beg you not to. If anybody is to take a job it's *me*, not you. I intimated in a previous letter that when I get back I would do that. If it's only on my account you want to do this, then don't. That would take the ground from under me. I understand how you feel—about the humiliation, etc. But you have a husband to look after you. You don't need a job. If you do this I'll feel terrible. It's the last straw.

If [Samuel] Goldberg [of the Gotham Book Mart] will act promptly on receipt of the MSS I'll be able to get back to N.Y. with what he sends me. (There's a chance that [Glen] Jocelyn† will come across too.)

Let's say I'm on my own now, from this moment on. I don't give a damn either, what I do, if work it's got to be. I'll come back to N.Y. like an immigrant from abroad. There never was a better time to get work. I'm sure I'll find a place rent free too.

---

*Dated subsequently, apparently, in A. N.'s handwriting.
†New York editor who had expressed an interest in H. M.'s work and to whom H. M. had sent a number of manuscripts.

I'm absolutely serious about this. You give me a shock. It's as though you wrote and said that you could get along without arms or legs.

I don't agree with you about the "irresponsibility and Bohemianism." (Anyway, that only applies to me, not to you! You've been more than responsible, always.) But I won't quarrel with you about that.

Perhaps if I take a job I can help you to do with that press what you really wanted to do—*print your own work!*

Listen, for me it's settled. Don't write me tomorrow that you see a way out, or that you were just depressed. Things must be very bad with you to force you to such a conclusion.

And remember this—I have had one long vacation—since the year 1924, when I quit the Western Union. It will be a pleasure to "rejoin the herd," doing the fatuous work of the world. It's so simple. You only need half a brain, one leg, and a few muscles. I really feel gay about it, now that I'm face to face with it. To do only as you please—that's really the hard thing. This other any imbecile can qualify for.

I don't direct this irony against *you.* I'm just telling you how easy it seems. But it's definite—*you're not going to look for a job!* If you are, you'll have to find a better excuse—*entendu?* Goldberg just wrote me a nice letter. He's waiting for the MSS. I'll write him again seductively.

> *HVM*

P.S. I'm really very happy it's come to this. I'm sure all your illnesses are due to mental anguish—too much sense of responsibility. You've got to take it easy again, dress up, loaf, do the things you like. I'm afraid I was driving you to an early grave.

> [Beverly Glen]
> New Year's Day [1943]

Anaïs—

I read [William Carlos] Williams' review of *Winter of Artifice* the other day at the Satyr Shop.* I thought on the whole it was good. I

---

*"Men . . . Have No Tenderness," in *New Directions No. 7*, edited by James Laughlin (Norfolk, CT: New Directions, 1942).

like his *dubiety*—it's honest. Apparently he seems to forget you wrote a diary—says you have only written a little. Without that at his elbow he must be a little nonplussed. But he pays you a high compliment as a woman—and says almost what you yourself say—what you told Rank—about woman as creator.

The Rudhyar book [*The Pulse of Life: New Dynamics in Astrology*] I haven't seen. Miss Steloff sent me an interesting little book which I'm sending you. There are things in it which you may appreciate. The biggest things you've said yourself. You'll see. It's by Mabel Collins—a quite famous person, incidentally.*

I'll write Eduardo, and if I can, send him a box of fruits and candies, such as they make up out here very well. I don't believe they'll retain him long.† See if I'm not right!

Yes, I received everything—and very grateful. No need to continue now—I'm sure of something these next few days.

About the "crucifixion" theme. Yes, I do understand what happened. (Curiously enough, the book I am sending you may throw a different light on it for you.) Why you persist in thinking I am blind or indifferent to your suffering I don't understand, nor am I going to argue with you about the relative merits of Stalin & Ramakrishna. They operate on different levels. Time will prove whose efforts were the most effective, the most lasting.

When you mention Christ being satisfied with a "symbolical" meal, I must say you don't read deeply enough. To give the wine of eternal life instead of real wine is not just a symbolical act. Though you are now accusing me of having sucked your very blood, you are mistaken if you think that is what nourished me. When you fear that harm will come to me if the material needs are denied me, isn't it proof that you yourself do not attach enough importance to the real gifts you make? The terrible urge which leads one to sacrifice "beyond one's strength" comes, I do believe, from a lack of faith in the cosmic processes. While doing one's utmost one has also to realize, it seems to me, that one is probably not altering the condition of the

---

*Under the pseudonym Mabel Collins, Mrs. Keningale Cook (born in 1851) had written a small booklet of 96 pages, *Light on the Path and Karma* (New York: Pocket Library, McKay, 1934), which became a perennial best seller for the Theosophical Society during the 1940s.

†Eduardo Sanchez was detained for a short while by U.S. military or immigration authorities, since he was still a Cuban citizen.

world a single iota. One is actually doing good for one's self—piling up credit, as it were. The only ones who can truly affect the world and the destinies of man are those who are completely dedicated to sacrifice, because they have emancipated themselves, lived out their personal problems, found true anonymity and realized that there is nothing beyond giving. They want nothing and expect nothing. For all lesser individuals sacrifice is only a lesson, an expiation, a purgation, etc. It is to their own interest not for the benefit of others. For the former it has no terrors, nor can it deplete them. They have learned, as it were, the secret of harnessing themselves to the inexhaustible power which governs the universe. They are "insolated." All others are consumed in the process—*sacrificed*, in the truest sense of the word.

There is nothing wrong with sacrifice in itself. Quite the contrary, indeed. But it is a form of action reserved only for the highest. In them, it is transmuted—the death is converted into life. (Don't argue about this—think it over. There is nothing *personal* in it; it just is a truth.) And as sure as there is truth, you will emerge from your death with increased powers and increased understanding. Your Neptunian insight, your very accurate flair for truth, needs, I think, to be more exteriorized, diffused, over the whole surface of your being. You have the tendency to use it very much as a medium uses his extraordinary gifts. You rely on the flash—but then every so often the commentator gets out of order. Don't you agree?

Believe me, I'm not trying to *criticize* you. I am trying to help you. Or do you believe I am incapable of helping you?

Later . . . Was interrupted by visitors, and now am getting a flood of letters in reply to my queries. Some book reviews already promised me—and more suggestions offered. I have gone thru a siege similar to Paris when I decided not to let the *Tropics* die out.

Today another letter from you. God, you seem to be in for it. I'll see Pierce [Harwell]* soon as possible to see what he can discover in the way of good for you. Everything seems to point to a change in life—I had that suspicion before. I remember mine, in Paris. You have to submit to it—not fight it. As in *Here Comes Mr. Jordan!*

I'm trying to get a most interesting almanac on herbs for you. Also something from the famous Dr. Chew's Chinese herboristerie here.

---

*A young astrologer who wanted an astrological chart for A. N. and visited her in New York later in 1943.

Miss Steloff sent me the ten dollars for X-mas. Said the reader has not yet called for the Diary. More soon.

HVM

By the way, when you are able, go to see Bette Davis in *Now, Voyager*—her best role. Another picture based on analysis, the ugly duckling etc. In a way better than *King's Row*. Her last line is interesting. By the way, you make a good psychological mispelling [*sic*] always when you write "comma" for "coma."

[Beverly Glen]
Sunday night—1/31 [1943]

Anaïs—

It's been a hectic ten days—more like ten weeks—and I don't think I've written you. Lots of unexpected visitors, winding up with Margaret & Gilbert's return for a few days again. Was ill for a few days but recovered quickly. And all the time more and more good news—I can't keep up with the recording of it all.

Hope you received the Blake book meanwhile.* Pierce said he got yours and wrote you a big letter. He found all sorts of marvellous things in your book, as he does in everything. Indeed, he seems to look only for the marvellous. He's a wizard in the body of an adolescent. More like Rimbaud than anyone I can think of—and with all of R's faults, too. To have him around is like having a comet in the house. But I never met anyone who can offer—and at lightning speed—more amazing interpretations. Finally, though, you have to throw him out, like a dirty sock. He knows no laws, no limits. Burns like a geyser. Knows no fatigue. Has no handovers. He's free, if ever a person was, but it's not an enviable freedom. All of which in no wise lessens the power of his words.

Your last letter ended in a riddle. For some strange reason I picked up your book [*Winter of Artifice*] this evening and was reading the last 30 or so pages. I understood more than I ever had before—but again, towards the end of the experience with the "Voice," I felt a mystifying element. This time I had the feeling that the original difficulty with the father expressed itself here too. I can see so far and then I am utterly baffled. The only clue I can give you is this, that whenever in

*William Blake's Circle of Destiny, by Milton O. Percival (New York: Columbia University Press, 1938).

speech or writing you stress the word "human," the secret becomes palpable, though never fully revealed. It's almost as though the more frank and revelatory you become the more you succeed in remaining inscrutable. Which reminds me of Moricand's definition of *"révéler"*—do you remember? One of the strangest words in the human language, I think.

Funny that you mention music. Gilbert has a wonderful library of records here. I haven't exhausted it yet. By the way, do they have in N.Y., as they do here, a rental library of records? Here they charge $4.00 for 3 months, which allows one to take out an album every day if he chooses. You might inquire—it's certainly worth it.

It's like Spring here now. We went from Fall to Spring without a Winter!

HVM

P.S. One day when alone here Angelino [Ravagli], who lives with Frieda Lawrence, called—to see Gilbert & Margaret. A fine earthy, vital Italian—just the opposite of Lawrence. And of course he asked me to come & stay a while at the ranch. I'm getting reviews now to do and *Town & Country* are taking a fragment of the burlesque on the Hollywood astrologer.*

Rudhyar is here in Hollywood & wants to send me a copy of his book. Do look up Arthur Koestler's books—*Dialogue with Death, Scum of the Earth & Darkness at Noon.*

[Beverly Glen]
2/13/43

Anaïs—

Won't send you the Kierkegaard book yet [Walter Lowrie, *A Short Life*], as I hope to be able to review it again elsewhere—at greater length. Send you copy of my first draft—of my first paid review—from *New Republic.* † I can't recommend the book too highly. There is a great and terrible father theme, a Hamlet theme, and a great "Journal"—all of which will interest you. There is also the subject of "The Sacrificed Ones"—see last pages of the book—2 marvellous "Symbols"—which cover everything.

*"Hello June 26th! Yoohoo!" published in June 1943.
†"Prince of Denmark," *The New Republic*, May 10, 1943.

Curious that you should return to music—a way of returning to the Father, I imagine. Fine! I don't doubt but that you will make a unique composer. You seem inexhaustible in your talents. Another Rudhyar come to judgment! (Or, rather, "fruition.")

I don't believe you will succumb to a murmuring heart. You will lie down and die—of your own volition—of no known malady—when you are ready to join the dead. You will enter the gates with cymbals in your hands. But do move! Anyone would get heart trouble climbing those stairs.*

Everything is rolling along superbly with me. I haven't time to do all I wish, that's all. It's tumultuously full—this period—which began just after Xmas. I wish I had an Amelia now—as at Louveciennes. Everything I send out now, every suggestion I make, seems to be accepted. I think it's because I gave in utterly. All that is happening is a response. It was I probably who created the dike. Now, good God, I need the strength and energy of ten men.

If you take up with [John] Cage, give Xenia my love. She's a bit of a phenomenon, as you will discover. I never saw anyone dance (alone) as she does, when she is in the mood. She's a virtuoso. But she needs the stimulus of alcohol. And I think you overawe her just a little. Her luminosity is somewhere in her bowels.

HVM

P.S. If you have a victrola, and can rent records, I'd like to send you the necessary for a year's subscription. Do let me know—you could accept it as a birthday gift. (*Gift* is "poison" in German!)

[215 W. 13th Street, New York]
[February 1943]

[Henry:]

Today I received your gift. I didn't want you to send so much— you may need it. I did two things with it. I took my radio out of the repair shop, and I bought paper to print my short stories on. When I finish the book for Caresse, I will print the stories.† When you wrote

---

*A. N.'s Greenwich Village studio was on the fifth floor.
†A. N.'s Gemor Press printed Paul Eluard's *Misfortunes of the Immortals*, translated by Hugh Chisholm, illustrated by Max Ernst. It was published in March 1943. The paper was used for an edition of 300 copies of *Under a Glass Bell*, which appeared

me what [John] Dudley said, I felt sad and [it seemed] ironic. Yes, I was wonderful, he said, wonderful enough to use, to take from, to feed on. His rich nature demanded freedom to be an artist, but at the cost of mine. He helped to cause the collapse.

[Anaïs]

[Beverly Glen]
Monday [February 1943]

Anaïs—

I somehow manage to keep the $200.00 loan [from the National Institute of Arts and Letters] in the bank, living off the checks that come in. When you get ready to do your book—if you need more—just let me know. It's only symbolical, this money in the bank. I know now that I don't need it. It's like the day you sent the huge quantity of food supplies to me at Villa Seurat. That cured me. And so, as regards making money—I know I don't have to worry about it, or even do it. The fact that I am willing is enough. It's only the attitude that matters. As I always say—there is no real security, certainly not in this material realm. There's only *inner* security—and that I have.

It saddens me to hear you speak of my "philosophy" having such a disastrous effect on you. Are you sure it is my philosophy—or your own doubts and fears? To me it's sad *and* ironical, because in this time between I have really made great strides—as a man, a person. I know I am not worse than before. I don't know if I should say that I'm *better*, but certainly I have made some vital conquests, always in the direction of fear and anguish. I think we must each follow our natural bent, our true instincts, our desires—and see what happens. I am not combatting phantoms, I assure you. I believe so much in liberty that I would risk all on it. Whatever you do with your whole heart and soul is right. Try to believe the same of me.

Glad to hear it was a "resurrection" party you gave. Curious to know your impressions of Carson McCullers.

You're hard on Dudley—as you always are on those whom you

in February 1944. H. M.'s gift was, apparently, a check for $100. He later stated (in "An Open Letter to All and Sundry," April 1944) that he had earned $1,400 in 1943—from his writing and the sale of his watercolors—and had given it all away. He listed his debts at the time as $24,000.

think are using you. He doesn't act that way with me, though he knows I have money—I offered it freely, all he wants. Instead, however, he takes a certain pride in keeping his end up. I think you are inclined to lose faith just two minutes too soon. Naturally you are more sorely tried than we others—but only because you have more to give. You're born with these vast obligations. It's for you to solve this problem—that's your grand life's problem. But you won't solve it, I fear, by evading it. You will have to give and give—till your dying day. I'm not sermonizing—I think about it constantly. It's one of the greatest problems a human being has to face. [Claude] Houghton has a character in *Hudson Rejoins the Herd*—a Dr. Bond—who is most interesting to study in this connection. Incidentally, Dudley Nichols, after reading *All Change, Humanity!* was most enthusiastic about Houghton. Thinks he will do something.

If you want a victrola and records get them. Just tell me in advance. I'm doing reviews—hard work—takes too much time. I read too slowly & conscientiously. But I continue to get more and more offers. Today I'm all cleaned up for a change. Could go back to my book or write a story—a breathing spell. I work like a demon.

Am reading [Jean-Marie] Carré's *Life of Rimbaud*—never knew what happened to him in Africa. I must say that he had the worst destiny of any man I ever read about. Far worse than Nietzsche, Dostoevsky or Nijinsky. To find that he was *"avare"*—that shocked me. What retribution!

HVM

Big Sur, Calif.
Sunday [April 1944]*

Dear Anaïs,

I enclose a letter from my anonymous benefactor which has a genuine ring to it. If, as he says, I hear from him in the next few days,

*After spending most of 1943 in West Los Angeles, where he shared the former Neiman cabin for a while with John Dudley, and a short stay with the painter Yanko Varda in New Monterey, H. M. was introduced, early in 1944, to Linda Sargent, who offered him a free room in her log cabin on the coast south of Carmel, since Miller's plans to live in Mexico had not materialized. For more on Varda, see Biographical Notes.

this is what I will do. I will send you each month one hundred dollars, for the printing of the first few volumes of the Diary in French—which is what I hope you wish to do too. If you don't, you may of course do as you please with the money. I hope for your sake that it comes through. I don't know how far that sum will carry you in this work, but it's the most I can do just now. There is still another chance I m:, receive an equal or bigger sum from a patron in Wash. D.C., through Cairns' overtures. That will have to be a gift, as I am signing over all returns from my writings to R[ussell] & V[olkening] to pay this first benefactor back.*

Meanwhile, I had another letter from the Pantheon Press asking me to be patient, and again I have written him [Kurt Wolff] to get in touch with you—about the Diary. I am hoping, though, that it will be my privilege to give you what is needed to get this particular work started. I am certain that once an opening wedge is made there will spring up other people to supply you with the money necessary to complete the great work. I will not rest till it is done.

Please keep this confidential, about the patron, because I shall be swamped with requests for aid. I am already, people being led to believe—why, I don't know—that I am already affluent. As it is, after splitting with you, I shall have to split again with someone [Harry Herschkovitz] who helped me greatly these few last months. And I have debts to pay off, too—but that will come out of other rewards— watercolors etc. The worse it gets the more resourceful I become. The law is that the more you give the more you receive. It works. And if it works for me, and others, it will for you. You have given to the utmost limits. You will not be overlooked or neglected, believe me.

One of the letters (to you), about one of your books, which will appear in [James] Laughlin's new book has just been printed in a small magazine in Berkeley.† I edited the one for the book (same one),

*Responding to H. M.'s various appeals for support, which had received national attention through a number of magazines, a benefactor hiding behind the name Harry Koverr offered to supply $2,500, in monthly installments of $200, to be paid back only if and when H. M. could afford to do so.
†The "Letter to Anaïs Nin (regarding one of her books)," written in Clichy in 1933 about the "Mona" pages and material later incorporated in House of Incest, appeared first in Circle (Vol. 1, No. 2, April 1944) and subsequently in the collection Sunday After the War (Norfolk, CT: New Directions, 1944). A. N. contributed two stories, later incorporated in Under a Glass Bell, to Leite's magazine, "The All-Seeing" (Vol. 1, No. 4, 1944) and "Hejda" (No. 7/8, 1946).

forgetting I had also given it to the magazine. The young man who runs it, George T. Leite, is a Portuguese and a most well-meaning and not unintelligent boy. I saw him the other day when I was up that way. He thinks he may be able to *print* the magazine next issue. He may also ask you to contribute something. He can't pay yet—he pays the entire cost of the mag. himself—works as a taxi driver, has wife and child. I think he has sent you a copy of it. You won't think much of it, but I am going now to help him get good writers and artists to make something of it. Dudley, I am told, received $5,000 to start his magazine. I doubt that he will make anything worthwhile of it. I am waiting for him to send me 500 dollars before writing him again. He owes me that and more. And I want it, not for myself, but for better purposes.

I won't go to Mexico with this money. I will stay here. I have the new place rent free—and it is just ideal. Later, when I finish the [Air-Conditioned] *Nightmare,* I may go down there.

Please return this letter, will you? I haven't any idea who he can be—but he is American, I suspect, and probably Jewish.

Henry

Big Sur, Calif.
May 3rd [1944]

Dear Anaïs:

In this same mail you will get another letter which I don't bother to open. This is the sequel to it. The patron came through. I am to get the two hundred a month for a year, unless in the meantime someone else steps in and wishes to aid me. No interest to be paid, nothing to be deducted from royalties. Pay back when and how or if I like.

So here is a hundred, and if nothing goes amiss, you'll get a hundred each month. This hundred, which was in addition to the two hundred, was to have gone for travelling expenses—to Mexico. But I am not going. I have the house (ten dollars a month, or free, if I choose), and it suits me to the ground. I am alone and I am working. So I won't budge until I finish one book at least. Then I may think of Guatemala, where, I am told, the exchange is 15 to 1, our favor. In that way I can do more for all concerned with what comes to me. I don't count on good fortune (material fortune) to last very long—it's not in my destiny, I feel.

[Bern] Porter writes me that you have abandoned all thought of bringing out the Diary here in America. Because your lawyer advises that it will get you into trouble. But—if you began at the beginning, as I always hoped you would, if you bring out the first volumes (in French), nothing could happen to you. And I am sure the next ten or fifteen will cause no trouble with the censors either. *Why don't you begin*—and trust in providence that money will be forthcoming to publish further editions? By the time you are ready to leave America you may have everything published but the difficult parts, which you can then complete in Europe. I am certain you will receive help. You must use me as a wedge. And even I may be able to do more—who knows?

I am living on the same scale as always. I have no big needs. But I am called on to help frequently now—and I do all I can. So, the more I get the more I will shell out. I am just a distributor.

If the printing is too much for you to do yourself, perhaps Bern Porter will help you solve that problem. I understand you are now writing a "Proustian novel"—so he says. Good. So don't try to do any printing now. Farm it out. Your two books from your own press are causing a stir everywhere.* You should never have to set type again. People should come to you, and they will! asking to let them do this work for you. Have faith!

May I ask how many volumes the Diary now includes?

Anyway, you are not to worry about the disposition of the enclosed check. Use it as you will. Perhaps you ought just to enjoy yourself with it. Why not? Also—I notice the check is on the National City Bank. I am tempted to inquire who my benefactor is. But perhaps it is better to remain ignorant. I know now that he is a painter and lives in California—and not French!

Henry

215 West 13, New York City
[July 1944]

Henry:

I left without speaking to Harry [Herschkovitz] about the wrongness of his taking from you because I feel how, after all, I should no

---

*A revised version of *Winter of Artifice* and the first edition of the stories collected as *Under a Glass Bell.*

longer feel about these things. I always knew that the day you obtained what you wanted (a year of peace from the money problems, time to write) you would throw it away. I am quite ready to give up my share but I know that too will go to some weak person and that the Dudleys, the Patchens etc. will always be given—not me. I was about to give 100 pages of the Diary to the linotypist and refrained, because you will need [the money].

The mail is being forwarded so don't bother, if you don't want to, about the change of address. (Until Sept. 5 I will be [at] Box 445, Amagansett, Long Island.)

It's a lovely peaceful place—real wild ocean—and the predominance of Europeans has changed its character. In the evenings there are always visitors.

Madame Chareau* is translating *Under a Glass Bell*—with the hope that [André] Schiffrin† might be interested. [Charles] Duits reads to us from *Finnegans Wake*. Matta talks more and more fantastically.

We bicycle, sleep etc.

Hugo has left the bank—a new life now, of denial and poverty— but independence. It was a big step. The name of "Guiler" is dead.‡

Will you be going to Mexico?

I talked over the radio Monday—was interviewed. Your name was mentioned by the woman who read my clipping book, and Varda's.

Have you read *Science & Sanity* [by] Korzybski—strange—half-fake—belongs to the Semantic Group.§ But it's like the [Charles Henri] Ford book—half crazy, half genius—half illuminated, half accurate.

How do you feel now?

Is your work lightened? Can you write? Tell me how you feel about Harry's manuscript.

Anaïs

*A former neighbor in Louveciennes.
†Born in Paris in 1935, Schiffrin had come to the U.S. in 1941 and become involved in publishing. He eventually headed Pantheon Books as editor.
‡This seems to have been a temporary change. According to Hugh Guiler's own recollections (see *Anaïs: An International Journal*, Vol. 4, 1986, p. 28), he finally left the bank in 1949, when he was fifty-one. As an artist (engraver and filmmaker), he used the name Ian Hugo.
§Alfred Korzybski (1879–1950) created the system of General Semantics, and his book, first published in 1933, had gone through a number of editions.

215 West 13, New York City
[August 1944]

Henry:

Your last letter sounded sad. How I wish I had followed my first impulse to keep what you sent me for the time you would need it. But actually it didn't help you very much to have it. You gave it all away. And I, pressed by debts on all sides, paid them, as, at the same time, Hugo left the bank and I knew I would never pay them later. I believe the man who sent you the money may have heard what happened to it, and everybody talked about it, about Harry being your protégé and others etc. Before you told me, I had heard that you only kept $25. He may have felt badly that he wasn't really helping you. The whole situation sounds mad to me and I wish I could help you but no one can and the realization of how little my words counted was one of the seeds of death of the relationship—your self-destruction was only disguised by my covering while we were together but it was there in all your acts, and is again clearer now that I am gone—and no one can help you.

Your gesture towards me and the diary I appreciated deeply but somehow the meaning of it became less the day I discovered you put it on a par with Harry's writing. It is a lack of differentiation (your first gesture should have been in relation to your own work) which in the end negates all values and ends in chaos. This income which should & could have meant your freedom you handled so that today you write me you are *relieved* to no longer have it.

Futile words, mine, which you never heard. Which soon will be coming to you from Europe.

We all await, this summer, our release from this American camp. It is coming soon now.

I hope before I leave I will hear that you are where you want to be.

Anaïs

[Cyril] Connolly's wife, Jean, is here with Laurence Vail. Asked to be remembered to you.

215 West 13, New York City
[September 1944]

Henry:

My intuitions were right and it is possible that within a month I may be leaving for France. I have felt it coming, and wished for it. I am sorry if some of my rebellions persisted in our correspondence. I should not have written you until they were transmuted—remember how I resisted writing at first? But now I am leaving and there are some things I want to ask you.

I shall be travelling very light and will not be able to take your watercolors, at least for the present. Shall I leave them with you or Huntington Cairns for safe keeping?

I have some books such as *Spirit of Zen, Interlinear to Cabeza de Vaca, Root and the Flower, Guide to Paris,* the Houghton—do you want them? I have some erotica of yours—shall I mail it by American Express, or to Cairns?

In Paris I have a box of your belongings. (If they exist.) I remember there were books mostly. If I can, shall I send it back to you? The bank was not occupied by the Germans, so I might find the diaries after all.*

The liberation I feel is undescribable—as if I had been living in a concentration camp. Five years of eclipse. Every year in America an eclipse. We all felt the change coming. The month at the beach was strange—a colony of "foreigners," none of them having taken root, all restless and ready to leave, regretting nothing; certainly none of them will make the renaissance. I know that. That will come from those who faced the drama, the reality, the pain.

Do you want a few *Glass Bells & Winters.*

Write me soon. Your last letter sounded sad.

Anaïs

---

*A. N. had left the originals of the diaries in the vault of the Paris branch of the First National Bank at which her husband worked when she was evacuated after the outbreak of war in 1939.

[New York]
[October 1944]

[Anaïs:]

For some strange reason I have not been able to telephone you. I seem to feel you do not want to see me. I don't understand it myself. I am at a loss to say where to meet you. I am staying with Harry as there is no other place available; it's far from ideal. Now I am leaving for Bryn Mawr College. Should be back Monday. I'll be in New York (in and out, as I have trips to make while I am here) until Thanksgiving. Then I return to the West Coast, as my mother is recovering and may live another few years.* I hope to get out of my present psychological morass about you the next few days. It may be only fear of hearing you reproach me. I wanted to see you first of all, and here I am writing you instead.

[Henry]

215 West 13, New York City
[April 1945]

Henry—

You wrote me just as I was thinking of writing you. I am completely free of all forms of torments and swimming in so large and so luminous an atmosphere that I cannot remember what separated us but only what brought us together.

In fact I am more like you in mood now than I was before.

Much has happened, thanks to you. The English publishers are going to do *Winter* and *Bell* together in one volume and I signed my contract and will receive $80 advance! They will reproduce the engravings [by Ian Hugo].†

---

*When H. M. learned that his mother was to undergo an operation for cancer, he rushed to New York, mindful that he had arrived two hours too late when his father died, on February 8, 1941. From there he visited a number of friends at various colleges—Herbert West at Dartmouth, Wallace Fowlie at Yale. He also met Janina Martha Lepska, a graduate student transferring from Bryn Mawr to Yale, who became his third wife on December 18, 1944. For more on Fowlie and Lepska, see Biographical Notes.

†Editions Poetry London published, in 1947, a volume that contained *The House of Incest, The Winter of Artifice* and collected stories, with the title *Under a Glass Bell* and without illustrations.

Also thanks to you I met [Wallace] Fowlie, whose work I like deeply—all but the Catholicism—but, better still, through him I met the nearest of all my sons, William Pinchard, a Neptunian. Another son has taken a houseboat and they are living out all my stories. (We had an evening of hypnotism in which we danced dances we didn't know awake. Sang songs in unknown languages etc.) I believe the young America has chosen you and me to follow. Yin and Yan!

Today I heard from France—*Winter of A.* has been translated and will be published.*

I liked your article in *Tricolor* on Obscenity†—full of a sort of cosmic noblesse and wisdom.

I get letters from the front from soldiers who have bought your books but you must be tired of hearing their reactions so I won't quote them.

Please send me Durrell's address.

I heard from Claude Houghton when you asked me to send him *U.A.G. Bell* but so English a letter, so inhibited in spite of his praise that I didn't answer it. Write me.

Anaïs

[215 W. 13th Street, New York]
[May 1945]

Henry:

Pierre Mabille's book [*Miroir du Merveilleux*] was loaned to me by Yves *(Qui Tangue)* Tanguy, as I call him—and I too tried to find a copy but couldn't. If I ever do I'll let you know.

David Moore came—a tall, pale, tubercular young man, interesting, difficult, and I believe on a quest of discovery of you. I was amazed that Fraenkel spent an afternoon convincing him *Tropic of Cancer* would not have been written but for Michael Fraenkel's books and influence—amazed and couldn't help laughing, knowing Fraenkel—at the falsity of this—but more, when I heard that Fraenkel wrote an essay on this to which it seems you wholly assented. I can hardly believe this when I think of Fraenkel['s] Lilliputian stature and fake value. Is

---

*A French edition, translated by Elisabeth Janvier, was published in Paris in 1976 by Editions des Femmes. Apparently there was no earlier edition.
†"Obscenity and the Law of Reflection," *Tricolor*, II, February 1945.

it so? *Incidentally he told Moore that after my book on Lawrence my talent became "perverted" and that I have done nothing good ever since! I have seen him around the Village, and once when I was at the movies watching Eisenstein's film on Mexico he put his hands on my shoulders—but I have carefully avoided him.

Moore I believe is worth your interest and I hope his work on you will satisfy you. I know you're overloaded with mail so I don't send you his 13-page letter mostly about you. He has great earnestness.

Today I received a letter from Edmund Wilson from London. You know he is very unhappy over his wife [Mary McCarthy] and they may separate. I consoled him the day before he left and helped him choose his uniform and camp mattress.

You asked about the Press. Although I share it with Gonzalo, share work and expenses, I still am always on the verge of losing it, and after I print this new book [*This Hunger*] (doing it by stages as I obtain a little loan here and there) I will then give it up—I shall be able to return to Europe after making this last effort free of indebtedness to America—as I came. Owing it nothing.

Alice Paalen came last night. She is very interesting, mature. Did you hear how I got interested in Givor's writing in *Dyn* and wanted to write him and how it was [Wolfgang] Paalen (whose ideological writing I didn't like) who was writing under this name. Because of my encouragement he continued and has now a book on secret Mexico. He often says: "Givor had an idea today!" He feels *freer* writing as Givor.

Did you like Rudhyar's article on Neptune? I read others too— apparently reducible to the word: magic. Our Neptunian month when Pinchard was here (he is now in the Army—has a horoscope like Blake's) had tragic consequences for Fowlie and probably spoiled my friendship with him. I don't know. The enraged and powerful father went to Yale and publicly accused Fowlie of corrupting his pupils with corrupt literature (Miller, Lautréamont, Nin). Fowlie was openly blamed. I don't know whether he lost his position. I don't dare write him. The father also tried to find a way to make me leave USA but couldn't. Sent detectives to my house. Meanwhile all of us, Pablo, and Duits the French poet, Alice, Luise Rainer, the Haitians, were creating

---

*First published as a pamphlet (by Bern Porter in 1946), "The Genesis of *Tropic of Cancer*" was subsequently included in the celebratory volume *The Happy Rock* (published by Bern Porter in 1947), with contributions by many of Miller's friends.

a marvellous atmosphere like that of our best days in Paris. We re-painted the windows, painted tapestries, carved birds out of copper which shine and whirl in the dark, wrote, danced, hypnotized, etc. A real real *Miroir du Merveilleux.*

While I print Volume 1, I'm writing II.*

I won't lose my friends when I leave, they will all follow me to Europe. Some are waiting there for me. They do not want to come home (some of the writers who were in the Army). Do you ever think of returning?

I didn't receive the Cuban magazine.

Saw Harry Bull at a cocktail [party] and he told me how extremely pleased he was with your war book reviews†—"very professional."

Anaïs

[215 W. 13th Street, New York]
[June 10, 1945]

[Henry:]

Here is Eduardo's address: Hotel Lucia, 82 Bank Street. I know he has Rimbaud's horoscope because he often mentions our points of similitude. I'm very interested that you're writing about him. I'm often haunted by his "break" and departure but it is not inexplicable to me or even mysterious. Nor is it, as you say, a "defection." I think some people swing violently into new dimensions and can make breaks like this when they have gone to the very *end* of an experience and perhaps he felt that writing was an unrequited love affair and turned his back and entered direct action—was not able to make the transition be-tween the death of the romantic past into maturity, died in the passage-way. Others, most of the romantics, died actually because that is the only outcome of romanticism, don't you think? Rimbaud didn't have the courage to die and be reborn. He chose the slow lingering neurotic

---

*In a preface, *This Hunger* was identified as "volume one, which deals with the aspect of destruction in woman." Portions of this volume were later incorporated in *Ladders to Fire*, the first of the five novels that made up *Cities of the Interior*, the "Proustian novel" Bern Porter had mentioned to H. M. in May 1944.

†"On Wartime Literature in English," *Town & Country*, August 1945; "On French Wartime Literature," *Town & Country*, September 1945. Harry Bull was editor of the magazine.

death. I read his letters of that second period. You notice he has no living joy in his adventure. *He is dead.* He did not live it as Cendrars did.

I understand how you feel about nursing the young! After a month or two of seeing nothing but these young people (now they come to my door directly, not even telephoning or seeking to be introduced; two rang the bell last night—hitch-hiked from the coast to see me), I spent an evening with two European men—a German painter and an Austrian musician—and felt all that I am missing each day I stay here.

Do you ever read the *Kenyon Review?* It has the best and only serious articles I've seen besides *Partisan Review.* They would like your critical studies. Fowlie has had articles in it—one beautiful one on recollections of France.

To raise money to print my new book [*This Hunger*] we're selling portfolios of the colored woodcuts done by Hugo for it. I'm sending you the announcement.

Cairns is trying to get me a loan from a friend but I have not heard from him yet.

I'm sending Leite some of the mummy photos as you asked me to.

I told you that I heard the boxes in storage in Paris are safe and one of them was filled with books etc. by you.

Since Hugo left the Bank he works at the Press all day and we will return to France as publishers, engravers etc. Queer, isn't it? I nearly married an American poet but escaped by a hair's breadth. The next one will be a European I know now. At 32 this man was actually like a boy of 17. Imagine me spending the rest of my life here.

You say you didn't know what I wanted people to feel about the Arabian woman. What did you feel? I felt her as pitiable and ridiculous too. It was my first caricature.*

Anaïs

P.S. Eduardo said he would write you about Rimbaud's horoscope. I gave him your address.

---

*The story "Hejda," obviously based on a couple A. N. knew in New York, appeared as the first section of *This Hunger,* and was later included in the collected stories of *Under a Glass Bell.* In 1946 it was reprinted in *Circle* magazine.

Big Sur, California
July 2, 1945

Anaïs—

The other day I sent you Fowlie's letter about Pinchard—without anything else—I was so busy. Now, by separate mail, I'm sending you [Albert] Cossery's book [*Men God Forgot*]. I just received the original French version—with illustrations—and also his *La Maison de la Mort Certaine*—which I find even stronger. I've written a review of the former for George [Leite], who will print the book.

You mention going to Gotham [Book Mart] to get my latest book. I'm sorry to hear that. I intend sending you one—if you mean *Semblance*. Trouble is that on the last four books Bern refuses to give me a single free copy—says he can't afford it. I have to pay $5.50 each for *Semblance* and for *Miscellanea*. Did you see the *Chronology and Bibliography?** Things are still pending in Paris—a great race going on between Gallimard, [Maurice] Girodias and Denoël over the books. I want Girodias to have it. He sounds very earnest and sincere.† In his last letter he offers to pay me *complete* royalties on reprints of English editions within two months after their publication. This would make, a/c to him, 410,000 frs. Sounds staggering. (Then there could be the French royalties too.) I told him to hold them until situation clarifies. No monies can be sent out yet. Also, the 50-to-the-dollar present arrangement of the franc is but temporary. I feel it won't be worth even a *sou* later. No European money will. There will be an almighty collapse.

However, what I wanted to say was this. If he is not "dreaming" all this, if he does get contract and does put this sum aside, and if it is worth anything, I want you to have half of it at least—all, if you need it. This isn't a gesture—I'm serious. It might be just the thing to set you up over there. Myself, I'm beginning to despair of ever seeing Europe. I'm obsessed with the work I've mapped out, refuse to budge

---

*Bern Porter had published a number of items of Millerana in small editions, which in 1945 were listed with various prices: *Semblance of a Devoted Past*, 61 or 62 pages, $7.50 and $12.50; *Henry Miller Miscellanea*, 41 pages, $7.50 and $10.00; *Henry Miller: A Chronology and Bibliography*, paper, $1.50.

†Girodias, the son of Jack Kahane, had revived the Obelisk Press as Editions du Chêne, which later became Olympia Press. See Biographical Notes.

until I'm forced out, and don't care if I go to the grave finishing it. So long as I finish! That's all I care about.

Henry

[215 W. 13th Street, New York]
[Late 1945]

Dear Henry:

Hugo wrote this* and for you because I can't remember all the details—[see] the enclosed.

How much you have helped me, Henry. Thanks to you my books are being done in England. Now I'm signing with Dutton and getting $1,000 for *This Hunger* and the next part [*Bread and the Wafer*].† I must say I enjoyed getting out of debt—the respite. Thanks for the name of the French publisher.

I'm getting your books from the Gotham now—and will write you.

Hugo is going to South America for 3 months in February with the Pan American exhibit branch—taking engravings around etc. and I'll be free to go somewhere and write—perhaps Mexico.

I envy your little girl having you for a father.‡

This Hunger [in the Gemor Press edition] is nearly sold out.

Wilson called me—was enthusiastic about your book—will tell me about it tomorrow when I go to his house for dinner.

Anaïs

[215 West 13th Street, New York]
[Late 1945]

Dear Henry:

This is the letter Hugo got this morning! What Kafka-esque obstructions! Even if Girodias can't produce a statement why can't he

*A memo concerning H. M.'s French royalties.
†Published together as *Ladders to Fire*.
‡Janina Martha Lepska, Miller's third wife, had borne a daughter, Valentine, on November 19, 1945.

at least produce part payment, something on account. Even Caresse spoke of the difficulties of reaching him. Hugo has another suggestion now. He suggests you put it all in the hands of the bank lawyers, who, for a small fee, will do the thing more persistently, are not overworked as Mr. [Russell] Porter seems to be. (Porter was a clever lawyer too.)

With your new child you must be in need of this. It is so baffling, these difficulties. Girodias told me he owed me money too, but never said how much. What does he write you? They all hide from direct action behind a smoke screen of technicalities.

Hugo tried to cut through the maze by saying he wanted a payment made on account (since the total involved years of accounting it seems), anything.

Thank you for the name of the French publisher. There is *one* kind of person you and I seem unable to master and that is the economic one, which now and then chokes one!

I read Fowlie's article on you in *Modern Reading*. Found it very interesting—intuitively he always strikes at basic truths. But he can't stick to them and he trails off into fog. But he always takes the biggest meaning, which is wonderful. Did you like it? I mean that he nearly got you all if he had a firmer grip.

Anaïs

[215 W. 13th Street, New York]
[March 1946]

Dear Henry:

I'm glad of all the news you give me. Wonderful about Girodias. (I'll do the diary with it)—and so you will have a house! You're taking roots, I see.

About [Marius] Battedou. We have written him that we want everything shipped. (Joaquin had all his music there.) He doesn't answer. I will have to ask a friend to go to Louveciennes and see. I may ask my other storage man, as he is shipping me my furniture and books. At the same time my original MSS are arriving—symbolically the day I decided to make USA [my base]. My work is here and possibly a remarriage—but twice now I couldn't make up my mind to marry men of 20 or 30. But I'm taking a separate apartment at least in the hope of being able to stand on my own feet economically *et puis on verra*. I do want to make a new life.

So you too may go to Europe on visits. I never thought you'd make your home in America.

Yes, the critics. If you could see the "roasting" I got in the *Nation* and *New Republic*—you would laugh.* We're both arousing them, disturbing them out of their sleep.

I haven't met Sartre but my intuition is that he is no leader of a new current—merely a deviation—doesn't go deep enough, represents France's transitional state. His movement is no creation. I heard his best friend Blaise Alain expound his philosophy. But [Raymond] Queneau I would like to see. Would you remember to give him my address, Henry? And Camus too—please.

Until I let you know, it will be 215 W. 13.

I lectured and read at Amherst. The responsiveness is amazing. I read from the "new" section [of *Ladders to Fire*], and they asked for more.

Everyone is going home to France: Helion, Pegine [Vail], Allanah Harper, [William] Hayter, Masson, Tanguy, Max Ernst, [his son] Jimmy Ernst etc. I was at a big party at Peggy Guggenheim's. It's a real exodus. Farewells. Caresse is going in April.

[Canada] Lee—you remember—who made the movies. He's back with photos of Paris, of Picasso, of Dominguez. He revived the entire scene we knew so well. It will be difficult to stay away. After Dutton brings out *This Hunger* with its completed 2nd part—the overall title will be *Cities of the Interior*—then it would be wonderful to go on a visit.† I'm glad all is well with you.

Anaïs

---

*Apparently a reference to Isaac Rosenfeld's "Psychoanalysis as Literature," *The New Republic,* December 17, 1945, and Diana Trilling's "Fiction in Review," *The Nation,* January 26, 1946, both of which reviewed *This Hunger* with emphasis on Anaïs Nin's "psychoanalytical" orientation. Rosenfeld found that her characters remained "personifications of neurotic anxiety," and Trilling saw in them "clinical history" used for the purpose of supporting her sexual "chauvinism" and her female self-pity.
†The E. P. Dutton edition, published in the fall of 1946, was entitled *Ladders to Fire,* and the overall title for the five novels of the *roman fleuve* A. N. had conceived was used for the first time in 1959, when she offset her previously published fiction in one volume, as *Cities of the Interior.*

[215 W. 13th Street, New York]
[April 1946]

Dear Henry:

I danced around when I received your check.* It made me very happy—in a deep way. Your giving to me means something to me that is even greater than the pleasure and freedom the money brings me.

I'm looking now for my own place, to begin my own life and also may get a rest, July and August, which I need. I hope by Fall to go on a lecture tour and pass by and see you.

Did you know Hans Reichel† had an exhibit here, by Jeanne Bouchard?

I'm sending you one of the stills from Maya [Deren]'s movie, which isn't finished yet but which you may see someday.‡

Tell me about your new house.

Anaïs

Anderson Creek, Big Sur
May 17, 1946

Dear Anaïs:

Yes, writing that script I knew finally it would not be necessary to send it out. But I had to write it out before I could see it clearly. When you surrender, the problem ceases to exist. Try to solve it, or conquer it, and you only set up more resistance. I am very certain now that, as I said therein, if I truly become what I wish to be, the burden will fall away. The most difficult thing to admit, and to realize with one's whole being is that you alone control nothing. To be able to put yourself in tune or rhythm with the forces beyond, which are the truly operative ones, that is the task—and the solution, if we can speak of "solutions." The guilt feeling is, as we both agree, based on the *real* knowledge that one is not giving himself completely. I say it one way, you another.

One thing I don't worry about, however, is what people think,

---

*H. M. had received a partial payment from Girodias of 300,000 francs, which came to $2,000. He used some of the money as a down payment on a piece of land where he wanted to build a house.
†See Biographical Notes.
‡A. N. and a number of her friends acted in Deren's film *Ritual in Transfigured Time*.

how they misinterpret things. There's nothing you can do about that. It was so curious to read your words about "only initiates understanding what was meant." There I think you are only half right. What amazes me more and more is how much people do understand when you give them the full dose, when you hold back nothing. [. . .]

I seem to see one other thing—that one has to permit people to become desperate, to become wholly lost, that only then are they ready for the right word, only then can they avail themselves of the truth. To withhold it then is a crime. But to nurse them along is a worse crime. And there is where much of the conflict centers, about that point. The *human* instinct to spare the other person his agony (which is his means of salvation, in any sense of the word) is a fallacious instinct. Here the subtle temptations, the vicious and insidious ones, because so confused and entangled, enter in. On this so-called human plane it is the ego which commands—often in the most amazing disguises. The temptation to be good, to do good, gets us all some time or other. It's the last ruse, I feel, of the ego.

You are the only one I ever knew who used silence effectively. It was really devastating sometimes—but I don't think you were aware of it. But people got more answers, and effective ones, from you than they ever did from me, with all my shouting and ranting, or cajoling and persuading. You threw them back on themselves. To do that consciously is another thing. I was never sure you did do it thus: Did you?

But this clamor and agitation which I seem to create all about me, even from a distance, proceeds from *me*. I know it.

I told you I am getting a piece of property—a home. It came about strangely. It *is* almost impossible to get land or house here. There was a neighbor on the hill where I lived, a Mrs. [Jean Page] Wharton, who seems to understand me—without reading the books. She is supposed to be a Christian Scientist—but she's outgrown that. She's the only person I know who uses the word "Reality" as I do. That's our meeting ground. What happened is that she is virtually offering me her place. She's done everything to make it easy for me—the price is ridiculous. She even gets out of her house and will build another as soon as she can get material. That's the only reason we are not up there now. She has an absolute faith—and it's not in *me*, I feel, but in all humanity. She works magic around her.

Add to this that the spot itself is the very one I crave, the site which deeply satisfies me, and which I thought unobtainable. Sometimes I think, in offering me my dream, she is only teaching me another lesson. She says, for instance, in explaining her willingness to relinquish it, that it is now inside her, can't be lost. This doesn't fail to impress me, you can well believe. Have I not become more and more aware latterly that the things I deeply desire come without struggle? (I haven't spoken enough to you of the increasing magic going on in my life—of desires being almost instantaneously answered. It would amaze you.) All the struggle, then, is phantom play. The fighting with shadows. *This I know.*

So maybe to answer a question you put to me recently, what I am about to learn is simply the meaning of "home," the one thing I have never known. And when that finally becomes a part of me it won't matter where or how I live. That home in Brooklyn, which I always see when the word home is mentioned, is the insane asylum! That was never my home. And from that I suppose I extended the notness until I almost eliminated the idea. . . .

Henry

P.S. Must be a P.S. to this! The best news is that I am really approaching *The Rosy Crucifixion*. Another two weeks' work and I should be free to resume it. And then I really believe I will write only that, just everything into one vessel, even if it requires six more volumes. I begin to see daylight again. What a struggle!

[215 W. 13th Street, New York]
[May 1946]

Dear Henry:

A very good friend of mine, Dolly Chareau, wife of the architect of the Maison de Verre near Louveciennes, do you remember (she was my neighbor there), is going to France soon. Is there anything she can do for you? Any errand? She will be there in preparation for a definite return home and will come back in September. She is dependable.

She has translated my stories from *Under a Glass Bell* and they sound as if they never had been written in English.

As you seem to be able to get an answer from Girodias could you please ask him why he doesn't answer me ever? He asked me for copies of the new books and I sent them. No answer. He wrote me about my own royalties. When I wrote him, no answer.

I am very desperate to get printed in France where I intend to return definitely as soon as I can. I thought I had taken roots here but I see it is not so. I'm homesick and lonely in spite of all the worshippers. Have been working hard in Maya's movie. If you want to see it, recommend it to someone in Hollywood or near you. Enclosing literature on the old one. The new one will be shown June One.

You forgot to tell me what to do with your M.S. for [Oscar] Baradinski.* Shall I return it to you? He came with his wife and we had dinner together. A man of good will.

If Girodias could at least tell me how much he has for me in France I might have gone over in July for two months and spent it there.

Where is Lawrence Durrell now?

Did you like the still from the movie? *Comme toujours,*

Anaïs

[Anderson Creek, Big Sur]
May 21st [1946]

Dear Anaïs:

There are two things your friend Dolly Chareau might do for me, yes. One is to investigate the missing trunk chez [Marius] Battedou. The other is to pick up royalties from Girodias. Today I had a letter from him saying he expects to send another 200,000 or 300,000 frs. to me in about a month. There would still be a balance when she gets there, and he might pay just before she leaves.

I just wrote Girodias for you about money and translations. As your money is [a] pre-war affair it may be difficult. Perhaps you could suggest a sum (round sum) to settle the matter. His accounts for that period were either balled up or lost, I don't know which. I am still dickering with him about mine. Durrell should get his too. Here is Larry's address: Public Information Officer, M.I.O.-B.M.A.-Rhodes, Dodecanese Islands, M.E.F.

If Girodias won't publish you, there are others in Paris who will, I'm sure. Robert Laffont, for one, was warmly recommended to me. But I think Gallimard would do it—and they are bigger.

Is the Maya movie the one Duchamps and Ernst and Léger had a hand in? Very vague about it. You did not enclose literature on it.

*New York bookseller and publisher of both H. M. and A. N.

That photo you sent me recently—was that the movie still? Looked very Renaissance—à la Botticelli, I thought.

Yes, please return that script to me. But I am not using it.

Have you seen Patience Ross* yet? Has she placed any of your books abroad? I just signed up one book in Denmark and have offers now from Sweden and Norway. And what about Italy?—Mondadori there, a big publisher? Did you ever try Spain or any Spanish country? I have offers from Brazil and Argentina, but none direct from Spain. China too is a possibility for you now. They recently took one of D. H. Lawrence's books. And there is Australia—Reed & Harris (publishers of *Angry Penguins* in Melbourne).

I got a book from your friend [Gore Vidal] at Dutton's. Got six books and three long mss. from unknown authors the same day. Which reminds me that, though accepting your criticism of my proposed pamphlet, you never suggested a remedy, did you? What would *you* do about it? Every mail day I fight the same battle over again.

Did you ever look up Franz Werfel's last book—*Star of the Unborn?* It would probably bore you, but I can't be too sure. There is lots in it that fascinated me. I have been reading [Charles] Péguy lately. Find him quite wonderful. (How late I am coming to these men!) And Ramuz' *The End of All Men* (a Pantheon book), I thought quite superb. I want to read more of him.

Today a ms. in pen and ink from a young woman in a whorehouse in Australia, asking if I could help get it published. She is a poet and has a strong religious bent; went there in search of love. Very strange document. Not a moron either. A Welsh girl. What things drift in here! [The remainder of this letter is missing.]

[215 W. 13th Street, New York]
[June 1946]

[Henry:]

I allowed Gore Vidal to send you a copy of his book [*In a Yellow Wood*], remarkable because he is 20. I know you have no time to read it. I only allowed it because he has done a great deal for me, being one of the editors at Dutton—given me full editorial freedom, helped writers I sent in and tried to rescue from oblivion such as [James] Agee,

*London literary agent.

William Carlos Williams etc. You can send him ms. by people you want to help anytime. He is intelligent and helpful. One line from you would mean a great deal. His true role for me is that of a loyal son. And whatever child I have always chooses you for the male. Symbol of this Trinity!

He has a side very much like you. We could have made him: half you, half me. So give him your blessing please!

Seems ironic, I asking you this when this is what you fight off—but I have never done it! And you can send your burdens to him *par contre!*

Yes, I feel confident I will travel—be able to—freely—soon.

Will let you know plan for the diary with your money. I have the originals now. Can print first volumes—next fall perhaps.

What a life you have! I thought only in the city one suffered interruptions—amazing to read.

But to return to the article: you owe the world no apology. As far as the world goes you have given generously, more than it could digest with its meagre paltry stomach. So I don't like to see you in that role. *Bonne chance.*

I noticed too that just as I prefer to write about the present and have reluctance to turn back, you always have to clear the present, like a diarist, really, because actually it's the present you love, and going back is going back to what hurts. The present is always healing, at worst—the past is the abscess. I feel the same way. *C'est là le secret.* Love

Anaïs

Easthampton, L.I.
[July 1946]

Dear Henry:

I can't tell you how pleased I was with the French review of [*Tropic of*] *Cancer.* To read again people who can hear, see and evaluate you. One can write for such people. I'm sorry I kept it so long. The last weeks before coming here were taken up by the last efforts to keep the little Press afloat in the hope of printing the Diary soon but I only lost out with debts and finally had to close it. It was just another dream. As soon as I stopped working in it (last November) it collapsed. You know what a worker I am—but I couldn't write *and* print—my strength gave out. So no more Press. But your friends came to see me on my last few days in N.Y. Zoe [?] and her husband. And they seemed interested. I gave them all my books—not the Diary because it was in storage already—and we'll talk in September. I think now the best thing would be to print it in France, as Caresse did the portfolio. So much easier for the linotype, proofing errors etc.

Perhaps when you send me the next royalties I could go to France and do it all there—all the parts in French—and dedicated to you whose persistent dream it was to see it out. Boss. (I'm holding what you already sent for that and no other use.)

Resting here because I couldn't afford to travel, had wanted to pass by and see you and go to Mexico. The Press drained me—just because I hated to give it up.

Hearing a lot about you, your life, child, wife, house etc.

Dutton can't do anything for foreign publications. Someday ask Emil if he has time to send me whatever names and addresses of foreign publishers you think might want me, and I'll send them the English edition and the new Dutton book [*Ladders to Fire*]. You are already the cause of my being published in England. Now perhaps in France through Zoe's husband. I know no one in South America. Do you?

I'm trying (this is a secret) to work on Dutton to take you up openly and face the consequent legal battle. If they only had the guts! I may yet accomplish this someday. Love

Anaïs

[215 W. 13th Street, New York]
[Fall 1946]

Dear Henry:

I couldn't help laughing—when you write me so much about being burdened with correspondence and you yourself start one with Vidal—an absolutely unnecessary one, really—most of these people merely interested in boasting they have a correspondence with a famous man, you, very few really aware of you with any sincerity. Oh, Henry—now you see how it is you who starts this and you like it because it gives you a feeling of contact. You couldn't live without it. The whole thing was enacted before my eyes. I write you and ask you merely to say one word about a book by someone who has done a lot for me. You didn't even have to read the book. You write him encouraging a correspondence. And there it goes. You want this and you called for it and you can't live without it!

So sorry about Mme Chareau—she can't go to France—not this year. But everybody else is [going]. That is what makes me change my plans. I get attacks of homesickness, as each one leaves, and then I master it and try again to live here. But last night reread some old diaries and saw clearly how much bigger life was there. So again I hope to leave, holding back only because of the great difficulties to live there—people spend their days waiting in line for food. No coal etc. But now no matter what happens we will go back next year.

Miss Ross has been fine to me. The volume done by Nicholson [& Watson] will be out next Fall, I guess.

The Rimbaud section was *magnificent.* You brought out an interesting point—that of holding on to the adolescent attitude of rebellion. But the mystery remains, I feel. And you too. You must have asked Laughlin to send me *New Directions.* Thank you. I wanted to read this.* I think you did him with real fire and faith.

Anaïs

[Anderson Creek]
Friday morning [Fall 1946]†

Dear Anaïs—

Went to bed last night with an excellent idea about your Diary. Suddenly I sat up in bed and asked myself why had we never thought of Girodias as a publisher for the Diary? Why should you have to do this gargantuan task of printing yourself? It's absurd. I'm almost positive Girodias will agree to do it—and without cuts and so on. And only he, of all the publishers we know, can publish in both English and French. When it comes to the English-written volumes, he can sell them all over the world—*and* in America too. If he balks for any

---

*H. M.'s essay on Arthur Rimbaud, "When Do Angels Cease to Resemble Themselves," appeared in the *New Directions Annual,* #9, edited by James Laughlin, in 1946. The second installment, "Rimbaud," was included in the *New Directions Annual,* #11, in 1949.

†Though this letter is partially quoted in A. N.'s *Diary, 1944–1947,* under the date May, 1945, some of the items discussed indicate that it was written after July 1946. French translations of *Tropic of Cancer, Black Spring,* and *Max and the White Phagocites* appeared during the course of that year.

reason, I can guarantee to cover him against loss out of my royalties. What do you think? Should I write him about it at length?

I had an idea that when printing each volume he could bring out a small de luxe edition by *facsimile* process, which would establish the authenticity of the work and be a handsome product at the same time. Many of your friends will like to have these.

Anyway, there would be no need for translating from one language to another. *And*—you would be assured of an excellent distribution—thru Hachette. Not until half the Diary is published would there be any question of censorship in France. The only thing you would have to do, in my case, is to alter the names, to protect him and yourself from libel charges, I suppose.

Incidentally, don't think that I am suggesting this to avoid giving you money. Please! I will continue to share with you no matter what you do. It's for practical reasons I suggest Girodias.

I see that the publicity created by the French versions of my books has had tremendous repercussions—they reach all over Europe. The clippings pour in—in batches. Now recently I notice that Robert Laffont (the new publisher) has a revue called [*Le*] *Magasin du Spectacle* (devoted to theater & cinema) in the 3rd number of which [July 1946] he has published my "Scenario." The "Max" book will be out any day now, in French, with my critique of the Diary.* The time is ripe, I think. So do think it over. I suppose the original volumes are still in the vault in Paris, yes? But you could go over and arrange all that, couldn't you?

If, by the way, Girodias has made no answer on your three books, why don't you offer them to Robert Laffont—or Denoël or Gallimard?

Reichel has just sent me a photo of one of his watercolors and asks on the back what news of *you*, where are *you?* His address is still Impasse du Rouet (14). He has a fiancé now—Nathalie Romaine. Some friends in Carmel tried to buy *This Hunger* from "The Nation" but say it is exhausted. Is that true? And will Putnam publish the three in one, as you said? Wait to hear from you.

Henry

Max and the White Phagocytes, first published by Obelisk Press in Paris in 1938, contained the essay "Un Etre Etoilique," which had originally appeared in *The Criterion*, in London, in October 1937, and revealed the existence of A. N.'s Diary.

Girodias now publishes a revue edited by Georges Bataille called *Critique* (of French and foreign books)—rather interesting! He has taken every book I recommended [to] him thus far!*

[Big Sur]
Oct. 5, 1946

Dear Anaïs—

Thought these 2 letters might interest you. [Jacques] den Haan is a good, sincere and intelligent chap. (Return this please.) I answered and gave him your address for further information.

The university editor I had to turn down—can't possibly do more now. But told him you might be able to suggest someone.

I don't think you should despair about Girodias. His letters and responses are always sincere and honest, I feel. He hasn't paid me either on pre-war royalties, nor Durrell, I suppose. But I still hope for a settlement.

Now action has been taken against the translated volumes of my 3 books & all three publishers go to trial in a few months—and will be found guilty, thinks Girodias—perhaps imprisoned for a month or two. He is now printing 20,000 more of *Capricorn* (this will make about 45,000 altogether, I believe). Sales continue until trial begins. I think it will result favorably for every one, no matter what the verdict.†

Look for more money in a few weeks. In haste, and glad everything goes well!

Henry

---

*The first issue, June 1946, of *Critique* contained an essay by Georges Bataille entitled *"La Morale de Miller."*
†An action against H. M. was instituted in March 1946 by the Cartel d'Action Sociale et Morale, under a 1939 French antipornography law. He was found guilty, but a group of French writers, including André Breton, Albert Camus, Paul Eluard, Maurice Nadeau, Jean-Paul Sartre, and André Gide, came to his defense and eventually prevailed. When an American bookseller received a three-year prison term for selling the banned *Tropic of Cancer* and *Tropic of Capricorn*, no American writer spoke up. Only in the early 1960s, when Grove Press defended its publication of *Tropic of Cancer* in numerous court cases, did a group of U.S. writers, including Edmund Wilson, John Dos Passos, and Alfred Kazin, issue a statement supporting Miller and opposing censorship.

[215 W. 13th Street, New York]
[June 1947]

Dear Henry:

Got your letter and leaving the money problem to you and Hugo, as he is leaving for France July 12. I can't go because the bank won't pay my trip and also because as you know I am trying to live alone. So I'm finally going to Mexico July 12 hoping something will turn out and that this time I won't go broke again. I do so much want to stand on my own feet. Your gift to me will have the same purpose mine to you had: it will give me freedom.

I had a small taste of this freedom last month—the only one I've had in my whole life!

Keep writing to 215 [West 13th Street]. The super will forward my mail, as my plans in Mexico are without premeditation.

I hope to be able to visit you all again in October.

The *House of Incest* was printed on what you once sent me. I'm trying to revive and sustain Gemor Press—ultimately to do Child-[hood] Diary as you wished it—all the French in one volume. In the Fall will do this.

Love

Anaïs

Big Sur
September 14, 1947

Dear Anaïs—

This is the first chance I've had to write you. Lots has happened recently. Lots of difficulties. Now a bit better. Everyone I know seems to be in trouble. Climax came when I heard that June was ill and destitute, deserted by her husband. Weighs only 75 lbs.!! Has ulcerated colitis, as I understand it. Sent her what I could—not very much—and got friends to aid a bit with doctors, food & medicine. Don't know if you wish to see her, but thought I ought to let you know, at least. She lives at 196 Clinton Avenue, Brooklyn (5), N.Y. Apt. 55D. Says she needs to get to a dry climate. Needs rest and nourishment above all, I gather.

It looks now as if I shall truly get some money out of France very soon. In my own miraculous way, all by accident, I met the French consul in S.F., who apparently is untying the knots. Fine chap—a writer, too, I believe.* All those bank men and specialists got absolutely nowhere—full of negation and frustration—quite as I suspected. My luck always comes from the unexpected source, as you know. Anyway, I feel confident now you will have what you need when it comes time to go to Mexico—or first to come West, if you intended that.

You have seen me in many straits and complications, but never was there anything like these last few months. I almost gave up.

What would straighten me out enormously would be to find a person who could be part secretary and part governess. I can't go on doing all the things demanded of me without aid. I shall have soon a separate studio four miles down the road where I will be able to work in peace a few hours each day. I need a car for that, but now a friend promises me a gift of a jeep. (8 miles up & down these hills is too much on foot.)

I hope things are better for you too. At least you are freeing yourself. Wherein our freedom lies precisely is sometimes difficult to know. I make progress in some directions and fall back in others. The problems are greater, always. And should be so, I guess. I seem to be sent back to school to learn over and over again—the school of life, *bien entendu.*

Oh yes—when I mentioned above about a secretary, it was because I thought you might sometime run across such a person. It takes a very special individual, to be sure. I can't *pay* anything. Can only offer this life here at Big Sur—meaningless to some, a paradise to others.

I am not sure you are back at 215 W 13th St. So let me know what address when you write again, yes? Forgive my silence and brief notes. One day I'll give you a bird's-eye view of it all. Love.

Henry

P.S. Lepska reads *all* the mail—one of her pleasures. And tries to help me answering. But she has plenty to do. The child alone is a great job. I give her much time myself. There ought to be more children here, flocks of them.

*Romain Kacew, who wrote as Roman Gary (1914–1980), served as First Secretary of the French delegation to the U. N. in San Francisco at the time, and later became French consul in Los Angeles. Gary had published his first book, *A European Education*, in 1945.

[Big Sur]
Sept. 18 [1947]

Dear Anaïs—

Your three notes came just after I had written you. Feel more than ever certain now I can send you money in time to travel West. Am inquiring tonight or tomorrow at Anderson Creek—4 miles down the road, where Margaret and Gilbert lived, if you can stay there—not with them—they are all leaving shortly—but with a girl named Betty Frank. It's a large, very large place, that Varda originally built—you'll like it, I'm sure.

Offhand I think of two people in L.A. for a lecture, by all means write to Dr. Lawrence Clark Powell—Librarian at U.C.L.A. He knows your work well and has everything in the library.

A person who might put you up is Mrs. Dorothea Ramsay. She admires your work greatly. There are many admirers of yours in L.A. or Hollywood, but it's hard for me to recall names now. (May give more later.)

Also, you have a friend in Attilio & Paola Bowinkel of Westwood Village, L.A.—near University, who have an art & frame store and possibly room in their house.

Don't go to Carmel, especially John Ney's—that's a frightful place—like Greenwich Village. Have a feeling lots of foreign people in Carmel know you from abroad. Have friends at Pebble Beach— beautiful restricted spot—where you will be invited too, if you wish. But Anderson Creek would be more *intime,* and as you like it.

Don't try to drive across country if you are not a good driver—it's nerve-racking. Someone may give me a jeep any day now. In which case you'll have transportation here. And Lilik Schatz, my collaborator,* is here down the road now. He too has a car. Someone will bring you down from Berkeley after your lectures. *When* must you be there?

I am expecting to have one of those places (cabins) at Anderson Creek too. Soon as they all leave—they're going on a long cruise. Will use it as a work place. Difficult to do anything here, with all the interruptions.

---

*A neighbor, the Israeli-born artist Bezalel Schatz, had worked with H. M. since February 1946 to produce an illustrated volume based on the dream chapter in *Black Spring*. After a year of work, *Into the Night Life,* a beautifully hand-crafted book of eighty pages, appeared in an edition of 800 copies, which sold for $100 each.

Soon as money comes will wire it to you or air-mail a money order. I may not get one large sum immediately—it may come in smallish sums of 250 or so. If I wire only $250.00 that means to use it for fare. Will *surely* have what you need for indefinite period when you get here. You won't have rent to pay, we can take care of your food bill, if necessary, and there won't be any other expenses to speak of—so rest easy on that score. And everybody—Lepska too—is eager for you to come.

More very soon. Love. And don't get cold feet at the last minute!

Henry

[215 W. 13th Street, New York]
[September 1947]

Dear Henry:

I just want to tell you where I'm going to be and when on my slow indirect way to the Coast:

Oct. 21   Black Mountain College (Dutton will pay my trip.)
Nov. 3   New York for bookshop party
Nov. 6   Bennington
Nov. 10   Washington—School of Creative Arts
Nov. 13   Chicago University
and after that?
I'll get to Berkeley I hope.
I have your $100 and that is all for the moment—but hopeful.
Keep writing here—until I let you know otherwise.
I hope you are less troubled now.
Love

Anaïs

[Summer 1948]

Dear Henry:

Here I am in Guatemala—but dreaming of being able to return to Acapulco. This is an amazing city, at the foot of a volcano—half ruins of the 16 and 17th century. It is muted, windless, still and drugged. People dressed beautifully, like Hindus, Balinese, Mongolians. Carry everything on their heads and trot like little horses. I'm staying for two weeks at Vidal's house—a monastery which was part of the ruined church. There is a bell tower and a chapel, and vast manorial rooms. I've just returned from the market—so variegated, primitive. In one arched long room they all cook food on braseros for sale—and it is smoky and they sit there utterly mute, static. They speak so little, do not dance, though at night the marimbas play in the square. It is feudal, and oriental—almost like Tibet. At night you see the tip of the volcano. Next to it is one still active, which causes earthquakes.

As in Corfu, the whites drift and drink and disintegrate.

Write me care of my brother, Thorvald Nin, Augustin Ahumada 109, Lomas, Mexico, as that is my base. In a week I'll be back in Acapulco—which is where I could stay the rest of my life.

I may see you again on my way home*—as I may read at Berkeley, October. I'll let you know.

If you have news, write me.

Love

A.

[San Francisco]
[Fall 1948]†

Dear Henry:

Someone loaned me the new book.‡ It's the most beautiful thing you've ever written and I was moved. A completely different region of you which I had once seen, believed in, vividly, and which had been erased and destroyed by other aspects—now recovered, and so simple and perfect.

Anaïs

---

*A. N. had visited the Millers at Big Sur when she first went to California.
†After her auto trip to the West Coast, A. N. had taken an apartment in San Francisco, which she kept till January 1950. During this period, a limited edition of *House of Incest* was published, apparently by Centaur Press, of 1726 Baker St., San Francisco, at $2.50. This press also published, in 1950, a collection of poems, *Medieval Scenes*, by her friend Robert Duncan.
‡*The Smile at the Foot of the Ladder.* With watercolors by H. M. and a Preface by Edwin Corle. (New York: A Merle Armitage Book, Duell, Sloane & Pearce, 124 pp., $5.00.)

[San Francisco]
[Early 1949]

Dear Henry:

Now that James Broughton and Kermit Sheets are going to do Volume One [of the original diary] on their Centaur Press and that I am trying to raise funds, I wrote to Walter Zivi, who once wrote me he wanted to publish [the] diary and he does not answer. Do you know what happened to him? At the time he wrote me I had lost my Press through debts etc. and couldn't print anything. Centaur has a good plan for several books, including one by Leonora Carrington—and we are looking for subscriptions of $25.00 to all the books that will come out—or writers with good literary MS who will lend 100, which will be returned together with a larger share of royalties than other presses do, as here only the printer gets paid and it's non-profit.*

I hope your luck has changed. I wrote to Larry Powell to do all he could for you at the time your second child was born.†

Does Emil White still sell books?

How have you been doing with the watercolors?

I finished a new novel—*Four-Chambered Heart.* Leading a completely secluded life [. . .] only go to a movie now and then.

Anaïs

35 West 9th [Street], New York City
[Summer 1952]

Dear Henry:

I have heard rumors which rather saddened me, of a separation between you and Lepska. Is it true?‡

I have a feeling we are all going back to Paris ultimately, where we were happiest. I don't think America has anything to love and I have grown to despise it. All those who have gone back tell me they are no longer "angry. . . ."

*Nothing came of this plan to begin publication of the early diaries, written in French. An abridged English version, *Linotte,* was published by Harcourt Brace Jovanovich in New York in 1978. In 1979, Editions Stock, in Paris, published them in full, covering the years 1914 to 1920, as the two-volume *Journal d'Enfance.*

†A son, Tony, was born on August 28, 1948, to Lepska and H. M.

‡H. M. and Lepska separated in 1951 and were divorced a year later.

Well, here is to the day I will be walking down the boulevard and see you at a café table among your loyal friends.

I expected you in Los Angeles for a while. I'm here now taking care of Hugo, who is flat on his back with a ruptured disk.

Kathryn Winslow was here the other night—very busy collecting data on flying for a book—first woman to fly a jet plane etc.

I also met Paolo Milano,* who admires you. I wrote a new book on Sabina [*A Spy in the House of Love*] but can't get it published. Trying to find someone in France who would do it in English. Is there anyone aside from Obelisk Press? Have been mailing out our records announcements to new names and colleges—as Barrons don't do anything to push them themselves.†

Met painter who wanted to give you his paintings (in L.A.), married to a Greek. Not a good painter but sincere and pathetically struggling to get free.

Anaïs

[35 W. 9th Street, New York]
[Summer 1952]

Dear Henry—

Isn't it strange that [Lawrence Clark] Powell, who has children, cannot see the injustice of taking a gift MS from you when that is a work, more important than his, which if you were paid for, as you should [be], would support your wife and children? I wrote him this when he celebrated his haul at your place and he admitted I was right. He should pay you. He will raise the money. UCLA is wealthy and there is no reason for this continuation of the artist's masochism [. . .]. On the one hand you know the world should support you, on the other you allow exploitation. I was given a friendly lunch by Powell to obtain the Diary for the Library. Such injustice! Yet when I tried to live alone this last year and a half I had to fall back on my husband again for help.

*Young Italian writer.
†In June 1949, A. N. had read a complete version of *House of Incest* and four stories from *Under a Glass Bell* for the "Contemporary Classic" record label of Louis and Bebe Barron.

Do you have a record-playing machine? Let me know as I wanted to send you some records of mine as a present.

Anaïs

I keep finding magazines & books of yours among my books and keep sending them to you.

Was it Mondadori you wrote to? He has all my books now and wrote me a fine letter.

Big Sur
[August 2, 1952]

Dear Anaïs—

Was glad to hear from you. Heard about library business from someone at the library.

Things are quite different for me here now. Schatz's sister-in-law [Eve McClure] has come to live with me, the children are back (I hope for good) and we have a real, full, happy life & only after 16 months of no work I've just begun to write again—*Nexus*. If you ever pass by this way do stop in. I think you'll like Eve.* I expect to get a divorce soon—in Mexico. We would like to go to France, all over, in fact, but there is no extra cash. I earn just enough to get by.

The Books in My Life is out in England but not yet here. Is the present address a good one to mail books to? *Plexus* came out in French (Correa, Paris) but no English edition in sight yet. Have you tried Denoël or Correa or Gallimard with your books? Girodias is out of the picture now—firm taken over by Hachette.

I still have a job squeezing in a couple of hours a day writing. So very much to do around here.

All the best to you.

Henry

P.S. June is still ill and always broke. But shows more desire now to get well.

———

*Eve McClure eventually became Miller's fourth wife. See Biographical Notes.

P.S. Have you tried Sweden for publishing? And did Mondadori ever take anything.* Latter has just contracted for *Plexus*.

I've improved this place considerably since you were here. I really feel at home.

P.S. The French radio (Paris) made a transcription of *Scenario* (called it "Alraune") and it made a sensation, I am told. I sent the tape recordings to Powell to get changed to our speed. Cendrars gave it an "introduction" on the air. His last six books I find marvelous.

La Ciotat (B. du R.)
Chez Michel Simon
[February 10, 1953]

Dear Anaïs—

Just got your letter here in this strange place—Simon offered it to us in his absence. Met him in Paris for just a few minutes—and struck it off at once. Am going to Vienne (Isère) from here, then back to Paris & Brussels, then home. Frankly I'm homesick. The first time in my life. There's nothing new for me in Europe and I don't want any more the cultural, intellectual life. Too too much talk, rehash, etc. Besides, I don't see how Europe can survive much longer. The whole system is now crazy—it must collapse. Nothing has changed here, as I see it, except the *fantastic* cost of living. It's incredible. Worse than you may think. I have been marvelously treated everywhere—no complaints. But I am a different person and Big Sur is where I want to stay. I miss the children too—they mean more to me than places and people. All that divorce business has been tragic.

No, I did not mention your other books because it was not the moment—only singled out special ones, as you see. And I can't expand too much. Hachette took over Girodias' edition & print me in English. But Girodias, who is starting up again, may get *Plexus*. Frankly, I don't care much anymore who prints or doesn't print. The whole bloody business is a farce. I even begin to question the value of writing itself.

Children of the Albatross and *The Four-Chambered Heart* were published by Wahlström & Widstrand in Stockholm in 1950. Mondadori published an Italian edition of *Under a Glass Bell* in 1951.

If my book is a "success," as you say, it must be *intime*. I worked as hard to launch it as I did with *Cancer*. Just as though nothing had happened in between. I almost believe it would be more "honorable" to sit back and beg for alms. Of course here I am taken seriously and enthusiastically. But I don't need it. I have no vanity left.

This sounds discouraging. Forgive me.

And I do hope your star continues to rise.

All the best to you.

Henry

P.S. My best & most reliable (also intelligent) publisher is Edmond Buchet of Corréa, Paris. He's Swiss. If only you could bring yourself to publish the Diary! or unmutilated big fragments of it. Also—I spoke to Simon about you—the *péniche, les suiges à Paris*, etc. A wonderful warm being, he!

[35 West 9th Street, N.Y.]
[October 1953]

Dear Henry—

I wonder if you are back from Europe. Your letter from France sounded very sad and disappointed. I thought you would be happy there. Please tell me whether your books have been translated into German.

A nephew of Jacob Wassermann came to see me. He is a Dr. Rosen. He once owned a literary magazine in Germany, has much to tell about Wassermann and would like to translate you. He is in contact with a big German publisher. He was interested in the Diary too. I promised to write you and ask you.

Did you see the New Story Press when you were in Paris? They are doing my new book, *Spy in the House of Love*. *

To let Maxwell Geismar read (he will someday write about you) I had to re-open Diaries and the Henry who emerged from them is wonderful and it truly is so alive and permanent a portrait that it blotted out the dark last part of the relationship, its disintegration etc. The *causes* are so clear, too, that if we had seen them then they could have been remedied. At least I see you clear of distortions and it makes

---

*Published in New York in 1954 by the British Book Centre.

me write you for the first time without the stiltedness due to hardening of the personal vision. Probably if I had then the sense of humor I have today and if you had *then* the qualities you have today, nothing would have broken. I have changed enormously. Have begun to open diary and let it be read, to realize it's my major work, and seeking to solve human problems of its publication. *On verra!* I can always let it be done in Chinese, Hebrew, German etc. . . .

Anaïs

BIOGRAPHICAL NOTES

Allendy, Dr. René Felix: (1889–1942.) French psychoanalyst, founder of the Société Française de Psychoanalyse, author, and lecturer at the Sorbonne. Among his patients were Anaïs Nin, Eduardo Sanchez, and Hugh Guiler. He was interested in a wide range of subjects, including alchemy and astrology. Well acquainted with numerous French writers and publishers, he was particularly close to Antonin Artaud; his wife, Yvonne, served as treasurer of Artaud's short-lived experimental theater, and he raised the funds for Artaud's first film, *La Coquille et le Clergyman*. He took Artaud to Louveciennes to meet the Guilers. Anaïs Nin described Allendy as being tall and looking like a Russian muzhik. His books include *La Psychoanalyse* (Paris: Denoël & Steele, 1931), *Capitalisme et Sexualité* (Paris: Denoël & Steele, 1932), and *Aristote, ou le complex de trahison,* which appeared in English as *The Treason Complex* (New York: Social Science Publishing Co., 1949).

Bachman, Rudolf: Austrian refugee in France who sought support from Anaïs Nin and Henry Miller by eliciting sympathy with stories of his vagabondage and prison experiences.

Bald, Wambly: American newspaperman, born in Chicago in 1902, who, after graduating from the University of Chicago, went to France and worked on the staff of the Paris edition of the Chicago *Tribune,* which provided a haven for many expatriates, including Alfred Perlès; the young American novelist Edgar Calmer; and literary editor Waverly Root, who later became known for his three-volume *Secret History of World War II.* Irving Schwerke, a friend of Joaquin Nin-Culmell, was the *Tribune's* music editor. In his weekly column, "La Vie de Bohème," Bald reported on the activities of the English-speaking community in a gossipy style, and Miller at times apparently collaborated with him. Collected in a volume edited by Benjamin Franklin V, *On the Left Bank, 1929–1933* (Athens,

OH: Ohio University Press, 1987), these columns also contain several items on June Miller and a brief sketch, dated October 14, 1931, presents Miller as "a legitimate child of Montparnasse, the salt of the Quarter," sleeping on park benches and living on handouts, but cheerful.

Bradley, William Aspenwall: (1878–1939.) American poet and translator who went to France after World War I and established, with his French wife, a literary salon and agency on the Ile Saint-Louis. At the suggestion of Dr. Krans, of the American-French Exchange program, who had helped Miller get a job at the Lycée Carnot in Dijon, Bradley read the manuscript of *Tropic of Cancer* and eventually introduced Miller to Jack Kahane. For a number of years, he also tried to place Anaïs Nin's work with American publishers.

Brassai (Gyula Halasz): Hungarian photographer and painter who became known especially for candidly chronicling Parisian night life in the 1930s. He photographed June Miller and Anaïs Nin. Miller's essay about him, "The Eye of Paris," was included in *The Wisdom of the Heart* (Norfolk, CT: New Directions, 1941). Some of Brassai's photographs appeared in Miller's *Quiet Days in Clichy* (Paris: Olympia Press, 1956) and on the cover of the 1984 reissue of two volumes by Alfred Perlès.

Cairns, Huntington: American lawyer, born 1904, who served between 1933 and 1943 as a legal adviser to the U.S. Treasury Department, which ruled on the importation of "obscene" books. An admirer of Miller's work, he tried to help him in various ways, including planning a showing of his watercolors in the late 1930s. In 1943, Cairns became manager of the National Gallery of Art, in Washington, D.C.

Cendrars, Blaise: (1887–1961.) French writer and adventurer who lost his right arm in World War I and became known in the United States for his book *L'Or*, translated as *Sutter's Gold.* An early champion of Miller's work, he praised *Tropic of Cancer*, and Miller wrote of him: "With the exception of John Cowper Powys, I have never met another writer who has given me more than he."

Conason, Dr. Emil (Seymour Emil Cohen): American physician who met Miller when he was working at the "Cosmodemonic Telegraph Company" (i.e., Western Union) as a young psychiatrist for the personnel department, of which Miller was the manager, between 1920 and 1924. They became lifelong friends.

Crosby, Caresse (Mary Phelps Jacob): (1892–1970.) American publisher and editor, widow of Harry Crosby (1889–1929), who started the Black Sun

Press in France in the late 1920s. She had befriended many writers, among them Joyce, Lawrence, Hart Crane, and, later, Miller, though she had initially disliked *Tropic of Cancer* when Anaïs Nin had shown her the manuscript in 1934. In 1940, Miller stayed at her New York apartment, on East 54th Street, and at "Hampton Manor," her country home in Virginia, where he wrote *The Colossus of Maroussi* and *The World of Sex.* In 1944, she exhibited Miller's watercolors and Hugh Guiler's copper engravings at her "G" Gallery in Washington, D.C. Anaïs Nin, at her Gemor Press, printed several books for Crosby. Her memoirs, up to 1940, *The Passionate Years,* first published in 1952, were reissued in 1979 by The Ecco Press in New York.

de Vilmorin, Louise (Mrs. Henry Hunt): French writer and novelist. A member of an old aristocratic family, she was deeply attached to her brothers. She first met Anaïs Nin in November 1931 and served as the model for "Jeanne" in some of Nin's fiction, notably the story "Under a Glass Bell."

Dudley, Dorothy (Mrs. Harry Harvey): American critic and journalist, born in 1884. First biographer of Theodore Dreiser (*Forgotten Frontiers: A Novel of Facts,* 1932), and translator of Auguste Rodin's *Venus* (1912). She covered the French literary and artistic scene during the 1930s for various U.S. publications, including *American Magazine of Art* and *The Nation.* Her daughter Caroline married the French writer Joseph Delteil, whose work (*Cholera, Le Cinq Sens, Jeanne d'Arc,* among others) Miller discovered in the 1930s, and who later became a personal friend.

Erskine, John: (1879–1951.) American educator, pianist, and novelist, who taught English literature at Columbia University from 1909 to 1937 and became director of the Juilliard School of Music. He appeared as soloist with the Philharmonic-Symphony Orchestra of New York, but achieved fame as the author of numerous books, notably the best seller *The Private Life of Helen of Troy* (1925). Admired by Hugh Guiler, who studied under him, Erskine became a family friend and vacationed in France in 1928 with the Guilers and his two children, Anna and Graham. Anaïs Nin became romantically infatuated with Erskine, which precipitated the first major crisis in her marriage, though the relationship never developed and ended in disillusionment after a trip to New York in October 1931. (See *The Early Diary of Anaïs Nin, 1927–1931.*)

Faure, Elie: (1873–1937.) French author and traveler, who wrote a multivolume *History of Art* and numerous other books, including *Dance Over Fire and Water* (1926) and *The Spirit of Japan* (1930), which deeply impressed Anaïs Nin and Henry Miller.

Flandrau, Grace (Mrs. G. C. Hodgson): American author and novelist, born in 1889, who lived in France and contributed to various magazines, including *Scribner's*. Though Miller apparently never commented on her work (*Then I Saw the Congo*, 1929; *Indeed the Flesh*, 1934; *Under the Sun*, 1936), he considered her a potential go-between for him with American publishers.

Fowlie, Wallace: American educator, critic, and specialist in French literature, born in 1908, who taught at Bennington College (1936–1941, 1950–1952), Yale, and the University of Chicago. He was an early champion of Miller's work in the United States, and their correspondence was published by Grove Press in 1975 *(Letters of Henry Miller and Wallace Fowlie: 1943–1972)*. Before Fowlie left for a year in France (1948–1949), Miller introduced him to Anaïs Nin, and she recalls their first meeting in March 1945 in Volume Four of her *Diary*.

Fraenkel, Michael: American book dealer and writer, born in 1896 in Kopul, Lithuania. He settled in France, after acquiring a small fortune from bookselling and the stock market, to write and publish some of his own work under the imprint Carrefour, at the St. Catherine Press in Bruges, Belgium (*Werther's Younger Brother*, 1930; *Anonymous: The Need for Anonymity*, with Walter Lowenfels, 1930; *Bastard Death: The Autobiography of an Idea*, with an introduction by Henry Miller, 1936, among others). Fraenkel, who is Boris in *Tropic of Cancer*, sheltered Miller in 1930 at his house, 18 Villa Seurat, which also contained the studio Anaïs Nin rented in 1934, where Miller lived until May 1939, and where Lawrence and Nancy Durrell briefly stayed in 1938. Fraenkel became involved in the publishing activities of the Siana Press, which printed *House of Incest*, at the St. Catherine Press, in 1936. He sublet Louveciennes for a while, and took up residence in Mexico in 1940. In a lengthy essay, "The Genesis of *Tropic of Cancer*" (Berkeley: Bern Porter, 1946), he claimed his decisive influence on Miller's work, and when the first French edition (Paris: Denoël, 1946) came under attack, he published *"Défense du Tropique"* (Paris: Variété, 1947). After his death in 1957, Walter Lowenfels and Howard McCord brought out a brief summary of his life and his ideas, *The Life of Fraenkel's Death* (Pullman, WA: Washington State University Press, 1970).

Girodias, Maurice: French publisher, born in 1920, was the son of Jack Kahane. He took his mother's maiden name during the German occupation of France. After the war he resumed his father's business as Editions du Chêne, which eventually became the Olympia Press, and continued publishing some of Miller's work as well as such "risqué" titles as Vladimir Nabokov's *Lolita* and *Candy* by Terry Southern and Mason Hoffenberg.

Guiler, Hugh Parker ("Hugo"): Anaïs Nin's husband from 1923. Born in Boston, February 15, 1889, he spent his childhood in Puerto Rico before his Scottish parents sent him to the Edinburgh Academy when he was ten years old. He studied English literature and economics at Columbia University, graduated in 1920, and joined the First National Bank as a trainee. He met Anaïs Nin when she, her mother, and her two brothers were living in Queens, N.Y. The young couple left Richmond, N.Y. in 1924, when Guiler was assigned to the bank's Paris office. Except for occasional visits to New York, the Guilers lived in France for the next fourteen years, in various Paris apartments and for several years in an old house in Louveciennes, a brief train ride from the Gare St. Lazare. A. N.'s mother and younger brother, Joaquin, shared the house in the late 1920s and early 1930s, and Guiler contributed to their upkeep. Working for the bank and, encouraged by his wife, pursuing his artistic impulses (music, dancing) created tensions ("The dissatisfactions of my life were a result of a good deal of internal strain," he once wrote, "of being pulled in two directions"). Guiler went into analysis with Dr. Allendy and later with Dr. Rank. Repatriated, at the outbreak of the war, from London, where he kept an apartment and eventually became manager of the newly merged City Bank and Farmers Trust, he returned to New York with his wife. A student of William S. Hayter at the famous Studio 17, Guiler, under the pseudonym Ian Hugo, became an accomplished engraver on copper plates and, in the early 1950s, a maker of renowned experimental films, which often featured Anaïs Nin. He resigned from the bank in 1949, but for economic reasons resumed work as a financial adviser, which he continued until shortly before his death, on January 7, 1985.

Hiler, Hilaire: American painter, color theorist, musician, and writer, born in 1898, and once owner of the Jockey bar in Paris, which displayed some of his murals. He lived in France for many years and in California during the 1940s. Exponent of "Neonaturism" in painting, he gave Miller art lessons at his studio in the Rue Broca. Anaïs Nin met him in June 1934 at Dr. Rank's Psychological Center at the Cité Université in Paris. Author of numerous books (*From Nudity to Raiment,* 1929; *Notes on the Technique of Painting,* 1934; *Painter's Pocketbook of Methods and Materials,* 1938), he got Miller and William Saroyan to contribute to his volume *Why Abstract?* (New York: New Directions, 1945). Miller devoted a chapter in *The Air-Conditioned Nightmare* to "Hiler and His Mural" (in the Aquatic Park Building in San Francisco). Wambly Bald, in his column, occasionally reported the goings on in Hiler's studio.

Kahane, Jack: Textile manufacturer, born in 1887, in Manchester, England, who went to Paris in the 1920s to pursue a writing career. There, his Obelisk Press published English-language books, catering to the tourist trade, with somewhat salacious titles, some of which he wrote himself under the pseudonym Cecil Barr (*Suzy Falls Off,* 1929; *Amour=French for Love,* 1932; *Bright Pink Youth,* 1934; *Daffodil,* 1934; *It's Hard to Sin,* 1935). Frank Harris's *My Life and Loves* was his first major success. The literary reputation of the firm was established by such authors as Miller, Cyril Connolly (*The Rock Pool,* 1935), and Lawrence Durrell (*The Black Book,* 1938), who, for censorship reasons, could not be published in England or the United States. Kahane died suddenly in September 1939, the year Obelisk published *Tropic of Capricorn* and Anaïs Nin's *The Winter of Artifice.* Michael Joseph, in London, published Kahane's own *Memoirs of a Booklegger.*

Lepska, Janina Martha: Polish-born (1924) student of history and philosophy. Henry Miller's third wife. They met during the summer of 1944, shortly after she was graduated from Bryn Mawr, and were married on December 18, 1944, at the new home of the Neimans in Boulder, Colorado. They went on to Big Sur, where Miller had decided to settle. Lepska gave birth to a daughter, Valentine, on November 19, 1945, and to a son, Henry Tony, on August 28, 1948. She and Miller separated in 1951 and were divorced in 1952.

Lowenfels, Walter: American poet and writer, born in 1897. He and his wife, Lillian, lived in Paris in the early 1930s. His first book, a sixteen-page elegy for Apollinaire, was set by hand and printed privately (150 copies), with covers designed by Yves Tanguy (Paris: Hours Press, 1930). Under the Carrefour imprint, his friend Michael Fraenkel published 150 copies of his *Elegy in the Manner of a Requiem for D. H. Lawrence* (1932) and 110 copies of *The Suicide* (1934), which was part of an unfinished book, "Some Deaths." Miller presented him as "Jabberwhorl Cronstadt" in *Tropic of Cancer.*

Mansfield, June: See Smith, June Edith.

McClure, Eve: Actress and painter, born in 1924, who married actor Lyle Talbot, when she was seventeen. She met Henry Miller through her sister Louise, who was married to artist Bezalel Schatz. She moved to Big Sur in April 1952 to look after Miller's two children. She became his fourth wife, and for most of 1953 they traveled through Europe and visited many of Miller's old friends. They were separated in the late 1950s, and she died, after a bout with alcoholism, in August 1965.

Morand, Paul: French writer and lecturer born in 1888. Among his numerous books were *Europe at Love,* 1927; *Black Magic,* 1929; *Closed All Night,* 1932; and *Paris de Nuit,* 1933. Miller approached him with the idea of translating some of Morand's works into English. Morand was a friend of Jean Giraudoux and of Marcel Proust, who had written a preface to Morand's *Tendre Stocks,* 1921.

Moricand, Conrad: French astrologer, occultist, and author of *Miroir d'Astrologie* (Paris: Au san Pareil, 1928). Miller met him, through the Guilers, in Paris in 1936. He went to California in 1947, a visit that Miller recalled in *A Devil in Paradise.* Miller called him "an incurable dandy, living the life of a beggar." Born in 1887, he died, penniless, in Paris in 1954.

Neagoe, Peter: American writer and editor who, with Hilaire Hiler and Richard Thoma, among others, worked on Samuel Putnam's *The New Review,* a short-lived literary magazine, published in France. He edited the anthology *Americans Abroad* (The Hague: Seroire, 1932), and eventually returned to the U.S. In an unsolicited letter, Miller panned Neagoe's book *Storm,* published in 1932.

Neiman, Gilbert: American writer, translator, and man of many trades who, with his wife, Margaret, met Miller in Los Angeles in 1941 and offered him shelter in their small bungalow on Beverly Glen Boulevard in June 1942. When they moved to Colorado, Miller (who had lived for a while over Richard Thoma's garage) shared the house with the painter John Dudley until late 1943. An expert in Spanish and French literature, Neiman encouraged Miller's interest in Rimbaud, and Miller helped him with his novel, *There Is a Tyrant in Every Country* (New York: Harcourt, Brace and Co., 1947), a suspense story set in Mexico. Neiman devoted his doctoral thesis to Miller's work ("Henry Miller: A Semi-Critical Approach," University of New Mexico, 1958–1959), and Miller dedicated *The Air-Conditioned Nightmare* to Margaret and Gilbert Neiman ". . . so utterly and perfectly human." Of himself Neiman wrote: "I have lived in two countries, Mexico and the U.S. My real birth took place in Mexico, long before I was born. It's been my home for three thousand years."

Nin y Castellanos, Joaquin ("Padre"): Anaïs Nin's father; Spanish composer, concert pianist, and musicologist, who was born in Havana, Cuba, in 1879. After the breakup of his marriage, which caused Anaïs's mother to emigrate, with her three children, to America in 1914, he lived mostly in France, with his second wife, Maruca. He became reconciled with his daughter in 1932, and visited her at Louveciennes. Anaïs's early letters to her father became the basis of her now famous diary, and her efforts to recover the lost father are a consistent theme in her work, especially in *The Winter of Artifice*. He eventually returned to Havana, and died there in 1949.

Nin-Culmell, Joaquin: Anaïs Nin's younger brother, born in Berlin in 1908, while his father was working there. He studied piano and composition in Paris at the Schola Cantorum and at the Conservatory under Paul Dukas. He was a private pupil of Alfred Cortot and Ricardo Viñez and became an assistant to Manuel de Falla. In January 1936, he made his debut in New York at Town Hall, and concertized in France, Italy, and Spain before the war. After his return to the United States in 1939, he taught and became head of the music department at Williams College and later at the University of California, Berkeley.

Norman, Dorothy: Born in 1905. American writer, editor, and long-time associate of photographer Alfred Stieglitz. She started a publication, *Twice a Year*, in 1938, in which Anaïs Nin's recollection of the stillbirth of her daughter in 1934, "Birth," (Fall–Winter, 1938) and Henry Miller's "Balzac and His Double" (No. 5–6, 1940–1941) and "Stieglitz and Marin" (No. 8–9, 1942) appeared. A tenth-anniversary issue, *Art and Action*, was printed on her own press in 1948.

Osborn, Richard Galen: American lawyer from Bridgeport, Connecticut, who worked in the Paris office of the First National Bank in the early 1930s with Hugh Guiler. When Henry Miller was homeless during the winter of 1931, Osborn let him stay at his apartment, at 2 Rue Auguste Bartoldi, and he introduced him to Anaïs Nin. Miller dedicated *The Wisdom of the Heart* to Osborn, "who rescued me from starvation." Osborn suffered a number of breakdowns during this period and was hospitalized after his return to the United States. He tried to write about his Paris experiences and asked for criticism from Miller, who had saved him from marrying a French girl who turned out to be a *femme du trottoir*. Osborn's greatest worry, Miller told Nin in May 1932, "was to have introduced us. He thinks you are wonderful and that you may be in danger from the 'gangster author.'"

Perlès, Alfred ("Fred"): Austrian journalist and writer, born in 1897. He met Miller and his wife, June, in Paris in 1928. After Miller returned to Paris, Perlès shared a flat with him at 4 Avenue Anatole France, from March 1932 to late 1933; it provided the setting for Miller's recollection *Quiet Days in Clichy*. Perlès worked on the Paris edition of the Chicago *Tribune* until the paper's demise in 1934. He emigrated to

England in 1939. As Private A. J. Barret, he joined the British army and became a British subject. During the early 1930s, he captured some of his amorous adventures in *Sentiments Limitrophes* and *Le Quatuor en Ré Majeur* (reissued in Paris in 1984), in which are glimpses of Henry Miller and Anaïs Nin at Clichy. Of his book *My Friend Henry Miller* (New York: John Day, 1956), Miller, in his introduction, wrote: "It may often be at variance with dates, facts and events. But it is the authentic record—the soul's memory." They met again in Barcelona in 1953, and Perlès visited Miller in California in November 1954, an event he described in *Reunion at Big Sur* (Northwood, England: The Scorpion Press, 1959).

Powell, Lawrence Clark: American librarian and writer, born in 1906. He met Henry Miller at the Lycée Carnot, in 1932, where he taught while earning his Ph.D. at the university in Dijon. He wrote *An Introduction to Robinson Jeffers* (Dijon: Derningnard & Privat, 1932) and *Robinson Jeffers: The Man and His Work* (Los Angeles: Primavera Press, 1934). After he became head librarian at the University of California, Los Angeles, he established the major collection devoted to Henry Miller and, eventually, to Anaïs Nin.

Rank, Dr. Otto (Otto Rosenfeld): (1884–1939.) Austrian psychoanalyst, pupil and "adopted son" of Sigmund Freud, secretary of the Psychoanalytical Society in Vienna until their break in 1926, when Rank left for Paris. Of his many books (*The Trauma of Birth*, 1924; *Technik der Psychoanalyse*, 1926; and *Das Inzestmotif*, 1926) Henry Miller and Anaïs Nin were most influenced by *Art and Artist* (New York: Knopf, 1932), which prompted Miller to arrange an interview with him, in March 1932, and to show him some of his work. Nin became his patient in November 1932 and finished her analysis early in 1933. When Rank was forced by economics to move to New York, in October 1934, Nin followed him, in November, and worked for him until February 1935, when their relationship terminated. She saw Rank only once more, for a brief visit at his apartment on Riverside Drive in April 1936. Rank died suddenly, three years later, shortly after he had remarried and decided to live in California.

Reichel, Hans: German painter in Paris who became a member of the Villa Seurat circle between 1934 and 1939. Miller wrote an essay about him, "The Cosmological Eye" (*transition*, April–May, 1938), which provided the title for the first collection of writings by Miller published in the United States (Norfolk, CT: James Laughlin, 1939). Reichel died in 1958.

Sanchez, Eduardo: Astrologer and writer who was Anaïs Nin's cousin and played an important part in her life prior to her marriage in 1923. (See *The Early Diary of Anais Nin,* 1920–1923 and 1927–1931.) He underwent analysis in New York and went to Paris in 1930, where he kindled Nin's and her husband's interest in psychoanalysis and astrology. He was briefly associated with Bernard Berenson at the Villa I Tatti in Florence in the 1930s. In the 1940s, in the United States, he shared Nin's interest in printing at the Gemor Press and, tutored by James Cooney, in Ashfield, Massachusetts, he handset his own book, *The Round,* published under the pseudonym Eduardo Santiago.

Schnellock, Emil: American artist, teacher, classmate of Henry Miller at P.S. 85 in Brooklyn, and a lifelong friend. They carried on a voluminous correspondence over the years. Some of the letters were published in various little magazines and in the collection *Semblance of a Devoted Past* (Berkeley, CA: Bern Porter, 1944). For many years, before his death in 1960, Schnellock directed the art program at Mary Washington College of the University of Virginia in Fredericksburg.

Smith, June Edith (also known as June Mansfield): Miller's second wife, who appears, as "Mona," "Mara," and others, as the central figure in the body of Miller's work, especially in *Tropic of Capricorn* (dedicated "To Her") and the three volumes of *The Rosy Crucifixion (Nexus, Plexus, Sexus).* They first met in 1923, when she worked as a taxi dancer on Broadway in New York, and Miller was employed as personnel manager of Western Union. After Miller divorced his first wife, Beatrice Wickens, a pianist and piano teacher, with whom he had a daughter, Barbara, in 1918, he married June, in 1924, and left his job to devote himself fully to writing, while June developed various schemes, including a speakeasy, to support them. In 1928, the Millers embarked on a lengthy tour of Europe, which included France, Austria, Hungary, and Germany. Their economic circumstances did not improve after their return, and in 1930 Miller went back to Paris, without June, desperately poor but buoyed in spirit, a period later recalled in *Tropic of Cancer.* When June arrived for a brief visit in December 1931, Miller introduced her to Anaïs Nin, at Louveciennes, and the two women immediately fell under each other's spell; the passionate involvement continued until June sailed for New York in the last week of January 1932. When June returned in October 1932, a complicated emotional struggle erupted. Miller, with the help of Nin and Alfred Perlès, tried to escape to London, but in a final confrontation June asked for a divorce and left for New York, late in December 1932. The divorce came through in December 1934, via lawyers in Mexico, but June remained an obsessive riddle to Miller. Nin's work, notably *House of Incest* and *Winter of Artifice*, reflects her own efforts to come to grips with this mythomaniacal character. See also Anaïs Nin's *Henry and June* (New York: Harcourt Brace Jovanovich, 1986). June remarried and for some time was employed as a social worker in Queens, N.Y.

Troubetskoia, Princess Natasha: Russian émigré painter and decorator, who had fled to Paris after the Bolshevik revolution. She met Anaïs Nin in January 1929 and painted several portraits of her, including a large canvas showing her seated on an ornamental chair. She also used Nin as a model for other paintings, and Nin used the Princess's studio as a mailing address and meeting place in Paris.

Varda, Jean ("Yanko"): American painter and collage artist. Born in Smyrna, Turkey, of Greek parents, he studied in Paris and trained, early in life, as a dancer. He moved from London to the United States in 1939. After reading Henry Miller's public appeal for help in late 1943, he invited Miller to stay with him and his wife, Virginia, in their converted barn in New Monterey, California. Early in 1944, he introduced Miller to Lynda Sargent, who let Miller stay in her log cabin and introduced him to the Big Sur country. Miller's essay "Varda, the Master Builder" appeared in the magazine *Circle* in December 1944, and was later included in *Remember to Remember* (Norfolk, CT: New Directions, 1947). Miller introduced him to Anaïs Nin, who later used some of his collages on her book jackets.

INDEX

Aaron's Rod (Lawrence), 186

Abramson, Ben, 335

Adams, Eve, 248

Admiral, Virginia, 337

Against the Grain (Huysmans), 38

Agee, James, 379

The Air-Conditioned Nightmare
        (Miller), 343 n., 361
    travel experiences described in,
        324 n.

Alain, Blaise, 374

Albertine Disparue (Proust), 46, 277

All Change, Humanity! (Houghton),
        359

Allégret, Marc, 279

Allendy, René Felix, 98, 106
    Nin in analysis with, 61, 101, 102,
        111–12
    Nin's work for, 133
    on neuroses, 115
    on the planets' influence, 107,
        109–10
    writings, 128

Aller Retour New York (Miller), 303

"The All-Seeing" (Nin), 360 n.

Alraune (film), 127 n.

"Alraune" (Nin), 129
    Bradley's assessment of, 153, 213
    division into two parts, 226–27
    June portrayed in, 126–27
    Miller's criticism of, 104–5, 142–44,
        146–47, 148, 271–72, 276, 279
    Miller's *Scenario* inspired by, 262,
        267, 287–88

preface for, 145
Rank's introduction for, 288 n.
writing of, 233

Also sprach Zarathustra (Nietzsche), 12

Amicitia Amorque (Bradley), 152 n.

Amok (film), 255

Andard, Louis, 246, 250, 261–62,
        277

Aphrodite (Louÿs), 128

Apocalypse (Lawrence), 164

Artaud, Antonin, 38 n., 138, 151, 221,
        231 n.

Bachman, Rudolf, 146, 147, 149, 150,
        165–66, 178, 181, 189

Balanchine, George, 239 n.

Bald, Wambly, 28–30, 47, 49, 50,
        97–98, 105, 149, 182

Baradinski, Oscar, 378

Baron, Jacques, 235

Bataille, Georges, 384

Battedou, Marius, 373

Baumann, Henry, 229

Beach, Sylvia, 231

Beckett, Samuel, 167–68

Beggars' Opera (film), 36

"Benno, the Wild Man from Borneo"
        (Miller), 237 n.

Beyond the Street (Calmer), 45 n.

Black Spring (Miller), 164 n., 260
    illustrations for, 387 n.
    Nin's comments on, 194, 200,
        206–7, 208–9
    publication of, 248, 303

Black Spring (Miller) *(cont.)*
  rejections by publishers, 231 n.,
    282–83
  sections for magazine publication,
    237, 248–49
  translated into French, 382 n.
  writing of, 219, 236, 249–50, 293 n.,
    298 n.
Blavatsky, Helena Petrovna, 317
Bodenheim, Maxwell, 50
Bonaparte, Marie, 135
The Books of My Life (Miller), 392
The Booster magazine, 34 n., 237 n.
Borowski, Stanley J., 229
Bouchard, Jeanne, 375
Boussinesq, Hélène, 150
Bowinkel, Attilio and Paola, 387
Boyle, Kay, 212, 213, 214, 216, 249
  Miller's letter to, 219, 222
Bradley, William Aspenwall, xvi, 80,
    100, 113, 150
  "Alraune," assessment of, 153, 213
  editorial work, love for, 152–53
  as Miller's agent, 202–3, 248
  on Miller's writings, 152, 167
  Nin's diary, interest in, 109, 146,
    147, 152, 153, 155, 200 n.,
    215–16
Brassai, 233, 234
Bread and the Wafer (Nin), 372
Breton, André, 384 n.
Brett, Dorothy, 151
Brett and Lawrence (Brett), 151
Breuer, Bessie, 318
"Brochure" on D. H. Lawrence
    (Miller), 134, 135, 139, 141,
    156
  Nin's comments on, 148, 186, 194
The Brothers Karamazov (Dostoevsky),
    71, 76, 85, 92
Broughton, James, 390
Buchet, Edmond, 394
Bull, Harry, 369
Buñuel, Luis, 23, 89, 236
"Buñuel or Thus Cometh to an End
    Everywhere the Golden Age"
    (Miller), xi, 59 n., 69
  Nin's criticism of, 75, 93

Buzby, George C., 69, 229
Bye, George, 236, 237

Cage, John, 357
Cairns, Huntington, 312, 323, 324,
    360, 370
Calloway, Cab, 208
Calmer, Edgar ("Ned"), 38, 44–45
Calmy, Jacques, 69
Camus, Albert, 374, 384 n.
Carré, Jean-Marie, 359
Carrington, Leonora, 390
Carteret, Jean, 313
Casanova, Giovanni, 4, 8, 11
Céline, Louis-Ferdinand, 150, 151,
    152
Cendrars, Blaise, 235, 261, 263 n., 370,
    393
  meetings with Miller, 248, 258, 259,
    267, 275
Centaur Press, 390
C'est le Printemps (film), 56–57
Chagall, Marc, 192
Challenge to Defeat (Hale), 142
Chareau, Dolly, 377, 378, 382
Chennevière, Daniel. *See* Rudhyar,
    Dane
Chicago Tribune, Miller's job with, 11,
    42, 51
Children of the Albatross (Nin),
    393 n.
Chisholm, Hugh, 358 n.
Chopin, Frédéric, 117
"Cinema Vanves" (Miller), 179
  Nin's comments on, 190, 199–200
Circle magazine, 360–61, 370 n.
Cities of the Interior (Nin), 362, 369 n.,
    374
Cocteau, Jean, 47
Coeurs Farouches (film), 108
Colette, 48
Collins, Mabel, 353
The Colossus of Maroussi (Miller), xvi,
    xx, 327 n., 334, 341, 342 n.
Colt Press, 327 n.
Conason, Emil, 134, 242
Connolly, Jean, 364
Conrad, Joseph, 153

Cooney, James, 312
Corle, Edwin, 389 n.
The Cosmological Eye (Miller), 132 n., 263 n., 323 n.
Cossery, Albert, 371
Count Bruga (Hecht), 337, 338
"Counter Nettles" (Nin), 59–60
Crawford, Joan, 138
"Crazy Cock" (Miller), 3 n.
The Criterion magazine, xvi, 259
Critique magazine, 384
Crosby, Caresse, 67, 70, 83, 349 n., 373
Crowley, Aleister, 235, 268, 286
"The Crown" (Lawrence), 153
Cummings, E. E., 32

Dagover, Lil, 200
Dali, Salvador and Gala, 236
Dandieu, Arnaud, 168
Da Vinci, Leonardo, 93
Davis, Bette, 355
Delta of Venus (Nin), 325 n.
De Mille, Cecil B., 298
Denoël, Robert, 203, 371
Deren, Maya, 375
Deux Hommes (Duhamel), 204
De Vilmorin, Louise, 127, 228
Devil's Shadow (Thiess), 38, 39 n.
De Vogüe, Comtesse, 138
D. H. Lawrence: An Unprofessional Study (Nin), vii, xii
  Miller's criticism of, 2, 66–67, 68, 69, 80, 83
  Nin's comments on, 71–72, 76–77, 90
  reviews of, 42, 44–45, 49
Diary of Anaïs Nin
  abandonment of, Miller's encouragement regarding, 217–18, 223
  "adaptation," Miller's opposition to, 200–202
  Bradley's interest in, 109, 146, 147, 152, 153, 155, 200 n., 215–16
  Childhood Diary, 385, 390 n.
  cruel things in, 160
  defects of, 216–17

French publication of, possible, 382–83
  Gemor Press' attempted printing of, 380
  imaginary journal parallel to, 212
  Miller's admiration for, xv–xvi, 19, 55, 98, 201, 314–15
  Miller's criticism of, 56, 215–19, 223–26
  Nin's reaction to, 219–23
  Miller portrayed in, x, xv, xxi, 394–95
  Miller stops reading, 73, 79
  name changes in, 215–16 n.
  Nin's assessment of, 114
  preface by Miller, 87, 153, 202, 213
  publication, Miller's insistence on, 339–40, 362
  publication of, vii–viii
  reason for, 167
  as refuge and workshop, vii
  "story" in conflict with diary structure, 216
  typing of, 113, 122, 145–46
  wartime storage of, 365
Dickson, Lovat, 283
Dinesen, Isak, 348
Dobo, Frank, 248
Dos Passos, John, 249, 318, 384 n.
Dostoevsky, Feodor, 2, 8, 13, 71, 85, 90, 92, 186
  on relativity of love, 76
  sexuality of his writings, 11
Drake, Lawrence, 70
Draper, Ruth, 62–63
Duchamp, Marcel, 235
Dudley, Dorothy, 234, 235
Dudley, John, 358, 359, 361
Duhamel, Georges, 179, 184, 185, 189, 204
Duits, Charles, 363
Duncan, Robert, 337, 338
Duran, Gustavo, 138, 151 n.
Durrell, Lawrence, 312, 313 n., 342 n., 378, 384
  with Miller in Greece, 317 n., 321, 322
Durrell, Nancy, 313 n., 317 n.

Edgar, David, 323
Elegy for D. H. Lawrence (Lowenfels), 70
Eliot, T. S., 259, 312
Elkus, A. M., 228, 229
Ellis, Havelock, 38
Eluard, Paul, 357 n., 384 n.
Emerson, Ralph Waldo, 72, 246, 300
The End of All Men (Ramuz), 379
Ernst, Max, 358 n.
Erskine, John, 98, 116
    correspondence with Nin, 12-13, 77, 87
    Nin's "affair" with, ix
    Nin's unpublished novel about, 5
Esquire magazine, 237
European Caravan, 81
Europe magazine, 303 n.
Expression in America (Lewisohn), 119
Extase (film), 139

Family Cinema, The (theater, Paris), 108
Farrère, Claude, 67
Faure, Elie, 32, 122, 124, 125, 171, 174, 188, 189, 193
Fernandez, Ramon, 123
Feuchtwanger, Lion, 344
Flandrau, Grace, 48
Fluchère, Henri, 320
Ford, Charles Henri, 227, 258, 363
Ford, Ford Madox, 153
The Four-Chambered Heart (Nin), 390, 392 n.
Fournier, Alain, 36
Fowlie, Wallace, xx, 366 n., 367, 368, 370, 373
Fraenkel, Michael, 47, 50, 59, 79, 207, 299, 312, 327, 341
    on *Black Spring*, 249-50
    on dreams, 68, 71
    Miller's attitude toward, 58
    on Miller's writings, 81
    money problems, 66, 68
    move to London, 304
    on Nin's beauty, 57
    Nin's feelings for, 70, 72

psychoanalysis, interest in, 84
Tropic of Cancer
    comments on, 58, 367-68
    efforts on behalf of, 65, 66, 67, 100
Frank, Betty, 387
Frank, Waldo, 75
Freeman, Walter, 56
Freud, Sigmund, 84, 236
Friedman, Marcel, 347, 348, 348 n.

Gallimard (French publisher), 371
Garbo, Greta, 140
Gary, Roman, 386 n.
Gautier, Théophile, 117
Geismar, Maxwell, 394
Gemor Press, 349, 352, 357-58 n., 362, 368, 380-81, 385
"The Genesis of *Tropic of Cancer*" (Fraenkel), 367
Gide, André, 9, 71, 85, 384 n.
Gide (Fernandez), 123
Giono, Jean, 320
Giraudoux, Jean, 316
Girodias, Maurice, 371, 372-73, 377, 378, 382-83, 384, 392, 393
Goethe, J. W. von, 12, 39, 47, 48, 142
Goldberg, Samuel, 351, 352
Goldman, Emma, 235
Gone With the Wind (film), 323
Gorulov trial, 85
Greece, Miller's visit to, 315-17, 321-22
Greenstein, Benno, 237
Grove Press, 259 n.
Guiler, Ethel, 328
Guiler, Hugh Parker (Hugo), 17, 88, 93, 105, 119, 138, 154, 168, 180, 190, 334-35, 373
    artistic career, ix, 363, 366, 370, 372
    banking career, viii-ix, 363
    Brazil, interest in, 72, 74
    marriage to Nin, vii
    Miller's feelings for, 7, 62
    Miller's teaching job, arrangement of, 1

Nin's letter for Miller sent to, by
mistake, 240–41, 243–44, 266,
267
Nin's loyalty to, viii, 90–91
Nin's relationship with June, reaction
to, 121
Nin's social calendar, 227–28

Haan, Jacques den, 384
Hale, William Harlan, 142
Hamsun, Knut, 259
The Happy Rock (celebratory volume
on Miller), 368 n.
Hardy, Thomas, 19, 38
Harvey, Harry, 214
Harwell, Pierce, 354, 355
Hecht, Ben, 318, 337
"Hejda" (Nin), 360 n., 370 n.
"Hello June 26th! Yoohoo!" (Miller),
356
Helm, Brigitte, 85
Hemingway, Ernest, 251
*Henry Miller: A Chronology and
Bibliography*, 371
Henry Miller Miscellanea, 371
Heraklitos, 78
Here Comes Mr. Jordan! (film),
354
Herschkovitz, Harry, 68 n., 360,
362
Hiler, Hilaire, 225–26, 234
Holty, Carl, 312
Houghton, Claude, 359, 367
The House of Incest (Nin), 216 n., 226,
336, 366 n.
limited edition publication, 389 n.
Miller's editorial work on, 117
"Mona" pages, 117 n., 119
recorded reading of, 391 n.
truth told as fairy tale, viii
See also "Alraune" (Nin)
Hudson Rejoins the Herd (Houghton),
359
Hugo, Ian. *See* Guiler, Hugh Parker
Hunt, Henry, 228
Huxley, Aldous, 235
Huysmans, J. K., 38, 117

In a Yellow Wood (Vidal), 379
Interlude (Thiess), 38, 39 n.
Into the Night Life (Miller and
Schatz), 387 n.

Jaloux, Edmond, 138
James, William, 129
Jeffers, Robinson, 8, 328
Jesus Christ, 353
Je Vous Aimerai Toujours (film), 179
Jocelyn, Glen, 351
Jolas, Eugene, 47, 48
Journal of Anaïs Nin. *See* Diary of
Anais Nin
Joyce, James, 78 n., 126
June. *See* Smith, June Edith
Jung, Carl, 84, 115, 116, 127, 128,
140, 268
Miller's assessment of, 236

Kahane, Jack, 150, 202–3, 258, 259
Black Spring publication, 248, 283,
303
business problems, 152, 230
funds for Miller, assistance with, 310,
312, 316, 317
Miller's attitude toward, 230–31
Tropic of Cancer publication, xv,
109, 134, 146
Kamasutra, 126
Kann, Frederick, 225, 226
Kazin, Alfred, 350, 384 n.
Kenyon Review, 370
Kerkhoven novels (Wasserman),
341–43, 344
Kierkegaard, Søren, 356
King, James, 26–28, 30, 68, 97
King's Row (film), 355
Klein, Roger, 278, 279, 304
Knopf, Alfred, 152, 155
Knopf, Blanche, 236
Koestler, Arthur, 356
Korzybski, Alfred, 363 n.
Koverr, Harry, 360 n.
Krans, Dr., 1, 80
Kriss (film), 45
Kronski, Jean, xi, 14, 47, 338

La Bataille (Farrèrre), 67
La Bête Humaine (film), 313
La Chienne (film), 108
Ladders to Fire (Nin), 369 n., 372 n.
Lady Chatterley's Lover (Lawrence), 92, 93
Laffont, Robert, 378, 383
Laforgue, Jules, 143
L'Age d'Or (film), 23, 66, 93, 94
La Maison de la Mort Certaine (Cossery), 371
La Mandragore (film), 127 n.
Land Without Bread (film), 236
Lang, Fritz, 78n.
"The Language of Night" (Jolas), 48
Laplanders, 313
Larnac, Jean, 48
Latimer, Margery, 30
Laughlin, James, 259–60, 312, 360
Lawrence, D. H., 78 n., 164, 184
  criticism by, 155, 156
  homosexuality, attitude toward, 76
  Lawrence, Frieda, and, 53
  Miller's assessment of, 81, 87
  Miller's identification with, 151–52
  Nin's assessment of, 92–93
  sexuality of his writings, 11
  solitariness of, 75–76
  See also "Brochure" on D. H. Lawrence (Miller); *D. H. Lawrence: An Unprofessional Study* (Nin)
Lawrence, Frieda, 53, 338
Lee, Canada, 374
Le Grand Meaulnes (Fournier), 36
Leite, George T., 361, 370, 371
Leonard, Dave, 177
Le Problème de la Destinée (Allendy), 128
Lepska, Janina Martha (Miller's third wife), 366 n., 372 n., 386, 390
Lerner Quartet, 298
Les Chants de Maldoror (Lautréamont), 67
Les Frontières Humaines (Ribemont-Dessaigne), 108
Le Signe de la Croix (film), 298

Letters to Anaïs Nin (Miller), vi
"Letter to Anaïs Nin" (Miller), 360 n.
Lewisohn, Ludwig, 115, 119
Life of Rimbaud (Carré), 359
Light of the Path and Karma (Collins), 353 n.
Linotte (Nin), 390 n.
Little Birds (Nin), 325 n.
Liveright, Horace, 48
L'Opéra de Quat'sous (film), 38, 108
Lorenzo in Taos (Luhan), 47
Louis Lambert, 316
Louÿs, Pierre, 128
Lowenfels, Walter, 50, 70, 139, 207 n., 224
  Nin's attitude toward, 210
Lowrie, Walter, 356
Lucienne (Romain), 92
Luhan, Mabel Dodge, 47 n., 52, 53
Lumière Bleue (film), 107–8

Mabille, Pierre, 367
McAlmon, Bob, 50
McCarthy, Mary, 368
McClure, Eve (Miller's fourth wife), 392
McCullers, Carson, 358
McKinley, Hazel, 334
"Mademoiselle Claude" (Miller), xi, 59 n.
Mandrake and Mandragora (Powys), 129
Marcel Proust, Sa Révélation Psychologique (Dandieu), 168
Marcienne (friend of Perlès), 44, 52
Marius (film), 17, 41
Martines Sierra, Gregorio, 137
The Maurizius Case (Miller's film script), 347, 348
Maurizius Forever (Miller), 342 n.
Ma Vie (Chagall), 192
Max and the White Phagocytes (Miller), 132 n., 382 n., 383
Melville, Herman, 155
"Men . . . Have No Tenderness" (Williams), 352–53
Men God Forgot (Cossery), 371

Metropolis (film), 78 n., 84–85
Milano, Paolo, 391
Miller, Henry
  on artistic creation, 143–44, 224–26
  on astrology, 109–10, 246, 339
  on auto driving, 333
  Avignon, visit to, 174, 175, 176
  benefactor of, 359–60, 361, 362
  bicycle riding, 105, 170, 177–78
  book reviews by, 356–57, 359, 369, 371
  borrowings from friends, 283, 312
  Carcassonne, visit to, 171–72
  on champagne, 168
  on children, 52
  Christmas crisis, 277–78
  Clichy apartment, 26–28, 44, 182, 198
  on criticism, 81
  on death, 155
  death premonition, 228
  depressions, 169
  on deserted villages, 183–84
  on desperation in people, 376
  on diary writing, 218–19
  doing nothing preferred over "making a living," 345–47
  dreams recorded by, 166
  on duty toward others, 315
  as Ego in a crowd, 308
  employment, planned return to, 351–52
  England visit, aborted, 129 n., 131–32
  Europe, departure for (1930), xi, 41–43
  European, visit to (1953), 393–94
  failure as a writer, feelings about, 58, 282–83
  on film actors, 140
  France, sightseeing in, 171–77, 317, 318, 319–21
  freedom in writing, need for, 53
  French writers, admiration for, 81, 92–93
  on the future, 246
  German despair of, 38

  ghost-writing job offer, 347
  Greece, visit to, 315–17, 321–22
  on health, 159
  homesickness for the U.S., 273
  on homosexuality, 86–87
  hypersexuality of, 4, 8, 11–12, 307–8
  on illness, 159
  inner security of, 358
  as intellectual writer, 194–95
  jealousy of, 244
  laziness, enjoyment of, 182
  legal problems in the U.S., 258–59, 384
  letter writing, need for, xvii, 381–82
  Louveciennes, impact of, xiii–xiv
  on love within friendship, 184
  Midi country, visit to, 172–73
  money given away by, 358 n., 360, 362–63, 364
  mother of, 136
  New Orleans, visit to, 325
  on newspapermen, 49–50
  New York, dislike for, 338
  New York, return to (1935), 292, 293 n.
  desire to be with Nin, 276, 279, 280, 281–82, 286, 288
  work plans, 284–85
  nightlife in Paris, 28–30
  Nin's English, correction of, 6, 10, 117, 143–45
  Nin's letter for Miller sent to Guiler by mistake, 240–41, 243–44, 247–48, 266, 267
  Nin's photographs, reaction to, 42, 43, 74
  obstacles, passion for, 275
  Osborn's breakdown, interest in, 197
  Paris, love for, 182–83
  payments from publishers, 371–72, 373, 378, 384, 385–86
  proofreading job, 11, 42, 51
  property purchase in California, 376–77
  psychoanalysis, interest in, 84
  psychotherapy work, 292 n.
  publisher, search for, 45

Miller *(cont.)*
record-buying, 165
role as writer, questioning of, 344,
346–47
on sacrifice, 353–54
scriptwriting work, 343, 344–45
secretary, need for, 386
self-creation through writing, v–vi
self-destructiveness, 85
selfishness, 50–52, 134, 156–62,
196–97, 232, 306–9, 329–30,
331, 332, 345
seven-year cycles of his life, xx
simple life, preference for, 332,
333–34
Spanish lessons, 338–39
Tarascon, visit to, 183–84
teaching job at Dijon, 1–2, 11
the Touraine, visit to, 179
on traveling, 170, 173
traveling with Perlès, 177–78
Trèves, visit to, 174
in Virginia, 323–34
U.S. cross-country trip, 324 n.,
325–26
watercolors by, 226, 365
weakness of, 270, 281, 285
wills written by, 228–29
on woman as evil, 42
working card in Paris, 23, 25, 26, 30
World War II
departure from France due to,
310–13, 322–23
indifference toward, 347
writing, obsession with, 3
writing block, 139
on writing habitually, 37
on writing while traveling, 183,
195–96
See also Miller-Nin relationship;
under other headings
Miller, Henry, writings of
Bradley's assessment of, 152, 167
early failures, x–xi
erotica for a private collector, 325,
326, 338, 340
film book, 107–8, 110, 119, 140
Fraenkel's assessment of, 81

international publication of, 379
Lawrence, proposed article on, 49
Mexican publication of, 327
Montparnasse article, 47, 48–49, 53
Nin introduced to, xi–xii
Nin's assessment of, xii–xiii, 125–26
revealing the writer in the process of
writing, 126
short pieces, publication of, 59 n.
See also specific works
Miller, June. *See* Smith, June Edith
Miller, Tony (son), 390 n.
Miller, Valentine (daughter), 372 n.,
386
Miller-Nin relationship
betrayal, possibility of, 33, 46
in California together, 387–88,
389 n.
estrangement, xx–xxi, 329–30, 334,
335–36, 364, 394–95
family and friends' reaction to,
xiv–xv
financial support for Miller, xiv, xv,
8, 45, 119, 127, 169, 176, 227,
330
first meeting, v, x, xiii
foreign places to live together,
Miller's thoughts on, 97,
286–87
interdependence between them,
180
June's return to Paris and, 46, 61,
69, 99, 100, 101–3, 110,
121–22, 130–31, 132
living together in the U.S., Miller's
proposal regarding, 250,
257–58, 289–90
Miller's anxiety at possible loss of
Nin, 293–98
Miller's callousness regarding Nin's
illness, argument about, 156–64
Miller's forced letters, 187
Miller's happiness as Nin's main
concern, 127, 154
Miller's love for Nin, 16–17, 18–20,
23–24, 63, 64–65, 74–75, 78,
96, 253, 261, 263, 268–69
Nin's reaction to, 202, 274

Miller's notes on Nin's departure,
37–38
Miller's protection of Nin, 202, 332
Miller's sadness at separation, 25–26,
167, 168, 204–5, 214, 256–57,
264–65, 266
Miller's wish for sole possession of
Nin, 269
money for Miller to hire prostitutes,
73
New York, visit to (1936), 299 n.
Nin as substitute for June, 101–2
Nin in New York (1934)
lies to Miller, 252, 256, 264–65,
277, 279, 284
Miller's fear for Nin's well-being,
278–79
Miller's unhappiness with their
correspondence, 251–53, 256,
263–65, 267–68, 276–77
voyage from Europe, 233–34
Nin's certainty about, 132
Nin's loneliness, 215
Nin's love for Miller, 20–22, 31,
77–78, 94–95, 99, 104, 106,
153
Miller's reaction to, 22–23
Nin's self-sacrifice, 348, 349–50, 351
published material about, vi
reunion after Nin's Tyrolean
vacation, 91, 95–96
sexual longing, 20, 25, 32, 33–34,
46, 75, 82, 95
support for the other's literary work,
xv–xvi
toughness of, 158
vacation together, 176–77, 178,
180–81
writing collaboration, 107–8, 110,
119
Miroir du Merveilleux (Mabille), 367
Misfortunes of the Immortals (Eluard),
357–58 n.
Moby Dick (Melville), 156
Modern Reading magazine, 373
Mondadori (Italian publisher), 392, 393
Mon Périple (Faure), 171, 174, 193
Moore, David, 367–68

Morand, Paul, 69, 70, 82
More, Gonzalo, 306 n., 368
Moricand, Conrad, 316
Murry, John Middleton, 77
"The Mystic of Sex" (Nin), vii

Nadeau, Maurice, 384 n.
Napoleon, 190–91
The Nation, 374
Neagoe, Peter, 34 n., 59 n., 78 n., 85
Neiman, Gilbert, 328, 329, 336, 343 n.,
356
Nerval, Gérard de, 190
"The New Instinctivism (A Duet in
Creative Violence, 1930)"
(Miller and Perlès), 34–35
The New Republic, 356, 374
The New Review, xi, 59
Nexus (Miller), 392
Niarchos, Melpomene, 350
Nichols, Dudley, 359
Nichols, John, 197
Nicolas, Prince of Rumania, 191
Nietzsche, Friedrich, 12, 135
Nijinsky, Vaslav, 320
Nin, Anaïs
on astrology, 107
auto ride in the mountains, 181
beauty of, 57
Cadiz, visit to, 306
Chamonix, visit to, 181
color preferences, 13
Connecticut, tour of, 272
critical method of, 221
on domination, 5–6
dream about Miller, 302
English corrected by Miller, 6, 10,
117, 143–45
explaining herself, dislike of, 71
father's desertion, impact of, vi–vii
Fez, visit to, 300–303, 305
financial independence, wish for,
232, 233 n., 265–66, 270, 385
gambling by, 186, 190, 233, 234
Gemor Press venture, 349, 352,
357–58 n., 362, 368, 380–81,
385
on god, 36

Nin *(cont.)*
on gossip, 83–84
Guatemala, visit to, 388–89
heart trouble, 357
on homosexuality, 76–77
houseboats of, 306 n., 313 n.
imaginary journal, 212
legal problems due to Miller's books,
    258–59
on lesbianism, 77, 307
letter for Miller sent to Guiler by
    mistake, 240–41, 243–44, 266,
    267
on letter writing, 89
on love within friendship, 185
on madness, 8–9, 12, 119
male friends, 31
Marseilles visit, 299–300
masculine elements, xvii, 54
on Miller as intellectual writer,
    194–95
on Miller as the Sun, 164–65
Miller's Brooklyn neighborhood, visit
    to, 254, 280
on Miller's selfishness, 306–9,
    329–30
on Miller's wish to live in California,
    329–30
mistress sensibilities, x
mother, relationship with, 15
on "moving on," 115–16
on necrophilia, 136, 137
neuralgia of, 135
on New York, 238–39, 242, 255
obstacles, passion for, 275
the past, absorption of, 193, 197–98
payments from publishers, 372–73,
    377, 378
philosophy of life carried with her,
    196
promotional efforts on Miller's
    behalf, 231 n., 236, 258–59,
    291
in Provincetown, 337
on psychoanalysis, 9, 90, 111–12, 116
psychoanalysis with Allendy, 61 n.,
    111–12

psychoanalysis with Rank, 229–30
as psychotherapist, 292 n.
recorded readings by, 391
on religion, 77
return to France after the war,
    interest in, 365, 377–78, 382,
    390
"roles" of, 203–4
Russian lessons, 13
self-abnegation by, 165, 166
self-creation through writing, v–vi
on sexual desire for one's parents,
    191
silence used by, 376
social calendar, 227–28
on solitariness, 75–76
suicide, thoughts of, 21
thirtieth birthday, 134
traveling, enthusiasm for, 193
truth, desire for, 54
U.S. citizenship, 257, 258, 259, 280
unhappiness in America, 334, 335
on walking, 83, 88
weakened physical condition, 348,
    349–50, 352
on woman as penetrator, 31–32
on works in progress, 126
on writer's need to struggle, 115–16
writing desks of, 65
writing process of, 71, 76
See also Miller-Nin relationship;
    under other headings
Nin, Anaïs, writings of
biographical facts disguised in, viii
early failures, vii
erotica for a private collector, 325,
    326, 327 n., 337
Erskine, unpublished novel about, 5
female essence of, 118
as ingrown and restricted, 147
international publication of, 379, 381
language of, 117, 143
Miller's criticism of, xii, 3, 117–18,
    143, 147, 217–18, 219, 223–25
loyalty and understanding lacking
    in, 219–23
poetry, 59–60

short stories, 60
See also specific works
Nin, Thorvald (brother), 389
Nin-Culmell, Joaquin (brother), vii, 15,
  92, 94, 114, 116, 158, 227,
  299 n.
Nin y Castellanos, Joaquin (father), vi,
  189, 203, 227
  discovering talent, flair for, 209
  horoscope of, 190
  illness, 175, 205
  letters to Nin, 150, 162
  Miller's attitude toward, 158
  Paderewski and, 205
  reunion with Nin, 151, 154, 167,
    170, 171, 203
  travels with Nin, 204 n., 205–6, 207,
    209
Norman, Dorothy, 327
The Notebooks of Malte Laurids Brigge
  (Rilke), 15, 92
Now, Voyager (film), 355

O'Brien, Edward, 313
"Obscenity and the Law of Reflection"
  (Miller), 367
O'Connor, Nell, 28–29
Ondine (Giraudoux), 316
O'Neill, Eugene, 235
"On French Wartime Literature"
  (Miller), 369 n.
On Native Grounds (Kazin), 350
"On Wartime Literature in English"
  (Miller), 369 n.
"An Open Letter to All and Sundry"
  (Miller), 358 n.
O'Regan, Joe, 229
Ortega y Gasset, José, 81, 92
Osborn, Richard Galen, 56, 78 n., 85
  breakdown of, 197
  on Miller, 196–97
  Miller introduced to Nin by, x, xi, xv
  Miller's criticism of his writings, 140,
    195

Paalen, Alice, 368
Paalen, Wolfgang, 368

Pabst, G. W., 36 n.
Pach, Walter, 32, 33
Pachoutinsky, Anatole and Leon, 199
Paderewski, Ignace Jan, 205, 206, 209
Pagnol, Marcel, 17
Paiva, Mona, 57
Pantheon Press, 360
Paris Was Our Mistress (Putnam), xi
Partisan Review, 370
Patchen, Kenneth, 340
Paulette (friend of Perlès), 65, 86, 106,
  109
Péguy, Charles, 379
Penny Serenade (film), 339
Percival, Milton O., 355 n.
Perlès, Alfred (Fred), xi, 11, 30, 42, 47,
  54, 67, 82, 106, 132, 267, 277,
  304
  Andard, work for, 250–51, 261
  astrological reading for, 246
  Clichy apartment, 27, 28
  disagreements with Miller, 68
  June, attitude toward, 39, 40, 100
  lovers of, 44, 52, 65, 109
  with Miller at Villa Seurat, 289
  on Miller's ability to love, 51
  in Miller's will, 229
  money problems, 250–51
  Nin and, 48, 50
  Nin's diary, typing of, 113, 145
  portrait of Miller, 36
  singing by, 39
  traveling with Miller, 177–78
  writing collaboration with Miller,
    34 n.
  writings, Miller's assessment of, 24,
    44, 52
Pickering family, 234–35
Pinchard, William, 367
Plexus (Miller), 392, 393
Poe, Edgar Allan, 135–36, 155
Porter, Bern, 350 n., 361, 362, 369 n.,
  371
Porter, Katherine Anne, 237
Porter, Russell, 373
Portman, Eric, 78 n.
The Possessed (Dostoevsky), 9

Pound, Ezra, 235, 249, 250
  Tropic of Cancer review, 259
Powell, Lawrence Clark, 328, 387, 390,
  391, 393
Powys, John Cowper, 129
Proust, Marcel, 4, 7, 81, 167–68
  Miller's comments on, 40, 42
The Pulse of Life (Rudhyar), 353
Putnam, Samuel, xi, 34 n., 38, 59 n.

Queneau, Raymond, 235, 374

Rabelais, François, 179
Rain (film), 138
Rainer, Luise, 331–32, 337, 339, 368
Ramakrishna, 353
Ramsay, Dorothea, 387
Rank, Otto, 133, 135, 190, 263
  "Alraune" introduction, 288 n.
  Miller's dislike of, 250
  Miller's interest in working for,
    284–85
  Miller's interview with, 136 n.
  Nin in analysis with, 191, 229–30
  Nin's final meeting with, 299 n.
  Nin's work for, 233 n., 238, 239,
    243, 270, 292 n.
Rattner, Abraham, 262 n., 324 n.
Ravagli, Angelino, 356
Reavey, George, 249
Reflections on the Maurizius Case
  (Miller), 342 n.
Reichel, Hans, 375, 383
Renaud, Jean, 104, 105, 106
Renoir, Jean, 108, 313
Rilke, Rainer Maria, 15, 43, 92
Rimbaud, Arthur, 143, 359
  Miller's essay on, 369, 382
  Nin's comments on, 369–70
Ritual in Transfigured Time (film), 375,
  378–79
Rivas, Humberto, 338–39
Romain, Jules, 92
Root, Waverley, 42, 49–50
Rosenfeld, Isaac, 374 n.
Ross, Harolde O., 229, 249, 258, 286
Ross, Patience, 379

The Rosy Crucifixion (Miller), 343 n.,
  350, 377
Roth, William, 327, 334, 335
Rudhyar, Dane, 331, 353, 356, 368

Salavin (Duhamel), 179–80, 184, 185
Sanchez, Eduardo, vii, 84, 107,
  109–10, 135, 138, 243, 247,
  304, 315, 353, 369, 370
Sargent, Linda, 359 n.
Sartre, Jean-Paul, 374, 384 n.
Sassoon, Victor, 328
Scenario (Miller), 262, 263, 267,
  287–88, 298
  radio performance of, 263 n., 393
Schatz, Bezalel, 387
Schiffrin, André, 363
Schiller, J. C. F. von, 39
Schnellock, Emil, xvii, 86, 100, 101,
  179, 215, 229, 273, 282, 286
  Nin's meeting with, 254, 265, 280
Schrank, Bertha, 13, 83–84
Science & Sanity (Korzybski), 363
Secret Doctrine (Blavatsky), 317
Segovia, Andrés, 209
"Self-Portrait" (Miller), 164 n.
Semblance of a Devoted Past (Miller),
  350 n., 371
Seven Gothic Tales (Dinesen), 348
Shakespeare, William, 100
Sheets, Kermit, 390
A Short Life (Lowrie), 356–57
Siana Press, 298 n.
Simon, Michel, 393
Six Immoral Tales (Laforgue), 143
The Smile at the Foot of the Ladder
  (Miller), 389
Smith, Harrison, 255
Smith, June Edith (Miller's second
  wife), 3, 19
  "Alraune," portrayed in, 126–27
  color preferences, 13
  divorce from Miller, 129 n., 132, 279
  drug taking by, 73
  horoscope of, 213
  "Hundred Years War" with Miller,
    124–25

illness, 385, 392
life with Miller, xi
love for Miller, 211
male friends, 50
with Miller in Vienna, 39
Miller-Nin relationship and, 46, 61,
  69, 99, 100, 101–3, 110,
  121–22, 130–31, 132
Miller's departure for Europe (1930),
  41–43
Miller's feelings for, 39–42
Miller's imaginary conversation with,
  65
Miller's influence on, 14
Miller's inquiries about, 8–10
on Miller's selfishness, 51
in Miller's will, 228
Miller's writings, portrayed in, 61,
  125
neuroses of, 13
Nin, relationship with, xvi–xviii,
  8–10, 12, 14, 19
Perlès' attitude toward, 39, 40, 100
return to Paris (1932), xv, 61, 69,
  100, 110, 119–24, 129–31
Société du Champ de Mars, 27, 28
Spengler, Oswald, 78, 87, 88, 197
on the Faustian soul, 75, 93
Nin's enthusiasm for, 70, 71, 77,
  89–90, 193
A Spy in the House of Love (Nin),
  391, 394
Stalin, Josif, 353
Star of the Unborn (Werfel),
  379
Steele, Bernard, 151, 227
Stein, Gertrude, 208
Steloff, Frances, 316–17, 353, 355
Storm (Neagoe), 78 n., 85
Stuerme der Leidenschaft (film), 78 n.
Sunday After the War (Miller), 201 n.,
  360 n.
Swasey, Robert, 304
Symons, W. T., 313

Tanguy, Yves, 367
Theosophical Society, 353 n.

Thiess, Frank, 38
"This Gentle World" (Miller), 4–5, 7
This Hunger (Nin), 368, 369 n., 370,
  372, 383
reviews of, 374 n.
Thomas, Calvin, 48
"Time, Distance and Form in Proust"
  (Ortega y Gasset), 81
Titus, Edward, 83
Toomer, Jean, 30
Tricolor magazine, 367
Trilling, Diana, 374 n.
Tropic of Cancer (Miller)
banned in the U.S., 259 n.
Fraenkel's comments on, 58, 367–68
legal actions against, 384 n.
material from other works
  incorporated in, 3
Miller's assessment of, 231
Miller's experiences portrayed in, 1 n.
Nin's criticism of, 61, 71, 87–88
Nin's underwriting of, xv, 121, 134,
  231 n.
Nin's promotional efforts, 234,
  291
Pound's review of, 259
publication efforts, 66, 67, 69, 80,
  83, 100, 109, 146, 291
reviews of, 380
Russian publication of, 249
sales of, 279, 303, 318
smuggling of copies into the U.S.,
  235, 242, 249, 258
Surrealists' interest in, 235–36
title for, 80
translation into French, 382 n.
U.S. printing of, possible, 234
writing of, 18, 65–66, 79, 230 n.
Tropic of Capricorn (Miller), xiii, 307
banned in the U.S., 259 n.
legal actions against, 384 n.
Nin's assistance in writing, 148–49
publication of, 322
truth about June in, 125
writing of, 98
Troubetskoia, Natasha, 13, 51
Tuer pour Vivre (film), 188

Uhland, Ludwig, 73 n.
"Uhland Ballads," 73
Ulysses (Joyce), 134
Unamuno y Jugo, Miguel de, 82, 86, 93
Under a Glass Bell (Nin), 358 n., 360 n., 362 n., 370 n.
  English publication of, 366
  Italian publication of, 393 n.
  recorded reading of, 391 n.
  translated into French, 363, 377
"Une Etre Etoilique" (Miller), xvi

Vail, Lawrence, 364
Valéry, Paul, 15
Vanity Fair magazine, 237
Varda, Jean "Yanko," 359 n.
Verdaguer, Mosén Vacinto, 207
"Via Dieppe-Newhaven" (Miller), 132 n.
Vidal, Gore, 379–80, 381–82
Volkening, Henry, 334
Voyage au Bout de la Nuit (Céline), 150, 151, 152

Walsh, Ernest, 213 n.
Wasserman, Jacob, 342 n., 394
The Weather Paper (Fraenkel), 68
The Well of Loneliness (Hall), 54
Werfel, Franz, 379
West, Herbert, 366 n.
West, Rebecca, 70, 86, 99, 231 n., 299
Wharton, Jean Page, 376–77
"When Do Angels Cease to Resemble Themselves" (Miller), 382 n.

White, Emil, 390
Whitman, Walt, 155, 156
Wickens, Beatrice Sylvas (Miller's first wife), 4 n., 229
Wilde, Oscar, 190, 191
William Blake's Circle of Destiny (Percival), 355
Williams, William Carlos, 352–53, 380
Wilson, Edmund, v, 368, 372, 384 n.
Winner Takes Nothing (Hemingway), 251
Winslow, Katherine, 391
Winter of Artifice (Nin), 216 n., 226, 362 n.
  Miller's comments on, 355–56
  Miller's promotional efforts, 327
  publication of, 317, 349 n., 366, 367
  review of, 352–53
  translated into French, 367
The Wisdom of the Heart (Miller), x, 237 n., 341
Wolff, Kurt, 360
The Woman at Point Sur (Jeffers), 8
Woolf, Virginia, 99
The World of Sex (Miller), 324 n., 325 n., 335

Year Before Last (Boyle), 213, 215
Young, Lafayette, 327
The Young and the Evil (Ford), 258

Zivi, Walter, 390

Made in the USA
Middletown, DE
22 September 2019